THE EDUCATION OF TEACHERS

THE EDUCATION
OF TEACHERS

Ninety-eighth Yearbook of the
National Society for the Study of Education

PART I

Edited by

GARY A. GRIFFIN

Editor for the Society

MARGARET EARLY

19 NSSE 99

Distributed by THE UNIVERSITY OF CHICAGO PRESS • CHICAGO, ILLINOIS

The National Society for the Study of Education

The National Society for the Study of Education was founded in 1901 as successor to the National Herbart Society. It publishes a two-volume Yearbook, each volume dealing with a separate topic of concern to educators. The Society's series of Yearbooks, now in its ninety-eighth year, contains chapters written by scholars and practitioners noted for their significant work on the topics about which they write.

The Society welcomes as members all individuals who wish to receive its publications. Current membership includes educators in the United States, Canada, and elsewhere throughout the world—professors, researchers, administrators, and graduate students in colleges and universities and teachers, administrators, supervisors, and curriculum specialists in elementary and secondary schools.

Members of the Society elect a Board of Directors. Its responsibilities include reviewing proposals for Yearbooks, authorizing the preparation of Yearbooks based on accepted proposals, and appointing an editor or editors to oversee the preparation of manuscripts.

Current (1999) dues are a modest $30 ($25 for retired members and for students in their first year of membership). Members whose dues are paid for the current calendar year receive the Society's Yearbook, are eligible for election to the Board of Directors, and are entitled to a 33 percent discount when purchasing past Yearbooks from the Society's distributor, the University of Chicago Press.

Each year the Society arranges for meetings to be held in conjunction with the annual conferences of one or more of the national educational organizations. At these meetings, the current Yearbook is presented and critiqued. All members are urged to attend these meetings. Members are encouraged to submit proposals for future Yearbooks.

The Education of Teachers is Part 1 of the 98th Yearbook. Part 2, published simultaneously, is entitled *Issues in Curriculum*.

For further information, write to the Secretary, NSSE, College of Education, University of Illinois at Chicago, 1040 W. Harrison St., Chicago, Illinois 60607-7133.

ISSN: 0077-5762

Published 1999 by the
NATIONAL SOCIETY FOR THE STUDY OF EDUCATION
1040 W. Harrison St., Chicago, Illinois 60607-7133

Second Printing, 2001

Printed in the United States of America

Acknowledgments

At a time when politicians and policymakers throughout the United States are focusing major attention on issues of school reform, the National Society for the Study of Education is indeed grateful to Gary A. Griffin, editor of this volume, and to his team of authors for producing a volume that addresses perhaps the key issue in the debate: the education of teachers along the continuum from recruitment to retirement. Professor Griffin and his authors undertook this crucial assignment, giving freely of their time, energy, and expertise, when demands on all three have been intensified as a result of the public's mounting concern for the effectiveness of their children's education.

At the request of the Society, Professor Griffin identified the issues, designated the order in which they would be treated, and persuaded highly qualified (and busy) authorities to prepare the chapters that comprise *The Education of Teachers*. From first draft to page proofs, they have paid careful attention to the many tasks that go into publishing a volume as timely and significant as this one.

This is the first NSSE volume for which I have had major responsibility. I am, therefore, especially grateful for the patient and prompt cooperation of Gary Griffin and all fifteen authors, but without Kenneth Rehage's constant and willing guidance Volume 98:1 would never have seen the light of day.

MARGARET EARLY
Editor for the Society

Editor's Preface

The National Society for the Study of Education, through its Yearbooks, has charted the course of educational thought and activity for most of the twentieth century. As we approach a new millennium, the education of teachers has become a topic of national significance in ways that are unprecedented. The public concern with educational issues is high. Policymakers are focusing their attention on teacher preparation and instructional competence through such vehicles as the promulgation of standards for students and teachers, renewed attention to accreditation of teacher education programs of study, raising the expectations for teacher candidates' licensure requirements, and attempting to establish the link between teachers' work and student performance.

At the same time, the research community has redirected considerable energy to studying how teachers are prepared, investigating the results of particular approaches to that preparation, developing research-based programs of professional development for experienced teachers, and focusing on the relationships between teacher cognition and pedagogy. There has been a marked, though not universally adopted, shift from a technocratic view of teaching to one that is rooted in conceptions of learning based on long-standing views that learning is the consequence of social constructions between and among students and teachers.

Persistent questions are asked in different ways: What is it to be a teacher in a time of educational reform? What is the nature of knowledge and how is it acquired in instructional settings? How does one redefine teaching competence as classrooms and schools are characterized by ever more diverse student groups? What are the relationships between teaching and the nation's economic and social status? How does the organization of schools affect teaching and learning and, reciprocally, how do teachers influence a school culture? These and other such questions guided the preparation of this Yearbook.

This volume is an attempt to gather together a set of emerging views about the education of teachers, in part to attend to the recommendations for reform and in part to suggest promising practices that may not yet be strongly rooted in the national consciousness. As has been the admirable stance of the Society over the years, this volume includes a rich mix of proposals—some rooted in research, some resulting from rigorous observations of and experience in practice, and some the consequence of thoughtful reconsiderations of persistent threads in discourse about teacher education. Because of this, the Yearbook brings together a variety of orientations to what it is to be a teacher, how expertise is defined and promoted, and how the education of teachers should be conducted and regulated.

For those who believe that the education of teachers begins and ends with a college- or university-based instructional program, I hope the arguments here will be sufficiently convincing to move them to reconsider teacher education as a long-term enterprise, beginning with participation in a higher education setting but extending into the first years of teaching and continuing on as teachers achieve veteran status. The point of view that guided the development of the Yearbook is that learning to teach should not be considered as a time- and experience-bound event but an ongoing process that gives serious attention to new understandings, rests on refinement of practice, contributes to the construction of teaching as a profession, depends for success upon membership in a community of dedicated and expert colleagues, and is characterized by ongoing inquiry.

The Yearbook has three sections. The first is devoted to perspectives about teacher education that provide both historical and current understandings about the education of teachers in relation to the changing face of teacher education, the dilemma of linking teacher education to classroom and school reform agendas, the possibilities and problems associated with considering teacher education in concert with realizing professional status for teachers, and linking how teachers are prepared and supported in their careers to issues of standards and licensure.

The second section is devoted to persistent questions about teacher education and new ways of responding to them. Attention is given to preparing teachers to work for social justice, considering the education of teachers in terms of construction of meaning rather than only demonstrating technique, struggling with the dilemmas of engaging in teacher education from the perspective of a scholar-teacher, reconsidering what knowledge for teacher education is and should be, and framing teacher education as a means to recreate educational settings as caring and civil communities.

The final section considers the future of teacher education from the perspectives of policy development and implementation, the creation of professional development schools as supportive sites for learning to teach, and both recalling and anticipating the problems and dilemmas the field faces today and will face in the future.

My hope is that the Yearbook will focus attention on both the ongoing tensions that have characterized teacher education and point the field to the future with some sense of positive anticipation. Perhaps more so now than ever before, policymakers, researchers, the public, and school professionals are focused on educational issues and on the role that teachers play in ensuring that our children and youth will have satisfying, productive, and meaningful futures. For these futures to be realized, the education of teachers must be considered a priority of major proportion as we move into the twenty-first century.

I am grateful to the authors who contributed with professional generosity and personal commitment to this Yearbook. I am also grateful to Karen Zumwalt, who asked me to consider taking on the editor's role, although that gratitude was occasionally tinged with resentment as deadlines came and passed and as the magnitude of the task became ever more apparent. Margaret Early provided ongoing good-humored technical assistance characterized by attention to detail as well as a patient understanding of the difficulties of gathering into one volume the work of already overcommitted leaders in the field. Finally, Kenneth Rehage, it must be noted, has been the life's blood of the Society for more years than either of us want to count, and his devotion to ensuring that the Yearbooks are both timely and on the mark is exceeded only by his patience, good humor, and gentility.

GARY A. GRIFFIN

Table of Contents

Section One
Perspectives on Teacher Education

Section Two
Practices in Teacher Education

Section One

PERSPECTIVES ON TEACHER EDUCATION

CHAPTER I

Changes in Teacher Education: Looking to the Future

GARY A. GRIFFIN

Teacher education has changed considerably in the years that have passed since NSSE devoted its 74th Yearbook exclusively to this topic.[1] The changes include practices associated with the education of teachers, conceptions of what teacher education is and should be for, considerations of who should be considered teacher educators, the contexts of professional education, perspectives about what teachers should know and how they should come to know it, policies governing the enterprise, and research support to guide decision making and practice. This chapter includes some of the more significant alterations associated with the education of teachers and suggests why they have captured the imagination of those of us concerned with ensuring that the nation's children and youth have access to "caring, competent, and qualified" teachers.[2] Throughout, other chapters in this Yearbook treat these issues in greater detail.

Reforming Teacher Education

The past several decades have been times of widespread change. We have seen unprecedented alterations in almost every aspect of our social institutions. Long-standing beliefs, values, and practices associated with governmental, cultural, and institutional regularities have been challenged and contested, sometimes with considerable attention and sometimes just beneath the surface of the public consciousness. The education of teachers has not been neglected in these times of

Gary A. Griffin is Professor of Education and Co-director of the National Center for Restructuring Education, Schools, and Teaching (NCREST) at Teachers College, Columbia University.

reform and reconsideration, even though some long-held beliefs and practices persist in both thought and action.

For the most part, however, we have witnessed dramatic transformations in how teachers are prepared, how they are encouraged and supported in their ongoing professional development, the ways in which they are expected to shape their professional practice, and the manner in which they play out their professional roles in schools and other educational settings. Although there are still widely held beliefs about teaching that probably could never be supported empirically (e.g., "don't smile until Christmas"), it is encouraging to many of us that teaching has come to be seen more fully by professionals and some of the public alike as work that is important, socially vital, complex, and intellectually rigorous. How teachers are prepared and how they continue to grow as professionals, then, become matters of serious consequence for the broader society as well as deserving of considerable investment of time, energy, political will, intellectual rigor, and material support.

Having noted the changing climate of teaching and teacher education, however, it is important to acknowledge that the United States has experienced a perennial struggle between stability and reform, a tension between what is believed to "work" and what is imagined as "working better and smarter."[3] The changes in how teachers are prepared and how their subsequent professional growth takes place have not come easily. In fact, many believe that schools and related institutions such as colleges of education, for example, are among the most difficult social institutions to alter in any significant and long-lasting ways. Ironically, when few citizens attended schools, in the early days of this country's history, changes were considerable, cutting deeply into the structure and ideologies of educational experience that had been brought here from abroad. However, as universal public compulsory education took hold, in itself a changed perspective on schooling of enormous magnitude and far-reaching influence, larger and larger numbers of the nation's citizens became self-proclaimed experts on education. After all, they had experienced schooling, engaged with teachers, and in many cases achieved social and economic success. The watchwords, then, became "the schooling and teaching that I experienced worked for me, therefore it should work for all." Thus, a dramatic and successful deep-seated change in schooling became one of the primary arguments to maintain a firmly entrenched *status quo*.

As a nation we once considered it reasonable that schooling should be for the few; came to expand that notion to include schooling for the many; recognized that teaching is the primary influence upon the achievement of children and youth; engaged one another around contested claims about what kinds of teaching and teachers contribute to that achievement; debated or deplored, depending upon the times and the varying civility of the discourse, how teachers should be educated to ensure achievement; and in recent years subjected our claims for teaching, schooling, and teacher education to intellectual, ideological, and political litmus tests. This arc of change and some of its persistent strands are what this Yearbook is about. Without attending to all of the issues associated with the education of teachers, the Yearbook features a number of them that have currency at the end of the twentieth century and that will persist, we believe, as we move into the next millennium.

As is so often the case with social institutions, the experts of a particular time are often seen in retrospect as anachronistic, uninformed, generally off the mark, or naïve about what they profess for their times and for the future. It is likely that this volume and its contributors will be viewed similarly when twenty-five years have passed if intellectual, cultural, and social changes continue at their current pace. Revisiting the 1974 Yearbook, as a particularly relevant example, one finds that teachers were consistently referred to as female, that teacher education was predicted to be today much as it was at the time the Yearbook was produced, that prospective teachers were believed to enter teaching as a means for upward social mobility, that teacher education would be almost exclusively controlled by higher education institutions, that teacher education was rooted primarily in a training model, that the specification of teacher performance superseded attention to teacher thinking and decision making, that research on teacher education focused less on how teacher education influences prospective and practicing teachers than on issues of selection and placement and satisfaction of graduates of teacher preparation programs, and other claims that simply do not hold today.[4]

In contrast to the 1974 view and as this Yearbook demonstrates, the education of teachers has changed, many would say, considerably for the better over the past twenty-five years. Of course, this does not mean that there aren't those who, for reasons of ideological persistence or distance from the field, might still hold allegiance to some or all of the ideas presented a quarter-century ago. For most people concerned with teacher education, though, this is a time of considerable promise based upon at least two decades of equally considerable effort to strengthen, enliven, and dignify a field of study and practice that we see as central to the well-being of individuals and institutions in today's and tomorrow's shared human experience.

Teacher Education, Teaching, and Schooling:
Interactive Understandings and Practices

Despite views and practices to the contrary, there is an unfortunate persistence in the beliefs of many that it is possible to separate teacher education from the realities of teaching in schools, that it is reasonable to consider the education of teachers as largely college and university activity divorced from what some refer to as "real life teaching." By embracing this notion, it is reasonable to place blame or praise upon schools, departments, and colleges of education for what is wrong or, less often, what is right about educational practice that takes place in tens of thousands of the nation's classrooms. Although there was a time when teacher preparation was almost exclusively carried forward in college and university settings, it is now much more common for teachers-to-be to spend considerable time and intellectual, psychological, and physical energy in representative public school settings. This is in stark contrast to the conventions of earlier times when many colleges and universities created greenhouse-like laboratory schools, most often populated by students of privilege, to serve as opportunities for teacher candidates to engage in what was called "practice teaching."

As the connections between and among higher education and elementary, middle, and secondary schools have increased and strengthened, it has become much more difficult than it once was to think of teacher education as the exclusive purview of colleges and universities. (This theme pervades much of what appears in this Yearbook.) Because of tighter intellectual, practical, and organizational connections across higher education and the schools, it has become almost impossible in recent years to isolate teacher education as a distinct and separate phenomenon, a set of efforts guided and implemented solely by university professors. Instead, it is now coin of the realm that teacher education is the focus of partnerships, of new amalgams of institutional collaboration marked by shared expectations and mutually reinforcing education strategies.

Certainly, there can be found instances where the historical dominance of higher education over teacher preparation persists, but the number of such cases decreases each year. Gradually we have moved from lengthy periods of "learning to teach" in colleges and universities, interrupted by only occasional forays into schools and classrooms to observe and engage in limited apprentice-oriented practice, to program-long opportunities to blend theory and practice as a consequence of parallel and interactive engagement in higher education programs of study and in the practical settings of public or private schools.

Consequently, the changes in teacher education included in this chapter and the content of most of the other chapters in this Yearbook are embedded in a conception of learning to teach as shared responsibility; a purposeful coming together of men and women aiming toward or already in teaching positions, higher education faculty, and teachers and administrators in schools. At the same time, there is also a pervading sense that providing prospective teachers with ways of thinking and acting that show promise to enhance educational opportunity for all children and youth continues to be an important resource for schools. There is, I believe, an important lesson here: Teacher education has become a more responsive activity in terms of what is needed and desired in elementary, middle, and secondary schools as well as remaining a potentially powerful lever for change in the schools.

With the understanding that the education of teachers is in a period of extensive re-examination and reform, I offer tentative and in-progress answers to what I believe are four important questions. They are: Who should teach? How should teachers be taught? Where and when should teacher education take place? What should teachers be prepared to do? I do not claim that my responses to these questions are definitive. Rather, I offer them as contributions to the important national discourse about the future character and quality of education in the nation.

Who Should Teach?

The United States faces a crisis of extraordinary proportions in terms of the anticipated need for teachers. It is estimated that half of the teachers in the nation will leave teaching in the decade that began in 1996. At the same time, there has been what some have called a "baby boomlet" as women have waited longer to have children than was once the case and as the birth rate of segments of the population rises as a consequence of a number of social and cultural beliefs and values. What this means in real numbers is the looming need for approximately 1.25 million teachers to work with the next several generations of children and youth.[5] Importantly, significant numbers of newborns will be raised in family settings with different cultural and linguistic customs, traditions, and values than those of the historically dominant group of American teachers who continue to be primarily middle-class white women. We have already seen the culture clashes that are certain to continue to pervade social and political debates about what is important for the nation, including what is best for the nation's children. A recent dramatic example is the controversy surrounding whether or not bilingual education should be strengthened, maintained, altered, or discarded as a major educational activity.

Who will teach our children? Attempts to answer that question create a number of possible scenarios. Most pessimistically, if United States history repeats itself as the anticipated teacher shortage becomes acute, as was the case after armed forces personnel returned from World War II, anyone who holds a bachelor's degree and is not a convicted or sought criminal may be allowed to fill "vacant" teaching posts. A similar dark picture is that teacher education may return to its high-income/low-cost status in colleges and universities, and short-term add-ons to conventional baccalaureate programs will provide some modest preparation for those who wish to "try teaching." Although states and local districts have made some attempts to mount their own teacher education programs, these efforts have turned out to be less than successful in terms of the perceptions of those who moved through them and in terms of the impact these teachers have on student outcomes.

We are witnessing an unfortunate confluence of, on the one hand, a need for teachers that considerably outpaces the capacity of teacher education institutions to prepare them in sufficient number and, on the other hand, growing research evidence that supports the conclusion that graduates of teacher education programs are more effective with students than persons occupying teacher roles who have had little or no formal preparation for those roles.[6]

In terms of the "who should teach" question, it now seems reasonable to conclude that teachers who have successfully completed a rigorous teacher education program should be our candidates of choice. But, as we know, the supply and demand sides of the equation are bound to be in increasing imbalance over the coming decades. It may be necessary to fill the gap with so-called "emergency credentialed" teachers, persons who demonstrate interest in and some initial capacity for teaching. What we must not do, however, is ignore the need of these teacher candidates for solid practical and intellectual guidance as they begin their careers, something we did forty years ago when an "emergency" credential eventually became a permanent license to teach without accountability or competence-assessment procedures to ensure teacher quality. It may be necessary to create mentoring systems, invent school-based school and university collaboration focused on providing teacher education as teachers are engaged in practice, refocus school districts' resources and will on strong professional development programs, and otherwise make up the difference between the quality of prepared and unprepared teachers. We must resist the temptation to allow unqualified teachers to work with our children and youth simply because to do so is less demanding than to face the supply-and-demand problems head on.

Whoever teaches in our schools, we must reaffirm and strengthen our intentions to recruit into teacher education the capable rather than settle on the available. At issue, of course, is the initial determination and subsequent monitoring of capability. At one time, it was believed that someone who had experienced at least one grade in school above the one she or he would teach defined capability. Another conception that seems to guide some public discourse is that the primary, if not sole, criterion for a teaching career is some demonstration of "love of children." These and other simplistic understandings of what it takes to be effective with groups of children in institutions called schools persist, even though they have never been shown to be adequate determiners of teaching quality.

By contrast, if one accepts the research-based conclusion that teaching is complex intellectual activity played out in equally complex social settings, the recruitment into teacher education becomes a formidable task. Certainly, it is reasonable under this formulation to attempt to draw into teaching persons who have demonstrated that they are competent learners themselves and, therefore, understand well what is required for students to achieve in school. However, this by itself is insufficient. Mastery of subject matter does not translate easily into making that mastery accessible and meaningful to students in classrooms, although there are teacher education programs that seem to make this assumption central. (A frequent rebuttal to this belief is that if subject matter mastery were the key to good teaching, we would recall as our best teachers our college and university professors. This recollection is rare, I have found.)

It is important to acknowledge that strong achievement in academics is a major factor in thinking about recruitment of the capable and appears as one component of a number of teacher education reform proposals.[7] At the same time, though, teacher education must address the issue of capability beyond demonstration of content acquisition. Several ways to do so appear reasonable to consider.

There is little doubt that teaching depends upon well-developed oral and written communication skills; yet few teacher education programs require candidates to submit writing samples and even fewer require an interview as part of the application process. In part, the belief that teachers must be proficient in communication rests on the understanding that teaching depends for success largely on how clearly intentions, expectations, responses, and the like are expressed with students. An additional rationale, though, is the growing realization that teachers must be effective communicators with parents, community members, colleagues, and policymakers. For teacher education to succeed in positively influencing classrooms and schools, then, teacher candidates must have the capability to work well with language.

Although the stereotype of the staunch and stern teacher persists, it is increasingly clear that teachers who are unconcerned with how they affect students or parents or colleagues are not effective in their pedagogy or in their work outside the classroom. Part of the admonition to recruit capable candidates, then, is that we seek out and/or filter into teacher education programs those who have demonstrated or show promise of developing strong interpersonal skills. Certainly, it is possible to be tough-minded without being unduly stern and punishing. It is reasonable to expect teachers to stand up for what they believe to be solid educational opportunity without relegating others' views to the waste bin. It is important for well-conceptualized and finely honed practice to be set forth as exemplary without adopting a stance of "my way or the highway."

Many believe that teaching is or should be primarily a problem-solving activity. Those of us who teach gain some understanding of what problems may occur typically in a particular situation and develop means in advance of dealing with them, but no matter the level of our expertise, we do not have templates to guide our work, pat answers for every anticipated question, or automaton-like expectations for our engagement with students. Rather, we draw upon our repertoire of experience, our ways of approaching difficult situations, our consideration of options given the circumstances, and we then move ahead with the understanding that we may have to circle around the issue and try other approaches before our teaching problems are resolved.[8]

As we recruit women and men into teaching, we must search out those who demonstrate a willingness to confront complexity in their daily work lives. Teaching involves multiple, often simultaneous, decisions related to content, pedagogy, student relationships, praise and censure, materials of instruction, interactions with colleagues and others, and on and on. Obviously, we cannot depend upon teacher candidates to have well-honed ways of coping with and capitalizing upon this complexity; we must provide them with opportunities to analyze, reflect, and try out a variety of ways of working well in a complicated social and intellectual environment. But we will be ahead of the game if we anticipate the need for prospective teachers to understand, accept, and interact capably in a classroom characterized by multiple meanings, conflicting expectations, widely varying degrees of student accomplishment, and the other daily dilemmas that are characteristic of student groups in the nation's schools.

In our search for the capable teacher candidate, we should be seeking out those who are comfortable with self-awareness and reflection as bases for continued professional growth. Stereotypically, it is believed by some that receiving a recommendation for licensure from a college or university marks the end of learning to teach and that all that must be known about working well with students can be accomplished in a time-bound period of study. We know that this is not the case. We know that teachers who maintain a carefully thought-through journey to expert status are aware of themselves as people and as teachers and use that awareness for ongoing reflection about the problematic, the probable, and the possible. It is important that our conception of the capable teacher candidate give serious attention to whether or not prospective teachers are disposed to be or to become self-conscious about their practice.

Also, I have long believed that the cosmopolitan teacher is more effective than the teacher whose understandings of the world are neatly bundled into manageable and retrievable packages of knowledge and skill. By cosmopolitan, I do not mean urban or metropolitan. Instead, I mean the term to refer to the teacher who sees connections across disparate fields like mathematics and music and language, who can help students make sense of the enormous range of stimuli with which they are bombarded every day. In teacher education, it seems to me imperative that we seek out prospective teachers who are not narrowly focused on pieces of school curriculum or approaches to teaching or ways of knowing but, instead, have come to see the world around them as connective, as an amalgam of thoughts and actions and events and artifacts that together compose the cultures and societies we share.

Another capability that should be sought out in prospective teachers is what has been called social conscience. In some ways similar to cosmopolitanism but defined more by a set of values about the world we live in, social conscience helps prospective teachers be disposed to, rather than just accept at an abstract level of knowing, working with others to break the restrictions on some of our students' opportunities to learn, to realize democracy in classrooms and schools, to work for justice, to construct meaning that is inclusive, and to see their prospective students as partners in working "to change the world."[9]

This discussion of recruiting the capable into teacher education programs, if accepted, would focus not only on the typically addressed prior academic achievement, although that is central to this formulation, but would also give serious attention to teacher candidates' oral and written communication, interpersonal skills, willingness to confront and deal with social and cultural complexity, self-awareness and disposition toward reflection, cosmopolitanism, and a well-developed social conscience.

The question of who should teach also causes us to think again of the dominant racial, ethnic, and gender characteristics of the nation's teachers who are today predominantly white, female, and middle class. There are those who believe for a variety of reasons that we should be attracting to teacher education programs women and men of color who would represent student populations in larger measure than is currently the case. This issue is one that has been addressed in a variety of forms, from specific and targeted recruitment programs in some colleges and universities to the eagerness of some school districts to by-pass teacher education programs in favor of attracting people of color into the teaching ranks and then offering professional development to ensure that they are competent in their pedagogy and that they stay in teaching.

It is widely believed that teaching is no longer the attractive occupation it once was for the three historical candidates for teaching: women, minorities, and men from lower socioeconomic levels. It was not so many years ago that members of these three groups were barred from the more mature professions such as medicine or law. In today's world, despite the persistence in some settings of barriers to professions other than teaching, it is far more possible for members of that traditional pool of prospective teachers to have a wider array of options for their adult work lives.

A number of arguments for changing the face of the teaching workforce are compelling. Many consider it desirable for students to have ongoing contact with teacher mentors and academic and social role models who understand diverse cultures and are ethnically sensitive. It is believed that curriculum making and interpretations of subject matter can be considerably more considerate of the nation's diverse population than is typical. Connections between the home, the school, and the community may be strengthened if there are education professionals who have a sense of the experiences that shape students' and parents' understandings of and expectations for schooling. And a current issue in recruiting and retaining teachers is the degree to which there is a concerted effort to recognize and celebrate the differences that mark our nation and set aside the presumption that these differences are problems to be faced down and solved.[10]

While the broadening of options for previously under-represented groups in traditionally exclusive occupations is an important social change with far-reaching consequences, it dismays teacher educators and school system officers who are seeking to create and sustain a teaching force that mirrors the student population to a larger extent than is presently the case and who must now compete with professions that provide greater economic security and are believed to have higher status. There are no easy answers here, but I do not think it trivial or overly sentimental to capitalize on what many see as a modest resurgence in commitment to working toward social change on the part of many young people. Similarly, we are seeing more and more women and men seeking out teaching as early- or mid-career changes, realizing that aspirations long held—often from childhood—are simply not being realized in their first-choice occupations.

Although this is not the place for an extended discussion of what deters highly desirable and culturally representative teacher candidates from pursuing teaching careers, it is not unreasonable to urge the continuation of efforts to alter positively such deterrents to teaching as salary, conditions of work, semi-professional status, and views of teaching as a job rather than a career.[11] Significant changes in these features will help to attract capable candidates, including those who would enhance the diversity of the teaching force.

Although I could advance a number of other claims about who should teach and, therefore, who should be recruited into teacher education programs, I will end this section with what in some circles may be professional heresy. When research on teaching became a priority of the Federal government in the 1970s and 1980s, concerted attention was turned from conventional wisdom about the personal characteristics that were believed to contribute to good teaching to a detailed determination of what effective teachers (as determined by their students' scores on standardized tests) do that ineffective teachers do not do. This so-called "effective teaching" research movement was the first widespread attempt to understand teaching as a consequence of detailed examination of teacher behavior (rather than speculation on what teachers ought to do versus what they actually did). Researchers were careful to control for student characteristics and other features of classrooms that were beyond teachers' influence and determined that, independent of the nature of student groups and other context variables, "effective" teachers behaved markedly differently with students than did less effective teachers. The results of these studies, with mixed impact and for a complicated set of reasons, were influential on state and local teacher education policies, professional development programs, and teacher evaluation approaches.[12] In some cases, this influence continues as teachers are expected to behave with students as did the teachers labeled effective in the research studies.

Although I have continuing respect and admiration for many of the features of the research-on-teaching movement even while I have been dismayed by the use to which the findings were often put, I believe that our about-face from "who teachers are" to "what teachers do" has been a mistake of unimagined proportions. Although conventional wisdom suggests that certain personality traits would contribute to positive interactions with students, most teacher education programs ignore them as required or at least desirable attributes for admission and little attempt appears to be made to foster them in professional development programs.

Yet, when most of us recall the teachers who influenced us most, we remember the teachers who consistently demonstrated personal concern for our well-being, the teachers who surrounded our work together with good humor, women and men whose warm acceptance of us demonstrated a belief that we were individuals of worth, and others who were persistent in their in- and out-of-school admonitions for us to aim higher than we may have imagined reasonable or possible. Instead of seeking out and nurturing these qualities in prospective teachers, we have been caught up almost exclusively with searching for the high academic achievers and then providing them with opportunities to "do" teaching rather than "be" teachers of warmth, humor, compassion, and commitment. Teaching, like most other human endeavors, is not emotionless.

Clearly, I believe it is time to think in multiple and overlapping ways about who should teach, giving as serious attention to human qualities as we do to the potential for demonstrating the techniques of teaching. Is it possible to identify and nurture prospective teachers who care, who comfort, who engage students beyond technique? I am hopeful that this is a reasonable question and that it can be used to guide the education of teachers.

How Should Teachers Be Taught?

There are few models for teacher education that have withstood the test of time and experience. We have witnessed the technique-driven competency movement, the dominance of a kind of counseling or interpersonal-relations perspective, the "try this" apprenticeship model, the "think about this" theoretical approach, and so on. Still we continue to search for guidelines that can help us introduce newcomers into a complex professional arena and then support them in their journeys toward expert status.

There is a growing understanding that it is important for teachers to be able to understand a variety of ways to both think about and act before, during, and after engagement with teaching. The theory-research-practice formula has helped us to realize that there is considerable truth in an old exaggeration about any human enterprise: Thought without action is futile, action without thought is fatal. Although teaching is in large measure the demonstration of technique, it also requires attention that is more purposefully thoughtful than a naïve observer might believe to be so. At issue, then, is how teachers can be educated to be concerned with conscious attention to both grand theories and theories-in-use, careful consideration of teaching activity in relation to theoretical underpinnings and justifications, and enactment of ongoing inquiry into their own work.

A commonly expressed view of teacher education by recently licensed teachers is that they learned little in their college and university courses but came to understand teaching more thoroughly and helpfully during their student teaching and their first years of practice. This perceived dominance of practice over theory, in terms of influence of teacher education programs, is widespread but has received little disciplined attention from those who plan, implement, and assess the effects of opportunities to learn to teach. Despite the current attention to constructivist theories as guides for teacher education, it is difficult to locate professional preparation efforts that demonstrate those theories in practice. Instead, we continue to depend largely upon a sequence of learning to teach that moves from engagement with theories of teaching through opportunities to learn about and test out teaching practices in higher education settings to an opportunity to be an apprentice teacher under the supervision of a teacher who has been identified as expert.

This linear model, from considerations of theory to supervised practice, is in need of considerable reconsideration. If we expect teachers to be thoughtful about their practice, we should provide opportunities for guided practice to be informed by theory and theory to be tested against guided practice. If we expect teachers to be constantly inquiring into the nature and consequences of their work, we should provide individual and group opportunities to ask serious questions about practice and search for answers *in* practice as well as in theory. If we expect teacher education graduates to have an influence on the schools they enter as novices, we should work with them in ways that raise penetrating and thought-provoking questions rather than perpetuate acceptance of the norms of the schools and classrooms in which they find themselves.

A number of scholars, pre-eminently Daniel Lortie and John Goodlad, have concluded that we teach the way we were taught.[13] This helps to explain the persistence of certain practices in the nation's schools despite admonitions and recommendations for change. After all, those of us who teach have successfully moved through thousands of hours of observations of teachers at work in the classrooms where we were students. These cumulative experiences must be considered as a major source of our understandings of what teaching is and, in many cases, should be. Following the logic that experience shapes behavior, many of us become imitators of the dominant teaching patterns we have encountered over a period of twelve or thirteen years in schools.

For those who want to alter the persistence of what they believe is outmoded, ineffective, or insensitive teaching, it becomes important to devise teacher education programs that push back against the authority of prospective teachers' experiential learning. How to do that is a preoccupation of change-oriented teacher educators. Two proposals are offered here.

First, it is important for us to focus much of our early work with teacher candidates on altering their conception of teaching and schooling from that of a student to that of a teacher. This must be conscious and public. That is, we must declare in a number of activities (e.g., analysis of videotapes, practicum-related observations of practice, discussions of the nature and strategies of teaching) that what goes on in instructional settings has very different meanings for teachers and students. I have found that one of the issues that helps drive these interactions is a conception of "fairness." Teacher education students who view a teacher mediating a classroom discussion, for example, will often challenge the teacher's actions from the perspective of whether they appear to be "fair" to all students. When asked to support contentions that the teacher in question isn't behaving fairly to all in the class, prospective teachers initially present rationales based on their assuming the student's persona and projecting feelings like "why didn't I get called on in the discussion?"

When asked to take the perspective of the teacher who is working with a group of 25 students, however, teacher education students gradually begin to see the dilemmas associated with the need to devise multiple ways of moving an educational experience forward while also maintaining an orderly learning environment, ensuring that different levels of achievement are acknowledged, keeping track of the use of space and time and instructional materials, anticipating next steps, and participating in other myriad teaching occasions in a typical classroom. Helping prospective teachers to think like a teacher while also attending to what it is like to be a student with that teacher is difficult and often contentious work for the teacher educator, but it should be a central focus in teacher education programs, particularly those that intend for their graduates to alter the conventions of typical teaching practice.

A second focus in pushing back against business as usual in teaching has become a cliché even while it has considerable merit: teacher educators should model the teaching they hope their students will enact. If we believe that children and youth should be provided with multiple opportunities for problem solving as opposed to receiving and giving back prepackaged information, we must engage their prospective teachers in ways that both create a familiarity with what students will experience as well as how such approaches can be demonstrated. Similarly, recognizing the theoretical and practical advantages of using technology to enhance learning in the school subjects, we must provide teacher candidates with ways to see, as well as experience, technology-assisted instruction. In short, we must model with our teacher education students those practices that we hope they will carry with them into their own classrooms.

A significant alteration in thinking about engaging in school and teacher change is the growing understanding that effectiveness and excellence are largely dependent upon both individual *and* collective work. That is, teachers work with their students in relatively private settings but they also contribute to the well-being of the school in which that work occurs. Teachers are increasingly involved with one another in curriculum development work, school-based decision making, peer evaluation and mentoring, team teaching, and other school-wide activities that have become familiar practices during the past twenty or so years.

It is obvious that teacher education programs cannot fully prepare their students for all of the possible collegial interactions that may be required in an era of teacher participation in almost all arenas of school policy and decision making. Given that conclusion, however, we can teach our students, by example as well as in more direct ways, about the school as a culture, as a human organization with certain features, including that of collective activity. We can do this, in part, by working with our students in meaningful cohorts rather than as individuals, by requiring that practicum experiences give attention to the school as well as the classroom as an object of analytic attention, by insisting that student teaching assignments have a component of school-level activity rather than only classroom apprenticeship, and by providing similar opportunities to create a conception of being a teacher that includes but is not restricted to life in an individual classroom.

A final consideration regarding how teachers should be taught has to do with how programs of teacher education are planned and implemented. Elsewhere, I have argued for a research-based clinical teacher education model, one that has been shown to affect positively both how and what teacher candidates learn to teach.[14] Briefly, the model suggests that teacher education is best accomplished when it is context-sensitive (rather than exclusively or mainly abstract and unconnected to real-life teaching and learning situations), ongoing (rather than sporadic and disconnected in its components), cumulative in its intentions (rather than having a set of features that do not lead to and build upon one another), reflective (rather than prescriptive and promoted as a set of accepted truths), and knowledge-based (rather than rooted solely in conventional wisdom and untested proposals). The research studies that support this model suggest strongly that these features must all be present over time. Even though one or two of the components alone may be helpful to teacher educators and their students, for the model to achieve its full potential, all of them must be present in combination.

These proposals for how teachers should be prepared, among all that could be advanced, lead to a consideration of some of the contextual and temporal arrangements that influence teacher education.

Where and When Should Teacher Education Take Place?

I have already argued that teachers should be prepared in college or university teacher education settings rather than through alternate routes leading to a teaching career. In this section, I will give attention to issues that I believe must be addressed by the colleges and universities engaged with the preparation of teachers: baccalaureate and extended programs such as master's degree or a fifth year program, partnerships with elementary and secondary schools, the role of the teacher educator, and what has been called the continuum of teacher education.

A continuing debate centers on whether teacher education should be embedded in a conventional four-year bachelor's degree or whether it should be developed in either a five-year baccalaureate program or a focused master's degree. When the Holmes Group called for teacher licensure to be recommended by a college or university only after completion of a master's degree, a number of objections were voiced in higher education settings, in policy bodies such as state departments of education, and among organizations concerned with teaching and teacher education. These objections included the belief by some in colleges that it would be extremely difficult to enlist prospective teachers into post-baccalaureate programs to prepare for jobs that are traditionally not well paid, that the additional time spent learning to teach wasn't necessary because teaching isn't sufficiently demanding intellectually to justify the additional time and effort, that learning on the job was probably a more powerful vehicle for teacher learning than academically oriented programs, that since most states didn't require master's degrees this would be a waste of teacher candidates' time and money, and that hiring new teachers holding master's degrees would be too costly for school systems that had created salary structures providing greater financial rewards for those with extensive academic credentials.

Notwithstanding these and other objections, many of us believe that post-baccalaureate teacher education is an important avenue for teacher preparation and a powerful lever to influence teaching and learning in the nation's schools. Further, there appears to be growing agreement in state policy arenas that teacher licensure should rely on teachers demonstrating that they have engaged in specialized professional education beyond what can be offered in already crowded bachelor's degree programs.

There has been a persistent tension between those who believe that knowledge of subject matter is sufficient to license a teacher and those who believe that mastery of content must be enhanced with serious investments in learning about what might be called the "content of teaching." The proposals for extended teacher education programs are rooted in the second conception, a view that claims that the academic disciplines must be transformed into school subject matter that is developmentally appropriate. This view also considers pedagogy as a set of specialized ways of interacting with children. This perspective does not ignore subject matter. In fact, it honors academic achievement in its insistence that teachers must have solid authority over their school subjects, hence the insistence on successful completion of an academic major prior to beginning to learn to teach.

But those of us who align ourselves with an extended teacher education program do so with the understanding that teachers must also have serious command of a range of other ways of knowing. Teachers must know how to make content accessible to students, how to engage students so that they can make sense of the academic traditions, how to utilize students' developmental levels and interests as foundations upon which to create opportunities for understanding, how to assess the consequences of both students' and teachers' accomplishments, how to connect families to their students' school lives, and so on. Clearly, this view assumes that there is a content of teaching in much the same way that the content of medicine goes beyond anatomy and physiology and chemistry (a few of the "basics" of the healing professions) to include wielding a scalpel, explaining diagnoses to patients, understanding appropriate pharmaceutical dosages, and directing therapy regimens.

Another relatively recent change in the education of teachers is the growing belief that the field experiences that have been long-standing components of teacher education programs be linked more tightly to the college or university components. Instead of relying on often fragile institutional relationships between higher education and the schools, typically representing the theory-versus-practice dichotomy noted earlier, there should be an intellectual and practical connection that rests on shared assumptions about teaching, ongoing school-university discourse focused on what good teaching is conceived to be, and reinforcing policies and procedures that serve to strengthen teacher candidates' opportunities to enter the teaching force with a solid foundation of knowledge and skill.

This more conceptually and practically coherent approach to joining the abstract and concrete aspects of learning to teach is demonstrated powerfully by the formalization of professional development schools, a movement that is gaining authority but that is not without its own unique tensions and dilemmas. Despite the inherent problems that are logical and expected consequences of joining two heretofore only loosely connected educational institutions, the promise of the professional development school as a way to bring together the school and university perspectives on teaching around a set of shared values and understandings is being realized forcefully in hundreds of settings.

Another change regarding the enactment of teacher education programs is related to the partnerships being forged between the schools and colleges and universities. If one accepts that practicing teachers and other professional educators in the schools can and should be partners in the education of teachers, one must also accept the claim that these persons are teacher educators and must work alongside those who prepare teachers in higher education programs. The fifth grade teacher who welcomes student teachers to his classroom is an important partner in efforts designed to educate teachers. The school principal who invites teacher education students into her school as an occasion to understand how the school goes about its business is a teacher educator. The associate superintendent of instruction in a school district who involves prospective teachers in a curriculum development project is a teacher educator.

What has been missing from the practice of teacher education is not the participation of school professionals in the enterprise. Rather, there has been no formal recognition, preparation, ongoing dialogue, or inter-institutional agreements to guide the nature of the participation. The professional development school partnerships provide this foundation for collaboration and for acknowledging and rewarding the contributions of school professionals to the preparation of the next generations of the nation's teachers.

Until recently, conventional wisdom has had it that the role of the college or university teacher educator is played out only by those faculty who teach methods or educational foundation courses. In some universities, even those who teach specialized academic content (e.g., American history) to prospective teachers have not considered themselves or been considered by others as teacher educators. In part, this is a status issue and should be acknowledged as such. In most colleges and universities teacher education is something of a stepchild, with the more privileged faculty being lodged firmly within a typical academic discipline. To align oneself with preparation of members of what Amitai Etzioni has called the semi-professions (i.e., nursing, teaching, social work) reduces one's status in the academy.[15]

As teaching and teacher education have become central issues in national and state policy arenas, however, there appear to be some modest attempts to promote the education of teachers as a central function of colleges and universities and to enhance the status and associated reward structures of those who work with prospective teachers within and across the typical academic disciplines. Although universities, particularly the large state-supported land grant institutions, have long claimed that the education of teachers is the responsibility of all faculty, that claim has been a hollow one. A major influence on bringing teacher education to center stage in universities was the call to arms sent forth by the Holmes Group, which required that the university, rather than just the school of education, be the applicant for membership in that teacher education reform initiative.[16] This requirement was seen as imperative if teacher education were to be included in the core mission of higher education institutions and, along with the recognition that teacher education could once again become the heavily enrolled degree program it was before the so-called oversupply of teachers in the 1970s and 1980s, it caused university officials to re-think institutional priorities.

Finally, a time-and-place issue in teacher education is what has been called the teacher education continuum. As noted earlier, there has been widespread belief that newly minted graduates of teacher education programs are fully prepared to do the work of instructing the nation's children. Despite the historically ritualistic local requirements that teachers attend "inservice" or "institute" days as a means to enhance their knowledge and skills, the development of expertise has not been taken as seriously for teachers as it has, for example, in the more mature professions. Whereas it would be unthinkable that a doctor would not stay abreast of the latest developments in her field, it has been assumed that the knowledge base for teaching is so modest that it is achievable in a four-year program of study that is already focused primarily on the content of the liberal arts and sciences. If this is the case, then, why should it be important to take the ongoing development of teacher expertise seriously?

Several recent and current conditions have resulted in the erosion of this view of what it takes to be an expert teacher. Research, as well as anecdotally supported conclusions by teachers, has demonstrated that the first years of teaching are difficult and often result in teachers dropping out or giving in. Teachers move from a highly supervised and, in the best of circumstances, carefully supported program of study into the complex and multifaceted environments of classrooms and find that they are overwhelmed by the typical responsibilities of teaching. Because of seniority privileges granted to more experienced colleagues, the move from student of teaching to teacher is also accompanied by requirements to work with the students who are having the most difficulty, assume responsibility for extracurricular activities, and demonstrate the same levels of expertise as veteran teachers. Further, it is not unusual for new teachers to receive no targeted intellectual, practical, or personal support to help them in their transition into relatively autonomous practice.

These conditions and others that affect teachers over a career have prompted policymakers, scholars, and practitioners to call for considering teaching as a staged career, one that offers novices and expert teachers differentiated support, that takes into serious account the context-specific issues and dilemmas they face, and that has as its core the assumption that teaching is an ever-changing intellectual and practical activity in ongoing and cumulative need of refinement, development, and growth. In other words, we seem, finally, to be taking Franklin Parker's reflection seriously. He wrote:

I began to keep school forty-two years ago. I began to learn how to teach some twenty-five years ago. And, today, I feel deeply that I have not yet learned the fundamental principles of education.[17]

A simple illustration of the continuum of teacher education would begin with participation in a disciplined introduction to teaching in an extended baccalaureate or master's degree program based on a higher education/school partnership, joining a school system that provides a reduced-load teaching assignment accompanied by mentored opportunities to understand the realities of teaching, engaging with colleagues over time in ways that are supportive of continuing to develop teaching expertise, moving into mentoring and other professional roles as experience and accomplishment suggest, and earning recognition as an outstanding practitioner through vehicles such as the National Board for Professional Teaching Standards.[18]

When one considers expertise in teaching, it becomes essential to formulate expectations for what that expertise should encompass. This is the focus of the next section.

What Should Teachers Be Prepared to Do?

A number of historically valid expectations for teachers have received considerable attention and do not need additional support here. These include solid academic understanding of the disciplines, a wide repertoire of teaching strategies, dispositions to work solely for the benefit of students rather than one's self, clear and realistically high expectations for students, knowledge and skill related to student assessment, capability in curriculum work, and the like. This section takes these expectations as given but suggests additional current and anticipated requirements for the education of teachers that are rooted in changing conceptions of what it is to be an expert teacher in today's and tomorrow's schools, some of which have already been touched on in this chapter and are presented more comprehensively in other chapters in the Yearbook.

The issue of standards for teachers as well as students has captured the attention of policymakers, the public, and the profession of teaching. Prompted perhaps by beliefs that teachers are often ill- or underprepared, standards for students are seen by some as a way to force the issue of teachers' competence by holding them accountable for student performance. Of course, this equation assumes that teachers who meet performance and knowledge standards, by definition, will be capable of helping students achieve. An issue for teacher educators and the profession at large as well as for policymakers, then, becomes establishing the link between teacher standards and student standards, a difficult methodological and conceptual task.

If one accepts the conception of learning to teach as a continuum, as noted earlier, the issue of standards becomes even more complicated. Is it reasonable, for example, to hold first-year teachers to the same standards as their veteran colleagues? Should the demonstration of standards be related to the time and energy devoted by teacher education programs and school systems in support of teachers' acquisition of the performance and knowledge expectations embedded in the standards? Should teacher education programs be accredited in direct or proximate relation to the numbers or percentages of graduates who meet standards? These and other questions promise to preoccupy us in the coming years.

As I have suggested above, the education of teachers in both preservice and staff development programs (or "inservice education," a commonly used term for experienced teachers' opportunities for professional growth) has not been connected tightly to student achievement for a number of substantive and political reasons, the most obvious one being related to the belief that prospective teachers have less direct impact upon student outcomes than do the experienced teachers under whose supervision they do their student teaching. Similarly, it has not been common practice to link student achievement to individual teachers' efforts to improve practice or to the effects of school and school system on achievement.

I believe it is time to determine the degree to which there is a relationship between student outcomes and teacher education efforts. In terms of preservice programs, we should ask: Is there a connection between schools and classrooms in which student teachers begin their practice, for instance, and student achievement? If so, what accounts for this relationship? Is it the identification of expert teachers to serve as mentors to student teachers, the infusion of thought and practice from higher education into the classrooms, the identification of certain student groups as important encounters for prospective teachers, or some other factor that is unique to settings that prepare teachers?

Also, we should be bolder than we are in determining the relationship between student accomplishment and investments in teacher education for experienced teachers. There have been some studies of this interaction, but they tend to be on a cost-benefit basis rather than explorations that take fully into account the nature, extent, and depth of the professional growth experiences.[19] What is needed is a set of carefully designed studies that ask not just if there is a relationship and how much it costs but adds to these questions the important ones of what the educational opportunities are and how they are made present to teachers. We must open up the often closed box that sits between conventional "inputs" and "outputs." If we are to take seriously the continuum of teacher education and invest in strengthening opportunities to learn to teach over a career, we must be significantly more knowledgeable than we are about approaches to experienced teachers' continuing education and how they are related to student outcomes.

Another component of the repertoire of the expert teacher that has gained attention in recent years is knowledge and disposition to act related to the school as a particular form of human organization. Although some have urged schools and school systems to adopt organizational schema and management techniques from business and industry, these recommendations have been only partially enacted. In part, the reluctance of school professionals to look outside their own settings to learn of new ways of operating may be another manifestation of entrenched bureaucracies' habit of self-justification and rationalization. However, I do believe that there is sufficient differentiation between what schools are about and intended to accomplish and how business organizations function that we should resist supporting a wholesale adoption of organizational models from the private sector.

If my assumption about the significance of the differences between schools and other organizations is at all valid, it becomes imperative that school professionals, including new and experienced teachers, become sharply more understanding of schools as particular forms of societal organizations than I believe is usual.[20] It is very rare to find prospective students investing time and intellect in understanding the school as a culture. It is also unusual for experienced teachers to analyze, critique, and review their own settings in seriously thoughtful and intellectually solid ways. Instead, conventional wisdom, anecdotal reports, fragile claims, and data-free generalizations dot the landscape of school reform, largely because of either a lack of interest in or a disinclination to consider organizational understandings as important aspects of teacher education programs.

Recent experience with a number of school-focused reform activities has convinced me that considerable time would be saved and considerable progress could be made in school change if the primary participants—teachers—were more thoughtfully prepared to understand and act upon the conventions of schooling and question "business as usual" more sharply. I believe firmly that the school restructuring movement in this country, for example, is important content for teacher education, preservice and inservice. If teachers were engaged cumulatively in understanding the organizations in which they work, it would be more likely that they could see where their own workplaces were functioning well (and why) and where they must join with others to improve. It seems unreasonable to expect teachers to be both professionals and either unaware of, or reluctant to invest in becoming expert about, the human organizations in which they do their work.

Closely aligned with this emerging perspective on what counts as teacher knowledge and skill is the issue of teacher leadership. Although it has been widely acknowledged that there have always been teacher leaders in schools' informal systems, many of the recent reform initiatives have as centerpieces calls for teachers to assume greater responsibility for and activities aimed at school quality. We are moving, sometimes reluctantly and most often slowly, from a so-called factory model of schools in which administrators hold and wield all of the power and authority to a more collegial organization in which much of the work of the school is directed and monitored by faculty leaders in consultation and collaboration with school colleagues and school and system administrators.

Yet, teacher education in conventional settings like colleges, universities, and school systems only rarely provide teachers-to-be or veterans with the content, skills, and dispositions to prepare them for leadership positions. Rather, it seems to be an accepted assumption that effective leadership is more of an inborn human characteristic than a set of learned understandings and strategies. Intuitively, however, it seems reasonable to suggest that teachers should gain experience with such bodies of understanding as conflict management, coming to consensus, organizing adults for work, analysis and critique of educational practice, theories of change, and the like.

At the same time, though, many of us who work in graduate programs of study have observed with dismay that teachers who have worked with us to build these important understandings report that they become something akin to pariahs in their own schools, are sometimes considered trouble-makers, and eventually give in to the school or system requirements out of resignation rather than an erosion of a sense of the possible. Although there is a clear and public sense that teachers *should* be intimately engaged in the determination of what a school should be about, the persistence of the view of the teacher as worker and the administrator as leader gets in the way of realizing this expectation. Until we collectively both prepare for teacher leadership and appropriately recognize it as a function of being a teacher, it will be difficult to bring what seems to be an important contribution to remaking teaching as a career rather than a relatively "flat" job. Further, as schools become ever more complicated human organizations, it seems reasonable to consider distributing leadership throughout the professional school cadre rather than vesting it solely in the role of school principal.

A series of research studies over the past twenty years has consistently pointed to the importance of a collegial and collaborative culture as a foundation for school success. Programs that contribute to the education of teachers, it seems to me, should engage prospective, novice, and experienced teachers with opportunities to work together in ways that are supportive of professional learning as well as potentially influential upon building a school climate and culture that works. Collegiality is not easily understood or learned. And it is apparent to even the most naïve observer of schools that teaching continues to be a predominantly isolated activity. The old saying "behind the classroom door" says it all when the phrase implies that what individual teachers do with their students is largely private and, in fact, may be disconnected to what is happening behind the other classroom doors in a school.

Even though it is widely agreed that collaboration and collegiality are important features of both a profession and an individual school, insufficient attention is given to preparing prospective teachers to work effectively with one another or to devise meaningful ways for experienced teachers to have ongoing professional experiences that depend for success on sustained interaction. Again considering the continuum of teacher education, it is unreasonable, for instance, to expect experienced teachers to work collectively for the common good if they have not had opportunities to learn how to be collegial. And if we are serious about preparing novices for and sustaining veterans in supporting school reform initiatives rooted in conceptions of a healthy school organization, we do ourselves and our clients a disservice by continuing to embrace a conception of teaching as what Seymour Sarason has called the lonely profession.[21]

This chapter has touched in several instances on the issue of whether teaching is a career or a job, whether teachers are members of a *collegium* or of an occupation. Obviously, my point of view is that the preparation and continuing education of teachers should contribute to the realization of teaching as a career, as a set of staged opportunities for the continuous development of expertise, and as professional practice. If we continue to think of teacher education as the passing along of technique, as depending for the development of expert practice on an apprenticeship model, as viewing teachers as workers under the authority of a manager, and as drawing few distinctions between novices and experts, teaching will not achieve professional status.

Teacher education can contribute to the development of a profession if it is linked more seriously to the issues raised in this Yearbook than has been the case. In part, this is an intellectual issue and rests on the creation and use of knowledge that is derived from and targeted toward teaching as complex cognitive activity. There are ways of thinking, knowing, and doing teaching and teacher education that are not commonly shared with the broader population, despite rhetoric to the contrary. Similarly, the enhancement of teaching as professional activity will occur in some measure if we take seriously the admonition that teachers must invest, along with higher education institutions and schools, in ongoing efforts to develop expertise as a consequence of individual and collective engagement with new knowledge and participation in the creation of that new knowledge. Further, consideration and enactment of teaching as a staged career with benchmarks along the way (e.g., certification by the National Board for Professional Teaching Standards) will help to promote teaching as something other than what "anyone who loves children" can do.

At issue for me is how the education of teachers across a career, rather than only during a preservice program of study, can be linked to what teachers do and who teachers are in ways that strengthen both the authority of teachers in their work with students and enhances the role of teachers in the broader society.

Conclusion

This chapter has presented a number of issues that I believe deserve serious attention as we consider recent changes in teacher education thought and action. I am convinced that these issues and others that are discussed in the Yearbook chapters that follow can also provide bases for thinking about the future of the education of teachers. Of course, it is not enough for individuals, however well intentioned and thoughtful, to ponder how to move ahead; there must be a policy agenda and a collective will for progress to be made. Linda Darling-Hammond provides what might be considered a policy briefing in Chapter 10 and, along with other recommendations for action, helps us to create a preliminary roadmap for the future. Together, school and university faculties and thoughtful policymakers can work to test our recommendations for their validity and promise and create opportunities for teacher preparation and professional development that ". . . engage us in our own quests for answers and for meanings . . . and initiate us into the human community, in its largest and richest sense."[22]

NOTES

1. Kevin Ryan, ed., *Teacher Education: The Seventy-fourth Yearbook of the National Society for the Study of Education* (Chicago: University of Chicago Press, 1975).

2. National Commission on Teaching and America's Future, *What Matters Most: Teaching for America's Future* (New York: Author, 1996), p. vi.

3. Jeannie Oakes and Martin Lipton, *Teaching to Change the World* (Boston: McGraw-Hill, 1998).

4. Ryan, *Teacher Education: The Seventy-fourth Yearbook of the National Society for the Study of Education.*

5. Recent policy decisions by state governments, California being a major example, have also added to this issue by mandating that class size should be no greater than a set number (e.g., 25 in elementary schools). Consequently, the pressure on teacher recruitment is exacerbated by a policy decision that is, on face, desirable but contributes dramatically to an already widespread problem.

6. National Commission on Teaching and America's Future, pp. 50-52.

7. The Holmes Group, *Tomorrow's Teachers* (East Lansing: Author, 1986).

8. Mark A. Smylie, "Redesigning Teachers' Work: Connections to the Classroom," in *Review of Research in Education, Volume 20,* edited by Linda Darling-Hammond (Alexandria, VA: Association for Supervision and Curriculum Development, 1994).

9. Oakes and Lipton, *Teaching to Change the World.*

10. Mike Rose, *Possible Lives: The Promise of Public Education in America* (Boston: Houghton Mifflin Company, 1995).

11. National Commission on Teaching and America's Future, *Doing What Matters Most: Investing in Quality Teaching* (New York: Author, 1997).

12. Gary A. Griffin and Susan Barnes, "Using Research Findings to Change School and Classroom Practices: Results of an Experimental Study," *American Educational Research Journal,* 23(4): Winter, 1986; pp. 572-586.

13. Daniel C. Lortie, *Schoolteacher* (Chicago: University of Chicago Press, 1975); John I. Goodlad, *A Place Called School: Prospects for the Future* (New York: McGraw-Hill, 1984).

14. Gary A. Griffin, "Learning to Teach in Schools: A Framework for Clinical Teacher Education," in *Teaching: Theory into Practice,* ed. Allan C. Ornstein (Boston: Allyn and Bacon, 1995), pp. 385-402.

15. Amitai Etzioni, *The Semi-Professions and Their Organizations* (New York: Free Press, 1969).

16. The Holmes Group, *Tomorrow's Teachers.*

17. Franklin Parker, "My Pedagogic Creed," *The School Journal,* LIII(8): September, 1896; p. 1.

18. National Board for Professional Teaching Standards, *News of Note: A Publication for Friends of the National Board,* 2(8): October, 1998; p. 1.

19. National Commission on Teaching and America's Future, *Doing What Matters Most.*

20. Gary A. Griffin, "Influences of Shared Decision Making on School and Classroom Activity," *Elementary School Journal*, *96*(1), pp. 29-46.

21. Seymour B. Sarason, *The Culture of the School and the Problem of Change* (New York: Allyn and Bacon, 1971).

22. Maxine Greene, *Landscapes of Learning* (New York: Teachers College Press, 1978): p. 3.

CHAPTER II

Preparing Teachers as Agents of Change

MARK A. SMYLIE, MARY BAY, AND STEVEN E. TOZER

Teachers have long been expected to be agents of change. They are expected to evoke change in the students they teach. They are expected to carry out the broad missions of public education in the United States, including specific agendas for social change, and they are also expected to implement programs, policies, and innovations. Now, increasingly, they are expected to assume leadership of school reform.

It is one thing to expect teachers to be agents of change and yet another for them to perform this role successfully. Goals for teaching and for schooling are vague and often contested. The means to achieve those goals—the "technology" of teachers' work—are also ambiguous and uncertain. The entire enterprise is fraught with dilemmas that pit highly valued alternatives against one another. To be effective agents of change, teachers must be able to confront and manage these dilemmas. They must make meaning out of ambiguity; they must act in the midst of conflict.

It is often assumed that teacher educators know what capacities teachers need to be effective agents of change and can help them to develop these capacities. The research on preservice and inservice teacher education indicates, however, that these assumptions are not necessarily valid. Despite decades of effort to improve learning opportunities for teachers, the manner in which they are typically prepared and supported on the job falls short of developing the capacities they need to evoke change. If the expectation that teachers should be agents of change is taken seriously, the capacities this work requires of them must be considered more closely. Current practices of preservice and inservice teacher education must be examined more critically. And ways to enhance teachers' learning across their careers should be explored more thoughtfully.

Mark A. Smylie, Mary Bay, and Steven E. Tozer are Professors of Education at the College of Education, University of Illinois at Chicago.

These matters are the subject of this chapter. We approach them from two perspectives. First, we believe that initial preparation programs cannot be expected to develop all the capabilities teachers will need throughout their careers to be effective agents of change. While pre-service programs can play a crucial role, they must be considered in relation to other vital sources of teacher learning, including the experience of teaching, the school workplace, and programs for continuing professional development. In short, a complete agenda for teacher education must consider the particular contributions that different sources of learning can make at various times during a teacher's career.

Second, we focus our analysis on dilemmas that teachers face as they work to promote change. We chose this focus for several reasons. Dilemmas represent important points of uncertainty and ambiguity where multiple, often competing demands collide. Dilemmas reveal the capacities that make teachers effective agents of change and suggest the types of learning opportunities most conducive to developing these capacities.

We begin by examining the role of teachers as agents of student change, social change, and school change. We continue with a general discussion of dilemmas associated with each area of change and then illustrate these dilemmas with specific examples drawn from the complex and challenging context of public schooling in Chicago. Our examples are not meant to compose a comprehensive inventory of dilemmas teachers may face in their work nor to represent particular dilemmas all teachers may confront. Rather, the intent is to focus on particular capacities that teachers need to be effective agents of change. Our analysis of dilemmas points to the importance of particular types of knowledge, intellectual skills, and professional orientations for effective change agency. It is followed by an assessment of the prospects of preservice and inservice teacher education as generally practiced for developing them. We consider some ways that teachers' opportunities to learn might be improved. We argue that even strong preservice programs will not be sufficient to develop the qualities teachers will need to be effective as change agents in the classroom, society, and school. The nature and complexity of these qualities underscore the importance of ongoing professional learning and development. Schools must become more purposeful sites of professional learning and universities must support teachers more explicitly in developing their qualities as change agents in multiple contexts. We conclude with a discussion of why such changes may be difficult to achieve.

Teachers as Agents of Change

When teachers are thought of as agents of change, most people think about their efforts to promote student learning and development. Less often considered are teachers' roles in promoting broader purposes of schooling, particularly those associated with social change and school-level reform. Yet teachers' roles in effecting student change, social change, and school change are importantly related to each other. Teachers' efforts to work in one area are likely to be shaped by and have implications for the others.

PROMOTING STUDENT CHANGE

The notion of teaching as the purposeful fostering of change in individuals has historical roots that extend from Plato's *Republic* to John Dewey's *Democracy and Education*[1] and to more recent debates among educators. Dewey recognized, for example, that changes sought among students in the name of education are not random but lead toward a desired goal. For him, this goal was mature participation in democratic community life. The task of the teacher was to foster individual growth with this "end in view."

In the 1960s and 1970s, educational philosophers and curriculum theorists sought to clarify just what kinds of changes in individuals should be promoted by teachers and schools.[2] Debates ensued concerning the value of discipline-based knowledge, specific behavioral manifestations of cognitive and affective development, and personal growth and sense of self. By the late 1970s and early 1980s, these debates were joined by more critical perspectives which argued that teaching should promote personal empowerment and emancipation and develop students' critical skills to reflect and act upon social and economic injustices.

Stakeholders in schooling, including parents, the business community, and government leaders, have expected teachers to promote all manner of cognitive, social, and emotional growth among their students. Teachers have been expected to develop specific academic knowledge and skills, instill particular values, and prepare students for productive employment and civic participation. Some expectations for student change are bounded by the immediate contexts of local communities. Others reflect wider public interests. Currently, expectations for student change are expressed in the spate of student learning goals, standards, and assessments being developed at the national, state, and local levels. Their content is often hotly contested as is the authority of national and state governments to use them as means of local control and professional accountability. These initiatives and the contentiousness that surrounds them reflect a broader debate about the purposes of schooling and the role of schooling in social change. In the face of such debate, teachers must make their own choices about what social agendas their teaching will serve.

PROMOTING SOCIAL CHANGE

Throughout the history of American public education, schools have been assigned a variety of social missions, some explicitly embracing agendas for social change. Thomas Jefferson, Daniel Webster, and Benjamin Rush were among those who believed that public schools were essential to building the knowledge and values necessary for representative government to succeed. Horace Mann built support for common schools in part by arguing that public schooling could address economic, social, and moral problems of urban life. Dewey argued that America's future would be precarious if schools did not become laboratories for democratic participation.

Throughout the 1800s, "social efficiency" agendas for schooling developed in which the goals of vocational preparation, economic productivity, and social stability increasingly vied with classical democratic values in the rhetoric of school reform.[3] In the twentieth century, social efficiency advocates, like Harvard's president Charles Eliot, argued that schools should play a greater part in sorting students for their roles in the American work force. After World War II, James B. Conant led a national movement for comprehensive high schools that would advance American technical expertise and economic productivity in the Cold War. Education reform reports of the late 1970s and early 1980s called for increased rigor in schools so that they might better equip the nation to meet growing economic threats from western Europe and Asia.

In contrast to these social efficiency arguments, a more critical democratic agenda for schools emerged in the early 1900s. For example, W. E. B. DuBois called for an education for African Americans that would be defined not by the needs of the economy but by the needs of a free people to develop the capacities for "honest and earnest criticism" that constitute the "soul of democracy." In the 1930s and 1940s, social reconstructionists argued that teachers and administrators should be prepared to exercise their professional responsibility as leaders of democratic social change. By the 1950s and 1960s, schools had become sites of conflict as they were expected to remedy the harm caused by racial discrimination and segregation. For the past fifteen years, curriculum theorists have argued anew that schools should become sites of democratic action. Today, proponents of multicultural education, anti-racist education, and culturally responsive education have exhorted schools and teachers to serve a social mission that would eliminate racial, ethnic, socioeconomic, and gender-based domination and subordination.

Conservative forces have also brought pressure on schools to promote their images of society. These advocates of social change have variously emphasized the importance of schools in restoring fundamentalist Christian values, patriotism, respect for Eurocentric cultural and political traditions, and English as the national language. Some parents and community leaders have promoted such "traditional" values within neighborhood schools and school districts. Others have promoted this agenda through state and national policies that would support private Christian schools, expand and enable public school choice, and establish charter schools.

In sum, teachers have been expected to enact these various goals for social change. They have been expected to promote literacy and republican values to secure the future of democratic government and social institutions. They have been expected to instill Judeo-Christian values and vocational skills to promote social stability, remedy social and moral ills, and prepare students for their economic and civic roles in society. Teachers have also been expected to be agents of integration and social justice, attacking problems of discrimination and social inequality from their schools and classrooms.

PROMOTING SCHOOL CHANGE

Teachers have long been expected to implement new programs and policies designed to improve schools. They are, however, more than functional agents who simply act out new programs and policies. They are active interpreters of change initiatives, adapting them according to their own interests and abilities, and shaping them to their local contexts.[4] Indeed, teachers are often blamed for the failure of new programs and policies if they do not achieve their objectives.

Teachers are increasingly expected to assume leadership roles in school improvement. Since the mid-1980s, school districts and state education agencies throughout the United States have developed a wide variety of such roles, which have expanded work for teachers beyond the classroom, placing them with administrators at the center of school- and district-level decision making and providing teachers with opportunities to develop programs and policies and to work on staff development and school improvement. New opportunities for teacher leadership have come with career ladders and teacher mentoring programs and from efforts to decentralize and expand decision-making authority at the school level. Teachers who assume new leadership roles usually continue their classroom teaching. Moreover, in these new roles teachers often enter an already crowded field since in many states and school districts, teacher leadership initiatives share an uneasy co-existence with centralized bureaucratic reforms that preceded them.

Expectations for teachers to promote student change, social change, and school change are long standing and firmly established. At the same time, they are ambiguous, dynamic, often contradictory, and contested. They present dilemmas that must be confronted and managed if teachers are to be effective agents of change.

Dilemmas in Working for Change

Larry Cuban defines dilemmas as conflict-filled situations that have no clear resolution.[5] They involve trade-offs and pit highly valued alternatives against each other. They embody normative conflicts, not just technical hurdles. Responses often take the form of "good-enough compromises" rather than neat solutions. According to David Hansen and Nicholas Burbules, responses can be no more than provisional working resolutions,[6] "provisional" because no response can permanently dissolve a dilemma and "working" because the response provides at least a temporary way of addressing it. Dilemmas are recurrent and must be managed.

CLASSROOM DILEMMAS

Dilemmas are an inherent part of teachers' work and may arise from a number of sources. They often occur in the complex interactions between a teacher and his or her students.[7] For instance, in a given lesson, or series of lessons, how does the teacher balance attention to one child with attention to all children? How does he or she share authority with students in an effort to create a sense of community, yet maintain authority appropriate to teaching important elements of the curriculum? During the discussion of a science concept, does the teacher call on a girl in an effort to foster her interest in science, or on the boy who experiences an attention deficit disorder and needs to be pulled back into the lesson?

Such dilemmas arise because the teacher is expected to foster change—learning—among all students. They arise because there are no clear-cut choices among highly valued objectives, or because situations implicate the teacher's commitment to broader values, such as providing all children equitable opportunities to learn. In any given classroom, students' learning needs may be so different as to become competitive. Teachers know that to commit the time and attention required to optimize learning opportunities for some students would disadvantage other students.

DILEMMAS SURROUNDING THE PURPOSES OF SCHOOLING

In a related manner, dilemmas may arise from the uncertain and often contested purposes of schooling. More than forty years ago, William O. Stanley wrote in an essay entitled "The Present Dilemma of Education":

It is exceedingly difficult to establish or to maintain a consistent program of education in a society characterized by fundamental confusion and conflict. For, in such societies, there is no conclusive standard of the public welfare and, hence, no certain conception of the kind of character which the school should undertake to build. Consequently, the educator has no clear definition of the ends and purposes of education which is generally acknowledged or taken for granted by all parties to the educational enterprise.[8]

This dilemma is present with us today. As postmodern society becomes more pluralistic and as knowledge and assumptions which were once taken for granted are challenged, the dilemmas surrounding the purposes of schooling become more complex and ambiguous.[9] If teachers' work should serve democratic ideals, which version of democracy should prevail? If schools are so important to the public welfare that all taxpayers are required to support them, what vision of the public good are teachers to serve? Furthermore, it is rarely, if ever, that a vision embraces the *status quo*. Rather, visions address the need for change, whether in social, economic, moral, or political spheres. Then, toward what vision of society, toward what mission of change, are teachers to commit themselves?

DILEMMAS IN SCHOOL CHANGE

Dilemmas may arise when teachers are expected to implement new programs and policies that challenge prevailing norms and practices, both personal and organizational. Proposed innovations may conflict with current programs and policies. They may contradict or interfere with one another. When teachers are presented with choices for change within their schools, how do they decide which change to support, especially when confusion exists about the larger social agendas to be served? How do teachers decide when the proposed changes conflict with their own commitments or carry risks of unsettling hard-earned progress in their classrooms?

According to Michael Knapp and his colleagues, teachers face a number of dilemmas when reforms are not mutually reinforcing.[10] Either they must select among competing reforms, or they must try to adapt and reconcile those reforms. The dilemma is intensified when the aims of competing reforms are similarly valued. Dilemmas become even more complicated when the aims of a reform (for example, one involving standardized testing) are not highly valued by teachers but carry high stakes for students, such as being denied promotion or graduation.

Finally, teachers may confront a number of dilemmas when they assume new leadership roles for school improvement. Teacher leaders may face trade-offs in how they allocate time and energy between working for school-level change and working for the students they teach. They may confront situations where they must challenge the administrative prerogatives and priorities of their principals, the persons to whom they are finally accountable. Working for school change may challenge the norms and routines that govern collegial relations and a teacher leader's place in this "social order." For example, a teacher leader may need to consider how the collaborative work required for the success of an important curricular reform may challenge the norms of privacy, autonomy, and egalitarianism that govern teachers' working relationships.

PROFESSIONAL CONSIDERATIONS

Like other professions, teaching is characterized by identifiable aims and norms (e.g., teachers should be agents of change; they should care for their students; their teaching should serve democratic ideals), but those aims and norms are vague and often contested. Unlike law and medicine, teaching has no common, articulated code of professional conduct. At best, the aims and norms of teaching provide only a framework to help teachers manage the dilemmas they confront in their work. Indeed, the aims and norms of teaching may themselves become sources of dilemmas as teachers try to make meaning of them in particular settings and as they try to reconcile them with the commitments they bring as individuals to schools and classrooms.

The management of dilemmas is complicated, too, by the fact that the knowledge base of teaching is not systematically codified nor universally recognized. In other professions, such as law, medicine, architecture, and engineering, a technical or practical knowledge base is recognized and utilized and it is constantly undergoing revision as goals and practices are questioned and improved. In teaching, the body of relevant knowledge is more than in flux; there is substantial debate about what belongs in it. Indeed, the very legitimacy of a knowledge base for teaching is the source of contention among those who believe that patterns of effective teaching can be identified, codified, and serve as a guide for teacher preparation and practice,[11] and those who believe that teaching is such a personal and idiosyncratic endeavor that it defies the boundaries of a knowledge base.[12]

Thus for teachers dilemmas must be managed at several intersections: that of knowledge, norms, and practice, both standard and emergent; that of the individual, the professional, and the public; and that of the classroom, the school, the local community, and society. It is unreasonable to expect preservice teacher preparation programs to equip future teachers to manage effectively the dilemmas that arise in these complicated and shifting intersections. Certainly, stronger programs of initial teacher preparation are called for, but these need to be followed by purposeful programs of professional development that far exceed what the teaching field currently offers. A systematic relationship between the preservice and inservice phases of professional growth needs to be articulated and enacted if teachers are to manage dilemmas successfully.

Dilemmas in the Work of Chicago Teachers

The types of dilemmas we have sketched can be vividly and concretely illustrated in examples from teachers' work in the Chicago Public Schools (CPS). CPS is the third largest public school system in the United States, enrolling 424,500 students of various racial, ethnic, and linguistic groups in 557 schools. It is a large, complex, and challenging environment in which to work. In describing dilemmas that this environment poses for teachers, it is not our intent to criticize, but to highlight sources of dilemmas that teachers everywhere need to manage if they are to be successful agents of change.[13]

CHICAGO PUBLIC SCHOOL STUDENTS

The student population of CPS is much like those of other big city school systems. Many students are confronted with the familiar challenges of urban life: poverty and unemployment, shifting family structures, crime and violence, and inadequate housing.[14] Many experience traumatic events that challenge personal development and threaten academic success. In a recent study of one low-income Chicago neighborhood, about 45 percent of high school students interviewed reported having a parent who abused alcohol or drugs.[15] Almost half of these students had experienced physical or sexual abuse and about 45 percent reported involvement in gangs.

Chicago's student population is highly mobile. A typical elementary classroom of 30 students has a net turnover rate of five students a year.[16] On the average, only 38 percent of elementary students remain in the same school from first through sixth grade. Students who change schools tend to be lower achievers than those who do not, adding another dimension to the "churn" in classroom memberships.

Student absenteeism is high, particularly in secondary schools. For example, 26 percent of tenth grade students are absent more than 40 days of a 180-day school year.[17] Another 23 percent are absent between 21 and 40 days. Absenteeism is high among students of all achievement levels. Forty-two percent of the highest achieving ninth graders in the system miss two or more weeks of classes in at least one major subject per semester.[18] When students attend school, they are often not engaged. Between 48 percent and 56 percent of students report being only somewhat or minimally engaged in their classes.[19] Lack of engagement often manifests itself in classroom misbehavior and neglecting homework. About one-third of CPS teachers report that on the average their classrooms are disrupted three or four times a day by student misconduct, and another third report five or more interruptions a day.[20]

Chicago teachers also confront low levels of academic performance. While reading and mathematics achievement, as measured by the Iowa Test of Basic Skills (ITBS), has increased in most elementary grades during the past ten years, overall levels remain low.[21] According to 1997 ITBS test data, 70 percent of students in third through eighth grades are performing below national norms in reading and 64 percent are performing below national norms in math. According to scores on the Tests of Achievement and Proficiency (TAP), 75 percent of ninth and eleventh grade students scored below national norms in reading and 69 percent scored below national norms in math. Finally, large proportions of students fail to complete high school; in recent years dropout rates have ranged from 25 to 55 percent.[22]

WORKING CONDITIONS OF SCHOOLS

Working conditions in Chicago schools vary significantly by building and neighborhood and often pose significant and challenging dilemmas to teachers. Some schools operate in facilities that are clean and new; others operate in buildings that are literally falling down. Some schools possess the latest high-tech equipment and Internet connections while others have insufficient numbers of outdated textbooks. Many teachers must spend their own money to stock their classrooms with even the most basic instructional materials, such as paper, pencils, and art supplies. Some schools are so overcrowded that teachers meet with students in hall corners and storage closets; other schools are so under-utilized that they have been threatened with closure.[23]

Other aspects of school environments that significantly affect teachers and their work include substantial isolation among faculty.[24] Only about one-third of teachers in the system engage in regular dialog about instruction. One-quarter work in schools where teachers and administrators disagree about school goals and norms of practice. Half fail to see any real coherence and continuity across programs in their schools. Most believe that their schools have so many programs coming and going that they cannot keep track of them all.

Given these situations, it is not surprising that approaches to improvement in many schools lack coherence. In the early 1990s, 31 to 39 percent of CPS elementary schools had unfocused approaches to school improvement.[25] Another 20 to 35 percent had more coherent approaches but these could not be considered systemic. More recent evidence of fragmentation has been found in a study of the Chicago Annenberg Challenge.[26] Among the major challenges to school improvement reported by principals and external partners was the lack of coherence among multiple programs and innovations at their schools. These data indicate that multiple programs often compete for teachers' time and attention, pull faculties in different directions, and limit teachers' ability to fully participate in any program.

The problem of incoherence in school improvement is exacerbated by an orientation toward entrepreneurialism among system administrators. The amount of new resources—programs, personnel, materials, and equipment—that principals bring into their schools has become a presumed indicator of successful leadership.[27] This indicator is easily demonstrated and understood as progress by the central administration and the Local School Councils (LSCs), the school-level governing bodies that have the authority to hire and fire their principals.

WAVES OF REFORM

Chicago Public Schools have been subject to two major reforms in the past ten years.[28] In 1988, the Illinois legislature fundamentally altered the structure and governance of the Chicago school system by legislation that curtailed central office authority and placed responsibility for improving student achievement at the school level. The most widely publicized feature of this legislation was the creation of LSCs dominated by parents and the community. In addition to the authority to hire and fire principals, these "mini-school boards" were given control of their schools' Chapter One funds and academic programs. School-level Professional Personnel Advisory Committees (PPACs), made up of teachers, were legislatively mandated to advise principals on instructional and teacher-related matters.

Seven years later, the state legislature amended the 1988 reform with a second package that focused on the system's central management and local school's accountability. While LSCs and PPACs were preserved, the 1995 reform replaced the existing central office and school board with a corporate-style management team and a Reform Board of Trustees directly accountable to the mayor. The law gave the new management team substantially more authority to hold schools accountable for their performance. Failing schools could now be subject to remediation, probation, or reconstitution. The central administration could disband LSCs and fire, layoff, or reassign staff, including principals, in schools deemed in need of reconstitution.

Among the first policies introduced by the new central administration were new accountability mechanisms for students and schools. Student promotion became dependent on performance on the ITBS. Students scoring below a pre-set grade equivalent in reading and math are required to attend remedial summer school, after which a retesting determines if they will be promoted to the next grade. With this high-stakes use of standardized tests, the central administration and the mayor's office proclaimed the elimination of "social promotion" in Chicago's public schools. Scores on the ITBS have also been used as the primary (but not the only) indicator to determine which schools will be placed on probation or reconstituted. In 1996 and 1997, the system placed 115 schools on probation. Seven of 38 probationary high schools were later identified for reconstitution resulting in about one-quarter of the teachers in these schools being released from their positions.[29]

The new administration developed new student learning goals and standards, promoted a basic skills curriculum, and encouraged direct instruction. It established a mandatory homework policy and developed prescribed lesson plans for teachers who work in mandatory summer school programs for low-achieving students. The system allocated more resources to expand early childhood programs. It created summer "bridge" programs and freshman academies to better support student transition from elementary to high schools. As of this writing, the central administration is developing systemwide end-of-course examinations and course lesson plans keyed to the system's learning standards. At the same time that it has developed these policies, the central administration has left school improvement largely to the schools, and professional development to individual teachers. While the central administration has provided managers and support teams to work with probationary schools, and while it has encouraged area universities and human service organizations to join schools in partnerships, individual schools and teachers are by and large left on their own to improve themselves.

Complicating efforts to promote professional development and school improvement in Chicago is the problem of time. The teachers' contract with CPS calls for a 33-hour work week. The central administration has mandated that 300 minutes (five hours) of every day be devoted to instruction. With closed campuses compacting the school day into 330 minutes, teachers find it hard to satisfy this instructional mandate. They also find it extraordinarily difficult to find time within their contractual work week to engage in meaningful professional development or school improvement.[30] While individual schools may obtain waivers to the contract to extend teachers' work hours, faculties and school-level administrators must decide how additional time can best be spent, whether in the direct service of students (e.g., attending to individual student needs or preparing them to succeed on high-stakes standardized achievement tests), in professional development of teachers, or in school improvement. The issue of time may force teachers to seek professional development on their own, diminishing its importance in their regular work lives, reducing its potential to contribute to school change, and making it about impossible to develop schools as places for collaborative work and learning among teachers.

EXAMPLES OF DILEMMAS

From this context spring a number of dilemmas for Chicago teachers. They work in a system with newly developed student learning goals and standards, a high-stakes accountability system oriented toward acquisition of basic skills, and an emphasis on teacher-centered instruction. Teachers are required to teach in ways that supposedly ensure student success on criteria set by administrators. The consequences of students not achieving success are severe—mandatory remedial summer school and/or grade retention for students, probation and perhaps reconstitution for schools and teachers.

Chicago teachers may find that the basic skills focus of the curriculum and the direct instruction promoted by the system help students succeed on standardized tests but do little to foster student interest and engagement in learning. In preparing students for the ITBS, teachers may find little room for curriculum that reflects and responds to students' culture, experiences, and future interests and for instruction that moves to higher levels and more "authentic" forms of learning.[31] Thus, while Chicago teachers may recognize and support students' rights to succeed according to the system's administrative criteria, they may be frustrated in their ability to enact curriculum that engages students and promotes meaningful learning.

This dilemma evokes others related to the social purposes of schooling in Chicago. If the purposes of Chicago schools are primarily to sort and prepare students for diverse roles in an economically and socially stratified society, then assessing and ranking them according to performance on standardized tests of basic skills makes sense. It makes sense for students at an early age, and it makes sense even for students whose socioeconomic status, ethnicity, culture, or language may not be reflected in the dominant norms of "quality" reflected in the tests. However, the discouraging effects of not doing well on such assessments may be so great as to undermine teachers' efforts to motivate every child in learning, which is the democratic purpose of schooling, the "moral meaning" which Dewey once formulated as serving "the all around growth of every member of society."[32]

Chicago teachers are thus confronted with a dilemma about which social mission they are to serve in working in the context of high-stakes assessments. How can teachers support students, especially students from low-income, culturally diverse backgrounds, in reaching their intellectual, ethical, and creative potential, in finding fulfilling work, and becoming critical, active members of a democratic society, when the policies and sanctions of the school system seem to focus on preparing these students as dutiful voters and reliable workers? If a teacher believes that the primary purpose of schooling is to prepare students for the workplace and the voting booth, this dilemma may be diminished. For a teacher who sees in students the potential to develop interests and capacities that could motivate and sustain a fulfilling work life and active, informed democratic participation in local communities and beyond, the pressure to act as agents of ranking and sorting, using standardized tests, may be deeply troubling. Indeed, many teachers with whom we work in Chicago claim to feel frustrated and helpless in the face of this dilemma.

Chicago teachers confront other important dilemmas in promoting student learning. They must decide how much time to allocate to the personal crises that some students experience outside school. Attending to these crises would take time away from instruction and limit the attention that the teacher might give to other students. If left unattended, these crises would make it difficult for the students who experience them to benefit from whatever instruction is offered. Teachers face dilemmas around the pacing of instruction.[33] Given high rates of student absenteeism and mobility, and given the lack of programmatic coherence in many schools, how much time should teachers spend bringing absent students and newcomers up to speed at the expense of slowing down the introduction of new material and moving prepared students forward? How much time should a teacher spend responding to disengaged or misbehaving students, if this disengagement or misbehavior is not necessarily disruptive to the rest of the class, and if the teacher's efforts come at the expense of attentive students?

Similarly, Chicago teachers face dilemmas in working for school change. Teachers must decide how much time to allocate between working with students and working with PPACs, LSCs, and other teachers and administrators on particular school improvement initiatives. How might teachers reconcile their participation in school-level decision making with the norm that the primary focus of their work should be classroom instruction? In schools where privacy and individual autonomy are the norm, how much should a teacher encourage other teachers to work together on a particularly promising instructional program? How much leadership should a teacher exercise in a context where authority is shared (and sometimes contested) between the principals and the LSC but not with teachers? How far should a teacher go to advocate a particular initiative that has strong potential to promote student learning when that teacher's effort infringes on the leadership prerogatives of the principal or conflicts with the principal's own agenda for the school?

Further, how might teachers' interests in creating more focus and coherence in school improvement efforts be balanced against their principals' interests in and rewards for the accumulation of programs and resources? How can a teacher balance the value associated with decentralized, democratic governance involving parents and community members, and the value of acting in good faith on decisions made according to those processes, when the decisions are contrary to the teacher's best professional judgment? How can a teacher reconcile avoiding central office sanctions that are a disservice to students with the value of local determinism in striking a course for school improvement? Finally, and importantly, how should teachers decide which social goals and student learning goals are best served by different types of and approaches to school change? The capacities that teachers will need to address these various kinds of dilemmas are many and complex.

Capacities for Managing Dilemmas

The confrontation of dilemmas lies at the heart of Dewey's analysis of thinking and learning in his book *How We Think*.[34] Dewey tells of a traveler who comes to an unexpected fork in the road. Not knowing which way to go, the traveler is confronted with the question, "Which road is right?" Dewey argues that the traveler has two alternatives. He can blindly and arbitrarily choose his course, or he can look for signs and clues that can inform his decision. Dewey reasons that as long as activity "glides smoothly" along from one thing to another, there is no call for learning and reflection, but difficulty in achieving an objective stimulates learning.

As our analysis suggests, teachers repeatedly face such "forks in the road," and how they confront, reason about, and manage these dilemmas determines their success as change agents. We contend that managing dilemmas should be a central focus of teachers' initial preparation and their ongoing professional development. Professional knowledge, intellectual capacities, and a professional orientation toward work are three factors to be considered in developing teachers' management of dilemmas. In discussing these three factors in what follows, we recognize that there is much more to say about them than can be offered here.

PROFESSIONAL KNOWLEDGE

The professional knowledge required to manage dilemmas effectively includes familiarity with relevant facts, values, and ways of organizing knowledge in the service of change. Implicit is an understanding of formal theory and the findings of empirical research as well as the inferences that can be drawn from careful analysis and critique of one's experiences as a student and as a teacher. The understandings and "know how" that teachers must draw upon when managing most educational dilemmas pertain to knowledge of students; of curriculum, instruction, and assessment; of the organization and function of classrooms, schools, and school systems; and of the broad social, cultural, and historical contexts of schooling. We use the term "know how" to indicate the craft knowledge that is integral to professional knowledge. The professional not only knows *that* something is relevant but knows *how* to proceed.

Knowledge of students includes understandings of how children and youth develop and learn under various conditions. It includes understandings of the influence of language, culture, ability, family, and community on student learning and development. Knowledge of curriculum, instruction, and assessment includes understanding of the structure and content of academic subject matter, as well as commanding the strategies for organizing subject matter for student learning, designing or selecting appropriate activities to engage students and help them connect with subject matter, and devising methods to monitor student learning in ways that credibly demonstrate progress. Knowledge concerning schools and school systems as organizations embodies theories of leadership and change, including how leadership can be exercised to address social, organizational, and professional issues. It also embodies knowledge of how education programs and policies are formulated and implemented to respond to these issues. Finally, it is crucial to include in professional knowledge a set of understandings of the social, cultural, historical, and philosophical foundations of education, providing critical perspective on the purposes of schooling, the values and conflicts that characterize them, and the dilemmas that surround the roles of schools and teachers in promoting social change.

INTELLECTUAL CAPACITIES

To manage dilemmas effectively in the contexts of change that we have identified, teachers must be able to think critically about the relationships among classroom practices, student learning, social outcomes, and the ways in which the school facilitates desired learning. Teachers need to think acutely about how classroom practices serve student learning, how student learning may serve social outcomes, and what changes in the school might be necessary to facilitate student learning consistent with particular social outcomes.

To think well about these matters suggests certain intellectual capacities. Teachers must be able to analyze complex situations, that is, to inquire and observe, perceive relationships, and draw logical infer-ences. Teachers must have the ability to confront dilemmas by care-fully framing and reframing them, identifying and assessing possible responses, taking action, and evaluating consequences. Teachers must have the ability to make ethical judgments, understand their own val-ues, infer the values present in a particular situation, and relate these values to their professional knowledge.

A PROFESSIONAL ORIENTATION

Knowledge without values is aimless, and each profession is guided by a value orientation that concerns the needs of those served and the broader social goals which that service addresses. Teachers should have the character to act consistently with the highest values of their profes-sion. Four values stand out as necessary for addressing the types of dilemmas described earlier. First, teachers should hold a student-cen-tered orientation toward their work because many of the important dilemmas teachers face are recognizable as such only when the learner is at the center of their thinking. Without such an orientation, teaching becomes primarily a technical endeavor, one that is more concerned with teacher behaviors than with student experiences and outcomes.

Second, teachers must be willing to accept the uncertainty and ambi-guity that dilemmas present. They must develop a disposition toward critique, inquiry, and analysis. They should come to see professional learning and personal development as a continuous process. Something like a scientific open-mindedness is needed, to use Dewey's comparison, for teachers to be inclined to continue to learn about teaching. Such a disposition rejects the notion of teacher as infallible expert and accepts a willingness to be simultaneously teacher, leader, and learner.

Third, teachers should see their work as a collective enterprise in-volving other teachers, administrators, parents, and other stakehold-ers. Teachers should understand the value of collaboration for their success with students, for their own professional learning and develop-ment, and for school improvement. Teachers should also be disposed toward joint work, the public examination of practice, and mutual accountability. Teachers should understand the professional nature of teaching and what it means to be a member of a profession.

Fourth, teachers must care about the social consequences of their work, be it at the school or classroom level, and be committed to act on behalf of a more just society. It is not enough that teachers think clearly and in well-informed ways about social consequences. Nor is it enough to add the skills to teach in ways consistent with social justice.

Teachers must also care deeply enough to act consistently with their best social and ethical understandings. For some teachers with whom we work, such commitment has led to efforts to become change agents in their schools, so that these schools may better serve the educational and social ideals to which these teachers are committed.

The Practice of Teacher Education

Considering these capacities together—professional knowledge, ability to think and reason well, and a professional orientation—it becomes clear that becoming effective change agents requires considerable learning. Neither preservice teacher education programs nor classroom teaching experience alone can reasonably be expected to provide it.[35] Instead, these capacities must be supported by a constellation of learning experiences that begins with preservice preparation and extends to workplace learning and ongoing programs of professional development. How well does preservice education, as now generally practiced, help develop these capacities? How well do inservice opportunities for teacher learning continue to support the development of these capacities?

PRESERVICE TEACHER EDUCATION

From the evidence that exists, we find that despite recent efforts to improve preservice education, these programs typically provide insufficient opportunity for teachers to develop the capacities they need to manage dilemmas effectively as agents of change. Most evidence is anecdotal. Comprehensive, in-depth analyses of curriculum, instructional processes, and program organization are rare.[36]

Perhaps the most current and comprehensive assessment is John Goodlad's five-year study of teacher education programs in 29 representative public and private colleges and universities across the United States.[37] This analysis portrays preservice teacher education as an enterprise characterized by poorly conceived collages of courses, lack of a clear mission (beyond entitling graduates to state credentials), and a concentration on developing discrete skills and techniques.[38] Teacher education curricula focus primarily on practical or craft knowledge. The theoretical and research knowledge presented in educational psychology and social foundations courses most often stands disconnected from courses and fieldwork in teaching methodology. Concerns with technique and practical experiences dominate all else in the curriculum. The implicit emphasis of these programs is to prepare teachers to fit into existing schools and classrooms rather than to challenge and change them.

Goodlad's study found that preservice programs were typically fragmented, providing few opportunities for the development of in-depth knowledge or for synthesis and application of subject matter knowledge, educational theory and research, and practice. Few programs provided opportunities for preserve teachers to develop understanding of subject-specific pedagogy. Education courses typically reduced teaching to the mechanical application of generic classroom procedures. Little attention was paid to understanding why particular techniques might be applied in different situations or why they and not others might achieve certain objectives. Further, lack of coherence in liberal arts requirements provided but a weak foundation for subject matter expertise or for preparing teachers to be the "best educated citizens of the community."[39] As might be expected, this study found little emphasis on the social foundations of education. In very few instances did the study find programs oriented around a broader conception of the role of schools and teachers in a democratic society.

Goodlad's research was also critical of the failure of teacher education programs to promote the intellectual development of their students. The most prevalent methods of instruction found in these programs were lecture and instructor-directed discussion. There was little "intellectual wave-making." The study found little evidence of deliberate attempts to develop skills of discourse, debate, and analysis. There was little indication that future teachers were introduced to canons of inquiry by which individual opinions might be assessed. Instead, the evidence pointed to an ethos that everyone is entitled to have his or her own opinion and all opinions are to be equally valued.

Particularly troubling to Goodlad was the failure of preservice programs to introduce students to a professional ethos to guide their practice, to provoke them to address the problems of the schools in which they would work, or to address the problems of schooling in broader social context. Overall, preservice teachers were prepared to work as individual, autonomous practitioners within their classrooms. Little evidence was found of efforts to help teachers think of their work as a collective enterprise or to prepare them to work collaboratively. Little evidence was found that preservice programs acted to socialize teachers to think of themselves as members of a profession. Finally, these programs introduced preservice teachers to profound moral and ethical issues of schooling and teaching only briefly and in a desultory fashion.

While Goodlad's study provides a view of preservice preparation as generally practiced, Kenneth Howey and Nancy Zimpher's case studies of six programs present portraits of "good" teacher education.[40] These studies show that even among these exemplary cases, attributes considered crucial for program success were generally found wanting. In particular, these programs typically failed to model a critical pedagogy and a transforming role for schools in society. There was little dialogue between program faculty and preservice teachers about the mission of schools and the nature of teaching. Instead, these cases revealed a common emphasis on the technical aspects of teaching and a "pervasive conservative view of teaching and schools."[41] While Howey and Zimpher urge their readers not to make generalizations from these cases, they note that their findings are consistent with those of the Research About Teacher Education (RATE) studies sponsored by the American Association of Colleges for Teacher Education (AACTE), also conducted in the mid-1980s, that drew upon a nationally representative sample.[42]

More recent studies have examined the impact of teacher education reforms on preservice programs. The most notable of these was conducted by Michael Fullan and his colleagues.[43] This study focused on change that occurred between 1985 and 1995 in teacher preparation programs at more than one hundred research universities belonging to the Holmes Group, a national organization concerned with the reform of teacher preparation. In general, this study found little evidence of significant change in preservice programs at Holmes institutions. At many institutions, faculty reconsidered conceptual underpinnings of their programs. They developed more rigorous standards for program admission and for assessing preservice candidates. At many institutions, stronger relationships were developed with schools. Indeed, most institutions claimed to have established at least one professional development school. At the same time, the study noted little change in the basic structure and content of teacher education programs. The study concluded that even among those institutions making the most progress there was little evidence of systematic program redesign. These findings are consistent with Henrietta Schwartz's observation that the numerous changes instituted in teacher preparation programs during the 1980s and early 1990s amounted to "little more than adjusting on the margins."[44]

ONGOING PROFESSIONAL DEVELOPMENT

For decades, the practice of teachers' professional development has been considered woefully inadequate. It has been portrayed in many disparaging ways, including "a waste of time," "a joke," and "the slum of American education."[45] In his review of literature, Thomas Guskey noted that nearly every major work on the subject has emphasized its failings.[46] Criticisms of professional development have continued unabated through the late 1990s. While most observers are careful to note that not all professional development is horrific, and some present exemplars of innovative programs, Matthew Miles's characterization is fairly typical:

> It's everything that a learning environment shouldn't be: radically under-sourced, brief, not sustained, designed for "one size fits all," imposed rather than owned, lacking any intellectual coherence, treated as a special add-on event rather than as part of a natural process, and trapped in the constraints of the bureaucratic system we have come to call "school." In short, it's pedagogically naïve, a demeaning exercise that often leaves its participants more cynical and no more knowledgeable, skilled, or committed than before.[47]

While there is substantial consistency in the representations of professional development, few empirical studies document general practices or teachers' experiences with them. Case studies and anecdotal descriptions of individual programs abound; however, studies of typical experiences of teachers are sparse and dated.[48] Still, the portrait of practice that emerges is consistent. Professional development generally takes the form of brief one-shot, beginning-of-the-year workshops without follow-up. These sessions may offer ideas for classroom management or teaching techniques not tied to specific school or classroom goals, subject areas, or dilemmas of practice. They may offer packaged prescriptions from outside consultants that bear little relation to what teachers want to study. They offer few opportunities for ongoing work on specific classroom problems and few opportunities for practice and feedback. Most formal inservice programs provided by schools and school systems serve a "maintenance" function where teachers are taught to comply with preferred administrative routines or support organizationally preferred modes of operation.[49] Few programs provide teachers opportunities to deepen their professional knowledge or intellectual skills or engage dilemmas of practice in any meaningful way.

Opportunities for teachers' workplace learning are similarly limited. As Seymour Sarason has observed, schools have never assigned importance to the intellectual, professional, and career needs of their personnel.[50] They are organized in ways that discourage, if not prevent, productive teacher learning.[51] Work roles in schools are often structured in ways that enforce independence and isolation among teachers and limit their opportunities for collegial interaction and learning. Often, workplace norms of privacy, autonomy, and equality inhibit interactions by which problems of practice may be shared, studied, and solved. In many schools, teachers refrain from seeking and giving help because of the implications such behavior may have for their social relationships. Beyond these social and normative constraints, the very structure of the school day and the lack of coordination of teachers' schedules prevent faculties from working and learning together.

Enhancing Opportunities for Teacher Learning

Certainly, this research suggests that, in general, teachers are not being well prepared with the qualities of mind and character, or with the necessary skills, to act as effective agents of change in the classroom, school, or wider society. Nor are they generally supported later in their careers by opportunities for professional development and workplace learning. By this assessment we do not wish to suggest that preservice programs can or should be reformed to bear the full load of preparing teachers to be effective agents of change. In our view, preservice programs are already asked to assume too much responsibility for the learning and development of teachers. We agree with Guskey and others that preservice education is too short and has too many built-in limitations to accomplish the "awesome task" of adequately preparing new teachers for the demands of schools and classrooms.[52] Understanding the multiple change-agent roles of teachers underscores the enormity of that task. Like Guskey, we emphasize the importance of professional development beyond preservice programs.

PRESERVICE PROGRAMS

Preservice education can play a vital role in the early development of teachers, but perhaps its chief contributions lie in areas of learning best suited to the strengths and resources of colleges and universities such as the development of a broad base of liberal learning and the acquisition of professional knowledge. Preservice programs, then, should focus on in-depth subject matter knowledge; knowledge of the historical, philosophical, and social-cultural foundations of education; and knowledge of formal theories and empirical research about teaching, learning, schools as organizations, and change. This suggestion does not imply abandonment of the practical or craft knowledge which dominates preservice preparation currently. Rather, it calls for a renewal of "formal" knowledge in preservice curricula and a better integration of different elements of professional knowledge than now exists in most programs.

Among the areas of learning best suited to preservice programs is the introduction of dilemmas and the initial development of intellectual skills and professional orientations that, along with the acquisition of the types of knowledge outlined above, can help teachers manage dilemmas and begin their work as effective agents of change. We consider the latter area of learning below, discussing the types of experiences in which preservice teachers might be engaged. We do not address other critical dimensions of preservice programs, such as structure and governance.

In considering experiences that preservice teachers should have to develop the professional knowledge, intellectual abilities, and orientations described above, we draw on Bridges and Hallinger's work on models of problem-based learning.[53] These models were developed with an eye toward preparing school administrators; however, they are readily applicable to the preparation of teachers for their roles as change agents. In problem-based learning, predicaments or dilemmas stemming from the realities of the work setting are identified and presented to teams of students who are expected to define the dilemma, identify the knowledge that is relevant to its management, and delineate how the knowledge is to be used. Students are encouraged to address jointly such questions as: What do we know that will facilitate the management of this dilemma? How is what we know relevant? What more do we need to know? What should be the plan of action? Pursuing these questions leads to the development of an action plan and strengthens critical thinking skills.

We envision a program that regularly engages preservice teachers in this type of activity across the several domains of professional knowledge. The dilemmas presented would be embedded in descriptions of real world situations that they are likely to confront in their classrooms and schools. Teacher educators and practicing teachers who have in-depth understandings of schools and classrooms would describe predicaments that require the preservice teacher to make decisions and take actions in contexts of competing values and conflicting expectations. Collectively, the dilemmas would focus on issues of student learning, school change, and the intersection of these issues with the larger purposes of schooling. As preservice teachers explore these dilemmas, they are likely to construct deeper understandings of the problems embedded in them, their possible causes and resolutions, and the constraints that must be taken into account. Analyzing these dilemmas would not only create opportunities to apply the knowledge and intellectual skills students are learning in their courses and field work but would also stimulate the acquisition of new knowledge.

Several benefits should accrue. First, when preservice teachers confront and begin to understand the complexities of dilemmas, their views about the nature of teaching and the role of the teacher will be challenged. A substantial amount of research shows that students enter teacher preparation programs with deeply entrenched views about the nature of teaching and learning and the role of the teacher in this process.[54] Most preservice teachers define the teacher's role as transmitter of knowledge, and they expect to assimilate new techniques into their existing system of ideas about pedagogy and subject matter.[55] To prompt preservice teachers to examine their beliefs, to make explicit their images of teaching, and to consider the teacher's role as reaching beyond the primary role of facilitator of learning to that of change agent in school and society will promote such dissonance.[56]

A second benefit is the opportunity to visit and revisit a set of core concepts, such as the difference between skill level and intelligence, or the importance of varying teaching approaches in different contexts. Learning about teaching is a nonlinear process. It requires continual examination of ideas from multiple perspectives and at increasingly complex levels of difficulty.[57] Experiences like those described above provide opportunities for future teachers to develop ideas and organize them into a coherent, stable, and generalizable set of understandings.[58] Moreover, such experiences encourage preservice teachers to see the knowledge associated with teaching as a flexible network of ideas with many interconnections that can be approached in a variety of ways. Through these types of activities, theory can be melded with practice, and episodic or case knowledge can be formed. Research on teacher learning suggests that as preservice teachers develop episodic or case knowledge they gain a more intuitive sense of situations and can bring case knowledge to bear productively on future predicaments.[59]

Experiences with confronting dilemmas should also allow for multiple social interactions among preservice teachers, professors, and practicing teachers and perhaps administrators. Preservice teachers would be exposed to new ideas and different perspectives, share values and ideals, observe how others think, practice their abilities of analysis and reasoning, reach beyond their own frames of reference, and understand others' viewpoints. In requiring a dialogic rather than a transmittal approach to preservice preparation, these types of experiences mirror current developments in the psychology of learning and parallel what teachers are now learning is best for educating children.[60]

Finally, because of the collaborative nature of this activity, preservice teachers must learn certain professional norms of conduct. In instances where they have been assigned to be a team facilitator, they can practice functioning in a leadership role, facilitating group discussions, working toward consensus, and resolving conflicts. In short, they practice the abilities associated with collaboration, the co-construction of knowledge, cooperative problem solving, and leadership for change. They are exposed to a particular professional orientation that defines teaching not only in terms of what teachers do in classrooms but also in terms of the impact and influence they can have beyond the classroom. It is an orientation that embraces commitment to inclusion and professional community and that guides preservice teachers toward a sense of ownership of the processes and goals of change.

ONGOING PROFESSIONAL DEVELOPMENT

We want to underscore the point made earlier that these types of preservice learning experiences will prepare future teachers for *initial* efforts at managing dilemmas and affecting change. We recognize the need for continued professional development across the initial years of teaching and beyond, professional development that supports teachers' understanding of the complexities of teaching and schooling and their role in the process. We agree with those who have argued that the profession of teaching needs a structured continuum of professional growth—one that provides initial preparation in institutions of higher learning, that includes carefully structured programs of support and learning for new teachers, and that supports site-based professional development in learning communities throughout the teacher's career.[61]

Our recommendations for enhancing preservice preparation programs have implications for the professional development of experienced teachers. For practicing teachers, examining dilemmas arising from their own experiences presents an ideal learning opportunity because of teachers' intrinsic motivation to manage well these immediate and troublesome dilemmas. Engaging groups of practicing teachers in problem-solving teams (as we suggested for preservice teachers also) fosters the possibility of teacher inquiry and action research that can extend professional learning beyond the mere (but important) exchange of ideas.

These suggestions are consistent with an emerging consensus among scholars and professional educators alike of a model of high-quality professional development. This consensus is grounded in two related sources—theories of adult learning and learning to teach, and an increasing number of descriptions of "best practices."[62] This model suggests that teachers learn best when they are active in directing their own learning and when their opportunities to learn are focused on concrete tasks and dilemmas drawn from day-to-day work with students. Opportunities to learn should be grounded in inquiry, experimentation, and reflection. They should be collaborative, involving interaction with other teachers and educational professionals as sources of new ideas and feedback. These opportunities should be coherent, intensive, and ongoing. They should be connected to broader goals of student learning, school improvement, and social change.

The "best practices" literature points to other potentially effective structures and processes of professional development. These include individually guided study, clinical supervision and training; interactive learning from curriculum and instructional development and school improvement; and individual and collaborative inquiry, sometimes referred to as action research. This literature challenges notions that teacher learning can occur only through training, only in workshops and conferences, or only with the help of external consultants. It points to the school workplace as a potentially rich source of teacher learning. It also projects benefits of learning outside schools in collaboratives, networks, subject matter associations, and teacher centers.

Smylie has argued elsewhere that teacher learning in the workplace can be enhanced by developing certain organizational dimensions of schools.[63] One dimension is providing opportunities for teacher collaboration, involving joint problem solving; development of new programs and practices; and examination and critical analysis of current ideas, practices, and taken-for-granted beliefs and assumptions. Such collaboration would not be confined to traditionally defined groups of teachers within a school (e.g., grade-level teams, subject-area departments). Instead, it would cut across such groups when appropriate in order to provide teachers access to others with whom they might not have regular contact or working relationships. New opportunities for variation, challenge, autonomy, and choice in work can be created to provide more effective learning experiences. These opportunities include designing new curriculum, leading formal professional development for other teachers, and conducting research.

Teacher learning would be enhanced if schools were to develop clear goals to give direction and meaning to work, learning, and innovations. These goals would direct collective and individual activity and serve as referents for performance, outcomes, and learning needs. Goals would be developed jointly and be subject to ongoing critical reflection and analysis in collaborative working and learning relationships. Learning would also be enhanced by mechanisms for formative and summative feedback on teachers' work. Examination and assessment of practice would be an integral aspect of collaborative working and learning relationships. Learning experiences would arise from and feed back into work experiences. Learning would be considered part of teachers' work, not an ancillary activity bearing little relation to daily work with students and colleagues. Finally, schools should work actively to increase teacher access to information and ideas from external sources. These sources include but are not limited to teachers and administrators from other schools and districts, professional workshops and conferences, university faculty and external consultants, and individuals and agencies in the school's community. Information and ideas from external sources not only add to the intellectual resources available to teachers; they can challenge prevailing perspectives and provide new thinking.

One way to develop more systematic linkages between preservice preparation and ongoing professional development and learning in the workplace is for universities and schools to form collaborative partnerships around career-long teacher education and school improvement. Certain resources essential to teacher learning and development are naturally available from each partner. For example, universities are well situated to provide theoretical perspectives that can guide the process of interpreting, framing, and reframing dilemmas; research-derived knowledge that can distinguish effective from ineffective approaches; and systematic understandings of how teachers learn and what fosters their learning. There are important resources that schools can provide— the critically important context in which teachers work, the ways in which practitioners define dilemmas and build craft knowledge, and the power of professional development when viewed as an integral part of the life of the school.[64] In a world of growing complexity and rapid change, schools will increasingly need to be places that *thrive on uncertainty* and that have a greater capacity for dilemma management and collective work than they currently do. The future will require that university- and school-based teacher educators exploit the resources that are most naturally available through their respective institutions.

Conclusion

We have argued that in order for teachers to fulfill their roles as agents of student change, school change, and social change they must be able to manage effectively complex, recurring dilemmas that emerge from the uncertainties, ambiguities, and competing aims and values of schooling in American society. We have argued that to manage these dilemmas, teachers need to develop a body of professional knowledge, particular intellectual abilities, and a professional orientation. From our review of research, we have found that despite often intensive efforts to improve their quality and effectiveness, preservice and inservice teacher education programs provide little support to develop these capacities.

We have argued that preservice teacher education can play a much more productive role in preparing teachers to manage dilemmas and serve as agents of change, but we think that role is necessarily limited. Preservice education may best be seen as an initial source of teacher learning, not as the sole or even primary source. It should be considered the beginning of a career-long continuum of learning that draws from classroom experience, the school workplace, and formal programs of professional development. Preservice programs are perhaps best viewed as particular, not comprehensive, sources of learning that take advantage of resources peculiar to the institutions that administer them and prepare teachers for a good start and for later learning. We see preservice teacher education as a place to begin to develop a body of essential professional knowledge, where teacher candidates are introduced to dilemmas of change and to the intersections where those dilemmas must be managed. Preservice education is a place where teacher candidates can begin to develop intellectual skills and professional orientations to manage those dilemmas well.

We have argued also for a more concerted effort to develop a body of professional knowledge and to focus curriculum and instruction around problem-based learning. While we have not explored here the implications of these suggestions for the structure and governance of preservice programs and for the work of teacher education faculties, we may assume that the changes we suggest will not be easy to achieve for several reasons.

For one, our suggestions challenge the orientations and capacities of many teacher educators who themselves are former teachers, often not actively engaged in research or formal theory, and who believe the best way to prepare new teachers is to emphasize the practical. To achieve more coherence in curriculum, greater integration of knowledge, and clearer articulation of conceptual assumptions than now characterize most programs will require more collaboration than now exists among college and university faculty and K-12 teachers. Education faculty who teach social foundations courses and methods and field-based courses must collaborate with liberal arts and sciences faculty to achieve integration and coherence in preservice curricula and to create continuity between teacher learning at the preservice level and on the job. Finally, teacher educators must model the forms of collaborative work expected of teachers and develop in their students capacities for inquiry, analysis, and evaluation as they model these modes of thinking in their own teaching.[65]

The sources are few for developing new knowledge, intellectual skills, and professional orientations among teacher educators. Traditional strategies for reforming preservice programs through the bureaucratic processes of state accreditation do not help; indeed, they may be counterproductive. Furthermore, preservice programs have low status on many campuses.[66] We see better prospects for improving preservice education through the agency of accrediting associations, teachers' professional organizations, and research and dissemination of exemplary programs.

In seeking to increase the priority and quality of continuous teacher professional development, we face additional challenges. According to Sarason, we are bound tightly by production models of schools and conceptions of teaching as routinized labor which favor bureaucratic approaches to school and teacher improvement.[67] There are no simple solutions that might get us beyond these models and conceptions. While theories of adult learning, research on learning to teach, and descriptions of best practices point in consistent directions, they do not present precise solutions.

Further, it may be difficult to redirect policy and resources toward high-quality staff development and workplace learning because the implications are too complicated to understand or too "radical" to embrace. To do so, policymakers would need to think differently about schools as organizations, restructure time and adult-student relationships, and redesign teachers' roles. They would have to challenge the role of school systems, unions, and state education agencies in professional development, the ways it is funded, and the entrenched economic and political interests of those who now provide it.[68] Redirecting professional development would mean investing in the very people—teachers—who are considered by many to be the primary source of the problems we wish to solve.

Finally, would-be reformers do not readily comprehend or take seriously the problem of persistence in schools. They operate from naïve theories of change that suggest that institutionalized patterns of belief and practice can be altered through exhortation, sanctions, a new technology, or a series of workshops. More comprehensive mechanisms for change are needed, including systematic, ongoing opportunities for teacher learning, which must have the support of broad organizational, political, and economic contexts. Failure to confront these challenges effectively will undoubtedly compromise the ability of schools and school systems to support this and future generations of teachers in fulfilling the expectations we hold for them to serve as effective agents of change.

NOTES

1. John Dewey, *Democracy and Education* (New York: Macmillan, 1916).

2. William H. Schubert, *Curriculum: Perspective, Paradigm, and Possibility* (New York: Macmillan, 1986).

3. David F. Labaree, "Public Good and Private Goods: The American Struggle Over Educational Goals," *American Educational Research Journal* 34 (1997): pp. 39-81.

4. David K. Cohen and Deborah L. Ball, "Policy and Practice: An Overview," *Educational Evaluation and Policy Analysis* 12 (1990): 233-246; Michael Lipsky, *Street-level Bureaucracy* (New York: Russell Sage Foundation, 1980).

5. Larry Cuban, "Managing Dilemmas while Building Professional Communities," *Educational Researcher* 21, no. 1 (1992): pp. 4-11.

6. David T. Hansen and Nicholas C. Burbules, "Introduction," in Nicholas C. Burbules and David T. Hansen, eds., *Teaching and Its Predicaments* (Boulder, CO: Westview, 1997), pp. 1-10.

7. Magdalene Lampert, "How Do Teachers Manage to Teach? Perspectives on Problems in Practice," *Harvard Educational Review* 55 (1985): pp. 178-194.

8. William O. Stanley, "The Present Dilemma of Education," in William O. Stanley et al., *Social Foundations of Education* (New York: Holt, Rinehart and Winston, 1956), p. 442.

9. See Andy Hargreaves, *Changing Teachers, Changing Times: Teachers' Work and Culture in the Postmodern Age* (New York: Teachers College Press, 1994).

10. Michael S. Knapp, Jerry D. Bamburg, Michele C. Ferguson, and Paul T. Hill, "Converging Reforms and the Working Lives of Frontline Professionals in Schools," *Educational Policy* 12 (1998): pp. 397-418.

11. See, for example, Maynard C. Reynolds, ed., *Knowledge Base for the Beginning Teacher* (New York: Pergamon, 1989).

12. See, for example, William C. Ayers (1988). "Fact or Fancy? The Knowledge Base Quest in Teacher Education," *Journal of Teacher Education* 39, no. 5 (1988): pp. 24-31.

13. Our examples come from several sources: (a) findings of recent survey and case study research conducted or assisted by the Consortium on Chicago School Research; (b) our observations as university faculty working with Chicago teachers in professional development and other school improvement activities; and (c) reports from our own students, who include practicing teachers and preservice teachers completing field experiences in Chicago public schools and classrooms.

14. William J. Wilson, *When Work Disappears: The World of the New Urban Poor* (New York: Alfred Knopf, 1996).

15. Joseph Kahne and Kim Bailey, "The Role of Social Capital in Youth Development: The Case of 'I Have a Dream'." Paper presented at the annual meeting of the American Educational Research Association, San Diego, April 1998.

16. David Kerbow, *Pervasive Student Mobility: A Moving Target for School Improvement* (Chicago: University of Chicago, Center for School Improvement, n.d.).

17. Penny B. Sebring, Anthony S. Bryk, Melissa Roderick, Eric Camburn, Stuart Luppescu, Yeow Ming Thum, BetsAnn Smith, and Joseph Kahne, *Charting Reform in Chicago: The Students Speak* (Chicago: Consortium on Chicago School Research, 1996).

18. Melissa Roderick, *Habits Hard to Break: A New Look at Truancy in Chicago's Public High Schools* (Chicago: University of Chicago, School of Social Service Administration, 1997).

19. Sebring, et al., *Charting Reform in Chicago: The Students Speak*.

20. Penny B. Sebring, et al., *Charting Reform: Chicago Teachers Take Stock* (Chicago: Consortium on Chicago School Research, 1995).

21. Anthony S. Bryk, Yeow Ming Thum, John Q. Easton, and Stuart Luppescu, *Academic Productivity of Chicago Public Elementary Schools* (Chicago: Consortium on Chicago School Research, 1998).

22. Alfred B. Hess, Jr., *Restructuring Urban Schools: A Chicago Perspective* (New York: Teachers College Press, 1995).

23. Some of these problems are being addressed by new school construction and other capital improvements.

24. Sebring, et al., *Charting Reform: Chicago Teachers Take Stock*.

25. Anthony S. Bryk, et al., *Charting Chicago School Reform: Democratic Localism as a Lever for Change* (Boulder, CO: Westview, 1998).

26. Mark A. Smylie, Diane King Bilcer, Julie Kochanek, Karin Sconzert, Dorothy Shipps, and Holly Swyers, *Getting Started: A First Look at Chicago Annenberg Schools and Networks* (Chicago: Consortium on Chicago School Research, 1998).

27. Mark A. Smylie, Robert L. Crowson, Victoria Chou and Rebekah A. Levin, "The Principal and Community-School Connections in Chicago's Radical Reform," *Educational Administration Quarterly* 30 (1994): 342-364.

28. For more detailed information about these reforms, see Hess, *Restructuring Urban Schools*; Dorothy Shipps, Joseph Kahne, and Mark A. Smylie, "The Politics of Urban School Reform: Legitimacy, Urban Growth, and School Improvement in Chicago." Paper presented at the annual meeting of the American Educational Research Association, San Diego, April 1998.

29. Virtually all of these teachers remained employed in the school system. Most found positions in other schools or at the central office.

30. BetsAnn Smith, *School Improvement, Student Achievement, and the Time Problem* (Chicago: Consortium on Chicago School Research, 1998).

31. Fred M. Newmann, Gudelia Lopez, and Anthony S. Bryk, *The Quality of Intellectual Work in Chicago Schools: A Baseline Report* (Chicago: Consortium on Chicago School Research, 1998).

32. Dewey, *Democracy and Education*, p. 186.

33. Julia A. Smith and BetsAnn Smith, *Curriculum Pacing and Coherence in Chicago's Elementary Schools* (Chicago: Consortium on Chicago School Research, 1998).

34. John Dewey, *How We Think* (Lexington, MA: D. C. Heath, 1933).

35. See, for example, Margaret Buchmann and John Schwille, "Education: The Overcoming of Experience," *American Journal of Education* 92 (1983): pp. 30-51.

36. Richard E. Ishler, Kellah M. Edens, and Barnett W. Berry, "Elementary Education," in John Sikula, Thomas J. Buttery, and Edith Guyton, eds., *Handbook of Research on Teacher Education*, 2nd ed. (New York: Macmillan, 1996), pp. 348-377.

37. John I. Goodlad, *Teachers for Our Nation's Schools* (San Francisco: Jossey-Bass, 1990). See also John I. Goodlad, Roger Soder, and Kenneth A. Sirotnik, *Places Where Teachers Are Taught* (San Francisco: Jossey-Bass, 1990).

38. See also Kenneth M. Zeichner, "Traditions of Practice in U.S. Preservice Teacher Education Programs," *Teaching and Teacher Education* 9 (1993): pp. 1-13.

39. Goodlad, *Teachers for Our Nation's Schools*, p. 240.

40. Kenneth Howey and Nancy Zimpher, *Profiles of Preservice Teacher Education: Inquiry Into the Nature of Programs* (Albany: State University of New York Press, 1989).

41. Ibid., p. 252.

42. American Association of Colleges for Teacher Education, *Teacher Education Policy in the States: Fifty-State Survey of Legislative and Administrative Actions* (Washington, DC: American Association of Colleges for Teacher Education, 1987).

43. Michael Fullan, Gary Galluzzo, Patricia Morris, and Nancy Watson, *The Rise and Stall of Teacher Education Reform* (Washington, DC: American Association of Colleges for Teacher Education, 1998).

44. Henrietta Schwartz, "The Changing Nature of Teacher Education," in John Sikula, Thomas J. Buttery, and Edith Guyton, eds., *Handbook of Research on Teacher Education*, 2nd ed. (New York: Macmillan, 1996), pp. 3-13.

45. Thomas C. Corcoran, *Transforming Professional Development for Teachers: A Guide for State Policymakers* (Washington, DC: National Governors Association, 1995); L. J. Rubin, *The Inservice Education of Teachers* (Boston: Allyn and Bacon, 1978); National Commission on Teaching and America's Future, *What Matters Most: Teaching for America's Future* (New York: National Commission on Teaching and America's Future, 1996).

46. Thomas R. Guskey, "Staff Development and the Process of Teacher Change," *Educational Researcher* 15, no. 5 (1986): pp. 5-12.

47. Matthew B. Miles, "Foreword," in Thomas R. Guskey and Matthew Huberman, eds., *Professional Development in Education: New Paradigms and Practices* (New York: Teachers College Press, 1995), pp. vii-ix.

48. See Kenneth Howey and J. C. Vaughan, "Current Patterns of Staff Development," in Gary A. Griffin, ed., *Staff Development: Eighty-second Yearbook of the National Society for the Study of Education, Part II* (Chicago: University of Chicago Press, 1983), pp. 92-117; Bruce Joyce, Renee Bush, and Margaret McKibbon, *Information and Opinion from the California Staff Development Study* (Sacramento: California State Department of Education, 1981); Judith Little et al., *Staff Development in California: Public and Personal Investments, Program Patterns, and Policy Choices* (San Francisco: Far West Laboratory for Educational Research and Development, 1987).

49. Philip Schlechty and Betty Lou Whitford, "The Organizational Context of School Systems and the Functions of Staff Development," in Griffin, *Staff Development*, pp. 62-91.

50. Seymour Sarason, *The Predictable Failure of Educational Reform* (San Francisco: Jossey-Bass, 1990).

51. Mark A. Smylie, "Teachers' Views of the Effectiveness of Sources of Learning to Teach," *Elementary School Journal* 89 (1989): pp. 543-558; National Commission on Teaching and America's Future, *What Matters Most*.

52. Guskey and Huberman, eds., *Professional Development in Education*.

53. Edwin Bridges and Philip Hallinger, "Problem Based Learning: A Promising Approach to Professional Development," in Milbrey W. McLaughlin and Ida Oberman, ed., *Teacher Learning: New Policies, New Practices* (New York: Teachers College Press, 1996): pp. 145-160.

54. Donna M. Kagan, "Professional Growth Among Preservice and Beginning Teachers," *Review of Educational Research* 62 (1992): pp. 129-165.

55. Kenneth Zeichner, Susan Melnick, and Mary Louise Gomez, *Currents of Reform in Preservice Teacher Education* (New York: Teachers College Press, 1996).

56. See also D. Jean Clandinin and F. Michael Connelly, "Narrative and Story in Practice and Research," in Donald A. Schon, ed., *The Reflective Turn: Case Studies in and on Educational Practices* (New York: Teachers College Press, 1991), pp. 258-281.

57. Virginia Richardson, ed., *Constructivist Teacher Education* (Washington, DC: Falmer, 1997).

58. Beverly Falk, "Teaching the Way Children Learn," in McLaughlin and Oberman, eds., *Teacher Learning: New Policies and Practices*, pp. 22-29.

59. David C. Berliner, "In Pursuit of Expert Pedagogues," *Educational Researcher* 15, no. 7 (1986): pp. 5-13.

60. Luis C. Moll, *Vygotsky and Education* (New York: Cambridge University Press, 1990).

61. National Commission on Teaching and America's Future, *What Matters Most*.

62. See Mark A. Smylie, "From Bureaucratic Control to Building Human Capital," *Educational Researcher* 25, no. 9 (1996): pp. 9-11; Linda Darling-Hammond, *The Right to Learn* (San Francisco: Jossey-Bass, 1997); National Staff Development Council, *Standards for Staff Development* (Oxford, OH: National Staff Development Council, 1995).

63. Mark A. Smylie, "Teacher Learning in the Workplace: Implications for School Reform," in Guskey and Huberman, eds., *Professional Development in Education*, pp. 92-113; Smylie, "From Bureaucratic Control to Building Human Capital."

64. Ann Lieberman, "Practices that Support Teacher Development: Transforming Conceptions of Professional Learning," in McLaughlin and Oberman, *Teacher Learning: New Policies, New Practices*, pp. 185-201.

65. Goodlad, *Teachers for Our Nation's Schools*; Alan Thom, *Redesigning Teacher Education* (Albany: State University of New York Press, 1997).

66. National Commission on Teaching and America's Future, *What Matters Most*; Tom, *Redesigning Teacher Education*.

67. Sarason, *The Predictable Failure of Educational Reform*. See also Smylie, "From Bureaucratic Control to Building Human Capital."

68. Gary Sykes, "Reform of and as Professional Development," *Phi Delta Kappan* 77 (1996): pp. 465-467.

CHAPTER III

Unions, Teacher Development, and Professionalism

ROBERT M. McCLURE

What it means to be a teacher in most American public schools has changed during the current "school reform movement," which began in the mid-1980s and will probably extend past the turn of the century. During this time, the ranks of teachers became more female, mature, experienced, Caucasian, educated, and married.[1] Three other changes have affected the nature and extent of individual and collective teacher professionalism: the work of teachers, the culture of the school, and the views teachers have of themselves as practitioners.

Changes Affecting Professionalism

Teachers' Work. Two developments related to student learning—assessment and standards—are in the forefront of the current phase of school improvement activity and their effects are often at odds with one another. Increasing amounts of student testing and the advent of curriculum standards detailing much of what students need to learn in school have changed teachers' work. Student testing has impacted teaching, curriculum, and the ways teachers view student learning; what is testable in current psychometric practice often defines the level of student outcomes toward which teachers teach. Standards are increasingly used to define more sharply the content to be learned by students and, in most cases, require students to exhibit higher cognitive order outcomes than those called for by the tests. Thus, teachers and principals experience conflict between the pervasive state-mandated tests with their accompanying accountability measures and the curriculum standards seen by many educators as more consistent with what students need to learn to be successful. Alignment of content, pedagogy, and assessment is not yet common practice.[2]

School Culture. Conflicts among purpose, instructional practice, and evaluation spill over into everyday life in the school, affecting the

Robert M. McClure is Co-director of the Charter Schools Initiative of the National Education Association.

nature of professional discourse. Such dialogue defines the culture of the faculty and the school. There are questions about whose authority does and should prevail. Site-based decision making, seen as a cardinal component in the early days of the reform movement,[3] now seems a sham to many parents, teachers, and principals. After all, fundamental decisions about curriculum, assessment, and, in some cases, pedagogy are determined elsewhere, at distances increasingly far from the campus. The system in too many schools is disjointed, and the culture reflects this lack of substantive cohesiveness.

Teachers' Views of Themselves. Early in the reform movement, many teachers and their leaders saw the possibilities of a new kind of culture in the schools marked by changes in the traditional roles played by teachers. This aspect of the improvement effort, often labeled "teacher empowerment," meant to most reformers an increase in individual and collective professionalism. "Empowering people by connecting them to knowledge about teaching, learning, curriculum, and how to change and grow represents the best resource available to us for creating the schools our students need and deserve"[4] was a typical statement in the early days of the reform movement. For many of today's teachers, the resources they have for their growth and change come from the various bureaucracies which shape schooling and are not related to the needs of the specific students they teach or their own quest for growth. Although teachers define themselves as professionals, they increasingly describe their job as following directives from the state legislature and the district office.

There is a sense of powerlessness to deal with the issues which confront individual teachers and the faculty. For example, the resource of *time*—that is, the lack of it to do the job well—is the single subject mentioned most often by teachers when they talk about the difficulty of improving their schools.[5] There seems, however, a lack of authority to cause time to be used differently. Decisions with regard to curriculum matters, assessment, even pedagogical choices and their own professional development plans are seen by a great many teachers as the province of others.

An increase in teacher professionalism was at the heart of the reform agenda in the 80s. That goal is yet to be accomplished. There are, of course, many schools in which individual teachers and indeed entire faculties are autonomous and collegial, oriented to using research, producers of knowledge, systematically reflective about their practice, and active in improving the quality of their school and district. The number of these places, though, is far from a critical mass. If schools are to change and improve in the ways now being called for, high levels of teacher professionalism must prevail. This is not an easy transition to accomplish given the current state of practice in most schools. Later in this chapter, following a discussion of the nature of professionalism, I shall explore current efforts to achieve improved schools and note some institutional changes leading to further improvements.

Influence on Professionalism of Unions, Professional Organizations, and Teacher Networks

Professional work and its value to clients and society can be described in several ways. The most basic definition of a professional is one who, through education, experience, and credentialing, is competent to help others and who puts the client's welfare above other considerations. How a group becomes professional and the level of status enjoyed by that group is considerably more complex than this definition implies.[6] Factors that complicate the attainment of professionalism by any group of workers include issues of supply and demand, social status, the ease with which the group has access to and uses political and monetary power, the nature of the marketplace in which it operates, and the rewards it seeks. Medicine and law enjoy high status as professions; teaching is far behind. Disparity between professional groups occurs for several reasons including historical context, where authority is vested, numbers of people needed to provide the service, which gender dominates, and whether the service is one in which the government's responsibility to citizens is seen as direct or indirect.

The strength of the glue that holds a profession together and makes it cohesive is determined by broad agreement within the group about the knowledge base that undergirds and defines its work. From such a common base of knowledge comes a vocabulary. Doctors communicate with other health care workers and are understood: protocols are clear, appropriate actions agreed to in advance, "good" practice is defined. Lawyers, although they can differ on the definition of truth in particular instances, use a shared vocabulary and employ processes which lead to a resolution of their differences and an acceptance that the system can and will fairly determine the outcome. In the so-called senior professions, the experience of practitioners is systematically recorded, analyzed, and used as a basis to change practice.

THE TEACHING PROFESSION

For reasons too varied and numerous to discuss fully here, little of this holds for the profession of teaching. The knowledge which underlies curriculum decisions or pedagogical practice is not defined to the satisfaction of a significant number of practitioners or theorists; there is no commonly accepted definition of good practice or how processes which could lead to improvement are to be defined and carried out. When there are agreements about the nature of the knowledge undergirding teaching, they are generally encoded in licensure and requirements for institutional accreditation. Although there has been significant progress in these arenas,[7] a large gap remains between the definition of a body of knowledge guiding the practice of teaching and profession-wide understanding and acceptance of the proposed definition.

Decisions about how many people are needed in the teaching force, how to determine if prospective practitioners are competent, and the conditions that guide placement and retention of these individuals in schools and classrooms are almost entirely political. There are strong pressures to retain this system, given the perception that only state and local government can assure the public that schools are staffed and running. Defining quality and controlling supply and demand are not responsibilities delegated by government to the teaching profession, as is the case in most other professions. In short, views of what it is to be a professional are vastly different for a teacher than for those in other professions.

During the last two decades, some remarkable thinking about the subject of teacher professionalization has been produced by a new kind of academic. These researchers have immersed themselves in the lives of teachers and schools and have written about the profession of teaching from the perspective of an "insider." They would have teachers become increasingly analytical about their work and take leadership in reshaping the nature of schooling.[8] Their work fits well with other theorists and activists who want systems to change so that they more genuinely reflect what is known about teaching, learning, and healthy organizations.[9]

Virginia Richardson sums up much of the current thinking about how professional teachers should go about their work: "The current cognitively based conception of the teacher describes a person who mediates ideas, constructs meaning and knowledge, and acts upon them."[10] The lack of this kind of professionalism in the daily life of teachers is ultimately debilitating to all involved in the learning enterprise. Clients, whether they are parents, taxpayers, or students, are not well served when teachers are not able to act in "professional" ways. The academic community has been articulate about the need for increased professional behavior in the schools; there is, however, a lack of wide acceptance of their propositions by state and federal legislators, school boards, and by teachers, school administrators, and district office staff.

From my experience with a national school improvement project involving many teachers,[11] I conclude that most school-based educators do not readily envision an expanded definition of professionalism. They do not articulate different ways of working with students, with each other, and with the various communities that impact upon them. Teachers are critical about how the work of their school takes place, but when asked to construct different organizations (e.g., vision and goals, roles, uses of time, authority structures, reward mechanisms), they are often hard pressed to identify alternatives outside of current practice. Certainly, teachers' solutions are different from those proposed by policymakers who call, for instance, for more tests, students spending more time in school, and higher standards. They are different, too, from the proposals of academicians who favor inquiry, research-based decisions, and reflection as necessary to an expanded view of professionalism. And teachers' ideas about change differ also from those proposed by reformers who offer, among other solutions to the problems of ailing schools, site-based decision making, block scheduling, and "systemic thinking."

At the most basic level, teachers see their work as going into the classroom, closing the door, and doing the best job they know how to do for the students assigned to them. What goes on in the community, the district office, the state capitol, or elsewhere is not as deserving of their attention as that mental and physical space inhabited by them and their students. Perhaps teachers pay little attention to these other influences on the educational enterprise because they feel so powerless to affect them.

So the discourse which occurs in school among teachers focuses on the here and now of their teaching (a mostly solo act) and the learning successes and problems of their students. There are schools in which staff members discuss more powerful ways to reach and teach their students, spend time on research into teaching and learning that should influence policy, work on strategies to more fully engage the community, and study how the faculty can deal with its problems. But these schools represent a small percentage of all schools.

Leaders and staff of teacher unions see schooling more broadly than do their members. Both the American Federation of Teachers (AFT) and the National Education Association (NEA) have focused on making policy, influencing political decisions, and helping to assure that teaching is seen as an important public service. Historically, the unions' interests in professionalism have been expressed chiefly through seeking assurances that all teachers receive due process, that is, that their professional rights to teach and their individual employment rights are respected. Primarily, the role of unions has been to put policies and procedures into place to assure teachers that they could practice safely as long as they adhered to certain conditions negotiated on their behalf.[12]

Many reformers, academics, and policymakers have accused the unions of blocking reform and causing teachers to behave and to be seen as less than professional. In some cases, such accusations have been justified. Because unions reflect the structure of public schools, they are at their most powerful at local and state levels. Those in leadership positions as well as staff workers in teacher unions "went through the revolution" during the 1970s. They saw a school system in which the most important workers were not treated with dignity and were victimized by undemocratic, top-down hierarchies in which they had little voice. With great zeal and energy, union leaders set about to correct these injustices. They changed their organizations from relatively ineffective *teacher clubs* to aggressive defenders of academic freedom, wielders of political influence, proponents for human and civil rights, and, above all, bargainers for and protectors of the economic and social well-being of their members. As the reform movement began in the mid-80s, most unionists saw school improvement as the job for school management; their responsibility was to extend hard-won rights and benefits.

It must also be remembered that teacher unions, and indeed the entire education establishment, are conservative, that is, protective of what works until proposed innovations are proved better. Teachers at the beginning of the movement in the 80s had seen previous reform attempts come and go, often leaving behind schools which they saw as no better and, in some instances, worse. Teachers and those representing them often took a "show me" approach to those who would change their schools. Policymakers and some of the less patient reformers and academics did not like this resistant stance.

Many of the reform thrusts ignored teachers and their need to help shape change and to have the time and education necessary to carry out a given innovation as well as the tools to evaluate it. Too little was done to bring teachers into the decision-making process; their unions responded and put a brake on what many saw as more frills and less substance.[13] One view is that the unions blocked change; another is that school administrators and union leaders were not yet at a place to trust each other to change the institution to which they were both deeply committed. As will be discussed later, those conditions were soon to change.

PROFESSIONAL ORGANIZATIONS

Other teacher organizations were important forces in the movement to reform schools. These organizations represented educators' interest in subject matter (e.g., National Council of Teachers of Mathematics); in new ideas about teaching and learning (e.g., Association for Supervision and Curriculum Development); in teacher learning (e.g., the National Writing Project); and in knowledge development and research (e.g., the Teacher Researcher Special Interest Group of the American Educational Research Association).

Many teacher organizations have played a significant part in updating standards for the content area in which their members specialize and which now guide so many state efforts in curriculum reform.[14] They continue to update curriculum standards and to develop materials and education programs aimed at assuring sound implementation. This work on standards and implementation strategies has contributed greatly to the professional development of those teachers engaged in it. An increasing number are now involved as their organizations respond to requests to enlarge their efforts to affect curriculum, particularly to update content and to prioritize what is important for students to learn within that subject. It is hoped that recent calls to make the curriculum more cohesive will be heeded by the subject matter associations with teachers pointing the way to make standards more "teachable." Currently, the national standards, taken as a whole, would require more school time than could ever be made available, and states are having to make difficult choices about what constitutes a comprehensive basic curriculum. Through their various organizations, teachers can provide leadership on this issue.

Since their beginnings in the early decades of this century, teacher organizations have contributed greatly to their members' professional growth. They have operated through journals and other publications, national meetings, regional and state action programs, professional development programs, preparation and distribution of instructional material, assessment processes, and, in some cases, through certifying and publicizing the educational values of teaching materials.

TEACHER NETWORKS

Many efforts of these teacher organizations were strengthened by networks, electronic and personal, which created communities of teachers, often in different parts of the country, where teachers' hunger for improved ways of teaching, for intellectual stimulation, and for validation could be accommodated when conditions at their workplace or in their other organizations did not provide such sustenance.

Informal networks of teachers within schools and between them have existed since almost the beginnings of public education in the United States. The possibilities for such association grew in the early 1960s when federal funding for teacher centers became available, making possible places in which teachers could exchange ideas, develop materials, and test out innovations. Many of the curriculum reform efforts of those days were discussed and tested in these centers. With the decline of funding, the more formal centers disappeared except in Indianapolis, New York City, and a few other places, and were replaced by more informal means of exchanging ideas and materials for teaching. Ann Lieberman has written about teacher networks and their importance to improving the quality of schools in her introduction to a monograph written by teachers about their work: "This is a process that enables teachers to reinvent themselves, their profession, and their communities."[15]

Many colleges and universities sponsor teacher networks as a way to provide support for those in the early years of their teaching. In networks that are well conceived and supported, neophytes receive help from one another and from mentors at the college and in cooperating schools.

The most extensive use of networks is electronic, where communities of teachers with similar interests are bound together through the Internet and through electronic mail services provided by various organizations. In these electronic conversations, teachers explore ideas among themselves, present problems which they seek help in solving, and report on innovative practices they are using. In the NEA Mastery In Learning Project, discussed later in this chapter, each school was connected electronically to the other sites, to consulting researchers, and to the project staff. Initially, MIL's School Renewal Network[16] was created to move teachers closer to educational researchers so that decisions at the school could be based on data. Later, because teachers came to see it as a way to establish community and to solve problems, the network became a setting for individual exchanges among professionals. Many of these exchanges continued beyond the life of the project, some lasting until the equipment became obsolete and the network had to be closed down.

Enhanced Professionalism and Educational Reform in Selected Sites

Reform movements prior to the 1980s attempted to increase educational opportunities for underserved groups,[17] update or expand curriculum,[18] or improve teacher education.[19] An interesting characteristic of the current movement is its focus on schools and school systems. Field-based improvement projects are often networked to include several schools or school districts in order to create a critical mass of school personnel who learn from one another. Two such projects are described below to provide a perspective on the problems and opportunities associated with enhanced professionalism.

MASTERY IN LEARNING PROJECT

Among the earliest of the school improvement networks was the NEA Mastery In Learning Project (later the MIL Consortium).[20] This school-based effort began at the inception of the current reform movement, the year following publication of *A Nation at Risk* (1983) and concluded eleven years later in 1995. In MIL, participating schools and their faculties were asked to develop their own professionalism, through examining their practice, basing decisions on research and other resources, building an agenda for improvement based on their particular school contexts, and becoming more reflective and analytical as teachers and "reformers."

To help teachers in MIL schools to further develop their professionalism, resources were made available on topics and processes identified by them as being important: student assessment, curriculum development, shared decision making, developing workable "flat hierarchies," conflict resolution, planning strategies, student and teacher scheduling, and others. They also received help on matters outside of their usual interactions at the school: increasing parent involvement, developing community and university partnerships, forging more productive relationships with their central office, using the products of research and development, building their capacity to do action research and to use the results.

In an article I wrote at the conclusion of the work, I listed the following characteristics of MIL schools:

. . . more writing of a substantive nature; questioning; hands-on learning; problem solving; visual arts, music, and art as serious subjects as well as for recreation and celebration; real student government; cooperative learning; whole language integrated with healthy doses of phonics for those who need it; cross-age grouping; student self-discipline; independent study; reading of good books; use of film and other media; out-of-school experiences used in lessons; peer and cross-age tutoring; portfolios; performance-based assessment; use of fugitive materials; diversity of instruction; project-based instruction; arguing about ideas; interdisciplinary classes; depth over breadth; opportunities to learn in different ways; mainstreaming; attention to fairness and civility; energy; and technology, technology, technology.[21]

In 1997, three years after the MIL Consortium disbanded, and thirteen years after it began, I conducted an informal survey of teachers and others who had participated in the work. The response rate was low, partly because many envelopes were returned by the post office stamped "not able to forward." Of the 386 mailed to the person's previous school address, almost half were returned. And this occurred when teachers were less mobile than at any time in the last 25 years. It leads me to wonder if service in an innovative, changing school somehow caused teachers to move to other positions with greater frequency than their counterparts in other schools. Many teachers claim that innovative schools are "high stress" places, and it is difficult to stay in them over a long period. Other teachers who have been involved in changing practices move on to other interesting positions which provide them with fresh stimulation and increased responsibilities. In any case, 198 surveys reached the addressees, and 56 of them were completed and returned, yielding a 28 percent response rate.

Open-ended questions were asked about participants' current views of professionalism, with particular attention to the substance and sources of their professional growth. From these responses I drew the following generalizations. Without exception these teachers and school staff saw themselves as "highly" or "very highly" professional. There were mixed reactions to the quality of the various sources of professional development. Some found the university a good place for them to learn and just as many did not. (Since these were mature teachers most of whom no longer needed advanced college credit to maintain their license or to receive salary increases, their current experience with universities was probably limited.) Many rated "subject matter organizations" as helpful in their development. Most did not think that their local, state, or national unions contributed very much to their growth as teachers.

Clearly, the most significant source of professional growth for respondents to my survey was "study groups/teacher-led sessions." In such settings, these teachers had opportunities to reflect on their work and receive comment and advice from others in their school who shared their interests or who taught the same grade or subject. That teachers would prefer to learn in seminar-like settings, building their own agenda and securing the substantive resources they found helpful, is an important lesson.

The majority described themselves as working in hierarchical settings and in places where communication among staff was "negative." With only two exceptions, the old MIL schools were described negatively by those few who remained in them. The MIL experience had affected them positively as individual professionals, but in the long run they believed their school did not sustain the professionalism and action programs that had once characterized them.

This lack of institutional impact has several causes, many of which have to do with the complexities of school systems and, in particular, their need to bring those who deviate from current practice back into the center. Other deterrents to reform have to do with forces that define the schools and their *connectedness* with other parts of the system: teacher education, textbooks, tests, state and local curriculum mandates, employee contracts, expectations of the public, all of which interact to support a way of schooling that no longer fits today's students and society.

It now seems clear that school-by-school reform does not work unless accompanied by efforts to affect the entire system. This lesson emerged when comparisons were made between the MIL project with its exclusive focus on the school site and another NEA project, the Learning Laboratories program, which focused on the entire school system. Reform efforts have to be top-down *and* bottom-up if they are to be deep and lasting. Others involved in school reform have made similar observations.[22]

Still another reason that MIL did not effect significant institutional change may reside in the habits of faculties and administrators who are caught in the dailiness of keeping school. Teachers in MIL schools could envision specific modest innovations and they could act to improve current practices. They worked remarkably well within the construct of schooling as we know it, but their views of fundamental change in teaching and learning were restricted. Perhaps, given other opportunities, resources, and more time, they might have met more successfully the MIL exhortation to "challenge the regularities." Yet this very concept often seemed alien even in these schools whose faculties had chosen to engage in restructuring.

CHARTER SCHOOLS INITIATIVE

A second national project that involves a network of schools is newer and smaller than MIL. The aims of the NEA Charter Schools Initiative (CSI) are not entirely different from those of Mastery In Learning. CSI emphasizes high student achievement, teacher learning, and community engagement in schools and programs newly created to support these three purposes. Five sites are involved in a five-year program, which began in 1995.

In these schools, "founders" apply to an agency authorized by the state to grant a charter. Typically, charter schools do not have to adhere to most of the rules and regulations of other public schools. They are free to develop the program that best serves the students they wish to enroll. Public money follows the students to the school. Generally, charter schools receive a per-pupil allotment almost equal to other public schools.[23] Charter schools, currently a popular concept, may eventually provide an alternative to public education and its present organization. More immediately, though, these schools can become laboratories for public schools, providing places where ideas can be tried and results shared.

Still, there is a concern that charter schools may not be providing the breakthroughs that many political and educational leaders think are needed to educate American students for an information-age global society. Presently, the charter school *movement* enjoys strong bipartisan political support with a considerable investment, financial and rhetorical, in trying to make these schools catalysts for change. In CSI schools, innovative activity is centered primarily on focused curriculum orientation, improved teaching arrangements, individualization of student programs, increased parent involvement, changing administrators' roles, enhanced uses of technology, and new conceptions of governance. However, three of the most basic considerations that shape schools—allocation and use of time, curriculum content, and teacher development—tend to be treated in traditional ways. As in other schools, teachers in CSI schools report that they do not have the time to be more reflective, to think of long-term outcomes, to use research effectively, and to develop new knowledge. In one of the schools which is still in the planning stage, a staff position has been designated for facilitating a program in which time and resources are available for teachers to develop professionally. It will be informative to observe experiences in this school where teacher learning is to be an integral part of everyday life.

The future impact of charter schools will lie in their ability to affect the basic structure of American education, including having an impact on how teachers continue their professional education. Ray Budde, the initiator of the concept of charter schools in 1988, saw a future in which school districts would delegate considerable authority to individual schools. In his plan, all schools would be charter schools, responsible for designating their particular purposes within the framework of district goals, designing and implementing programs, specifying their personnel requirements, hiring and firing staff, and being rigorously accountable to the community. District administrators and teacher unions would be important players in regard to upholding democratic principles, but basic decisions about teaching, learning, and staff development would be made as close to learners and teachers as possible.[24]

Will teachers, parents, and others "step out of the box" and create charter schools that draw on conceptions of teaching and learning more geared to the future than the past? Will charter schools, only some of which are bold in conception, develop into laboratories from which we can learn? To become an important source of ideas for improving American education, charter schools will have to challenge the most basic conditions which define schooling today and provide in their everyday practices blueprints for change that will meet the needs of tomorrow's society.

What these needs are cannot be determined by schools, charter or otherwise, independently of the public they serve. Ultimately, the public has to define educational quality predicated on the ability of the school to prepare students to live happy and productive lives. Although too little can be predicted about the world in which students will live, we can identify several indicators of future needs: an increased life span and the implications thereof for work, recreation, and happiness; processing, using, and evaluating information wisely and efficiently; critical consumerism; living in a global society; strengthening our citizenship in a multicultural democracy, for example. Defining the school's role in helping citizens deal with such imperatives is an important public debate that must occur.[25]

As important as any of the conditions leading to a new definition of schooling are the qualities of the person who teaches. A discussion of a possible future for teachers and professionalism concludes this chapter.

Unions, the Future of Professionalism, and School Quality

The ways in which schools will be different in the future depend on the outcomes of two major thrusts. One thrust is *curricular* and presently focused on the standards-based education movement with its emphasis on explicitness, assessment, accountability, and perhaps most important, on defining the essentials of a basic education. In a school where standards are central, learners acquire depth in important content instead of experiencing a curriculum "a mile wide and an inch deep."[26]

The second thrust is *pedagogical* and focuses on teachers' work as an instrument of achieving quality. Here the nature of what is being discussed, the proposals being made, and the various efforts to produce change are many and diverse. They range from efforts to help practitioners become more reflective and change-oriented to very ambitious agendas to change the nature of recruitment, preparation, licensure, induction, and career patterns of teachers.[27]

Placing on top of the present system interventions such as higher level curriculum standards or new mandates for teacher education will not, by themselves, produce substantive change that is deep and lasting. Such change has to be supported by attention to the entire system, not ". . . focus on snapshots of isolated parts of the system, and wonder why our deepest problems never seem to get solved."[28] Some attention has gone to school and system reform which focuses on contextual matters aimed at bringing form and function into closer synchronization. Efforts along these lines include helping school staffs spend their time on matters more directly related to the purpose of the school; flattening hierarchies so that decisions can be improved and "owned" by those who will implement them; building data collection and analysis systems to guide decision making; developing improved ways for management, governance, and teachers to relate; and creating learning programs for educators that further the central purposes of the institution. Unfortunately, however, such system-affecting innovations are still few in number. If they are ever to become widespread, teacher unions will have to play even larger roles than they have so far in implementing system-oriented reforms.

The national unions and their state and local affiliates hold great influence over schools and their efforts to improve. "The massive 2.2 million-member National Education Association and the articulate, urban-centered 900,000-member American Federation of Teachers have arguably been the strongest forces in American public education over the last half-century," claim Kerchner, Koppich, and Weeres.[29] This influence emanates from collectively bargained agreements in many local communities. Teachers' influence also derives from their political prowess at the local, state, and federal level; from their ability to establish the environment in which reforms are implemented; from their reputation in parents' eyes; and from their sheer numbers.

At the beginning of the reform movement, the NEA tentatively reached beyond its usual professional program focused on teacher education to become instrumental in schoolwide reform. Through the Mastery In Learning project, it hoped to dispel its obstructionist image by playing a visible and constructive role in school improvement. That initial foray was the beginning of several experimental programs such as the National Center for Innovation, the Learning Laboratories, the Teacher Education Initiative, the Charter School Initiative, and the KEYS program.[30]

In 1997, NEA President Robert Chase placed the Association's school improvement activities in a larger context. In a speech announcing a major turn in the organization, he called for the reinvention of teacher unions for ". . . lifting up teachers as professionals and boosting the quality of schools."[31] Since the delivery of that speech, NEA has attempted to define more fully Chase's vision. The National Center for Innovation was expanded in size and scope, a school improvement strategy embedded in its KEYS program was developed, and the teacher education emphasis was enlarged to include more partnerships between schools and universities to affect preservice preparation and provide professional development opportunities for inservice teachers. Importantly, programs are in place to help NEA field staff gain the skills and attitudes necessary to the collaborative efforts that authentic school improvement demands. And it has taken what many consider to be a risk to public relations by supporting the Charter School Initiative, since this movement contains in its ranks many who would privatize the schools, a position that NEA has vigorously fought for decades.

Most revealing is that NEA now has a single strategic objective guiding the allocation of all resources: "NEA will focus the energy and resources of its 2.3 million members toward the restoration of public confidence in public education."[32] NEA is developing new ways of relating to the public school system, using its resources to "save" a system which many opinion leaders and policymakers see as being troubled and perhaps not worth saving.

Earlier than NEA, AFT saw the need to tackle the major issues confronting school quality. A very different organization with a working culture unlike NEA's, AFT proceeded in somewhat different directions because of the nature of its membership and leaders. But both NEA and AFT have changed dramatically since *A Nation at Risk* was issued.[33] They are more focused on the professional needs of their members; they are lobbyists for policies that support a centrist view of education; and they are more directly involved in the improvement of schools.

AFT and NEA continue their attempts to merge the two organizations, and when that occurs, it will impact the way in which teachers relate to issues of professionalism. It seems likely that union activism in school improvement will be accelerated. "Together, we can bridge old divides and start sharing the wisdom, talent, and experience that run throughout both our individual organizations. We can focus more energy on saving public education, joining with others who share our goal of empowering those who educate America's children," said the presidents of the two unions in a joint statement.[34] The rhetoric surrounding the merger negotiations implies but does not make specific how the new union, its members, and its work could be conceived in ways that will benefit educational quality, student achievement, and how communities relate productively to their schools. When a conception of new unionism is achieved and the new organization emerges to carry it out, will the result matter in the places that count—where students learn and teachers teach? The answer lies in the ability of a union of teachers to attend with equal effectiveness to the quality of members' working conditions *and* the quality of members' professional work. Unions know very well how to affect working conditions; they are learning how to influence professionalism.

The most concrete evidence of the increasing attention being paid to the quality of teachers' work lies in NEA policy documents published during the current effort to improve schools. In this twenty-year period, three proposals were vigorously debated which shaped the association's stance on professionalism: the earliest was about teacher education,[35] the second on the direction of school improvement,[36] and the third, and most recent, on peer assistance and review.[37]

The most interesting difference in these documents is the shift from teachers' dependence on others in changing their behaviors to a belief that teachers themselves must play a major role in their achieving high professional status.

Peer assistance and review programs provide a way for teachers to help other teachers improve their work and thereby assure greater competence in their ranks. NEA provides training, sample contractual language, and examples of what is working in various school districts where union representatives support local implementation of NEA's peer review/assistance policy. Local schools are already feeling the effects of this phase of the new unionism. The press recently reported that teachers and the board of education in the large, well-respected school system of Montgomery County, Maryland, negotiated a contract that gave teachers, ". . . an unusual influence in establishing education policy . . . aimed at resolving some of the most nettlesome problems facing schools."[38] The article went on to say, "School board and union officials said the bargaining process was dramatically different from the head-banging contentiousness that traditionally has dominated contract talks. [NEA president] Chase said that in other districts that have adopted a more collaborative approach to union negotiations, teachers have become 'co-managers' of schools."[39]

FUNDAMENTALS OF PROFESSIONALISM

In the future, unions will accompany their changes in bargaining with a definition of professionalism more consistent with members' work. They will focus on those fundamentals of professionalism having to do with authority, personal growth, and enhancement of the knowledge underlying teaching and learning. Four goals will drive unions' action in the future as they pay greater attention to helping members provide service of high quality to students.

1. *Autonomy Over Practice*. When those who are only indirectly involved with schools have undue authority over the nature of practice, students and teachers are not well served. School quality will be enhanced when professional teachers have the inclination, commitment, opportunity, intellectual resources, and authority to make basic decisions about their school, based on their students and community. This kind of *teacher empowerment* is different from previous conceptions held by the unions. The unions are well situated to increase teacher autonomy over practice because they have the organizational experience and the human resources to make it happen.

2. *Opportunities to Improve Practice.* Teachers do not have the opportunities that other professionals have to acquire new skills and knowledge; school improvement, therefore, takes a long time and in the end may be only temporary. Time, resources, and rewards are all key to designing teacher development programs which will bring about quality. Teacher unions, through collective bargaining, alliances with business, and the use of advanced technologies can radically change the ways in which inservice teachers learn and grow.

3. *Depth and Mastery in Teaching and Curriculum.* Schools in the future known for their high quality will have a core of faculty members who are senior professionals—teachers with lengthy service, advanced degrees, and, most important, the recognition by peers that they are accomplished leaders and mentors. They will be teachers certified by the National Board for Professional Teaching Standards who enjoy high status and receive rewards commensurate with their accomplishments. Both AFT and NEA have played significant roles in moving the National Board to its present state. The next step is to assure that these Board-certified teachers have opportunities to lead their schools and systems to higher quality. They must be there in sufficient numbers and with the authority to make a difference. Both NEA and AFT have the organizational experience and the human resources to achieve these goals.

4. *Opportunities to Contribute to Knowledge about Teaching, Learning, and Schooling.* Most people who are ill want to be treated in a teaching hospital because they are convinced that practitioners in these hospitals are acting on the best and newest research available. Schools could enjoy similar reputations if their faculties focused on current research, had the ability to translate these ideas into practice, and learned from systematic inquiry into their own work. This is a culture-changing endeavor. It is not one in which the unions have extensive experience, but they have the capacity and the responsibility to move in that direction.

As Kerchner and his colleagues suggest, teacher unions may be on the edge of transforming themselves into institutions that are capable of "constructing a successor to industrial-era education."[40] Teacher unions have a history in which principles of democracy have played a critical role, and Kerchner rightly calls for a reconnection of labor to the American dream. Certainly, teacher unions have the capacity to transform themselves and to increase the professionalism of their members and thereby improve educational opportunities for students. The survival of the unions and the health of public education depend on that transformation.

NOTES

1. *Status of the American Public School Teacher 1995-96* (Washington, DC: National Education Association, 1997).

2. Norman L. Webb, *Criteria for Alignment of Expectations and Assessments in Mathematics and Science Education*, Research Monograph No. 6 (Madison: National Institute for Science Education, University of Wisconsin, National Center for Improving Science Education, 1997).

3. Priscilla Wohlstetter and Susan Albers Mohrman, "School-Based Management: Promise and Process" in *CPRE Finance Briefs* (Rutgers: Consortium for Policy Research in Education, Rutgers University, December 1984).

4. Robert McClure, "From Tinkering to Transformation," in *If Minds Matter*, eds. Arthur Costa, James Bellanca, and Robin Fogarty (Palatine, IL: Skylight Publishing, 1992), p. 130.

5. Nancy E. Adelman, Karen Panton Walking Eagle, Andy Hargreaves, eds. *Racing with the Clock: Making Time for Teaching and Learning in School Reform* (New York: Teachers College Press, 1997).

6. Gary Sykes, "The Social Consequences of Standard-Setting in the Professions," Paper prepared for the Task Force on Teaching as a Profession (New York: Carnegie Foundation, Carnegie Forum on Education and the Economy, November 1986).

7. For example, see *What Matters Most: Teaching for America's Future* (New York: National Commission on Teaching and America's Future, 1996).

8. A body of literature appearing prior to the decades under consideration in this chapter suggested new ways of thinking about the work of teachers. See, for example, Robert J. Schaeffer, *The School as a Center of Inquiry* (New York: Harper and Row, 1967); Daniel C. Lortie, *Schoolteacher: A Sociological Study* (Chicago: University of Chicago Press, 1975); and William J. Tikunoff, Beatrice Ward, and Gary Griffin, *Interactive Research and Development on Teaching Study: Final Report* (San Francisco: Far West Laboratory for Educational Research and Development, 1979). More recent works on teacher learning and a different kind of practice include Donald A. Schon, *The Reflective Practitioner* (San Francisco: Jossey-Bass, 1983); Lawrence Stenhouse, *Research as a Basis for Teaching* (London: Heinemann, 1985); Patricia Wasley, *Teachers Who Lead* (New York: Teachers College Press, 1992); Marilyn Cochran-Smith, "Learning to Teach Against the Grain," *Harvard Educational Review* 61, no. 3 (1991); Sharon Feiman-Nemser, "Teacher Preparation: Structural and Conceptual Alternatives" in *Handbook of Research on Teacher Education*, ed. W. Robert Houston (New York: Macmillan, 1990); Virginia Richardson, "Teacher Inquiry as Professional Staff Development," in *Teacher Research and Educational Reform*, Ninety-third Yearbook of the National Society for the Study of Education, eds. Sandra Hollingsworth and Hugh Sockett (Chicago: University of Chicago Press, 1994); Judith Warren Little, "Teachers as Colleagues," in *Educators Handbook*, ed. Virginia Richardson-Koehler (New York:

Longman, 1987); Ann Lieberman and Lynne Miller, "Problems and Possibilities of Institutionalizing Teacher Research" in *Teacher Research and Educational Reform*; Gary A. Griffin, "Clinical Teacher Education," in *Reality and Reform in Clinical Teacher Education*, eds. James Hoffman and Sara Edwards (New York: Random House, 1986), pp. 1-24.

9. There is considerable discussion about new ways of maintaining organizations in a rapidly changing world. Writings which exerted influence on business and governmental organizations and eventually touched the school reformers include: Peter F. Drucker, *The Age of Discontinuity: Guidelines to our Changing Society* (New York: Harper and Row, 1969); Thomas J. Peters and Robert H. Waterman, Jr., *In Search of Excellence: Lessons from America's Best-Run Companies* (New York: Harper and Row, 1982); and Peter M. Senge, *The Fifth Discipline: The Art and Practice of the Learning Organization* (New York: Doubleday, 1990). In the same period, there emerged a considerable amount of writing more directly related to how the educational enterprise should be reconceived and organized: *A Nation at Risk* (Washington, DC: U.S. Department of Education, 1983); Howard Gardner, *Frames of Mind* (New York: Basic Books, 1983); John I. Goodlad, *A Place Called School* (New York: McGraw-Hill, 1984); *A Nation Prepared* (Washington, DC: Carnegie Forum on Education and the Economy, 1986); and Theodore Sizer, *Horace's Compromise: The Dilemma of the American High School* (Boston: Houghton Mifflin, 1992).

10. Virginia Richardson, "Teacher Inquiry as Professional Staff Development," p. 187.

11. The NEA Mastery in Learning Project and its successor, the NEA Mastery in Learning Consortium, existed from 1985 to 1995. It involved 38 schools, 1,800 teachers and other staff, and about 39,000 students. For further information, including discussions about teachers' interests and inclinations to engage in reconceptualizing their work, see eds. Carol Livingston and Shari Castle, *Teachers and Researchers in Action* (National Education Association Professional Library, 1989); Robert M. McClure, "Sharing a Decade's Lessons" in *Doubts & Certainties*, Vol. IX, no. 5, May/June 1995 (Washington, DC: The National Education Association, 1995); and Donna L. Jurich and Gary Griffin, "School Restructuring: More than the 'Third Wave' of School Change," (Paper presented to the American Educational Research Association, New York City, 1996.)

12. There are exceptions to this generalization. Albert Shanker, the late president of AFT, had considerable influence in the national debate about school quality and purpose. Mary Hatwood Futrell, president of NEA, 1984-89, moved her Association to become more involved in matters of teacher education and school improvement.

13. Lorraine M. McDonell and Anthony Pascal, *Teacher Unions and Education Reform* (Washington, DC: Rand Corporation, 1980).

14. See among many descriptions and guides: *Professional Standards for Teaching Mathematics* (Washington, DC: National Council of Teachers of Mathematics, 1991).

15. Martianne D'Emidio-Caston, Lynette Hill and John Snyder, *Teachers' Voices* (New York: National Center for Restructuring, Education, Schools, and Teaching, Columbia University, 1994), p. 4.

16. Carol Livingston and Shari Castle, eds., *Teachers and Research in Action* (Washington, D.C: National Education Association Professional Library, 1989).

17. For a description of the landmark Elementary and Secondary Education Act passed by the Congress in 1964, see Paul E. Peterson, *Making the Grade, Report of the Twentieth Century Fund Task Force on Federal Elementary and Secondary Education Policy* (New York: The Twentieth Century Fund, 1983).

18. Robert M. McClure, ed., *The Curriculum: Retrospect and Prospect*, Seventieth Yearbook of the National Society for the Study of Education (Chicago: University of Chicago Press, 1971).

19. James Bryant Conant, *The Education of American Teachers* (New York: McGraw-Hill, 1963).

20. Robert M. McClure, "The Evolution of Shared Leadership," *Educational Leadership* 46, no. 3 (November 1988): pp. 60-62. Association for Supervision and Curriculum Development.

21. Robert M. McClure, "Sharing a Decade's Lessons" in *Doubts and Certainties*, Vol. IX, no. 5, May/June 1995 (Washington, DC: The National Education Association, 1995).

22. Patrick M. Shields and Michael S. Knapp, "The Promise and Limits of School-Based Reform: A National Snapshot" *Phi Delta Kappan* 78, no. 4 (December 1997): pp. 288-294.

23. Erik W. Robelen, "Charter Schools and Public Education," an Association for Supervision and Curriculum Development *Infobrief*, Issue 12, January 1998.

24. Ray Budde, *Education by Charter: Restructuring School Districts* (Andover, MA: The Regional Laboratory for Educational Improvement of the Northeast and Islands, 1988).

25. The Education Commission of the States and the National Center on Education and the Economy have been leaders in the effort to articulate schooling and students' futures.

26. For an explication of the standards-based education reform movement, see Marc S. Tucker and Judy B. Codding, *Standards for our Schools: How to Set Them, Measure Them, and Reach Them* (San Francisco: Jossey-Bass, 1998).

27. For a view of how these characteristics should be manifest in the future, see *What Matters Most: Teaching for America's Future*.

28. Peter M. Senge, *The Fifth Discipline: The Art and Practice of the Learning Organization* (New York: Doubleday, 1990), p. 7.

29. Charles Taylor Kerchner, Julia P. Koppich, and Joseph G. Weeres, *United Mind Workers: Unions and Teaching in the Knowledge Society* (San Francisco: Jossey-Bass, 1997), p. 13.

30. The National Center for Innovation was begun in 1990 to provide an organizational home for the Association's experimental school improvement programs. For a description of the NEA Learning Laboratory Program, see *Rapporteur Experience: Field Studies in School District Systems Change* (Washington, DC: National Education Association, 1997). For a description of the Teacher Education Initiative, see "The NEA's Teacher Education Initiative" in *Doubts and Certainties*, Spring, 1997. For a description of the KEYS program, see Richard R. Verdugo, et al., "Statistical Quality Control, Quality Schools, and the NEA: Advocating for Quality," *Contemporary Education* 67, no. 2 (Winter 1996): pp. 88-93.

31. Robert Chase, "The New NEA: Reinventing Teacher Unions For a New Era." Speech before the National Press Club (Washington, DC: National Education Association, February 5, 1997), p. 3.

32. *NEA Handbook* (Washington, DC: National Education Association, 1997), p. 407.

33. Since I have spent most of my professional life as an NEA staff member, I know more about that organization than I do about AFT. AFT's views of professionalism, school reform, and other issues related to school quality are well represented in their publications and, most publicly, in the *New York Times* and *Education Week* columns by Albert Shanker and his successor as AFT President, Sandra Feldman.

34. Robert Chase and Sandra Feldman, "The AFT/NEA Unity Talks: A Joint Progress Report," January 21, 1998, available from both organizations.

35. *Excellence in our Schools: Teacher Education* (Washington, DC: National Education Association, 1982).

36. *An Open Letter to America on Schools, Students, and Tomorrow* (Washington, DC: National Education Association, 1987).

37. NEA Handbook, pp. 295-296.

38. Fern Shen and Michael E. Ruane, "Montgomery County Teachers Get Greater Say," *Washington Post*, February 11, 1998, p. B-1.

39. Ibid., p. B-4.

40. Charles Taylor Kerchner, Julia P. Koppich, and Joseph G. Weeres, *United Mind Workers: Unions and Teaching in the Knowledge Society* (San Francisco: Jossey-Bass, 1997), p. 15.

CHAPTER IV

The Role of Standards in Teaching and Teacher Education

ROBERT J. YINGER

In the United States today one rarely picks up the newspaper or tunes to the electronic media without finding some report of educational crisis, failure or, occasionally, some story of educational innovation or success. Education has been identified in numerous polls as one of the top concerns of the American public. Hundreds of analyses have been offered in the past fifteen years detailing the problems of public schools, urban school systems, school funding policies, and teaching practice. Parents, politicians, and professionals alike often point to one means for improving the educational state of affairs: standards. Standards for learners, standards for instruction, standards for curriculum, standards for teacher training, standards for teacher licensure, standards for performance, standards for testing, and even standards for standards have been proclaimed. Standards are developed, debated, legislated, repealed, promoted, demoted, waived, and winced at. Much of our hope for educational reform and renewal in the near future is pinned to a strategy of defining and applying new standards for teaching, learning, and schooling. Precious little of this strategy has been questioned or analyzed.

The purpose of this chapter is to foster a discussion on the role of standards in teacher education, licensure, and certification as we enter the twenty-first century. Robert Roth characterized the 1990s as the "age of standards" and generated a comprehensive history and analysis of research and policy in this area.[1] Likewise, others have published recent reviews of issues and challenges as standards are developed and applied.[2] The report of the National Commission on Teaching and America's Future based many of its recommendations for the improvement of teaching and learning on the use of professional standards as vehicles for improvement in teacher education, teacher licensure, and advanced teacher certification.[3]

Robert J. Yinger is Dean of the School of Education and Professor of Educational Psychology at Baylor University.

My strategy here is not to replicate or merely update the excellent reviews and critiques done by other teacher educators or policy analysts, though some updating will be important because of the rapid developments in the use of teaching standards in the past few years. Most of this chapter, however, will be devoted to framing the role of standards in the process we call professionalization. To do this, I will rely heavily on Andrew Abbott's sociological analysis of professionalization processes across various modern professions in the United States and Europe.[4] Aspects of his framework will be used to create a model of professional knowledge and jurisdictional authority for practice that highlights the role of standards in professionalization. This model will then be used to interpret historical and current trends in teacher education, licensure, and certification. Finally, lessons will be drawn from professionalization processes in other modern professions, and emergent issues and challenges will be identified for the field of teaching.

Professional Knowledge and Legitimacy

The study of professions, especially the modern professions of medicine, law, and accounting, has become a popular area for scholars in the past half century.[5] Most of this work has focused on trying to identify organizing features and developmental stages that distinguish professional occupations from other forms of work, especially other forms of skilled labor such as the crafts and trades. Most writers in this area have identified common features of established professions such as proprietary knowledge, autonomy of practice, internal control of training and entry into practice, licensure and certification standards, and a code of ethical practice. Several scholars have attempted to define stages that professions go through on their way to establishment and public recognition.[6]

Abbott has departed from these characterizations by shifting the focus of analysis from how professions are organized to a focus on the work itself. He defines a profession as an exclusive occupational group applying somewhat abstract knowledge to particular cases. For him the central issue of the professions is how a group obtains the right to practice; that is, how a profession claims and establishes a jurisdictional authority over particular kinds of knowledge and skill and over particular work with clients.

Like Terence Johnson and Magali Larson, Abbott rejects the notion that the history of professionalization reveals any general process or common developmental steps.[7] His strategy is to focus on the content of professional work, which case studies indicate undergoes continual change due to new knowledge, new technology, or social developments. For Abbott, it is the control of work that brings professions into conflict with each other and makes the histories of related professions interdependent. The central phenomenon of professional life, then, is the link between a profession and its work, a link Abbott calls jurisdiction.

<h2 style="text-align:center">PROFESSIONAL JURISDICTION</h2>

The work tasks of the professions are human problems amenable to expert service. "They may be problems for individuals, like sickness and salvation, or for groups, like fund raising and auditing. They may be disturbing problems to be cured, like vandalism or neurosis, or they may be creative problems to be solved, like a building design or a legislative program."[8] The reliance on experts varies widely across cultures, across problems, and over time. Experts seize new problems by defining and labeling them but also discard old problems with equal speed.

Professional jurisdiction refers to claims to control and authority for dealing with particular kinds of problems. Physicians have staked their claim to jurisdiction over sickness and disease. Psychiatrists have claimed mental illness (along with some psychologists). Clergy have claimed salvation. Accountants have claimed auditing. Architects and engineers have claimed design, and so forth. These jurisdictional claims are based on control of knowledge and skill, and practical skill is grounded in a particular form of knowledge—abstract knowledge.

<h2 style="text-align:center">KNOWLEDGE JURISDICTION</h2>

Abbott argues that the modern professions control their occupations by controlling abstract knowledge. In other words, professions control the abstractions that generate not only technique but also the definitions of problems in the first place. This use of abstract knowledge can be contrasted with crafts or trades that control their occupations with technique *per se*.

For me this characteristic of abstraction is the one that best identifies the professions. For abstraction is the quality that sets interprofessional competition apart from competition among occupations in general. Any occupation can obtain licensure (e.g., beauticians) or develop an ethics code (e.g., real estate). But only a knowledge system governed by abstractions can redefine its problems and tasks, defend them from interlopers, and seize new problems—as medicine has recently seized alcoholism, mental illness, hyperactivity in children, obesity, and numerous other things. Abstraction enables survival in the competitive system of professions. If auto mechanics had that kind of abstraction, if they 'contained' the relevant sections of what is currently the engineering profession, and had considered taking control of the repair of all internal combustion engines on abstract grounds, they would, for my purposes, be a profession.[9]

According to Abbott, jurisdictional claims of professional practice have three parts: (1) claims to classify a problem (what he calls "diagnosis"); (2) claims to reason about it ("inference"); and (3) claims to take action on it ("treatment"). Abbott sees these components as modalities of action, not always separate acts, but more importantly, they embody the essential cultural logic of professional practice. It is within this logic that tasks receive the subjective qualities (current cultural construction of the problem controlled by a profession) that form the cognitive structure of a jurisdictional claim.

There are objective foundations for professional tasks, such as technology (e.g., computers and the new information professions), organizational structures (e.g., the institutional contexts for teaching and social work), natural objects and facts (e.g., the human body for medicine and the weather for meteorologists), and established cultural structures (e.g., the concept of private property in law). Even these objective foundations are subject to change as can be witnessed in the work tasks of information science shifting from hardware-dominated to software-dominated and the effects on psychiatry of the mass closing of mental hospitals. This reshaping creates subjective foundations for professional tasks as the profession constructs new definitions of problems, accepted ways to reason about them, and authoritative modes of treatment.

Abbott argues that jurisdictional authority for professional practice is anchored in abstract knowledge rather than in technique. Successful professions have tied their work to a system of knowledge that formalizes the skills on which work proceeds. The ability of a profession to establish and sustain its jurisdictional authority lies partly in the power and prestige of its academic knowledge. Many professions have bolstered their jurisdictional authority by embedding professional training in university study and the academic disciplines. Abbott has defined three functions for academic, abstract knowledge systems. First, they play a cultural and social role in legitimizing professional work through the public's mistaken belief that abstract, academic knowledge is continuous with professional practical knowledge, and therefore more prestigious academic knowledge (e.g., university graduate study) implies

more effective practice. Abbott hypothesizes that the true use of academic knowledge is more symbolic than practical, as it legitimizes professional work by clarifying its foundations and tracing them to major
cultural values (e.g., health, learning, justice, safety). Second, abstract
knowledge contributes to the actual work of a profession by generating
new modes of action: new conceptions, new treatments, and new inference methods. Academic knowledge lends itself to research and invention because of its abstraction and the ability to find underlying patterns
across cases and situations. Third, the abstract theories and categorization systems found in textbooks often model most purely the knowledge
framework on which professions are based, but that never or rarely exist
in the world of practice. The teaching of abstract, academic knowledge,
then, creates a classification and reasoning system that justifies professional work with general cultural values and simultaneously generates
new means for professional work. As custodian of professional knowledge in its most abstract form, academic knowledge is uniquely situated
to make jurisdictional claims. But these claims are cognitive only and
must be bolstered by concrete social claims and legitimizing responses.

Diagnosis, treatment, inference, and academic frameworks provide
the cultural machinery of jurisdiction by constructing work tasks into
known "professional problems" that can be acted upon and researched.
To perform skillfully and to justify performance cognitively is not,
however, sufficient for holding professional jurisdiction.

SOCIAL JURISDICTION

In claiming jurisdiction, a profession asks society to recognize its cognitive
structure through exclusive rights; jurisdiction has not only a culture but a
social structure. These claimed rights may include absolute monopoly of practice and of public payments, rights of self-discipline and of unconstrained
employment, control of professional training, of recruitment, and of licensing,
to mention a few. Which of them are actually claimed depends in part on the
audience. Claims made in the legal and political systems generally involve
much more than do those in public media. The claims also depend on the
profession's own desires; not all professions aim for domination of practice in
all their jurisdictions. Finally, they depend on the social organization of the
professions themselves.[10]

A jurisdictional claim made before the public is a general claim for
the legitimate control of particular work. The general nature of this
claim has particular effects on how a profession is viewed and expected
to operate in the public arena. For instance, though jurisdiction may
confer authority and obligation (e.g., lawyers doing legal work as they

see fit), there is often only a secondary obligation to in fact accomplish the work claimed (e.g., serving the needs of justice). In the public arena the discourse about practice and jurisdiction is constrained by public stereotyping of professional practice and assumptions of homogeneity. Public discussions of "doctor-nurse relations," for example, assume that all doctors are the same and all nurses are the same. In addition, public discourse also assumes that work tasks are objectively defined and connected in fairly straightforward ways to reality. Each of these features causes public claims for jurisdiction to develop slowly and change slowly (taking a decade or more, according to Abbott). Though less than fifty percent of doctors and lawyers are in independent practice today, most public jurisdictional claims are grounded in images (often perpetuated by these professions) that draw upon simplified and romanticized images from the past such as Ben Casey and Perry Mason.

Jurisdictional claims made in legal arenas tend to be more specific than public claims. They may involve claiming monopolies of practice, monopolies of certain payments by third parties, control of certain work settings, and even control of what language is used to define the work. Claims of legal jurisdiction primarily occur in legislatures and the courts. The need for clear boundaries for law and legal rulings leads to more rigid treatment of legitimacy and jurisdiction than in the public arena. All members of a professional legal category are treated exactly the same, and professional tasks are rigidly defined. Once established, legal jurisdictions are extremely durable.

As a result of this extreme formality, the legally established world of jurisdiction is a fixed, static world that rejects the living complexity of professional life. Most importantly, its insistence on rigid definition forces it to ignore the ambiguities that professions can successfully enshrine in their professional images. As a result, legally established jurisdiction comes slowly and endures forever. Professions often attempt legal jurisdiction early in their development . . . But by the time a profession actually achieves legal establishment, it has usually long since won its public position.[11]

The third arena for establishing professional legitimacy is the workplace. It is in this arena where the complexities of practice are manifest and where issues of genuine efficacy are confronted. In an organizational context, where most professional practice exists today, jurisdiction is a fairly simple claim to control certain kinds of work. There is little debate about what the tasks are or how to construct them. The basic question is who can control and supervise the work and who is qualified to do it. In work sites where employees are overworked, professional boundaries become blurred because incompetence or understaffing requires other people to do parts or all of a professional's work. Abbott calls this process "workplace assimilation" as subordinate professionals or non-professionals learn on the job a craft version of a given profession's knowledge system and practice.

This assimilation is facilitated by the fact that professionals are not in reality a homogeneous group. In the jurisdictional system of the workplace, it is the real output of an individual, not his credentialed or non-credentialed status, that matters. Since some professionals are much more talented than others, the best of the subordinates often excel the worst of the superordinates; certain individuals in closely related professions end up knowing far more about a profession's actual work than do a fair number of its own practitioners.[12]

If the public knew the extent of workplace assimilation, claims for comprehensive jurisdiction would become much more suspect.

It is the workplace where connections between the profession and task must be demonstrated. The acts of a profession (Abbott's "modes of treatment") are most visible and practitioners must demonstrate such things as measurability of results, specificity of treatment, acceptability of treatment to clients, and overall efficacy of professional action. Though less visible to clients, diagnostic procedures must be able to employ clear diagnostic classifications, restrict relevant information, and reduce the amount of residual categorization. Likewise, inferential processes being used by professionals should be grounded in a sound logical structure, employ solid inferential chains, and balance inference against routine processing. Claims for workplace legitimacy are established somewhat by task accomplishment and effectiveness; more often, social control processes of formal preparation and credentialing establish rights to entry and the opportunity to practice legitimately.

INTERNAL SOCIAL CONTROL

Abbott identifies three major components of a profession's social organization: professional groups, professional controls, and professional work sites. In addition to forming official groups of professional practitioners (professional groups tend to show up early in the professionalization process), professions have lobbying groups, informational groups, and groups aimed at professional control. In the United States, professional associations such as the American Medical Association, American Bar Association, American Institute of Architects, and the National Education Association tend to embody all of these group functions.

Practice itself is more directly influenced by professional controls in the form of accredited professional schools, licensure and certification requirements, and codes of ethics and practice. There are also less formal social controls specific to particular work sites. Empirical studies of the professions show that licensure efforts tend to come early in a profession's efforts at legitimacy and codes of ethics later. Formalizing the examination requirements and establishing accreditation for training tend to take place in the middle of the process, but once established all of these activities develop in interaction with one another. Of all these processes, licensure is often most visible and has the most direct effect on others outside of a profession. This is because licensure carries certain preemptive rights over outsiders for a legitimate right to practice. It is also through establishing licensure standards that a profession publicly and legally demonstrates attention to standards for behavior and efficacy. Standards for approval or accreditation of training schools function in a similar manner, though restrictions are being exercised internally and have less impact on outsiders.

A MODEL OF PROFESSIONAL KNOWLEDGE AND JURISDICTION

Abbott's analysis of the professions provides a means for representing how standards fit into and influence the process of professionalization. Figure 1 illustrates the major components and processes discussed by Abbott. At the center is Jurisdictional Control of Work Tasks with the three components of work and with critical aspects of performance. Professional Knowledge, especially abstract and case knowledge, forms the basis for a profession's claim to cognitive jurisdiction, i.e., the right to conceptualize, categorize, and act upon professional problems. This abstract knowledge base is generated and legitimized by the academy as noted in the box top left of Figure 1. The formal rationality embodied in the academic disciplines and academic professional study provides culturally accepted formulations of the world of practice and, through the knowledge base, can generate new practice. The knowledge base also generates and legitimizes the establishment of standards for the profession. These standards (see box in lower left in Figure 1) establish internal control by the profession over training, entry to practice, and practice itself. By doing so, the profession consolidates its legitimacy and jurisdiction by demonstrating attention to performance and quality control. Though knowledge is sufficient for establishing cultural and cognitive jurisdiction, a profession has to interact with and

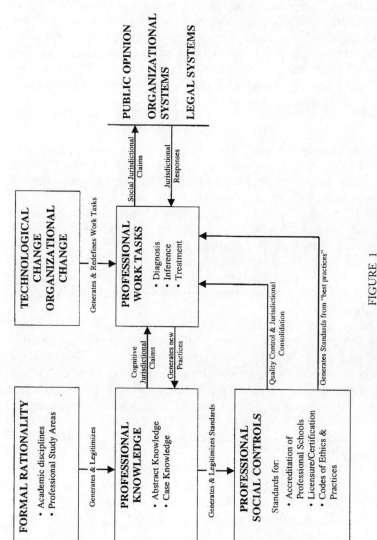

FIGURE 1

A Model of Professional Knowledge and Jurisdiction

claim social jurisdiction in the arenas of public opinion, the legal system, and organizational systems. This is especially true in the way the public, legal, and organizational arenas endorse the establishment of standards for professional training, licensure, and ethical practice. In addition to knowledge growth or change generating new practice, technological change and organizational change, especially the emergence of large-scale organizations, are two external forces that have created or redefined work tasks for the professions. This new work becomes a new site to establish jurisdictional authority and can become a basis for interprofessional competition.

THE ROLE OF STANDARDS

Using this professionalization framework, it is possible to create a model of the roles of standards in the professions. Figure 2 identifies two major areas where standards function. To function as a profession, a group must be able to demonstrate that their knowledge and skill make them uniquely suited to solve unique problems most effectively and receive jurisdictional recognition for that practice. Professional standards serve both this practice function and this legitimization function. Though these two functions are not independent, it is important to separate and assert that professionalization must involve both the creation of effective practice and the creation of a recognized jurisdiction.

By creating standards for practice from a recognized professional knowledge base, it is possible to establish public definitions for effectiveness through codes of practice and codes of ethics. Standards also can generate efficacy parameters for outcomes (treatment effects) and performance criteria for thinking and action. A third practice function of standards is that of defining inquiry frameworks for assessing and creating new knowledge and practices. Finally, standards can establish the goal and means for initial training and for continuing professional learning.

At the same time, knowledge-based standards can help legitimize practice by supporting cognitive, cultural, and social jurisdictional claims. The way in which standards define (and standardize) the problems of practice bolster the cognitive and cultural claims that professions make through the knowledge base. The shared definitions and expectations for practice embodied in standards create an image of formal rationality and underlying theoretical sophistication. Accreditation and licensure standards support social claims for jurisdiction by limiting the settings for training and limiting access to practice. Overall,

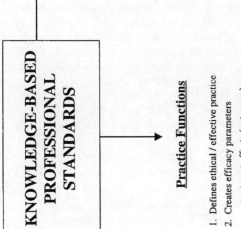

Cultural and Social

Legitimization Functions

1. Creates jurisdiction for particular tasks and problems
2. Shared definitions convey image of "rational practice"
3. Defines accepted educational and training process
4. Limits access to practice
5. Generates accepted norms for efficacy and safety

KNOWLEDGE-BASED
PROFESSIONAL
STANDARDS

Practice Functions

1. Defines ethical / effective practice
2. Creates efficacy parameters
   -treatment effects (outcomes)
   -performance criteria (knowledge, inference, action)
3. Defines inquiry framework for assessing and creating new knowledge and practices
4. Frames training and continued learning parameters

FIGURE 2

The Functions of Professional Standards

standards serve to legitimize professions by appealing to Western society's regard for scientific knowledge, higher education, specialization, and credentialing. They serve a further social function of addressing clients' expectations that practice will be safe and effective.

Standards in Teaching and Teacher Education

In the 1990s educators have witnessed a rapidly changing professional environment for teaching and teacher education. Much of this change has been a result of the increasing influence of knowledge-based standards on policy and practice as can be seen in the following excerpts, which contrast the policy contexts of the late 80s [A] with that of the mid-90s [B].

[A] Public policies adopted in the 1980s have had direct and unprecedented consequences for who will be allowed to teach and how they will be prepared. Although the making of teacher education policy is taking place in the context of multiple reports and studies, and although statistics are called upon frequently to justify the need for public action, it appears that most of the policies being adopted are not burdened by their fit with available knowledge or systematically developed theory.[13]

[B] The three-legged stool of quality assurance—teacher education program accreditation, initial teacher licensing, and advanced professional certification—is becoming more sturdy as a continuum of standards has been developed to guide teacher learning across the career. . . . The Commission recommends that this framework be used to guide education policy across the states so that every teacher prepares at an NCATE-accredited [National Council for Accreditation of Teacher Education] institution, demonstrates teaching competence as defined by INTASC [Interstate New Teacher Assessment and Support Consortium] standards for initial licensing, and pursues accomplished practice as defined by the National Board for Professional Teaching Standards.[14]

A policy context that was highly fractured and contentious in 1990 had by 1996 rapidly closed on a consensus on standards related to teacher education, initial licensure, and advanced teacher certification. Understanding how this happened requires a look at only fairly recent developments in the fields of teaching and teacher education.

RECENT DEVELOPMENTS

Unlike many other countries, the United States has historically resisted national efforts to set educational standards. The strong tradition of local school control has not only influenced expectations for student performance but also expectations for teacher performance as well. Though entry to teaching in the United States has been conditioned on a four-year baccalaureate degree and teaching credential since the 1930s, the influence of the school district's hiring, promotion, and tenure policies have only recently given way to the influence of state regulation and professional standards. Fundamental to this change is a shift in emphasis from trying to guarantee teacher "inputs" by way of certificates granted by approved teacher education programs to assessing teacher "outcomes" by way of performance-based professional licensure.

From the 1930s to the 1980s standards in the teaching profession were virtually unchanged. Licensure of teachers continued to be based primarily on credentials. Teacher education programs were approved based on the existence of prescribed course work. Though the National Teacher Examination (NTE) was developed in the 1940s, it was not until 1977 that the first states mandated testing for licensure. Beginning in the mid 1970s a surge of standards-setting activity began, driven largely by state policymakers' concerns about teacher quality and teacher supply. Gary Sykes has summarized well the danger signs in the profession at that time:

Enrollment in teacher education had declined 50 percent between 1972 and 1980, partly in response to the lack of jobs. Policymakers feared a teacher shortage, for salaries also declined throughout this period. Coupled with worry over supply was concern for teacher quality. Widely publicized reports at the time indicated that teaching recruited from the bottom of the academic ability distribution, as measured by the SAT and other tests. . . . At every point of choice from initial entry to teacher education through the decision to remain in teaching, the least academically able opted for teaching. . . . Others noted that, with expanding opportunities, talented women and minorities would no longer choose teaching, and some evidence bore out the exodus of these historically captive labor pools . . . And 20 years of survey data revealed a steady decline in teacher morale as measured by the question "Suppose you could go back to your college days and start over again: would you become a teacher?" The number responding "certainly not" or "probably not" grew from 9 percent in 1966 to 36 percent in 1981.[15]

State policy strategies in the 80s combined initiatives to strengthen licensure standards through competency testing with efforts to address teacher supply issues through recruitment incentives such as salary increases, forgivable student loans, and scholarships. By 1986 all but four states required competency tests for teachers (primarily the NTE). States also began developing more sophisticated forms of assessment such as portfolios, instituting tests for re-licensure, increasing mandates for more liberal education and subject matter studies in teacher preparation, and creating more specified credentialing to reduce teaching out of field.

At the same time, and in response to many of the same concerns about the quality of teaching and the schools, several new professional organizations were created to address these concerns nationally. Largely due to recommendations proposed by the Carnegie Forum on Education and the Economy in *A Nation Prepared: Teachers for the 21ˢᵗ Century*, the National Board for Professional Teaching Standards (NBPTS) was formed in 1987.[16] The goal of the NBPTS was to establish high and rigorous standards for what accomplished teachers should know and be able to do. Also in 1987, the Council of Chief State School Officers sponsored the formation of the Interstate New Teacher Assessment and Support Consortium (INTASC), the purpose of which was to facilitate collaboration among states that are interested in rethinking standards for initial teacher licensing and developing new techniques to assess teacher performance and to promote teacher professional development. That same year the Holmes Group (now Partnership), a consortium of approximately one hundred research universities involved in teacher education, was established to address concerns about the quality of teacher education and the ties of teacher education to the realities of public schools. The recommendations of the Holmes Group in *Tomorrow's Teachers*[17] reinforced calls for higher national standards for teacher education being made anew by established professional organizations such as the National Council for Accreditation of Teacher Education (NCATE).

Since 1987, standards for initial teacher licensure, advanced teacher certification, and accreditation have been developed in concert. By the mid-1990s the work of NBPTS, INTASC, and NCATE had produced a remarkable consensus which was becoming accepted nationally around definitions of professional teaching practice and preparation. This consensus was referred to as "the three-legged stool of teacher quality" by the National Commission on Teaching and America's Future and has become a template for change and research in education. The unity of this conception of professional teaching can be seen through an overview of these standards frameworks.

ADVANCED TEACHER CERTIFICATION

The primary mission of the National Board for Professional Teaching Standards is to develop and operate a national voluntary system to assess and certify accomplished teachers. This work is overseen by a 63-member board of directors, the majority of whom are classroom teachers. The National Board's policy position is based on five core propositions about teachers:

1. **Teachers are committed to students and their learning.** National Board-Certified teachers are dedicated to making knowledge accessible to all students. They adjust their practice based on students' interests, abilities, skills, and backgrounds. They understand how students develop and learn.

2. **Teachers know the subjects they teach and how to teach those subjects to students.** National Board-Certified teachers have a rich understanding of the subject(s) they teach, and they know how to reveal subject matter to students. They are aware of the knowledge and preconceptions that students typically bring. They create multiple paths to knowledge, and they can teach students how to pose and solve their own problems.

3. **Teachers are responsible for managing and monitoring student learning.** National Board-Certified teachers create settings that sustain the interest of their students. They command a range of instructional techniques and know when each is appropriate. They know how to motivate and engage groups of students. They use multiple methods for measuring student growth and can clearly explain student performance to parents.

4. **Teachers think systematically about their practice and learn from experience.** National Board-Certified teachers critically examine their practice, seek the advice of others, and draw on educational research to deepen their knowledge, sharpen their judgment, and adapt their teaching to new findings and ideas.

5. **Teachers are members of learning communities.** National Board-Certified teachers work collaboratively with other professionals. They use school and community resources for their students' benefit. They work creatively and collaboratively with parents, engaging them in the work of the school.[18]

Standards and assessments are being established in 34 certificate fields, framed by age levels and content areas such as Early Childhood Generalist (ages 3-8), Middle Childhood Mathematics (ages 7-12), and Social Studies/History (covering both early adolescence and young adulthood). As of January, 1998, standards and assessments have been developed in 21 certification fields and 595 teachers have received Board certification.

BEGINNING TEACHER LICENSURE

The Interstate New Teacher Assessment and Support Consortium is currently a consortium of more than 30 states and professional organizations. INTASC has developed performance-based standards for initial licensure of teachers that are built upon and compatible with the advanced certification standards of the National Board for Professional Teaching Standards (NBPTS). They articulate what entering teachers should know, be able to do, and be like in order to practice responsibly and begin their development towards accomplished, professional teaching. The task force drafting the standards addressed the question of what distinguishes the beginning practice of a competent, newly licensed teacher from the advanced levels of performance expected of a Board-Certified teacher and concluded that "the appropriate distinctions between beginning and advanced practice are in the degree of sophistication teachers exhibit in the application of knowledge rather than in the kind of knowledge needed."[19] They also decided that, like the NBPTS standards, the appropriate benchmark for teaching standards should be based on considerations of what students need in order to learn effectively, rather than on current systems of teacher preparation.

INTASC began its work by articulating standards for a common core of teaching knowledge and skill that should be acquired by all teachers and is articulating additional specific standards for disciplinary areas and levels of schooling. These core standards are expressed as ten principles:[20]

Principle 1: The teacher understands the central concepts, tools of inquiry, and structures of the discipline(s) he or she teaches and can create learning experiences that make these aspects of subject matter meaningful to students.

Principle 2: The teacher understands how children learn and develop and can provide learning opportunities that support their intellectual, social, and personal development.

Principle 3: The teacher understands how students differ in their approaches to learning and creates instructional opportunities that are adapted to diverse learners.

Principle 4: The teacher understands and uses a variety of instructional strategies to encourage students' development of critical thinking, problem solving, and performance skills.

Principle 5: The teacher uses an understanding of individual and group motivation and behavior to create a learning environment that encourages positive social interaction, active engagement in learning, and self-motivation.

Principle 6: The teacher uses knowledge of effective verbal, nonverbal, and media communication techniques to foster active inquiry, collaboration, and supportive interaction in the classroom.

Principle 7: The teacher plans instruction based on knowledge of subject matter, students, the community, and curriculum goals.

Principle 8: The teacher understands and uses formal and informal assessment strategies to evaluate and ensure the continuous intellectual, social, and physical development of the learner.

Principle 9: The teacher is a reflective practitioner who continually evaluates the effects of his/her choices and actions on others (students, parents, and other professionals in the learning community) and who actively seeks out opportunities to grow professionally.

Principle 10: The teacher fosters relationships with school colleagues, parents, and agencies in the larger community to support students' learning and well-being.

Since the 1992 release of the draft standards over 30 states have adapted and adopted the INTASC core standards to guide their teacher licensure reform efforts. Most state efforts are now focused on establishing performance-based licensing systems incorporating the following components:[21]

1. The adoption of clear standards for performance that are comprehensively evaluated through **performance-based assessments for licensing**. These assessments must be good representations of the actual tasks, knowledge, and skills needed for teaching and of what good teachers actually do in a learning setting.

2. **The replacement of course-counting strategies** for licensing and program approval with two kinds of standards:

- licensing based on successful completion of performance-based assessments and completion of an approved/accredited program;

- program review and accountability based on a demonstration that the [education] school's program provides learning opportunities that lead to the successful attainment of the knowledge, skills, and dispositions needed to teach and their demonstration on structured assessments that are based on the standards.

How these strategies mesh with new program accreditation standards will be seen below.

NATIONAL TEACHER PREPARATION PROGRAM ACCREDITATION

Founded in 1954, the National Council for Accreditation of Teacher Education (NCATE) is comprised of 30 professional associations and organizations of teachers, content area specialists, and local and state policymakers. As of March 1998, 540 of the approximately

1,200 teacher education institutions in the United States are NCATE accredited. The other non-accredited institutions are still able to offer approved teacher preparation programs under historical arrangements that have placed approval of teacher education programs in the hands of the states.

The NCATE standards emphasize prospective teacher performance in the context of solid preparation in liberal arts and professional studies. The standards focus on four categories: (1) design of professional education (e.g., conceptual framework, curriculum design, quality of instruction, quality of field experiences); (2) candidates in professional education (e.g., qualifications, diversity, assessment of competency); (3) professional education faculty (e.g., qualifications, diversity, assignments, professional development); and (4) the unit for professional education (e.g., governance, resources).

A current goal of NCATE is to increase collaboration with state departments of education to reduce or eliminate the redundancy of both state and NCATE program assessment, to integrate state and national professional standards, and to increase the rigor of the review of teacher preparation programs. As part of their State Partnership Program, NCATE has agreements with 40 of the 50 states to conduct joint reviews of schools of education. In these partnerships, states are now requiring all teacher education programs to undergo NCATE assessment or to undergo state assessment using the NCATE standards.

A third partnership option being actively pursued by NCATE as part of their New Professional Teacher Project is to help create a professional continuum for teaching that links program accreditation to initial licensure and to advance certification standards. In this framework a state would establish a comprehensive performance-based licensing system that meets NCATE criteria. In turn, when accrediting programs NCATE would consider the performance of the program's teacher candidates throughout their preparation and assess the success record of the program's graduates on standards-based licensure assessments. Currently, NCATE is working with both INTASC and NBPTS to develop compatible standards throughout the professional teaching career.

THE EMERGING IMAGE OF TEACHING

Through the work of the three organizations described above, a powerful consensus has emerged regarding the definition and assessment of good teaching throughout a career, from preservice education to advanced professional certification. The standards have framed an image of the professional teacher as a knowledgeable, reflective practitioner willing and able to engage in collaborative, contextually grounded learning activities. The NBPTS standards expect accomplished teachers to think systematically about their practice in the context of educational research and the experience of others (Standard 4) and to work creatively and collaboratively as a member of a learning community (Standard 5). Even beginning teachers are expected to meet the INTASC core standards of reflective practice and professional growth (Principle 9) and to develop professional and community relationships that support student learning (Principle 10).

In September of 1996 the National Commission on Teaching and America's Future (NCTAF) released its influential report, *What Matters Most: Teaching for America's Future*. The Commission's recommendations are based on three premises:

- What teachers know and can do is the most important influence on what students learn.
- Recruiting, preparing, and retaining good teachers is the central strategy for improving our schools.
- School reform cannot succeed unless it focuses on creating the conditions in which teachers can teach—and teach well.

NCTAF proposed the goal, "Within a decade—by the year 2006— we will provide every student in America with what should be his or her educational birthright: access to competent, caring, qualified teaching in schools organized for success."[22] To accomplish this goal, the Commission offers five major recommendations:

1. Get serious about standards, for both students and teachers.
2. Reinvent teacher preparation and professional development.
3. Fix teacher recruitment and put qualified teachers in every classroom.
4. Encourage and reward teacher knowledge and skill.
5. Create schools that are organized for student and teacher success.

In the late 1990s three trends have emerged in the development and application of standards in teaching. First, concerted efforts have begun to link standards for teaching to standards for school learning. The pressing question to be demonstrated by advocates of standards for teachers is whether properly educated, licensed, and certified teachers are more successful at facilitating the learning outcomes in students that we desire. Second, there is a continuous trend toward furthering the aims of professional standards by establishing partnerships among previously independent or isolated stakeholders. The alliance of NBPTS, INTASC, and NCATE mentioned above is one powerful partnership. As notable is the re-invention in 1997 of the Holmes Group as the Holmes Partnership, a transformation acknowledging that teacher education is unlikely to reform itself in significant ways without dedicated alliances with schools and school districts that are involved in reform activities themselves. Also, in 1997 the American Federation of Teachers and the National Education Association announced talks exploring the possibilities and processes involved in merging the two national teacher unions. The third notable trend in the standards-based professional education movement is the willingness of states, the federal government, and foundations to make sizable investments in research into standards and their application. In 1997, the United States Department of Education funded a five-year, 23-million-dollar contract with a consortium of research universities and professional organizations, National Partnership for Excellence and Accountability in Teaching (NPEAT) aimed at providing a research base supporting the implementation of the recommendations of the National Commission on Teaching and America's Future. This work has been furthered by significant investments by private and corporate foundations aimed at additional research and dissemination of effective practices.

Interpreting the Trends

Using the analysis and models developed at the beginning of this chapter, one could interpret the recent history of standards in teaching as a process of re-asserting claims for professional jurisdiction. Teaching has had difficulty establishing itself as a profession similar to the more established and high-status professions mainly because the jurisdiction for school teaching has historically been organizationally derived. Rather than making professional claims based on control of the unique work tasks of teaching and learning, the public has seen work of teachers as being a function primarily of the organizations (schools) in which it is conducted. In other words, the nature of the organization and the controls placed on it by the public generate and control the work of teaching, rather than teachers themselves. This is similar to the jurisdictional difficulties faced by social workers and nurses, where the work tasks of their professions are sustained by the organizations in which they work.

The major way in which the professions have asserted a claim for professional jurisdiction historically is by means of professional knowledge. Grounding this knowledge in the abstract and theoretical world of the disciplines and the university is the means for claiming both cognitive and cultural jurisdiction. Until the 1980s teaching made only weak claims to these jurisdictions. In 1930 requiring a four-year college degree for teachers to be licensed linked teaching to the academy and its knowledge, but by 1980 this special claim was eroded by the increased number of people attending college and by the migration of other professional preparation to the graduate level.

The establishment of research on teaching as a serious area of social science research in the 1960s and 1970s made possible the types of scientific claims recognized as legitimate in the university and the modern world of the professions and by the public. By 1986, three editions of the *Handbook of Research on Teaching* had been published by the American Educational Research Association, each over 1,000 pages in length.[23] In 1989 the American Association of Colleges of Teacher Education published the *Knowledge Base for the Beginning Teacher*,[24] and in 1990 the *Handbook of Research on Teacher Education* was published by the Association of Teacher Educators.[25] Both of these volumes chronicled hundreds, if not thousands, of research studies on teaching, learning, curriculum, and schooling. By 1987 NCATE had revised its accreditation standards to require programs to explicitly define a conceptual knowledge base for teacher education and to demonstrate how this knowledge framework was being implemented.

This emerging research framework gained additional professional prominence when the NBPTS commissioned scholars in the field of research on teaching to work with subject matter experts to develop the assessment instruments, strategies, and content of the National Board examinations. As NBPTS and INTASC wrestled with definitions and performance components of effective teaching, they grounded their claims in research on teaching and learning as well as in analyses of the work tasks of teaching. The work of the Educational Testing Service (ETS) to develop a reliable and valid performance assessment for beginning teachers (called Praxis III) similarly used both research and workplace analysis to determine a framework for best practice.[26] This performance examination has been indexed closely to the INTASC knowledge framework and may be in use by several states by 2000 as a component of performance-based licensure.

By 1996, the teaching profession was positioned to make persuasive claims for an abstract knowledge base underlying teaching. This claim was bolstered by a number of universities who were members of the Holmes Partnership (as well as some others) redesigning their teacher education programs to include extended undergraduate degree work or moving entirely to the master's level. The message that these universities were sending to the public was that effective teachers need to possess more academic knowledge in their subject matter and in their professional specialties. Like other respected professions, teaching is grounded in theories and specialized techniques for addressing the unique problems of practice. The importance of the academic knowledge underlying teaching has been further reinforced by a number of states now requiring the completion of master's degrees to receive continuing licensure.

Standards play an important role in claiming jurisdiction for the teaching profession because they intersect the interests of the academy and the public. To the degree that they are knowledge-based they reinforce and consolidate claims to cognitive and cultural jurisdiction. Because standards become the basis for licensure, certification, and accreditation requirements, they become recognized and established in policy and law. As legislative bodies and policymakers accept standards, this action becomes a powerful and public response to a profession's claim for social jurisdiction of the work tasks.

yes but will they [handwritten marginal note]

Importantly in the field of teaching today, standards for accreditation, licensure, and certification are being initiated by the profession and the academy. This is far different from even ten years ago when policies being adopted were "not burdened by their fit with available knowledge or systematically developed theory."[27] As consensus develops around national standards for teaching and teacher preparation, it fulfills the needs of both policymakers and the public for simplification of the image of teaching and issues of quality. There was no way teaching could have met these social needs for a unified, scientifically based perception of professional practice as long as academics were arguing publicly about conceptions of teaching and 50 state legislatures were deciding the matters for themselves.

Another trend influencing social jurisdictional claims by the teaching profession is the shift from focusing standards on professional inputs to focusing on demonstrated outcomes. Education has always found it easier to guarantee the quality of teaching inputs (e.g., instructor's credentials, curriculum, time, materials) than the quality of learner outcomes. This has been especially true of the university, where the incentives and rewards are oriented toward improving the knowledge of the professors rather than that of the students. A weakness that all professional preparation wrestles with is the tendency to measure the effectiveness of instructional programs by means of the courses taken, not the knowledge and skills acquired.

There is additional pressure on efficacy of practice in teaching because teaching is conducted in publicly supported institutions and the clients (students and parents) often have little choice in who delivers professional services. This is still further complicated in schools today, where there is often dissatisfaction or misunderstanding or even disagreement about how to measure learning outcomes and how these outcomes can be linked to the work of teaching. The fact that teachers historically have had weak jurisdictional claims to defining and framing the work tasks of teaching meant that views of teaching and learning were up for grabs and one person's assessment was as good as another's. To the degree that professional standards (along with professional codes of ethics and practice) can delineate (that is, take control of) the issues and solutions to problems of teaching and learning, there will be more acceptance of and satisfaction with the process of schooling.

Lessons and Issues for Standards-based Teacher Education, Certification, and Licensure

The analysis of the professionalization process points out a number of lessons that could benefit the teaching profession and highlights significant issues that must be addressed for teaching to mature. Confronting these lessons and issues will be important yet difficult because they require teachers and professional educators to enter arenas heretofore avoided because of their political, competitive, and public nature. Students of professionalization such as Abbott boil down the issues of a profession to those of (1) defining what are the work tasks and problems to be solved (knowledge control); (2) determining who gets to do the work (jurisdictional control); and (3) asserting how the work should be effectively accomplished (quality control). Words such as *control*, *authority*, *regulation*, and *standards* have negative connotations for many educators who prefer to envision themselves as independent operators engaged in liberating and empowering learners. If teaching is to develop as a profession under the banners of standards and effectiveness, educators must clearly understand and seek to influence the organizational, social, and political contexts in which they practice.

LESSONS FROM OTHER PROFESSIONS

Though there is little evidence to support common paths or required components for the development of the professions, historical analysis can point to commonalities in professionalization. For teaching in its current situation, five generalizations seem to be applicable:

1. Professionalization is a competitive and political jurisdictional process. The success of a profession depends on its ability to establish and consolidate jurisdictional claims in cognitive, cultural, and social arenas. Success seems to hinge on a profession's ability to clearly delineate a focus for its work and on the ability to adapt to changes in the workplace brought on by technological developments and organizational change.

2. The university plays an important role in producing and legitimizing professional knowledge. Cognitive jurisdictional claims asserted by a profession are grounded in academic disciplines and university professional programs. Additionally, successful professions have been able to develop settings for clinical education and practice that blend the world of academics and the world of practice. There are problems, however, in sustaining these connections because the reward system in research universities undervalues the teaching mission and resists efforts to connect more closely to real practice.

3. There are dangers arising from what some call "the convergence plot" of professionalization. As a profession stakes its claim and becomes established in a jurisdiction, there are increased opportunities for the exercise of self-interest and abuse of power. In recent decades medicine and law have been criticized for non-responsiveness to client needs and for the erosion of foundational professional values. Public support for cost containment and more institutional control over health care may be due, in part, to perceptions of professional abuse of their jurisdiction.

4. Professionalization is a slow, bumpy ride. The fact that jurisdictional claims are asserted in the context of complex social and cultural arenas such as public opinion, the legal system, and higher education makes rapid change and progress unlikely. It took nearly 50 years for medicine to consolidate its social jurisdiction for licensure in the mid-1800s, and the recommendation by the National Board of Medical Examiners in 1915 to tie all state licensure to a tripartite requirement of graduation from an accredited medical school, a three-part, staged examination, and completion of a year-long, supervised internship was not universally accepted until the mid-50s.

5. Technological change and changes in large-scale organizations pose the biggest challenges to professional jurisdictions. New technology, especially the rapidly changing information and communication technologies, raises work-task issues by allowing new forms of routinization, access to expertise, and client self-service. Some professions like law, architecture, and medicine face new pressures for institutionalization,

while others like teaching and nursing are reacting to opportunities for increased institutional autonomy.

The above lessons suggest that as teaching uses standards as a strategy to achieve professionalization, we should pay special attention to jurisdictional issues, the role of the universities, and sustained political and public engagement. Five issues seem crucial to address over the next ten years:

Issue 1: Consolidation of teaching's jurisdictional claims by defining teaching in terms of its core work rather than through its place in school organizations. Standards will play a crucial role in this activity as they convey a core set of knowledge, skills, and strategies that teachers should possess and as these are linked to valued learner outcomes. The debate should focus on the essential work tasks and efficacy measures for teaching, not on trying to preserve teaching by protecting the current organizational frameworks. Jurisdictional legitimacy will require educators to become more engaged politically and publicly, entering the messy world of debate, negotiation, and compromise. The "new work" of teachers must also become more public in the forms of codes of practice and codes of ethics.

Issue 2: Expanding the research knowledge base. Standards for teaching will become more persuasive as they can be more directly linked to learning standards and performance. Research on teaching and learning must focus more on "design experiments" where researchers and practitioners, especially teachers, collaborate in the design, implementation, and analysis of changes in instructional practices.[28] Also, research investigating teacher learning across the professional continuum should be expanded in order to better understand the professional learning and development processes. Social acceptance of the "new teacher" will depend in part on research-based demonstrations of increased effectiveness of teachers emerging from redesigned teacher education programs. It will also be important to demonstrate research-based strategies to address the needs of experienced teachers to learn to practice in new ways and in new roles.

Issue 3: Adapting to organizational change. New standards for teachers are aiming at a practitioner who is more knowledgeable about subject matter, more skilled in tailoring school content for diverse learners, more reflective, more collegial, and more directed toward continuous professional learning. School reform efforts are creating room, as well as need, for these kinds of individuals by establishing new leadership roles for classroom teachers, increasing school-based decision making, establishing team-based instructional models, reorganizing instructional delivery through multi-year grouping or block scheduling. Teacher education institutions are rapidly moving to more integrated ties to schools and school districts by creating Professional Development Schools, new clinical faculty roles, and expanded partnership agreements. All of these developments are driven by a new professional model of teaching, and all those involved—teachers, school administrators, teacher educators, and others—are going to have to redefine the nature of their work. This redefinition should be directed by knowledge-based standards and has already begun for teachers and school administrators. Teacher educators and other participants in higher education will face a much larger challenge because there are as yet, no knowledge-based standards established for new teacher education roles in professional programs. NCATE's newly proposed standards for Professional Development Schools is a first step toward standards for clinical education, and the work of the Holmes Partnership on the parameters of effective school-university partnerships points in the right direction. In research universities large barriers still remain to the realignment of the reward system so that it supports collaborative, clinical work of faculty, more effective instruction, and accountability for the performance of graduates. By focusing on and clearly defining the essential work of teacher educators as professionals, it may be possible to invent new faculty roles and new instructional processes that are currently thwarted by the organizational *status quo*.

Issue 4: Response to competition. Until recently, the near-monopoly of public schools has left little room for real competition in formal education. In the past two decades belief by both politicians and the public in the efficacy of the free-market system has created legitimate competitors in the form of home schooling, voucher programs, and charter schools. At the same time, teacher educators in traditional colleges and universities have lost their exclusive franchise for teacher preparation and professional development to proprietary colleges, school districts, and not-for-profit teaching academies. Lessons from other professions suggest that these jurisdictional challenges are inevitable and that they can only be successfully met by establishing strong claims to research-based professional knowledge and to demonstrations of effective professional performance backed by client satisfaction. Teachers and teacher educators should be less worried about preserving the current organizations in which they work and more concerned about first demonstrating their effectiveness and then determining what organizational frameworks would facilitate their delivery of services.

Issue 5: Organizational and systemic competence. Related to all the above issues is how to create healthy and competent organizational systems for carrying out the work of teaching and learning. The massive mission of free public education in this country virtually requires practice embedded in large-scale, complex systems. Many of the pressing difficulties that high-profile professions such as law and medicine currently confront are due to moving sizable portions of their practices into large organizations. In these frameworks, it is no longer sufficient for a profession to assure its efficacy by the competence of individuals. Communication, collaboration, and interdisciplinary and interprofessional conceptualizations and actions become increasingly necessary. Shared vision, common mental models, team-based learning, personal mastery, and systems thinking have become the hallmarks of adaptive work systems or "learning organizations.[29] Martha Hendricks-Lee applied a systems model to a ten-year case study of school district and teacher education reform and described the tasks of systemic learning as (1) developing internal coherence as a system through establishing means for creating holism and goal-seeking behavior, clarifying relations among subsystems, and establishing openness and dynamism; (2) making connections to larger systems; and (3) developing system competence by creating new roles, new structures, and new processes to deal with change.[30] This perspective has become a part of the developing standards for teaching as professional learning, and it is now characterized as organizationally embedded and entwined with social, cultural, and interactional issues. Just how to adequately address these issues of organizational learning and development in teaching must be a focus of research and developmental work in the near future.

Notes

1. Robert A. Roth, "Standards for Certification, Licensure, and Accreditation," in *Handbook of Research on Teacher Education*, 2d ed., edited by John Sikula, Thomas J. Buttery, and Edith Guyton (New York: Macmillan, 1996).

2. Maralyn M. Scannell and Dale P. Scannell, "Teacher Certification and Standards," in *International Encyclopedia of Education*, 2d ed., edited by Torsten Husen and T. Neville Postlethwaite (London: Pergamon, 1994); Gary Sykes, "Teacher Licensure and Certification," in *Encyclopedia of Educational Research*, 6th ed., edited by Marvin C. Alkin (New York: Macmillan, 1992).

3. National Commission on Teaching and America's Future, *What Matters Most: Teaching for America's Future* (New York: National Commission on Teaching and America's Future, 1996).

4. Andrew D. Abbott, *The system of professions: An essay on the division of expert labor* (Chicago: University of Chicago Press, 1988).

5. For example, A. P. Carr-Sanders and P. A. Wilson, *The Professions* (Oxford: Oxford University Press, 1933); Magali S. Larson, *The Rise of Professionalism* (Berkeley: University of California Press, 1977); Geoffrey Millerson, *The Qualifying Associations* (London: Routledge, 1964).

6. For example, Theodore Caplow, *The Sociology of Work* (Minneapolis: University of Minnesota, 1954); Harold L. Wilensky, "The professionalization of everyone?" *The American Journal of Sociology* 70 (1964): 137-158.

7. Terence J. Johnson, *Professions and Power* (London: Macmillan, 1967); Larson, *The Rise of Professionalism.*

8. Abbott, *The System of Professions*, p. 35.

9. Ibid., 9.

10. Ibid., 59.

11. Ibid., 64.

12. Ibid., 66.

13. Willis D. Hawley, "Systematic Analysis, Public Policy-Making, and Teacher Education," in *Handbook of Research on Teacher Education*, 2d ed., edited by W. Robert Houston (New York: Macmillan, 1990), 136.

14. National Commission on Teaching and America's Future, *What Matters Most*, 29.

15. Sykes, "Teacher Licensure and Certification," 1353.

16. Carnegie Forum on Education and the Economy. Task Force on Teaching as a Profession. *A Nation Prepared: Teachers for the 21st Century* (New York: Carnegie Forum on Education and the Economy, 1986).

17. The Holmes Group, *Tomorrow's Teachers* (E. Lansing, MI: The Holmes Group, 1986).

18. National Board of Professional Teaching Standards, *What Teachers Should Know and Be Able to Do* (Detroit: National Board of Professional Teaching Standards, 1994) as paraphrased in *What Matters Most*, 75.

19. Interstate New Teacher Assessment and Support Consortium, *Model Standards for Beginning Teacher Licensure and Development: A Resource for State Dialogue* (Washington, DC: Council of Chief State School Officers, 1992).

20. Interstate New Teacher Assessment and Support Consortium, *Next Steps: Moving Toward Performance-based Licensing in Teaching* (Washington, DC: Interstate New Teacher Assessment and Support Consortium, 1995).

21. Interstate New Teacher Assessment and Support Consortium, *Next Steps*, 5.

22. *What Matters Most*, 21.

23. Nathaniel L. Gage (Editor), *Handbook of Research on Teaching* (Chicago: Rand McNally, 1963); Robert M. W. Travers (Editor), *Second Handbook of Research on Teaching* (Chicago: Rand McNally, 1973); Merlin C. Wittrock (Editor), *Handbook of Research on Teaching*, 3d ed. (New York: Macmillan, 1986).

24. Maynard C. Reynolds (Editor), *Knowledge Base for the Beginning Teacher* (New York: Pergamon Press, 1989).

25. W. Robert Houston, Martin Haberman, and John Sikula (Editors), *Handbook of Research on Teacher Education* (New York: Macmillan, 1990).

26. Carol Anne Dwyer, *Development of the Knowledge Base for the Praxis III: Classroom Performance Assessments Criteria* (Princeton, NJ: Educational Testing Service, 1994).

27. Hawley, "Systematic Analysis, Public Policy Making, and Teacher Education," 136.

28. For example, Ann L. Brown, "Design Experiments: Theoretical and Methodological Challenges in Creating Complex Interventions in Classroom Settings," *Journal of Learning Sciences* 2 (1992): 141-178; Allan M. Collins, "Toward a Design Science of Education," in *New Directions in Educational Technology*, edited by Eileen Scanlon and Tim O'Shea (Berlin: Springer, 1992).

29. Peter M. Senge, *The Fifth Discipline: The Art and Practice of the Learning Organization* (New York: Doubleday/Currency, 1990).

30. Martha S. Hendricks-Lee, *A Simple Theory for Complex, Systemic Educational Reform* (Unpublished dissertation: University of Cincinnati, 1997).

Section Two
PRACTICES IN TEACHER EDUCATION

CHAPTER V

Learning to Teach for Social Justice

MARILYN COCHRAN-SMITH

For the past twenty years (eighteen in Philadelphia and the last two in Boston), I have worked with new and experienced teachers in urban teacher education programs. Throughout this period, I have taken the position that researchers, practitioners, and policymakers alike ought to acknowledge the inevitable political dimensions of teaching and teacher education. With others, I have argued that among the most important goals of teaching and teacher education are social responsibility, social change, and social justice.

My students—prospective teachers enrolled in preservice teacher education programs—and I have been fellow learners in this enterprise, all of us at times inspired to greater commitments as educators and activists, at times resistant to the very idea of teaching as a political activity, at times willing but deeply skeptical about the efficacy of individuals within a movement aimed at social change of such great scale, and at times profoundly confused about the whole endeavor. As a teacher educator committed to social justice, I have steadfastly insisted that there are no recipes, no best practices, no models of teaching that work across differences in schools, communities, cultures, subject matters, purposes, and home-school relationships. I have eschewed narrowly focused "methods" courses, claiming that teaching for social change is not a matter of method, particularly in the limited sense often referred to in the teacher education literature as something that can be divorced from content, theory, and perspective. Instead I have emphasized that the teacher is an intellectual who generates

Marilyn Cochran-Smith is Professor of Education and Chair of the Department of Teacher Education, Special Education, and Curriculum and Instruction.

knowledge, that teaching is a process of co-constructing knowledge and curriculum with students, and that the most promising ways of learning about teaching across the professional lifespan are based on inquiry within communities rather than training for individuals.[1]

Over two decades, my students have more or less accepted the idea of teaching for social justice. With their school-based and university-based mentors, they have struggled to interrogate their implicit assumptions about teaching and learning. They have developed critical perspectives about the arrangements of schooling and the roles schools and teachers play in maintaining or disrupting the inequitable distribution of material resources and access to opportunities in our society. As a central part of their learning, my students have written thousands of pages of inquiry about teaching and learning—pages that were almost always thoughtful and articulate, often compelling, and sometimes even brilliant in turn of phrase, use of example, or original weaving together of disparate threads of meaning. Programmatic emphasis on the construction of interpretive and political perspectives notwithstanding, the question my students inevitably asked was this one: "But what does teaching for social justice really mean—in a concrete way?" And its many variants: "What does it look like in the classroom?" "What do you actually do with the students?" "You can't really teach for social justice with five-year-olds, can you? Don't they have to be older?" and "When do we get to the part in the program where we actually learn how to do it?"

In this chapter I attempt to offer an answer to this question by analyzing examples of student teachers' work for social justice within urban classrooms. Drawing on the words of student teachers themselves, these examples are intended to help prospective teachers, experienced teachers, and teacher educators clarify what it means to learn to teach for social justice—both what it looks like within particular contexts and how the student teachers working in those contexts understand what they are doing. In the pages that follow, I briefly discuss the notion of teaching and teacher education for social justice as it has been conceptualized in the literature. Then I pose six guiding principles accompanied by examples of student teachers' work, each revealing something of what it means to learn to teach for social justice and at the same time demonstrating how a given principle is played out within a particular school setting. Finally, by zeroing in on one student teacher's experiences, I argue that ongoing inquiry within communities is one of the most promising strategies for preservice teachers learning to teach for social justice.

Reflection

Teaching and Teacher Education for Social Justice

Although not completely synonymous in the literature, the terms "teaching and teacher education for social justice" or ". . . social change" or ". . . social responsibility" bear a strong resemblance to one another. In this chapter, I use these terms more or less interchangeably to signify the following general argument: Teachers cannot fix the problems of society by "teaching better," nor can teachers alone, whether through individual or group efforts, alter the life chances of the children they teach,[2] particularly if the larger issues of structural and institutional racism and inequity are not addressed.[3] However, while teachers cannot *substitute for* social movements aimed at the transformation of society's fundamental inequities,[4] their work has the potential to *contribute to* those movements in essential ways.

Underlying all versions of this argument is the idea that teaching and teacher education are fundamentally political activities and that it is impossible to teach in ways that are not political and not value-laden.[5] This is not to suggest that we politicize teaching but rather, following many others[6] including Bruner in his recent argument about education in general, that we recognize "that it is already politicized and that its political side needs finally to be taken into account more explicitly, not simply as though it were 'public protest'."[7] Part of teaching for social justice, then, is deliberately claiming the role of educator as well as activist based on political consciousness and on ideological commitment to diminishing the inequities of American life.

Teaching for social justice is based on critical understandings of the larger social, historical, and political dynamics of teaching and schooling. These understandings are drawn from several different but interrelated political and intellectual movements, some more than a century old and others emerging more recently: European critical social and economic theory (for example, the work of Karl Marx, Antonio Gramsci, and the Frankfort School of Critical Theory); the American civil rights movement and subsequent efforts to develop multicultural, antiracist, and/or culturally relevant pedagogy (for example, the work of Gloria Ladson-Billings, Beverly Tatum, James Banks, and Christine Sleeter); struggles for liberatory education in Latin America, particularly as conceptualized in the literacy work of Paulo Freire;[8] North American critical educational theory (for example, the work of Michael Apple, Jean Anyon, Henry Giroux, Peter McLaren, and William Pinar); and critical ethnographic, sociocultural, and gender studies of language, learning, and schooling (for example, the work of Ray McDermott,

Shirley Brice Heath, Courtney Cazden, Hugh Mehan, Frederick Erickson, Catherine Weiler, Madeline Grumet).

Pulling together the various threads that weave in and out of these movements, I suggest that teaching for social justice is animated by several basic premises. Schools (and how "knowledge," "curriculum," "assessment," and "access" are constructed and understood in schools) are not neutral grounds but contested sites where power struggles are played out. The structural inequities embedded in the social, organizational, and financial arrangements of schools and schooling help to perpetuate dominance for dominant groups and oppression for oppressed groups. Power, privilege, and economic advantage and/or disadvantage play major roles in the school and home lives of students whether they are part of language, cultural, or gender majority groups or minority groups in our society. The history of racism and sexism in America and the ways "race" and "gender" have been constructed in schools and society are central, whether consciously or not, in the ways students, families, and communities make meaning of school phenomena as well as how they interact with school designates. Curriculum and instruction are neither neutral nor natural. The academic organization of information and inquiry reflects contested views about what knowledge is of most value; part of the curriculum is what is present or absent as well as whose perspectives are central or marginalized, and whose interests are served or undermined. The social and organizational structures of instruction, including classroom and other discourse patterns, grouping strategies, behavioral expectations, and interpretive perspectives are most congruent with white mainstream patterns of language use and socialization and are more conducive to the achievement of boys than girls.

Animated by these understandings, teaching for social justice is teaching that is openly committed to a more just social order.[9] Ladson-Billings provides some of the most coherent and useful work about teaching for social justice in K-12 contexts, particularly teaching African American students with culturally relevant pedagogy.[10] Other influential conceptions are "critical pedagogy,"[11] "anti-racist pedagogy,"[12] "feminist pedagogy"[13] and pedagogy that is "multicultural [as well as] socially reconstructionist."[14] Of course, these terms are not synonymous and, in fact, persuasive arguments have been made about the problems of linking these efforts.[15] Nevertheless, many of their concerns and goals are analogous, especially with respect to issues of educational access, equity, and excellence in a culturally pluralistic society. For the purposes of this chapter, it is most important to note that each of these terms is used to describe a kind of pedagogy that is intended to

help students understand and prepare to take action against the social
and institutional inequities that are embedded in our society.

Learning to Teach for Social Justice:
Six Principles of Practice

In a chapter published elsewhere in which I posited a grounded
theory of teaching and teacher education for social change, I argued
extensively that teachers' work is fundamentally interpretive, political,
and theoretical *as well as* strategic, practical, and local.[16] Building on
this argument in the present chapter, I use the term, "principles of
practice," and not terms like "best practice," "models of teaching," or
"essential teaching skills" to describe and analyze student teachers'
learning to teach for social justice. The language of "principles" is
intended to emphasize that teaching practice is tightly linked with
knowledge and interpretive frameworks, on the one hand, and with
politics and ideological commitments, on the other. Another way to
make this point is to emphasize that teaching for social justice is not so
much a matter of practice but of "praxis," a term used variously by
educational philosophers and social theorists to refer to "the interactive, reciprocal shaping of theory and practice."[17]

Although the examples that follow are intended to provide a way
to describe and understand practice, then, they are in no way intended
to suggest that there are generic methods or specific strategies that are
"typical" of student teachers working for social justice and hence generalizable—full-blown—to other contexts. To the contrary, my analysis does not follow from, and is in no way intended to bolster, formal/
practical or theory/practice distinctions about teachers' knowledge
and/or the activity of teaching.[18] Rather, what I am suggesting is that
across contexts, student teaching for social justice is guided by a set of
common principles that are instantiated differently in practice depending on the particularities of specific contexts.[19]

The six principles are:

- **Principle 1:** Enable significant work for all students within
  learning communities.
- **Principle 2:** Build on what students bring to school with them:
  knowledge and interests, cultural and linguistic
  resources.
- **Principle 3:** Teach skills, bridge gaps.
- **Principle 4:** Work with (not against) individuals, families, and
  communities.

- **Principle 5:** Diversify modes of assessment.
- **Principle 6:** Make activism, power, and inequity explicit parts of the curriculum.

Each of the examples below is based on the work of student teachers in urban public schools in Philadelphia where I directed an inquiry-centered teacher education program for many years.[20] I concentrate on urban examples here not to suggest that learning to teach for social justice should happen only in cities where there are large numbers of children of color and large numbers of children who are poor. To the contrary, I have argued elsewhere,[21] as have others,[22] that we need ways to help all students and teachers interrogate their experiences and construct practices that are effective in an increasingly multiracial and multicultural society. However, because urban teaching poses extremely difficult challenges for student teachers, this context renders student teachers' efforts to teach for social justice particularly vivid. In a number of the examples below, student teachers allude to the tensions of the preservice period during which, by definition, they are called upon to be both teachers and students, and during which they are, essentially, guests in other people's classrooms. The inherent tensions of the preservice period coupled with clashes between the teaching philosophies and styles of student teachers and those of experienced teachers often lead to misunderstandings and sometimes even to anger on the part of student teachers or their mentors. Although these and other aspects of school culture are palpable in some students' writing and are certainly among the most significant realities of the culture of student teaching, I do not elaborate on them in the current chapter.[23]

Principle 1:
Enable Significant Work within Learning Communities

I use the phrase, "enable significant work within learning communities," as shorthand for several interrelated features of social justice pedagogy. Specifically, student teachers who enable significant work assume that all students are makers of meaning and all are capable of dealing with complex ideas. They have high expectations for their students and provide opportunities for them to learn academically challenging knowledge and skills. As well as having high expectations for students, teachers for social justice have high expectations for themselves, working from a sense of their own efficacy as decision makers, knowledge generators, and change agents. Finally, enabling significant work means fostering learning communities, an approach that explicitly eschews homogeneous grouping and/or tracking and instead fosters a shared sense of responsibility for learning within collaborative groupings.

In the excerpts that follow, Gillian Maimon provides a striking example of what it actually "looks like" to enable significant work within a learning community and, just as important, what it looks like for a student teacher to struggle to make sense of that work.[24] Over the course of a year, Maimon was student teacher in a class of 16 first graders in a primarily working class elementary school in urban Philadelphia. Her class was uncharacteristically small because, as Maimon writes, the children "were skimmed from the perceived 'bottom' of the first grade population"—that is they were children who had been designated "at risk" by their teachers, earmarked for remedial instruction, and expected to spend at least two years in first grade.

In the excerpts that follow, Maimon analyzes her experiences with six of these children who worked as a literature study group to explore multiple versions of "The Three Little Pigs." Although she began with high expectations for the children and for herself, she also had doubts about both of these.

We had never attempted anything as open-ended as a literature study in this classroom because the teacher had assumed that the students would be overwhelmed by any activity that lacked strict, teacher-controlled structure. Though I believed that my teacher had woefully underestimated our students' potential throughout the year, I worried that six months in this classroom setting had conditioned the children to focus only on minutiae, like individual letters and words, rather than on ideas. I had to prepare myself for the possibility that the students would not be able to meet the challenge of a project which asked them to think deeply about books [and] to pose and wrestle with questions that had no clear-cut answers.

Maimon's report on the group's work as well as her title for that report, "Little Pigs and Big Ideas," make it clear that her high expectations were not disappointed. Her commentary also touches on the difficulties of trying to construct social justice pedagogy while still a student teacher, who by definition occupies an ambiguous and often low-status role in the classroom.

Maimon's analysis demonstrates that a small learning community of "at risk" first graders were indeed able to engage in quite sophisticated intellectual work, debating points of view, seeking textual evidence, and comparing and contrasting multiple versions. In one session, for example, Maimon had the children draw pictures and offer their opinions about story characters. She wrote:

I found Timmy's sympathy for the wolf so interesting that I wanted to include the entire class in our exchange. After Tim described his picture to everyone, I asked him, 'Do you think the wolf deserved to be eaten at the end of the book?' He answered with a definite no. He explained. 'You know why? Because the pig was mean. He came at different times and he wasn't waiting for the wolf [several times in the story, the wolf makes plans to meet the pig at a scheduled time, but the pig outsmarts him by arriving earlier]. It wasn't fair. That's why he shouldn't get eaten.' In response, Colleen stated strongly that the pig's deception was a necessary evil. 'He had to do that or he would have been eaten.' I quickly polled the room to see who stood where on this wolf issue. Based on the responses I received, I paired up individuals with classmates who held opposing opinions and asked each group member to try to convince the other.

In the days that followed, Maimon and her students discussed, wrote, drew, and read. In addition to versions of the classic story that varied in language and illustrations, they read or listened to several parodies of the tale that played with point of view, narrator reliability, and novel characters.

In commenting on the literature study project as a whole, Maimon reflected on her children's abilities as learners, the power of shared literary experience to turn a small group into a learning community, the problematic status of a teacher who is also a student, and the damaging effects of a learning culture based on low expectations. In concluding, she wrote:

As for my question about the children's ability to think independently, I have no doubt that my students are as insightful and courageous in their convictions as their counterparts at [any other school] . . . I rejoiced to see them articulate a variety of viewpoints, debate with each other, back up their ideas with examples from texts, change their minds when persuaded by classmates, refuse to accept information presented in a book at face value. . . .

In spite of my doubts about the good that can come out of this project while the students remain confined to our classroom, I am ecstatic about (and quite moved by) this experience we shared . . . I have been told so many times, 'You can't do this because they can't do this,' and 'You don't understand the way you have to teach *these* children.' . . . In response to these words of suppression, I hold up the powerful, angry, excited, exciting, deep, enlightening, funny, brave, complex, strong responses that these 'At Risk' students produced over the course of our literature study. Our exploration has been their and my vindication.

In one way, it may seem that what Maimon did in her student teaching classroom is just common sense—after all, how can students learn at high levels if their teachers do not support them and expect them to do so? In actuality, however, teachers frequently demonstrate just the opposite to their students—"dumbing-down" the curriculum,[25] especially for "the low group" and "at risk students." Rather than a pedagogy of social justice, then, what often occurs in urban schools is what Haberman has described as a "pedagogy of poverty"[26] emphasizing lower order skills, memorization, worksheets, and few opportunities to read connected texts while, at the same time, omitting higher order concepts, reading challenging texts, and exploring alternative points of view, the latter of which are commonplace in higher tracks and middle class schools.[27]

First and foremost, then, pedagogy for social justice means providing opportunities for all students to engage in significant intellectual work. To do so, as the above example suggests, a student teacher strives to:

- Work for a sense of efficacy.
- Hold high academic expectations for all students.
- Provide opportunities for learning academically challenging knowledge.
- Foster communities of learners.

Principle 2:
Build on What Students Bring to School with Them—
Knowledge and Interests, Cultural and Linguistic Resources

Building on what students bring to school means that student teachers acknowledge, value, and work from the cultural and linguistic resources as well as the interests and knowledge of their students. Especially in urban schools, classrooms increasingly contain widely diverse student populations or large numbers of students whose cultural backgrounds are similar to each other's but different from the teacher's. In each case, it is important to develop structures for social participation with narrative and questioning styles that are culturally and linguistically congruent with those of the students. In addition, it is important to construct curriculum that is multicultural and inclusive so that students can connect meanings in their own lives to innovative as well as more traditional content. Working for social justice explicitly rejects transmission models of teaching and instead operates from the twin premises that knowledge is fluid and socially constructed and that curriculum is co-constructed by teachers and students through their interactions with one another and with a variety of texts, materials, and experiences.

Marisol Sosa Booth taught for a year in a fourth grade urban classroom in a school that was almost completely Puerto Rican in population.[28] Her writing gives a sense of some of the issues faced by a student teacher attempting to construct curriculum connected to the children's cultural and linguistic backgrounds. Her writing also makes it clear that simply because the teacher and students share certain aspects of culture and language, they do no automatically connect with one another or with inclusive curricular materials that reflect varied perspectives, as sometimes seems assumed in the literature.

One of the first lessons I taught as a student teacher was about Christopher Columbus. This particular issue was especially sensitive because of the common Puerto Rican background of my students and me. I wrote in my journal, 'I want to present a traditional and then a contemporary revisionist story about Columbus because I want the children to begin understanding that sometimes stories change because of new facts and information.'

Encounter by Jane Yolen is a story documenting the Taino Indians' perspective on Columbus' arrival. I pointed out to my students that the Taino, Arawak, and Carib Indians are part of our heritage, that they were our ancestors. A few of them were disgusted by the thought. I was taken aback. My students' reaction of disgust was triggered by the first sight of illustrations depicting partially nude Taino Indians. There were remarks like, 'They're not *my* ancestors,' and 'They look funny.' I heard these reactions with a certain amount of irony and surprise. My children had internalized Eurocentric perceptions. They were disgusted by the faces of their own people.

Booth went on to describe how she talked about two different versions of the voyages of Christopher Columbus with her children, raising questions about history and "truth," perspectives and power. With the children she explored some of the information in primary documents including Columbus' own journal describing his voyages. Eventually, as Booth's words suggest, her children came to a different perspective about their ancestors and the Columbus story, and Booth understood somewhat better some of the complexities involved in constructing with children a curriculum that is inclusive, not only of stories from various cultures, but of varying perspectives and world views.

After I read [aloud] both the traditional telling and Yolen's revisionist version, some of the students called the traditional story 'phony' or said that it was 'telling lies.' To my surprise, they felt that Jane Yolen's *Encounter* was closer to the reality of what 'truly' transpired.

bell hooks said, 'Our struggle has not been to emerge from silence into speech but to change the nature . . . of our speech, to make a speech that compels listeners, one that is heard.' My goal was to place my students at the center of a curriculum that is inclusive of a Latino perspective and embraces their legacy as one that should be heard. This is by no means a simple task, but it's a challenge I'm willing to meet.

Reinventing the curriculum *vis-a-vis* more inclusive and multicultural texts and materials is only part of what goes on when teachers try to build on their students' resources and interests. What also seems to happen is that some of the more taboo topics of school life are explored and a different set of rules emerges about what one can and cannot discuss in school.[29] For young children, this may mean talking about hair texture and other physical features of racial groups. Along these lines, issues of race, racism and inequalities often become part of the curriculum (as discussed in the next section of this paper).

As the examples in this section suggest, then, part of teaching for social justice is building on what students bring to school with them. In order to do so, student teachers make efforts to:

- Co-construct knowledge with students by building on their interests and questions.
- Construct curriculum so that it includes multicultural and inclusive content and perspectives in addition to traditional content.
- Develop culturally and linguistically congruent interactional and questioning patterns.

Principle 3:
Teach Skills, Bridge Gaps

Learning to teach for social justice with its emphasis on co-construction of knowledge and on giving all children opportunities to deal with "big ideas" is sometimes taken to imply that there is no attention given to teaching and learning basic skills. To the contrary, an indispensable part of learning how to teach for social justice is learning how and where to help students connect what they know to what they do not know and how to use prior skills to learn new ones. Obviously this requires that teachers start wherever students are and, as is suggested in the discussion of Principle 2, build on prior experiences and knowledge to scaffold new learning. Some children, particularly those who live in poor urban areas, do not come to school with tacit knowledge of mainstream language patterns, as well as patterns of social participation, which are the invisible bases of classroom interaction. Many do not come with *a priori* knowledge of basic number and literacy concepts, which are the implicit starting point of much instruction in the primary grades. For these children, student teachers have to learn how to teach skills but also bridge gaps between what is often assumed children know and what they actually do know. To do so, first and foremost, student teachers have to learn to pay attention to children, to what they already know and do not know, and to the sense they are making of whatever it is student teachers think they are teaching.

Ronit Eliav provides an intriguing example of a student teacher's evolution in learning this aspect of teaching for social justice.[30] In an unusually candid essay about her own learning over the course of the preservice period, Eliav looked back on the year, pointing out that when it began, she had assumed that her role was to transmit knowledge and skills to children. She began her essay with a quotation from Vivian Paley about the journey involved in becoming a teacher:

In September, I thought I understood what Vivian Paley expressed [about gradually shifting attention away from oneself and toward children as learners] . . . Today, I realize that I did not. I did not truly comprehend what focusing on children meant and how that would affect me. Focusing on children, to my understanding, merely meant teaching them. I did not realize that focusing on children would open a window through which I could see things as the child does, that it actually meant learning from them.

This past year has been an amazing one. I have grown and developed both as an individual and as an educator. I have learned things about myself, my world, my education, and most importantly, my students. Growing up, I thought of teachers as the carriers of knowledge. I defined teaching as the transferring of knowledge. I viewed a good student as someone who studied that knowledge and was able to retrieve it upon demand. . . . As the year progressed, the sources from which I sought answers evolved. . . . As I started to think more about what it means to look at children, I realized that they were my greatest teachers. I began to see that when I understood how they learned and thought about a concept, I was better able to teach them that concept. This realization marked the turning point in my education and development as a student teacher.

Eliav provides access into the usually implicit and internal process of a student teacher's evolving sense of what it means to teach skills within the larger framework of teaching for social justice. There were specific moments in her experiences as a student teacher that were mileposts in the evolution of her ideas about connecting with children in order to teach skills effectively.

In one essay, Eliav reflected on her first "real" lesson—a mini-lesson in mathematics where the children contributed number sentences and answered questions about the number sentences Eliav posed. In the next part of the lesson, she switched to a more open discussion in which the children were to apply their knowledge of number sentences and do the practice work she provided. She hoped for greater participation and involvement in this part of the lesson.

I did not think to ask how the children were perceiving what I thought I was teaching them. Many children were coming up with the correct answers to my examples, which I saw as an indication that they were understanding the lesson. . . . I entered this experience thinking about myself, my teaching, and my lesson plan. At no point in this process did I consider the children's prior knowledge or needs until a little boy immediately raised his hand.

I was so excited that right away a student was participating and could answer my question. When I called on him with the expectation that he would have a response, he said, 'Miss Eliav, what does a number sentence mean?' It had never occurred to me that the children might not know what a number sentence was. I asked the class if anyone could define a number sentence and to my surprise, no hands went up. I began to think that this lesson was not appropriate for this class, this being the second time that they were not able to do what the lesson had assumed they could. At this point, I realized that children needed to be consulted and their understandings and work be reviewed before teaching a lesson. In choosing this lesson, however, I thought it was grade level appropriate. However, had I looked to the children prior to planning it, I would have seen that their needs and background knowledge had not prepared them for the lesson that I had planned. I did not meet my students where they were. Why did I assume that they were at a level at which they were not? Why did I not think to look at their prior knowledge and understanding before choosing this lesson?

As I have said before, in a certain way, it seems only common sense that student teachers must learn how to begin teaching where the children are. This is certainly one of the oldest and most commonly passed-along aphorisms in teacher education. In another sense, however, there is evidence that learning how to teach skills at the preservice level has been reduced to "the lesson plans" that student teachers, almost universally, are required to complete. In the traditional lesson plan assignments of preservice education, the skills student teachers are supposed to teach are pre-established in lists of curriculum standards and/or in teachers' manuals and often reduced to what amounts to a script for teaching and learning.[31] Variations in children's prior knowledge and skills are not accounted for in these. This failure to account for variation is reinforced in the curriculum and teaching frameworks used in many urban and other large school systems.

A major part of learning to teach for social justice, then, means taking into account students' understandings and prior learnings at the same time that one introduces and reinforces new skills. To do so, as the above example suggests, the student teacher strives to:

- Start where children are in terms of prior knowledge and skills.
- Teach skills by linking prior knowledge to new information.

- Pay attention to what sense students are making of what is being taught.

Principle 4:
Work With (Not Against) Individuals, Families, and Communities

I use the phrase, "working with (not against) individuals, families, and communities" to emphasize that teaching for social justice means drawing on family histories, traditions, and stories as well as demonstrating respect for all students' family and cultural values. It also means consciously avoiding functioning as a wedge between students and their families by conveying negative messages subtly and unintentionally or giving students the idea that to succeed is to escape from, ignore, or rise above their own communities or become "exceptions" to their race. Particularly important here is that the teacher demonstrate that she or he is connected to, rather than disengaged from, or (worse) afraid of, her or his students as individuals and as members of groups and larger communities.

Student teachers generally have few opportunities to work directly with parents or to become genuinely engaged in the communities in which they work. The relatively short duration of student teachers' time in schools coupled with their inescapable status as "guests" in other people's classrooms make it unlikely that student teachers can link with families and groups in the ways experienced teachers are sometimes able to do—living in the communities in which they work, learning the cultural references and language patterns of parents, visiting homes and taking children to religious or social events, or joining neighborhood efforts to challenge local regulations or fight crime.[32]

What student teachers can do, however, is notice and critique the implicit messages conveyed about students and their families, consciously rethinking their own identities and assumptions as well as vigilantly avoiding the imposition of their judgments on others. In the excerpts that follow, Susan Moore provides a glimpse of a student teacher attempting to work with (not against) families and communities.[33] Moore worked in a school located in a Puerto Rican neighborhood in Philadelphia. Despite "Puerto Rican History Month" and wonderful jointly sponsored parent-teacher celebrations, however, Moore realized that there were also powerful negative messages about Puerto Rican culture being sent to students.

Most egregious for me was the schoolwide celebration of Columbus Day in October. My classroom had been on a field trip during Puerto Rican History

Month in which we had discussed the fact that the Puerto Rican culture is a mix of Spanish, African, and Taino Indian cultures due to Columbus' importation of African slaves to obtain gold for him because the Tainos were dying off with his introduction of European diseases to the island; this led to the erroneous conclusion that a school with a majority of Puerto Rican students would not be apt to celebrate Columbus' conquest of the Americas . . . Columbus Day should never pass uncritically in a school populated by the descendants of those that this 'hero' oppressed.

As the year progressed, Moore also recognized subtle contradictions about the children's cultural heritage and about their very identities as people of color. She noticed, for example, that students' spontaneous comments about race or culture were diverted or silenced in the classroom. She also noticed that children were not encouraged to talk about their racial/cultural backgrounds and that when talking among themselves teachers proudly claimed to see "only children, not color" in the school. Books read aloud or displayed on classroom shelves had few African American characters and no Latino characters. She wrote:

I posit that it is crucial to explore issues of race and culture with our students at [this school] and to embed these issues in the curriculum. It is important that we white teachers recognize that aspect of our students' identity and resist denying it due to guilt over our own place in the hegemony. We simply must acknowledge our students' racial minority position in the United States if we are to begin to prepare them to negotiate a system which will be cruel to them. Furthermore, we must work to build on our students' cultural strengths in the work that we do with them in the classroom in order to foster pride in their culture and to encourage maintaining their cultural competence even as they become adept in the ways of the mainstream.

What is particularly interesting about Moore's experiences as a student teacher is that she did not simply spout liberal (or radical) ideology about the teacher's role in opening a discourse about racism and oppression. She also struggled with what it really meant to avoid being a wedge between children and their communities for even, as she termed it, "such a seemingly innocuous event" as Valentine's Day and such a minor issue as whether young children should celebrate this holiday in school. Moore's cooperating teacher had remarked that valentines were particularly important in Latino culture and that mothers went to great lengths to send gifts for teachers and valentines for children to trade with their classmates. Moore reflected in her journal:

This raises an important issue for me. Valentine's Day is one of those holidays in which I have lost complete interest as an adult. In my mind, it is just one big money-making venture . . . and I guess you could say that I am now a conscientious objector. . . . Yet if I teach in a place where the community loves to celebrate Valentine's Day, how will I make room for both their enthusiasm and my cynicism? My first strike at an answer to this question is that I will not ban all manifestations of the holiday from my room—I mean, I made sure to hand craft individual valentines for each of the kids this year—yet I will also not let the holiday pass uncritically. I will raise the issue with the kids of how much money is spent each year on candy, cards, etc. . . . I will raise the question of what else that money could be spent on. . . . I will try to get them to consider who profits from Valentine's Day expenditures. . . .

In the excerpts above, Moore reveals some of what it looks like when a student teacher tries to make sense of the tension between what she perceives as competing claims to social justice. She struggles to respect community traditions and family desires, on the one hand, and to teach her students to critique marketing campaigns that urge unnecessary and (for certain families and communities) unaffordable expenditures, on the other.

Part of learning to teach for social justice, then, means understanding the complexities of working with (not against) individuals, families, and communities. To do so, as the above excerpts suggest, the student teacher strives to:

- Respect the cultures and cultural traditions of families.
- Ensure that the messages about race and culture conveyed more subtly are consistent with those conveyed directly.
- Frame issues in terms of tensions between community values and social critique.
- Support (and join in) activities that strengthen rather than suggest escape from neighborhoods, communities, or cultural/racial groups.

Principle 5:
Diversify Modes of Assessment

It is now well documented that most standardized testing practices perpetuate inequities in the educational opportunities available to various groups, particularly that they limit opportunities for poor children and children of color. Beckum and others urge educators to "diversify assessment" as a partial response to this situation by using a wide variety of evaluation strategies for formative as well as cumulative assessments (e.g., portfolios, performances) and by not relying on standardized tests as the sole or primary indicator of students' abilities and achievement in schools.[34] Part of the idea here is that over time assessment and instruction can blend into one another, and ongoing assessments can be designed in ways that support students' learning rather than truncating it.

In many school contexts, however, student teachers have few opportunities to "diversify" assessment if the experienced teachers and administrators with whom they work are not already doing so. In fact, cumulative assessments of children's achievement are often out of student teachers' control completely, and although they may contribute to some more formative assessments of their students, student teachers seldom have the opportunity to do away with assessment systems or introduce new ones. Instead, student teachers who are struggling to teach for social justice must focus on understanding the assessment systems that are in place in their schools, and on interrogating the connections and discontinuities between assessment and educational opportunity, access, and standards.

Jamie Kim-Ross's experience as a student teacher is instructive along these lines, although clearly an interesting inversion of the usual situation.[35] Kim-Ross worked in a large and quite diverse public elementary school with children from a variety of cultural groups and many children for whom English was a second language. Unlike most of their colleagues, her two cooperating teachers, who worked as a team, had rejected the use of test scores and other numerical grading systems in their classrooms. Kim-Ross was unfamiliar with assessments that were not numerically based although she quickly saw their benefit for the children with whom she was working. Partly because she herself had many painful memories of her high school experiences as an ESL student who had come to the United States from Korea, however, Kim-Ross was also concerned about the implications of diversified assessments for non-native speakers.

When I started student teaching, I volunteered to build a data base to help my cooperating teachers keep track of their students' test scores. My cooperating teachers responded that they would have nothing to put into the data base because they did not make use of test scores or grades. Instead, the children are evaluated based on the progress they make over their three years in the program; progress is monitored by keeping a portfolio of each child's work. Likewise, the children are issued report cards that indicate their individual progress as opposed to measuring them against a common numerical standard. I initially found this method bizarre. How could a child's ability be measured objectively under such a system? How could the performance of different children be compared? Could not teachers' preferences be prejudicial to the fair evaluation of some children?

It was not long, however, when I realized that the system worked precisely because it was not designed to measure how much the children had learned versus a common standard; rather it was designed to monitor the progress of each child in a context that made sense given the particular facts and circumstances that related to that child. This aspect of the system was especially useful given the large numbers of ESL students for whom most standardized tests would be grossly inappropriate. Many of these students understood the underlying concepts being taught quite well but lacked the language skills to explain their understanding on paper. In assessing such students' knowledge, my cooperating teachers recognize that the language barrier should not prevent students from having their hard work praised.

This [individualized] assessment framework made my comments on the children's writing exercises more productive . . . The assessment system also allowed me to adapt my approach to the needs of each child . . . I quickly saw how the individualized nature of the assessment system helped build self-confidence. . . . However, I am still not sure . . . Can we really be sure students are progressing? If so, what about the ESL students? Can we really be sure that these children are keeping pace with their peers in traditional classrooms? Is there no chance that individual progress is being overemphasized to the detriment of high academic standards? How do we know the children are being challenged? How will the children cope when they are thrust back into a traditional classroom?

Kim-Ross's experiences touch on some of the issues involved in teaching for social justice by diversifying assessment. Many student teachers, however, have experiences that are quite different from hers, obligated to utilize assessments that they judge to be biased or struggling to introduce portfolios or other diversified means of assessment into even the smallest parts of curriculum and instruction. Although it is sometimes not possible, then, given the narrow realm of influence that most student teachers have, those who are working for social justice strive to:

- Critique standardized assessments.
- Use a range of alternative assessments that focus on students' abilities and achievements.
- Connect assessment and instruction.

Principle 6:
Make Activism, Power, and Inequity Explicit Parts of the Curriculum

Student teachers whose work is animated by a sense of social justice encourage their students to think critically about the information to which they are exposed and make explicit in the curriculum issues that are often kept underground. Part of what this means is helping students name and deal with individual instances of prejudice as well as structural and institutional inequities by making these issues "discussible" in school. This also means actively working against the grain[36] of many of the practices and assumptions that are taken for granted. Finally, making inequity explicit means modeling activism and helping students explore how they themselves can question the status quo.

In the excerpts that follow, Mark Paikoff reveals more fully what it looks like when a student teacher attempts to make power and inequity an explicit part of the curriculum, and, perhaps even more important, how that student teacher poses questions about the work and struggles to understand the complexities involved.[37] Paikoff was a student teacher over the course of one year at a large urban elementary school with an African American population. Prompted by his cooperating teacher to choose a novel with an African American theme for Black History Month, Paikoff chose Mildred Taylor's *The Friendship* for use with a reading group of five children in grade 3.

Black History Month is much more than George Washington Carver, Jesse Jackson, and Jackie Robinson. I wanted to insure the students knew—or at least began a process leading them to knowledge—of the biases that have been created against them. In this way, they will best be able to tear down the walls constructed to keep them from climbing society's ladder.

I had many questions. . . . How will the students react to a story that does not have a 'happy ending'? How will they deal with blatant racism present in the story? What will they say or do after reading the word 'nigger' in a story? . . . How will I help the students connect this story to other pieces of literature they have read? How can I most effectively guide them to a grand conversation about a topic I feel anxious about? . . . What will my reaction be to theirs? How do I as a white person teach five African Americans about racism?

As his experiences with the group reveal, this last question proved to be especially important. In vivid detail that stays close to the children's own words and to their unfolding understandings of the story, Paikoff described the group's responses after they had read the first section of the book.

I closed the lesson with a return to the journals, and the students wrote for a while. Ryanne was the first to share. 'I don't like the story because I am Black, and anyone Black who reads this story, *The Friendship*, will not like it either. It is a really sad story because Black people should be treated right and the Black people in the story aren't treated right.' She told me she did not want to read the story anymore.

Ultimately Ryanne decided to stay in the group, partly in response to Paikoff's explanation of how important it was to know about "what really happened." Throughout their reading of the novel, however, student teacher and students wrestled with the visceral emotional response the story evoked. Paikoff wrote:

I saw the word 'Nigger' approaching on the next page and warned the students, 'Something that will probably bother you is coming up on the next page.' . . . I posed one simple question, 'How does that word make you feel?' Ryanne said, 'It doesn't make me feel good because they called it to a Black person only because he's Black.' Regina said, 'I feel if the White people want respect, they got to earn respect.' Nicole said although the word bothered her a lot, she understood the usage: 'It adds to the story because we can tell it was the deep South and feel like we're there.'

[But] the students were visibly upset—eyes drooped and they looked angry. Tarell said, 'Why we reading this anyway?' Nicole, who only moments earlier had said she understood the word usage in the story said, 'What does this have to do with friendship? Why is the name *The Friendship?*'

Public discussions of inequities and injustices are difficult. Some student teachers worry that such discussions are depressing, making young children feel worse than they already do, while others are concerned that they may be inflammatory and divisive for older students. Paikoff's report reveals the anxiety involved in prompting children to think critically about topics that are difficult even for adults to discuss openly, and it also suggests that the race of the teacher *vis-a-vis* that of the students plays a complicated part in the ways each responds.

As these examples suggest, however, part of learning to teach for social justice is struggling to make visible and explicit—at whatever level is developmentally appropriate for students—the inequities of society and the institutional structures in which they are embedded. To do so, student teachers attempt to:

- Encourage critical thinking and activism about information, texts, and events.
- Openly discuss race and racism, equity and inequity, oppression and advantage.
- Work against the social, organizational, and structural arrangements of schooling and society that perpetuate inequity.

One Student Teacher's Experience:
Inquiring into Social Justice

The six examples above make it clear that learning to teach for social justice is as much a matter of learning how to make sense of one's experiences over time as it is learning how to act in particular ways in the classroom. It is the "making sense" aspect of learning to teach for social justice that the final section of this chapter emphasizes. By "making sense," I mean the kinds of questions student teachers ask about their work, the problems and dilemmas they pose, the interpretive frameworks they construct, the assumptions they are prompted to rethink, as well as the ways they connect emerging ideas to the theories, research, and experiences of other teachers and researchers. Each of these is part of what we have called an "inquiry stance" on teaching and learning to teach.[38] Inquiry is a central part of both the context within which learning to teach for social justice occurs and the vehicle through which much of that learning is worked through and expressed.

An inquiry stance is reflected, either implicitly or explicitly, in all of the examples I have already offered. Inquiry allowed Gill Maimon to raise questions about whether her "at risk" first graders could reason independently and debate the multiple perspectives of a story; it also fueled her belief that they had the right to try. Inquiry supported Marisol Sosa Booth's tentative explanations about her students' initial disgust at pictures of their own Taino ancestors as well as her determination to give them voice and place in the curriculum. Ronit Eliav's inquiry about her first "real" lesson prompted her to rethink the assumptions she had been making about her students' prior knowledge and also allowed her to shift her focus away from herself as teacher and toward the meaning the students were making of what was going on in the classroom. Susan Moore's inquiries allowed her to interrogate the overt as well as hidden messages in the curriculum and also to struggle with what she saw as conflicting claims to justice—respecting families' values, on the one hand, but also fostering critical perspectives about mass market practices, on the other. Likewise, through inquiry, Jamie Kim-Ross posed a problem with multiple and competing perspectives—she considered both the importance of assessing ESL students' learning in ways that tapped into their cognitive understandings rather than simply their (lack of) language skills and, at the same time, the need of parents and educators to have comparative assessments of progress. And finally, an inquiry stance legitimated Mark Paikoff's uncertainty about how young African American children would respond to a novel that focused on racism just as it legitimated his commitment to make that topic part of the curriculum.

To elaborate on the role of inquiry in learning to teach for social justice, I draw in this final section on the work of Mary Kate Cipriani, who was a student teacher for a year in a public elementary school in a working class neighborhood in Philadelphia. In the portfolio that represented Cipriani's work for the year, there are many examples that illustrate the six principles of teaching for social justice that I have outlined above.[39] I have selected the excerpts that follow, however, to focus more on the underlying intellectual stance that Cipriani developed as she struggled to work for social change.

Cipriani's words, excerpted here from the critical essay that introduced her portfolio, focus on this inquiry perspective. In this essay she sets out to describe not only what she learned about teaching over the course of a year but also how she learned it—that is, the internal processes that prompted her to think and rethink her experiences as well as the social and organizational structures that supported her learning.

> I am a twenty-seven-year-old white female. I am a student. I am a teacher. I am a teacher researcher. I am comfortable with myself and happy with my choice to return to school to become a teacher. I am coming to the end of a positive, fulfilling, difficult, rewarding, confusing and satisfying time of my life. I am, however, continuing upon an ongoing journey to teach, research, learn and be an agent for change. I am someone who in this past year has worked harder than I have ever worked in my entire life. I am certain that I will always work this hard as I continue on my journey. I am someone who has learned a lot but still has a lot to learn. . . .
>
> This essay evolved into a backwards autobiography of my experience as a graduate student, as a student teacher, and as a teacher researcher. It is the unpeeling of all the layers I have created and grown. I do not know how many layers I will shed. I do not know what is at the core. I do know that as you read this, we will learn about me together. This is not a 'how to' book on how to become a teacher in twelve months. This is not a paper that has a conclusion or an answer. It does not have neat endings, results or confirmations. This is a presentation of a process. It is an essay that comes with many tentative conclusions and questions. . . .

With these words, Cipriani makes it clear that she sees social change as part of the job of the teacher (and student teacher). But as importantly, she makes it clear that she sees learning to teach as an ongoing process—filled with questions—that will continue over the course of her lifetime as a teacher rather than one that will reach closure when she graduates from her preservice program.

Cipriani's use of the journey metaphor, which was a central image in many discussions of the program, emphasizes the continuous and distinctly non-linear character of the process of learning to teach. Cipriani describes part of the process as the "unpeeling of layers to make meaning." Her analyses suggest that the journey was a process of linking previous and present school experiences to the ideas and concepts of others, of responding to situations by rethinking expectations and assumptions, and of being uncomfortable sometimes with what she saw when she looked beneath the surface. It is worth noting also that Cipriani explicitly designates herself as learner as well as teacher as she suggests that a fluid relationship exists when students and teachers are partners in the endeavor called education.

> On Parents Night in September . . . I stood in an unfamiliar place, before a classroom of unknown parents, allied with a woman I knew nothing about and attempted to explain my philosophy, one that I hadn't even developed yet. In my speech, I emphasized that their children and I were going to learn from each other. This simple statement, made so early in my journey, was just about the most prophetic thing I could have said. I was in essence accepting the duality of our shared roles—as learners and as teachers. I was acknowledging that both my students and I would take turns as the givers and receivers of knowledge. In September I recognized that we would construct meaning together, and this paper is an attempt to understand and reflect on all the layers of meaning I have made about myself as a teacher researcher through the lived and learned experiences of myself and my students.

Part of being a learner (rather than an expert, a transmitter, or some sort of repository of knowledge) is acknowledging that one does not know everything and that, indeed, knowledge is not a "thing" that is accumulated like garbage or money in the bank.[40] As Cipriani's essay continues, she articulates her philosophy about learning how to teach, emphasizing that "not knowing" comes with the territory.

> Teachers are expected to know. We are expected to transmit what we know to the next generation. But teacher researchers believe that it is O.K. not to know . . . NOT TO KNOW? Could that be? Yes, because there is a difference between knowing and knowing how. We learn how to teach not by looking for answers, but by continuously searching for meaning in our classrooms. Our search for meaning is ongoing. We begin with uncertainty. Through observation and reflection we attempt to make meaning of this uncertainty. Based on our interpretations, we implement new strategies in our classrooms. In the end we are left with a new uncertainty which causes us to begin this process all over again . . . We have learned to look to our students to guide us. By understanding who they are and what they bring to our classrooms, we allow the children to teach us how to teach them.

Learning to teach for social justice is supported by inquiry that acknowledges ongoing uncertainties, confusions, misgivings, and concerns. An inquiry stance contradicts the certainty that many student teachers expect to find during their preservice programs. For some student teachers, this is unsettling, to say the least; others are more comfortable with the ambiguity.

Finally, Cipriani also writes specifically about the importance of being part of a learning or inquiry community as the context within which she learns to teach for social justice—various groupings of school children, preservice teachers, experienced teachers, and university-based supervisors and instructors, all of whom function as learners and researchers across the professional lifespan.[41] In a certain sense, this community is both the invisible "audience" for many of the reflections student teachers write and, at the same time, it is the context within which they work. Cipriani emphasized the importance of community by first discussing the isolation of teaching and the problem that it creates for so many teachers. Then she focused her discussion on the role of the many communities that interlocked to form the fabric of her experiences learning to teach.

> My salvation became the teacher communities I [was part of] . . . The term "communities" is used broadly because it encompasses many kinds of support groups and moments. It includes the mornings when [the other student teachers who taught with me at the school] would come by my classroom to ask me questions that ranged from, "Have you ever used pattern blocks?" to "How are things going in your life?" . . . It includes the ethnography paper group and Sunday nights we spent beside [our professor's] fireplace wrenching and writhing over our journals and papers, looking for themes. It includes [my cooperating teacher] and me chatting about our students' academic behavior and who likes who this week. It includes dinners at [my supervisor's] house, classes at Penn and special events like the Ethnography Forum and the AERA annual meeting . . . I am a teacher because we are a teacher community and because we are a teacher community, I am a teacher.

Reading between the lines of Cipriani's compelling essay and taking into account the social and organizational structures of her program provide more information about how inquiry supported her efforts to grow and develop as a teacher committed to social justice. Student teachers in her program read a wide variety of challenging literature from many perspectives—both university-based and school-based—about topics related to diversity, literacy and learning, culture and language, race and racism, privilege and oppression, and teacher inquiry itself. They developed and used structured formats for looking closely at individual children, reflecting on classroom practice and on the language of educational policy and practice, and confronting difficult personal and professional assumptions related to difference, culture, and the purposes of schooling. They wrote frequently about their experiences—their own histories, the teaching issues that were difficult, responses to the writings of other teacher researchers as well as university-based writers and scholars. Their work was deliberately structured so that multiple viewpoints and experiences were represented. They listened to presentations by many university-based and school-based teachers and researchers. Their schedule included long periods of time for groups to work together to hash out issues, talk and think through disagreements, and write about their experiences. They shared the data of their classrooms with one another, offering early thoughts on inquiry projects and shaping and reshaping both questions and interpretations.

Conclusion

Perhaps more than anything else, the excerpts used throughout this chapter emphasize that teaching for social justice is difficult and uncertain work. It is work that is profoundly practical in that it is located in the dailiness of classroom decisions and actions—in teachers' interactions with their students and families, in their choices of materials and texts, in their utilization of formal and informal assessments, and so on. At the same time, however, it is work that is deeply intellectual in that it involves a continuous and recursive process of constructing understandings, interpretations, and questions. To describe learning to teach for social justice, then, we must describe not simply "what it looks like"—the question my own student teachers so often asked, but also "how teachers make sense of it"—how they struggle to think about and understand what they are doing. In this sense, learning to teach for social justice is as much a matter of learning to construct particular practices as it is learning to understand, or theorize, those practices.

The principles of learning to teach for social justice, then, must be embedded inside a framework for helping student teachers learn to explore and reconsider their own assumptions and alliances, understand the values and practices of families and cultures that are different from their own, examine their ideological commitments about the purposes and goals of education, and construct pedagogy and curriculum that take all of these into account in ways that are locally appropriate, culturally sensitive, and globally aware. Figure 1, which synthesizes the six principles and their accompanying sub-principles as well as the ways inquiry functions in the learning process, is intended to emphasize both

FIGURE 1

LEARNING TO TEACH FOR SOCIAL JUSTICE THROUGH INQUIRY
- Teacher is learner, researcher, and agent for change
- Inquiry communities are the contexts for teachers' learning
- Learning to teach is an ongoing process across the professional lifespan

---

Principle 1
Enable significant work for all students within learning communities
- Work for a sense of efficacy
- Hold high academic expectations for all students
- Provide opportunities for learning academically challenging knowledge
- Foster communities of learners

Principle 2
Build on what students bring to school with them: knowledge and interests, cultural and linguistic resources
- Co-construct knowledge with students by building on their interests and questions
- Construct curriculum so that it includes multicultural and inclusive content and perspectives in addition to traditional content
- Develop culturally and linguistically congruent interactional and questioning patterns

Principle 3
Teach skills, bridge gaps
- Start where children are in terms of prior knowledge and skills
- Teach skills by linking prior knowledge to new information
- Pay attention to what sense students are making of what is being taught

Principle 4
Work with, not against individuals, families, and communities
- Respect the cultures and cultural traditions of families
- Ensure that the messages about race and culture conveyed more subtly are consistent with those conveyed directly
- Frame issues in terms of tensions between community values and social critique
- Support and join in activities that strengthen rather than suggest escape from neighborhoods, communities, or cultural/racial groups

Principle 5
Diversify modes of assessment
- Critique standardized assessments
- Use a range of alternative assessments that focus on students' abilities and achievements

Principle 6
Make activism, power, and inequity explicit parts of the curriculum
- Encourage critical thinking and activism about information, texts, and events
- Openly discuss race and racism, equity and inequity, oppression and advantage
- Work against the social, organizational, and structural arrangements of schooling and society that perpetuate inequity

---

student teachers' construction of practices for social justice and their construction of knowledge and understandings about those practices.

As a final note to this chapter, I want to extend the discussion from one that focuses particularly on learning to teach for social justice during the preservice period to one that centers more broadly on teaching

140   LEARNING TO TEACH FOR SOCIAL JUSTICE

for social justice across the professional lifespan. In this case, the leap
from preservice to inservice education comes easily. This is so because
the six principles I have proposed and elaborated in this chapter are
grounded in the first place in two distinct sources that document the
processes of teaching for social justice across the lifespan and not simply
at the early stages of the profession. As I mentioned at the outset of this
chapter, the six principles were informed by both the academic literature and the writing of new and experienced practitioners. Hence,
although the processes of understanding and the kinds of questions
asked by new and experienced teachers for social justice may well not be
the same, the principles of practice outlined in this chapter may be useful for consideration by both new and experienced teachers and teacher
educators.

The research for this chapter was supported by a major grant from the Spencer Foundation to Marilyn Cochran-Smith, Boston College, and Susan L. Lytle, University of
Pennsylvania, entitled "Teachers' Inquiry and the Epistemology of Teaching."
This paper was completed with the invaluable assistance of Marguerite Connolly
(Graduate Research Assistant, School of Education, Boston College) who located
resources, coded examples, provided editorial suggestions, and helped construct case studies from which the examples are excerpted.

Notes

1. Since 1986, I have worked with my colleague Susan L. Lytle to develop a conceptual framework for teacher research and its relationship to teacher education and
professional development within inquiry communities; see especially, Marilyn Cochran-
Smith and Susan Lytle, "Research on Teaching and Teacher Research: The Issues that
Divide," *Educational Researcher* 19 (1990): pp. 2-11; Marilyn Cochran-Smith and Susan
Lytle, *Inside/Outside: Teacher Research and Knowledge* (New York: Teachers College Press,
1993); Susan Lytle and Marilyn Cochran-Smith, "Inquiry, knowledge and practice" in
*Teacher Research and Educational Reform Ninety-third Yearbook of the National Society for the
Study of Education*, eds. Sandra Hollingsworth and Hugh Sockett (Chicago: N.S.S.E.,
1994); Marilyn Cochran-Smith and Susan Lytle, "Teacher Research: The Questions
that Persist," *Journal of Educational Leadership* 1, no. 1 (1998).

2. Jean Anyon, "Teacher Development and Reform in an Inner-city School,"
Teachers College Record 96, no. 1 (1994): pp. 14-34; Lawrence Cuban, *To Make a Difference: Teaching in the Inner City* (New York: Free Press, 1970).

3. Cameron McCarthy, "Multicultural Approaches to Racial Inequality in the
United States," in *Understanding Curriculum as Racial Text*, eds. Louis Anthony Castenell
and William F. Pinar (Albany: SUNY Press, 1993).

4. Stanley Aronowitz and Henry Giroux, *Education Under Siege* (New York: New
World Foundation, 1985); Kenneth Zeichner, "Preparing Reflective Teachers: An
Overview of Instructional Strategies Which Have Been Employed in Preservice
Teacher Education," *International Journal of Educational Research* 7 (1986): pp. 565-575.

5. Paulo Freire, *Pedagogy of the Oppressed* (New York: Seabury Press, 1970).

6. Mark Ginsberg and Beverly Lindsay, *Comparative Perspectives on Policy Formation,
Socialization, and Society* (Philadelphia: Falmer, 1995).

7. Jerome Bruner, *The Culture of Education* (Cambridge, MA: Harvard University Press, 1996).

8. Paulo Freire, *Pedagogy of the Oppressed.*

9. Paulo Freire, *Pedagogy of the Oppressed*; Sonia Nieto, *Affirming Diversity: The Sociopolitical Context of Multicultural Education* (White Plains, NY: Longman, 1996); Gloria Ladson-Billings, "Culturally Relevant Teaching: Effective Instruction for Black Students," *The College Board Review* 155 (1990): pp. 20-25; Gloria Ladson-Billings, "Liberatory consequences of literacy: A case of culturally relevant instruction for African-American students," *Journal of Negro Education* 61, no. 3 (1992): pp. 378-391; Gloria Ladson-Billings, *The Dream Keepers: Successful Teachers of African-American Children* (San Francisco: Jossey-Bass, 1994); Gloria Ladson-Billings, "Toward a Theory of Culturally Relevant Pedagogy," *American Educational Research Journal* 32, no. 3 (1995): pp. 465-491.

10. Also see Elliot Eisner, *Learning and Teaching the Ways of Knowing* (Chicago: The University of Chicago Press, 1985); Michele Foster, *Black Teachers on Teaching* (New York: The New Press, 1997); Janice E. Hale, *Unbank the Fire: Visions for the Education of All Children* (Baltimore: John Hopkins University Press, 1994); Jacqueline J. Irvine, *Black Students and School Failure: Policies, Practice and Prescriptions* (New York: Greenwood Press, 1990); Jacqueline J. Irvine and Darlene E. York, "Learning Styles and Culturally Diverse Students: A Literature Review," in *Handbook of Research on Multicultural Education*, eds. James A. Banks and Cherry A. McGee Banks (New York: MacMillan, 1995).

11. Aronowitz and Giroux, *Education Under Siege*; Ira Shor, *Critical Teaching for Everyday Life* (Boston: South End Press, 1980); Christine E. Sleeter and Peter L. McLaren, *Multicultural Education, Critical Pedagogy, and the Politics of Difference* (Albany: SUNY Press, 1995).

12. Christine E. Sleeter, "Restructuring Schools for Multicultural Education," *Journal of Teacher Education* 43, no. 2 (1992): pp. 141-148; Beverly Tatum, "Talking About Race, Learning About Racism: The Application of Racial Identity Development Theory in the Classroom," *Harvard Educational Review* 62 (1992): pp. 1-24.

13. Mary Field Belenky et al., *Women's Ways of Knowing: The Development of Self, Voice and Mind* (New York: Basic Books, 1986); Madeline Grumet, *Bitter Milk: Women and Teaching* (Amherst: University of Massachusetts Press, 1988); Kathleen Weiler, *Women Teaching for Change: Gender, Class and Power* (South Hadley, MA: Bergin and Garvey Publishers, 1988).

14. Christine E. Sleeter and Carl A. Grant, "An Analysis of Multicultural Education in the United States," *Harvard Educational Review* 57, no. 4 (1987): pp. 421-444; Christine E. Sleeter and Peter L. McLaren, *Multicultural Education, Critical Pedagogy, and the Politics of Difference* (Albany: SUNY Press, 1995).

15. Beverly Gordon, "Knowledge Construction, Competing Critical Theories, and Education," in *Handbook of Research on Multicultural Education*, ed. James Banks (New York: Macmillan, 1995).

16. Marilyn Cochran-Smith, "Inquiry as a Stance on Teaching: The Preservice Case" (Paper presented at American Research Educational Association Annual Meeting, San Diego, 1998).

17. Although Patti Lather in "Research as Praxis," *Harvard Educational Review* 56, no. 3 (1986): pp. 257-277 was describing social science "research as praxis" rather than teaching as praxis, her conceptualization is appropriate here.

18. Cochran-Smith and Lytle, "Teacher Research: The Questions that Persist."

19. These six principles of pedagogy are drawn from two sources that in turn draw on the work of many other sources: an extensive review of the literature related to the knowledge, skills, and experiences of teachers who work in the increasingly diverse contexts of urban schools (Marilyn Cochran-Smith, "Knowledge, Skills, and Experiences for Teaching Culturally Diverse Learners: A Perspective for Practicing Teachers," in

Constructing the Knowledge Base for Urban Teacher Education, ed. Jacqueline J. Irvine (Washington: AACTE, 1997) and a theoretical framework on teaching and teacher education for social change that links knowledge and interpretive frameworks, political perspectives, teaching practice, and inquiry contexts for professional development (Marilyn Cochran-Smith, "Teaching for Social Change: Toward a Grounded Theory of Teacher Education," in *The International Handbook of Educational Change*, eds. Andy Hargreaves, et al. (Netherlands: Kluwer Academic Publishers, 1997). These two papers are based on the literature of multicultural education, urban and minority education, culturally responsive curriculum and pedagogy, and related sociological, linguistic, and anthropological research on schools, classrooms, and community cultures. Both of these also draw on a body of lesser known writing and research by teachers on urban education. The six principles that I identify are informed by and intended to represent the major pedagogical themes that recur in this larger body of conceptual and empirical research by university-based and school-based researchers. In this sense they build on the work of many others, and each of the principles in this chapter represents a synthesis of other work. To describe each principle, however, I try to use relatively straightforward terms and a minimum of citations. Readers are directed to my two previous chapters for a more extensive discussion of the literature that informs these six principles as well as a complete bibliography of the related work.

20. These examples are excerpts from teacher research essays, studies, and journals that student teachers completed during their preservice program in classes that I taught at the University of Pennsylvania from 1994-96, the years of data collection for a major grant to Marilyn Cochran-Smith and Susan L. Lytle from the Spencer Foundation that investigates the interrelationships of inquiry, knowledge, and practice across the professional lifespan. (See Marilyn Cochran-Smith and Susan L. Lytle, "Teacher Learning in Professional Communities," *Review of Research in Education* 24 (in press); Marilyn Cochran-Smith, "Inquiry as a Stance on Teaching: The Preservice Case.") Excerpts are used here with the authors' permission.

21. Marilyn Cochran-Smith, "Uncertain Allies: Understanding the Boundaries of Race and Teaching," *Harvard Educational Review* 65, no. 4 (1995): pp. 541-570.

22. Nieto, *Affirming Diversity*.

23. The realities of the contexts of student teaching are explored in a series of case studies of urban student teachers learning to teach, which are products of the aforementioned Spencer grant (Marilyn Cochran-Smith, "Inquiry as Stance on Teaching: The preservice case," in preparation.

24. Gillian Maimon, "Little Pigs and Big Ideas" (Unpublished paper prepared for The University of Pennsylvania Graduate School of Education, 1996).

25. Jacqueline J. Irvine, *Black Students and School Failure: Policies, Practice and Prescriptions* (New York: Greenwood Press, 1990).

26. Martin Haberman, "The Pedagogy of Poverty versus Good Teaching," *Phi Delta Kappan* 73, no. 4 (1991): pp. 290-294.

27. Jean Anyon, "Teacher Development and Reform in an Inner-city School," *Teachers College Record* 96, no. 1 (1994): pp. 14-34.

28. Marisol Sosa Booth, "Literature Study," (Unpublished paper prepared for The University of Pennsylvania Graduate School of Education, 1994).

29. Michelle Fine, *Chartering Urban School Reform: Reflections on Public High Schools in the Midst of Change* (New York: Teachers College Press, 1994); Linda Powell, "Interpreting Social Defenses: Family Group in an Urban Setting," in *Chartering Urban School Reform*, ed. Michelle Fine (New York: Teachers College Press, 1994).

30. Ronit Eliav, "Learning about Learning: My Evolution from What I Thought I Thought about Teaching and Teachers to What I Think I Think about Learning and Children" (Unpublished paper prepared for The University of Pennsylvania Graduate School of Education, 1996).

31. Marilyn Cochran-Smith, "Color Blindness and Basket Making Are not the Answers: Fronting the Dilemmas of Race, Language and Culture in Teacher Education," *American Educational Research Journal* 32, no. 3 (1995): 493-552.

32. See the powerful examples offered in personal accounts of ethnographic studies by Cynthia Ballenger, "Because You Like Us: The Language of Control," *Harvard Educational Review* 62, no. 2 (1992): 199-208; S. Brown, "Lighting Fires," in *Inside/Outside: Teacher Research and Knowledge*, eds. Marilyn Cochran-Smith and Susan Lytle (New York: Teachers College Press, 1993); D. R. Dillon, "Showing Them that I Want Them to Learn and that I Care about Who They Are: A Microethnography of the Social Organization of a Secondary Low-track English-Reading Classroom. *American Educational Research Journal* 26, no. 2 (1989): 227-259; Robert Fecho, "Language Inquiry and Critical Pedagogy: Co-investigating Power in the Classroom," in *Chartering Urban School Reform*, ed. Michelle Fine (New York: Teachers College Press, 1994); Robert Fecho, "Learning from Laura" in *Cityscapes* (Berkeley: National Writing Project, 1996); Michele Foster, "The Politics of Race through African-American Teachers' Eyes," *Journal of Education* 172, no. 3 (1991): 123-141; Michele Foster, *Black Teachers on Teaching* (New York: The New Press, 1997); b. hooks, *Teaching to Transgress: Education as the Practice of Freedom* (New York: Routledge, 1994); Gladys Ladson-Billings, *The Dream Keepers: Successful Teachers of African-American Children* (San Francisco: Jossey-Bass, 1994); Diane Waff, "Romance in the Classroom: Inviting Discourse on Gender and Power, in *The Voice of the Philadelphia Writing Project* 3, no. 1 (1994): 15-18.

33. Susan Moore, "Masters Comprehensive Portfolio" (Unpublished paper prepared for The University of Pennsylvania Graduate School of Education, 1996).

34. L. C. Beckum, "Diversity in Assessment: Always Factoring the Reform Equation," in *Diversity in Teacher Education*, ed. M. Dilworth (San Francisco: AACTE/Jossey-Bass, 1992); Linda Darling-Hammond, "Inequality and Access to Knowledge," in *Handbook of Research on Multicultural Education*, eds. J. A. Banks and C. A. M. Banks (New York: Macmillan, 1995).

35. Jamie Kim-Ross, "Portfolio Narrative Essay Project START" (Unpublished paper prepared for The University of Pennsylvania Graduate School of Education, 1996).

36. Marilyn Cochran-Smith, "Learning to Teach Against the Grain," *Harvard Educational Review* 61, no. 3 (1991): 279-310.

37. Mark Paikoff, "Literature Study" (Unpublished paper prepared for The University of Pennsylvania Graduate School of Education, 1994).

38. Marilyn Cochran-Smith and Susan Lytle, *Inside/Outside: Teacher Research and Knowledge* (New York: Teachers College Press, 1993); Marilyn Cochran-Smith and Susan Lytle, "Knowledge for Teaching: Where It Comes From" (Paper presented at American Educational Research Association Annual Meeting, San Diego, 1998); Marilyn Cochran-Smith, "The Power of Teacher Research in Teacher Education," in *Teacher Research and Educational Reform*, eds. Sandra Hollingsworth and Hugh Sockett (Chicago: The University of Chicago Press, 1994); Marilyn Cochran-Smith, "Knowledge, Skills and Experiences for Teaching Culturally Diverse Learners: A Perspective for Practicing Teachers," in *Constructing the Knowledge Base for Urban Teacher Education*, ed. J. J. Irvine (Washington: AACTE, 1997); Marilyn Cochran-Smith and Susan Lytle, "Teacher Learning in Professional Communities."

39. M. K. Cipriani, "Communities of Learners Constructing the Meaning of Teachers" (Unpublished paper prepared for The University of Pennsylvania Graduate School of Education, 1996).

40. Elliot Eisner, *Learning and Teaching the Ways of Knowing* (Chicago: The University of Chicago Press, 1985).

41. The argument for teachers learning together within the context of inquiry communities across the professional lifespan has been developed in conceptual and empirical

research over more than a decade (see especially Marilyn Cochran-Smith and Susan Lytle, *Inside/Outside: Teacher Research and Knowledge*; Marilyn Cochran-Smith and Susan Lytle, "Teacher Learning in Professional Communities"; in addition, Cochran-Smith analyzes the preservice context in particular (Marilyn Cochran-Smith, "Color Blindness and Basket Making Are not the Answers: Fronting the Dilemmas of Race, Culture and Language Diversity in Teacher Education"; Marilyn Cochran-Smith, "Uncertain Allies: Understanding the Boundaries of Race and Teaching," *Harvard Educational Review* 65, no. 4 (1995): 541-570; Marilyn Cochran-Smith, "Inquiry as a Stance on Teaching: The preservice case").

CHAPTER VI

Teacher Education and the Construction of Meaning

VIRGINIA RICHARDSON

The cognitive revolution has changed our thinking about teaching and teacher education by focusing on cognitions, beliefs, and the making of meaning as the desired outcomes of interest rather than, or in addition to, prescribed skills and behaviors. This chapter describes and analyzes one form of teacher education that has been influenced heavily by this revolution: constructivist teacher education.

In this chapter, teacher education refers to inservice teacher education, also described as staff development, and initial or preservice teacher education. Constructivist views began to enter the literature on staff development about twenty years ago, perhaps the first description being found in the reports of a staff development project funded by the National Institute of Education and facilitated by Jean Bamberger, Eleanor Duckworth and Magdelene Lampert.[1] This project engaged teachers in long-term inquiries into issues of science, mathematics, and music as well as their own processes of learning. The participants were asked to consider how their learning about learning and inquiry could be used in their own classroom teaching. More recently, constructivist practices have been introduced into the scholarly literature on preservice teacher education.[2]

As so often happens in education, however, the term "constructivist" is used in many different ways. Like the term "reflective," *constructivist* has become a category term that describes programs with a few agreed-upon characteristics. In the case of constructivist teacher education, the term is thought to refer to current programs and to programs that are student-centered and are based on a theory of learning that focuses on how students develop understandings. Beyond these two characteristics, the term describes many different approaches to teacher education. In fact, the concept is quickly becoming a "slogan system," described by Michael Apple as a term that is ambiguous enough to unite people and

Virginia Richardson is the Chair of Educational Studies and Professor of Education in the School of Education at the University of Michigan. She is presently working with Gary Fenstermacher on a grant from the Spencer Foundation on Manner in Teaching.

groups with differing philosophical frameworks and world views around a common goal such as the improvement of instruction.[3]

In the following sections, I briefly review constructivist learning theory and its relationship to teaching and teacher education and then develop a description of constructivist teacher education. I conclude with two arguments: (1) constructivist teacher education is an important means for working with preservice and inservice teachers who are undergoing deep changes in their understanding of teaching and learning that will lead to quite different classroom actions; (2) there is a place, however, for other forms of teacher education that are designed for purposes other than deep changes in understanding. In the process of developing these arguments, I will suggest various approaches to constructivist teacher education, present a case of staff-development planning that uses a mixed-strategy approach, and conclude with issues still to be resolved in constructivist teacher education.

Constructivist Learning Theory

Constructivism refers to the belief that human knowledge is constructed. Knowledge is constructed within the minds of individuals and within social communities; and the bodies of knowledge that inform individuals as well as their means of acquisition are themselves human constructions.[4] Most empirical and instructional work emphasizes the first of the focuses mentioned above: the construction of knowledge, knowing, beliefs and meaning within the minds of individuals and within social communities. In this case, constructivism is a theory or set of theories of learning or meaning making. It suggests that individuals create their own new understandings, based upon the interactions of what they already know and believe, and the phenomena or ideas with which they come into contact. This is a descriptive theory of learning that suggests how people *do* learn or develop. It is not a prescriptive theory that would imply how people *should* learn.

Most constructivists would agree that the transmission approach to teaching, usually delivered through lecture or direct instruction, promotes neither the interaction between prior and new knowledge nor the conversations that are necessary for intense involvement in ideas, connections between and among ideas, and the development of deep and broad understandings. This is not to say that learning or making meaning does not necessarily take place during a lecture. It is always possible for an individual to make the ties between prior knowledge and newly introduced understandings during a lecture, just as it is while reading a book. However, the concern about the transmission model is that the new knowledge that is introduced to students may not become well integrated with existing knowledge and beliefs. This new knowledge, then, may be brought forth by the student for school tasks such as examinations and be ignored at other times. Developing a constructivist learning environment, it is thought, helps to promote active learning that acknowledges, inquires into, and corrects or adds to understandings that already exist.

When constructivist learning theory is considered in terms of teaching, the linking of students' prior knowledge to present activities is of paramount importance. Depending upon one's approach to constructivism, it is important to involve students in examining their beliefs and premises through the careful design of classroom tasks and activities. Dialogue is also an extremely important element of constructivist pedagogy, as are hands-on activities in which students are engaged in inquiry.

However, while there are some common understandings among constructivists, there are also disagreements. Jennifer Vadeboncoeur traces fundamental differences in constructivist approaches to variations in the goals of teaching. These different goals are linked to very different notions of the nature of knowledge and how it is acquired. Two major constructivist approaches—the individual and the social— are usually tied to Jean Piaget and Lev Vygotsky:

Piagetian constructivism is aligned with an emphasis on education for individual cognitive development while forms of Vygotskian constructivism are aligned with an emphasis on education for social transformation.[5]

Piagetian constructivism focuses on the making of meaning by individuals, and the purpose of teaching within this frame is to lead students toward higher levels of understanding and analytic capabilities. Classroom activities are designed to help students become actively engaged in questioning their existing understandings and restructuring their cognitive maps with reformed and/or new understandings. In this approach, cognitive dissonance is an important element in helping students grow, and this may be introduced through hands-on activities and dialogue about and questioning of existing understandings.[6]

On the other hand, those concerned with social learning and transformation focus on the environment in which learning is taking place (situated cognition)[7] and on learning that requires social interactions (Vygotskian sociocultural approach).[8] Within the situated cognition approach, learning is not separated from action, and there is no representation of reality that is privileged. Knowledge is not thought of as static, nor separable from the action in which knowledge is constructed. In both social approaches, language and dialogue are of paramount importance. For John Dewey, whose view of language is often referred to in descriptions of this constructivist approach, language conveys meaning through being used in a social situation.[9] In the Vygotskian sociocultural approach, knowledge, understood as signs and symbols, enters the learning situation as tools within the social interaction.

Constructivist classrooms of this form also rely considerably on dialogue. Discovery and inquiry activities are planned by the teacher, although the activities vary in the degree to which they are guided and scaffolded. For Luis Moll, the bringing together of two forms of situated knowledge—school and community—is extremely important in helping students construct worthwhile and useful meaning. He asks that teachers open the school doors, learn about sources of knowledge within the communities of their students, and bring community experts into the classrooms.[10] Dennis Newman, Peggy Griffin, and Michael Cole use after-school activities to help children learn subjects through involvement in everyday activities such as cooking.[11]

Besides the differences in the degree to which social aspects enter into the considerations of constructivist instruction and learning, subject matter also makes a difference. For example, mathematics as a discipline is quite different from other disciplines such as history, science, or reading. Mathematics is bounded by a relatively concise symbol system, the meaning of which is generally agreed upon within the mathematics community. On the other hand, reading comprehension is understood within the constructivist community to be based on individual or cultural interpretations of concepts and ideas. It is less bounded than mathematics, and while some interpretations of text are more or less appropriate, there are few that are "wrong." Writing as a subject matter is also less bounded than mathematics.

In all disciplines, the constructivist teacher focuses more on how individual students arrive at results than on the results themselves. However, the differences in the disciplines seem to affect the nature of the specific constructivist pedagogy used in the classroom. One way of describing these differences is to look at comparisons of constructivist and traditional teachers in two disciplines. For example, Paul Cobb and colleagues compared two mathematics teachers, one traditional and one constructivist;[12] and Sarah Freedman compared a constructivist and a traditional approach to writing.[13] The differences in approach, particularly in planning, between the constructivist teachers—one teaching mathematics and one writing—were quite dramatic. These researchers examined, for example, the degree to which the students were encouraged to explain and justify their answers to problems set by the constructivist teacher. The mathematical tasks and problems were carefully planned and developed by the teacher to reflect understandings in the discipline. On the other hand, Freedman's constructivist writing teacher did little pre-planning or development of set activities: "Her theoretical framework told her that activities must be planned anew with each class to meet their particular needs."[14] One could conclude from descriptions like this that the culture of the subject matter impacts strongly on the constructivist classroom. This should certainly be a consideration in thinking about the content of teacher education, which, while less bounded than mathematics, involves a set of constructs and strategies that are agreed upon, by and large, within the teacher education community.

The Constructivist Reform Movement

Constructivism in teacher education has only recently entered the writing and thinking of practitioners and scholars in this field. This has come about in large part because reformers interested in changing the nature of pedagogy in the schools from a transfer-of-knowledge model to constructivism began to realize the necessity of preparing teachers in the constructivist forms. Reform that asks teachers to think and teach in very different ways requires reform of teacher education at the preservice and inservice levels.[15] Before moving into a description of the promises and challenges of the various forms of constructivist teacher education, it is helpful to view teacher education within the larger context of reform of education.

In 1969, Robert Chin and Kenneth Benne described three strategies of planned change, two of which are appropriate in thinking about reform in education and teacher education.[16] The *Empirical-Rational* approach employs the development of change models based on utopian goals and a rational, linear approach to achieving them. In this approach, research is conducted by academics or professional researchers, and change agents are employed to give the results to those who, it is presumed, will use it. The educational system is viewed as something to analyze and change. The *Normative-Re-educative* strategy is naturalistic in that it focuses on providing autonomy for and cultivating growth in the persons who make up the system. The third of these approaches, *Power-Coercive*, attempts to affect change through the type of collective-action strategies advocated by Mahatma Ghandi and Martin Luther King, Jr. This strategy focuses on the use of political institutions to achieve change, and on the recomposition and manipulation of power elites. The teacher organization/labor movement is an example of such a strategy.

Until recently, the approach used to make changes in the educational system as it relates to teachers was located within the first strategy, *Empirical-Rational*. Within this approach, the perception of teachers among change agents, policymakers, and educators in general is that teachers are the recipients of research and practice. Someone outside the classroom decides that teachers should employ research-based practices, ways of thinking, assessment systems, and so forth. Teachers are told about the change, it is demonstrated to them, and the expectation is that teachers as rational human beings will employ the new practices in their classrooms. Teacher education and staff development conducted within this framework follow these lines. Knowledge about appropriate behaviors, practices, and methods are transmitted to preservice and inservice teachers; this telling may be accompanied by demonstration, practice, observation, and coaching.

Quite recently, the literature has shifted in the direction of the *Normative-Re-educative* approach to planned change. Within this approach, it is assumed that change is enhanced through deep reflection on beliefs and practices. Since the change process entails understanding one's beliefs and knowledge and determining whether or not to change practices, dialogue has become a critical element of this approach in both preservice and inservice teacher education. The dialogue could take place with other teachers, with a teacher educator, "other," or critical friend. This approach is part of a larger movement toward the study of how individuals make sense of and contribute to the situations in which they live and work.[17] Margaret Gallagher, Anne Goudvis and P. David Pearson suggest that this approach (which they call "mutual adaptation") is the best form for dramatic change such as shifts in orientations and beliefs.[18]

Power-Coercive approaches within the union movement have, until recently, focused on teaching conditions, rewards for teachers, and political change. Recently, unions have shifted to a concern for teaching in the classroom. For example, Robert McClure describes a situation in which teachers in 26 schools voted to reconstruct their schools to better serve students, with the support of project staff.[19] (See Chapter III in this volume.) A book of district case studies by Charles Kerchner and Julia Koppich emphasizes interdependency of workers and managers and protection of teaching rather than teachers.[20] And Nina Bascia's high school case studies also demonstrate this change in union strategies.[21]

[Handwritten marginal note: Isn't this Basic knowledge Transfer?]

Most teacher education processes are located within the first two of
Chin and Benne's approaches, the Empirical-Rational and the Normative-Re-educative; and constructivist teacher education fits within the
latter. In constructivist classrooms, it is thought that the students must
engage deeply and actively in the material, and this engagement is
helped if the students become aware of the background beliefs and understandings they bring to considerations of the material. Deep changes
in beliefs and understandings are expected in the constructivist classroom. In teacher education, a movement toward constructivist teaching
represents differences in the way inservice and preservice teachers have
experienced education and what is expected of them within the "new"
classroom. It also requires deep changes in what they have come to
believe about the roles of the teacher educator and teacher.

Constructivist Teacher Education

One can see why constructivist learning or meaning-making theory
is so appealing in considerations of teacher education. After all, it is not
academic knowledge alone that we want future teachers to learn.
Ensuring that our students do well on academic written examinations
is not usually the aim toward which we aspire. Nor is teacher education
simply about the acquisition of skills. We have shifted our concept of
teaching from one that suggests teaching as exhibiting a set of behaviors toward one that views teaching as requiring complex thought
and decision making within situations of uncertainty and diverse contexts. Notions of the complexity of teaching and the variability of the
context work together to help justify the view of the teacher as a thinking, decision-making, reflective, and autonomous professional. Since
teaching is complex and contexts vary, teachers need to make their own
decisions and reflect on their situations and teaching in order to act in
appropriate ways. Teacher education is a professional experience which
requires preparing students in actions, intentions, habits of mind, ways
of thinking about students, educational contexts and incidents, and
understandings about the teaching/learning process. In the literature, if
not always reflected in practice, training in particular practices is no
longer the dominant approach to teacher education and staff development. Training has given way to education, and the focus is on developing ways of thinking and exposure to many different strategies.

Teacher education, however, envelops an anomalous and complex
content. Teacher education programs teach how to teach. The process
(teaches) is closely related to the content (teaching). Teacher education

also focuses on the subjects that will be taught, on learning, on learn-ers, and on schooling and society. The complex and sometimes com-peting goals are difficult to negotiate, particularly within boundaries that are created by educational institutions as they are structured today. For example, in very large undergraduate teacher education classes, the subject matter (i.e., a model of teaching) is often taught in a way that is at odds with the content. In a large lecture hall, students may be lectured about constructivist teaching and learning, and subse-quently given a multiple-choice test to assess their learning.

I do not suggest that a classroom in constructivist teacher educa-tion is devoid of direct instruction. It is expected in most classrooms that new knowledge will be introduced through texts, guided experi-ments, direct instruction from the teacher, from other students within the classroom, and other sources. Knowledge from other teachers is particularly important within a staff development program. Fellow teachers possess much valuable knowledge about teaching, and other teachers may be introduced to this expert knowledge during presenta-tions by teacher participants. The issue is how and when the new material is introduced, and how it becomes related to deep under-standings that the participants already hold.

In analyzing constructivist teacher education, it is helpful initially to look separately at the content of teacher education and the process or methods used to instruct. The following analysis is, of course, somewhat static and should be viewed as an initial way of understand-ing the nature of constructivist teacher education, not necessarily as a frame to be used in planning and implementing a teacher education program. The *content* goals of constructivist teacher education revolve around methods of instructing preservice and inservice teachers in how to create constructivist classrooms and to teach in a constructivist manner. The focus is on methods designed to help teachers develop an understanding of the nature of constructivist learning and teaching. For example, the Cognitively Guided Instruction (CGI) program at the University of Wisconsin worked with teachers on learning how to study students' learning of mathematics, an important aspect of con-structivist teaching of mathematics.[22]

The *process* of a constructivist teacher education approach involves using constructivist methods in the education of preservice and inser-vice teachers. A process focus attempts to create a constructivist envi-ronment in the teacher education classroom that includes using the pedagogical tools of dialogue, the development of meaningful tasks, and "giving reason" to the participants.[23] These processes are often used by teacher educators to model how they want their students to eventually teach in their own classrooms. It is also often believed that whatever the content, constructivism is the most effective approach in teacher education. Virginia Richardson and Mary Lynn Hamilton describe a constructivist approach to staff development in which teachers are initially interviewed about their beliefs, and transcriptions of these interviews are given back to the teachers. In addition to videotapes of the teachers' classroom instruction, these transcriptions become the basis for exploring existing beliefs and practices and possible new ones.[24] Case-based discussion[25] also represents a constructivist approach to teacher education, although it may be possible to apply a more Empirical-Rational format to such discussions.

Teacher education programs may be viewed within the matrix shown in Figure 1.

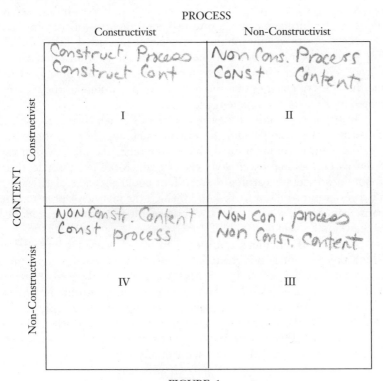

PROCESS

FIGURE 1
Approaches to Teacher Education

The *process* side of the matrix refers to the instructional approach or methods taken by the teacher educator. For example, the class could be largely lecture and recitation, or workshop-style "how to" (non-constructivist). On the other hand, it could focus on dialogues about teacher education students' beliefs and understandings of teaching in relation to what they are seeing in the classrooms and the new concepts and language that are being introduced (constructivist). The *content* side refers to the subject matter that is being explored, which could focus, for example, on standardized testing and issues of validity and reliability (non-constructivist), or, for a different example, on constructivist learning theory or the problems and promises of activating dialogue in large and small groups (constructivist).

Quadrant I would include programs or classes that use constructivist approaches in preparing inservice or preservice teachers in constructivist teaching. An example of this is a staff development program conducted by Francine Peterman. This program was a nine-month project in which she used Hilda Taba's theory of curriculum development for the process of changing teachers' theories of learning and classroom practices, and for the content that presented Taba's Teaching Strategies for developing higher order thinking.[26] Since Peterman's purposes included a strong research component, she was able to examine the kinds of changes that the teachers went through as they participated in the staff development program.

Quadrant II includes programs or classes in which the content is constructivist pedagogy, and the instructional approach is, for example, the lecture. As mentioned above, this may take place within the required educational psychology class in which the professor lectures about constructivist learning theory. This could also take place within a two-hour after-school workshop in which the instructor presents the participant teachers with a three-step model for determining students' background knowledge.

Quadrant III includes traditional forms of teacher education in which the content is not related to constructivist teacher education. An example would be a series of short workshops on the e-mail system within a particular school district. There would be no intent on the part of the staff developer to engage the participants deeply in the content or the theoretical aspects of the transmission process. She or he would provide a skill lesson—demonstration, trial, and practice. The content is expected to be useful in any type of classroom, constructivist or traditional. The participants may or may not engage deeply with the material; and may or may not tie the new knowledge to their own experiences in the past.

Quadrant IV includes situations in which non-constructivist teaching practices are being taught in a constructivist manner. To go back to the testing example used above, it is possible to approach the topic of standardized testing through the students' own experiences so that they can tie various forms of tests to examples in their own lives. It would also be possible to draw forth the emotions involved so that a discussion of test anxiety becomes more meaningful to the students. In this case, while the topic may not contribute to building a constructivist classroom, it is being introduced to students in a constructivist manner.

The next section presents a case of a hypothetical staff development program that requires approaches within several of the quadrants described above. This case is an amalgam of staff development processes in which I have been engaged and which I have studied.

Case: A Need for a Mixed Strategy

A medium-sized school district has made a commitment to bring current technology into all of its classrooms. The Board decided to start with a pilot project in the social studies classrooms of the four middle schools. This commitment has come about with the involvement of teams of teachers, administrators, parents and community people who agreed on both the overall goal and the nature of the pilot. The experience level of the social studies teachers ranges from less than one year to 30 years. The teachers also vary considerably on their use of technology within the classroom, as well as their interest in using it. The school district has purchased eight relatively advanced computers for each social studies classroom.

A team of staff developers, two teachers from each school, and two vice principals have been engaged for three weeks during the summer to plan the staff development that will start in the fall. The eight teachers on the planning team vary in how much they use technology in their classrooms. A facilitator from a local college of education has been engaged to work with the team. The team spends the first half of the three weeks exploring texts on how technology is used in the classroom and on staff development and the last half developing a plan for their district. They explore summaries of the research on the qualities needed in staff development processes.[27] They also examine literature that focuses on the nature of teacher change and the organizational context in which change takes place.[28] They read articles and view videotapes on the uses of technology in the classroom. They spend time relating this material to the needs of the teachers in their schools and the organizational context in which the proposed changes will take place.

The group members agree that there is not "one best way" to use the World Wide Web in the social studies classroom; however, they are able to gather interesting examples to be presented to their fellow teachers with the understanding that they would adapt some of these practices within their own curriculum approaches and for their particular students. This decision turns their attention to the individual differences among teachers and the need to provide teachers with individual help in their own classrooms. Further, incentives for the teachers are discussed. This is a complex topic since it is expected that teachers will vary in their involvement, depending, in part, on their prior knowledge and interest. They decide that each teacher will receive a bonus for participating in the project; teachers who participate actively in mentoring other teachers and leading workshops will receive an additional amount.

The group spends much time talking about the teachers who are going to be involved in the change effort. The variation among the teachers in knowledge, interest level, and even emotional response to a technological change is extreme. The group feels no need to ensure that all teachers reach the same level of expertise and use, or even a minimum level. They realize that change takes place faster with some teachers than with others, but that if the staff development is well structured, all of the teachers will be affected, hopefully in a worthwhile direction. Teachers who are already skilled at using technology will present their practices to others and will be available to help less experienced teachers as they begin to use the technology in their classrooms. The planning group also believes that the staff development will require large-group, small-group, and individual formats. Further, they believe that no teachers should have to sit through workshops whose content is already familiar to them, or for which they are not ready. Thus, it will be helpful to conduct initial individual assessments of the teachers' use of technology and their attitudes and beliefs.

The team produces a detailed plan which is summarized here. It is described under large-group, small-group and individual levels:

Large Group: The middle school social studies teachers usually meet once a year for one-half day to be presented with current curriculum issues such as the recently developed state standards. The panel plans two additional full-group afternoon meetings. The first meeting is designed to be inspirational and somewhat informational and will feature a dynamic speaker who will introduce the group to the wonders of the World Wide Web. The inspirational element would be placed within Quadrant III (Figure 1), unless the content were specifically about constructivist classrooms, which would place it in Quadrant II. At the next two meetings, the whole group will divide according to subject specialties (geography, social studies and United States history) to examine specific aspects of the use of technology within their own curricula. The first curriculum group meeting will involve lectures and demonstrations by teachers (Quadrant III), and the second, discussions about problems and possibilities (Quadrant IV).

In addition to the large-group meetings, there will be a series of short workshops for all interested teachers in aspects of technology, including initial computer skills, how to use e-mail, and connecting with the World Wide Web. There will also be a more advanced workshop on using search machines that focus specifically on social studies. These workshops represent Quadrant III.

Small Group: These meetings will take place within each school once every other week throughout the year. They will be constructivist in nature, focusing on such change issues as the role of the teacher in a technologically advanced classroom, the organization of the classroom and classroom management needs, and ethical and equity issues in computer use. Teachers will also be encouraged to discuss and diagnose their successes and failures in introducing the technology to their classes, and to develop an inquiry approach toward their experimentation. These meetings would be classified as Quadrants I and II.

In addition, each school will provide the teachers with the appropriate software for their home computers, and/or provide a number of computers that teachers can take home in the evenings and on the weekends.

Individual: At the beginning of the staff development program, a staff developer will meet with each teacher in his or her classroom. The purpose will be to assess the teacher's use of technology, curriculum approach, and attitudes and beliefs about changing in the direction of greater use of technology. From this assessment, the staff developer will work out an individual plan with the teacher concerning sessions of the staff development he or she should attend. For example, a teacher may be technologically sophisticated but still want to attend the search machine workshop. Another teacher may need a rudimentary workshop in using a computer.

After one full-group and several small-group meetings, the staff developer will again visit the teachers individually to determine how they are feeling about the staff development, and whether they need some specific help in the classroom. It may be suggested, for example, that a teacher visit a classroom in another school or talk via e-mail with another teacher in a similar situation. These will be individual and quite clinical meetings, and would also, by and large, be classified as Quadrants I and IV.

I leave it up to the reader to assess the likelihood of success of this program. Yes, it would be expensive and time-consuming. However, after years of trial and error, the educational community has learned that we need to expend time and money if planned changes are to take place. One of the aspects of this program that I feel is particularly important is that it entails a mixed strategy. It includes lectures, short "how-to" workshops, long-term dialogue sessions and inquiries, self-improvement, and individual clinical help. These varied approaches are tied closely to the form of knowledge, skills, and understandings that the school district is interested in developing in its teachers. For example, there may be little sense in involving teachers in deep conversations about the inner workings of the e-mail system.[29] Usually (but not always) people simply want to be shown how to use it. However, there probably is a reason to involve the teachers in inquiries into difficult contextual and ethical issues. For example, there may be some concern about the nature of the language used by students in their communications with others via e-mail, and questions concerning the point at which teachers should censor the use of certain language and encourage other forms. We hope also that the school district is willing to invite student teachers and interns from the local college of education to attend the workshops and work with the teachers who are implementing changes in their classrooms.

Issues in Constructivist Teacher Education

Three issues present problems and dilemmas in the development of constructivist teacher education and need to be resolved within programs like that described above. These relate to how new knowledge is introduced into the dialogue, the required knowledge, habits of mind, and skills of the teacher educator or staff developer, and the goals of constructivist teacher education.

HOW FORMAL KNOWLEDGE IS INTRODUCED INTO THE CONSTRUCTIVIST CLASSROOM

Allan MacKinnon and Carol Scarff-Seatter quote a student in a science methods class:

I am very anxious to return to my classroom and teach science. Constructivism has taught me [that] I do not need to know any science in order to teach it. I will simply allow my students to figure things out for themselves, for I know there is no *right* answer.[30]

In part, this troubling view of constructivism has been encouraged by some quite strident descriptions of constructivist pedagogy. Emphasis on moving teachers away from focusing instructional attention on "getting the right answers," moving them away from almost exclusive reliance on textbook teaching, and asking them to make sure students have reasons for learning has created a rhetoric that may have led to what MacKinnon and Scarff-Seatter believe is a reversion to the discovery approach to science teaching. It is also the case that constructivism as a learning theory is extraordinarily difficult to turn into pedagogical models. Further, and perhaps most pronounced, is that the epistemological foundations of constructivism are highly contested and quite confusing.

Questions concerning the nature of formal knowledge within a particular subject matter and, more particularly, how it should be introduced into a constructivist classroom have not been answered satisfactorily. These questions relate to issues of "teacher telling" and "correct answers." By formal knowledge, I am referring to concepts, premises and understandings that have been debated and agreed upon within discourse communities that relate closely to the particular subject matter. In order to bring students, including teacher education students, to a point of exploring deeply ideas of importance, the classroom environment should not provide the message that these ideas have been articulated by experts, nor that the knowledge that is present in textbooks, articles, or the teacher's head is the final word. Such an environment promotes the transfer model of teaching. At the same time, it is important to bring students into contact with formal knowledge as they work on their ideas. This tension is difficult to negotiate in the classroom. Deborah Ball, for example, laments the difficulties of valuing her mathematics students' interests at the same time that she is helping to connect them to ideas and traditions in the field of mathematics.[31]

We need to do a better job of describing the nature of a constructivist classroom in relation to the subject matter. When does it make sense to introduce a topic through direct instruction? How can we ask students to value formal knowledge within the field, but also to understand the possibilities of adding to and critiquing this knowledge? How can formal knowledge of subject matter be introduced without suggesting that it is something to be memorized in preparation for an examination?

Such questions are not so relevant when we move to inservice teacher education. In fact, here we have the opposite problem. Teachers are often suspicious of formal knowledge of classroom teaching, and often feel that it simply does not apply to their contexts. The question related to formal knowledge at the inservice stage concerns how we may help teachers value their own practical knowledge and to use formal knowledge of teaching in understanding, talking about, and inquiring into practical knowledge.

WHAT IS REQUIRED OF THE FACILITATOR

Within a constructivist teacher education environment, the teacher educator's role often is that of a facilitator. She facilitates the participants' learning and making of meaning and creates an environment that allows participants to link their background knowledge to the material that is being discussed. The teacher educator also is responsible for ensuring that new formal knowledge enters into the conversation. This does not mean that the teacher educator is always the one to introduce formal knowledge; it could be introduced in numerous ways. And this leads to a major issue in the constructivist movement related to teachers' knowledge of subject matter. The preservice student teacher's statement, quoted above from MacKinnon and Scarff-Seatter's study of science education, suggests the problem. Many believe that constructivist education does not require as extensive knowledge of subject matter as that required in a traditional classroom. After all, anything that the teacher does not know may be determined by the classroom group. However, as indicated in MacKinnon and Scarff-Seatter's study, teachers do not always know what they don't know.[32] In a constructivist classroom, a discussion of formal knowledge is not always planned but is introduced within the flow of the conversation. There is a need for "finger tip" knowledge that may quickly be brought into the conversation. Thus, it may be that constructivist teachers need a *better* grasp of subject matter than a more traditional teacher; in any case, problems with teachers' subject-matter knowledge may be more apparent in constructivist than in traditional classrooms.[33]

In addition to a firm and "finger tip" grasp of the subject matter, other skills and knowledge required by a constructivist teacher educator include:

- Knowledge of how teacher education students learn, and how to diagnose student learning.
- Ability to use this knowledge quickly and flexibly during the classroom lesson.

- Ability and interest in determining participants' beliefs about teaching and learning and particular practices.
- Skill in asking sometimes difficult questions that call for deep responses from students, and the ability to do so in a non-threatening way.
- Skills in keeping the conversation going in a direction that works toward the goals set by the teacher educator and/or the participants.
- Knowledge of teaching practice such that current examples of practices and classroom scenes may enter the conversation.

This represents a developing list of skills and knowledge. I hope that a research focus on the teacher educator will help expand this list and provide examples of particular practices.

BELIEFS, UNDERSTANDINGS, AND ACTIONS AS GOALS

The sea change in our thinking about cognition has brought about a renewed interest in different forms of cognition as the goals of interest in constructivist teacher education programs. Research that focuses on constructivist teacher education usually examines changes in teachers' beliefs, knowledge, and understandings. For example, Nancy Winitzky and Don Kauchak summarize a set of studies that examined the nature and structure of the knowledge acquired by preservice students in their constructivist teacher education program.[34]

While cognition is an important facet of teacher education, there are two other aspects that should not be forgotten. One revolves around what teachers actually do in classrooms, and one on what their students are learning. Classroom action, as a concept, combines behavior and intention. Knowledge of and ability to perform a variety of classroom actions should certainly be a goal in both preservice and inservice teacher education. Ultimately, however, we are interested in what happens to the students in classrooms with teachers who have been involved in a particular preservice or inservice program. At the preservice level, research on constructivist teacher education programs focuses almost exclusively on changes in how the preservice teachers think about teaching, subject matter, and students.[35] There are exceptions in which the research design measures outcomes of the program through observations during student teaching; but these studies are certainly in the minority.[36] And very often these studies indicate that changes in cognitive thinking and beliefs are extremely difficult to facilitate.

At the inservice level, a number of studies have examined changes in teaching. For example, Phyllis Blumenfeld and her colleagues were involved in a collaborative effort designed to help middle school teachers develop and implement project-based instruction in science. They studied teacher change in thinking and practice through extensive interviews, observations, and discourse analysis of their conversations with other teachers and with the university researchers.[37] However, there are very few studies that move to the next level of determining the effects of teachers' changes in practice on student learning.[38] If we are to suggest that constructivist teacher education is a significant and worthwhile approach, it is important that future research examine the effects of such programs not only on the ways teachers eventually teach, but also on the learning that goes on in their classrooms.

Conclusions

Constructivist teacher education holds great promise for deeply engaging preservice and inservice teachers in ideas and issues of importance in teaching. While such engagement may take place while listening to a lecture or reading a book, constructivist pedagogy may facilitate and encourage deep engagement in students who might otherwise treat the material as something to be quickly memorized for academic purposes.

At the same time, constructivist pedagogy requires the staff developer to have considerable subject-matter knowledge, cognitive flexibility, and the ability to quickly diagnose participants' thinking. Within such a classroom, deep inquiry into issues of interest to the group frequently sets up a tension with goals of content coverage. Further, constructivist pedagogy does not guarantee deep engagement with ideas, and it may be difficult to tell whether it is "working." Preservice teachers may develop deceptive ways of suggesting that they are deeply engaged when actually they are only trying to maintain their grade-point average,[39] and inservice teachers may simply try to make the staff developer feel good about his or her work.

We return to the original statement in this chapter that constructivism is a descriptive learning theory. Students may engage deeply in ideas of interest while listening to a lecture or reading a book, as well as when they are involved in a scaffolded group inquiry project in which dialogue is an important element. The point, however, is that constructivist pedagogy attempts to bring more students into such engagement and to engage them more deeply than would be the case in a traditional classroom.

However, not all topics require such time-consuming methods to achieve deep engagement. Some skills and knowledge may best be presented quickly and efficiently through a traditional transfer-of-learning model. Thus, in developing a course or program in teacher education, it is best to consider a mixed strategy that ties pedagogical approaches to the learning and understanding goals of the program and the needs of the students.

NOTES

1. Jean Bamberger, Eleanor Duckworth and Magdelene Lampert, *Final Report to the National Institute of Education: An Experiment in Teacher Development* (Cambridge: Massachusetts Institute of Technology, 1981); Magdelene Lampert, "How Do Teachers Manage to Teach? Perspectives on Problems in Practice," *Harvard Educational Review* 55 (1985): 178-84; Magdelene Lampert, "Teaching About Thinking and Thinking About Teaching, Revisited," *Constructivist Teacher Education: Building New Understandings*, ed. Virginia Richardson (London: Falmer, 1997): 84-107.

2. See, for example, the *Journal of Teacher Education*, *43*(5) and *Constructivist Teacher Education: Building New Understandings*.

3. Michael Apple, "Do the Standards Go Far Enough? Power, Policy, and Practice in Mathematics Education," *Journal for Research in Mathematics Education* 23, no. 5 (1992): 412-31. Apple refers to an article on slogan systems by B. P. Komisar and J. E. McClellan, "The Logic of Slogans," *Language and Concepts in Education*, eds. B. Othanel Smith and Robert H. Ennis (Chicago: Rand McNally, 1961): 195-214.

4. Dennis C. Phillips, "The Good, the Bad, and the Ugly: The Many Faces of Constructivism," *Educational Researcher* 24, no. 7 (1995): 5-12.

5. Jennifer Vadeboncoeur, "Child Development and the Purpose of Education: A Historical Context for Constructivism in Teacher Education," *Constructivist Teacher Education: Building New Understandings*, p. 15. See also, "The Good, the Bad, and the Ugly: 5-12; Eric Bredo, "Reconstructing Educational Psychology: Situated Cognition and Deweyan Pragmatism," *Educational Psychologist* 29, no. 1 (1994): 323-25; Paul Cobb, "Where is the Mind? Constructivist and Sociocultural Perspectives on Mathematical Development," *Educational Researcher* 23, no. 7 (1994): 13-20.

6. See, for example, Carl Bereiter, "Implications of Postmodernism for Science, or, Science as Progressive Discourse," *Educational Psychologist* 29, no. 1 (1994): 3-12; Deborah Schifter and M. A. Simon, "Assessing Teachers' Development of a Constructivist View of Mathematics Learning," *Teaching and Teacher Education* 8 (1992): 187-97.

7. John Dewey, *Democracy and Education* (New York: Macmillan, 1916); Jean Lave and E. Wenger, *Situated Learning: Legitimate Peripheral Participation* (Cambridge, UK: Cambridge University Press, 1991).

8. Luis Moll, ed., *Vygotsky and Education: Instructional Implications and Applications of Sociohistorical Psychology* (Cambridge, UK: Cambridge University Press, 1990); V. V. Davydov, "The Influence of L. A. Vygotsky on Education Theory, Research, and Practice," *Educational Researcher* 24, no. 3 (1995): 12-21; J. V. Wertsch, *Voices of the Mind: A Sociocultural Approach to Mediated Action* (Cambridge, MA: Harvard University Press, 1991).

9. Bredo, for example, quotes Dewey on how meaning can only be constructed through the use of language within a social context. Dewey, *Democracy and education*; Bredo, "Reconstructing Educational Psychology: Situated Cognition and Deweyan Pragmatism," 30.

10. Luis Moll, "Literacy Research in Community and Classrooms: A Sociocultural Context Approach," *Multidisciplinary Perspectives on Literacy Research*, eds. Richard Beach, et al. (Urbana, IL: National Council of Teachers of English, 1992): 211-44.

11. Dennis Newman, Peggy Griffin and Michael Cole, *The Construction Zone: Working for Cognitive Change in Schools* (Cambridge, UK: Cambridge University Press, 1989).

12. Paul Cobb, et al., "Characteristics of Classroom Mathematics Traditions: An Interactional Analysis," *American Educational Research Journal* 29, no. 3 (1992): 573-604.

13. Sarah W. Freedman, *Exchanging Writing, Exchanging Cultures* (Cambridge: Harvard University Press, 1994).

14. Ibid., 81.

15. However, examples of teacher education that encompass much of the constructivist philosophy have been around for some time: e.g., Lilian Katz, *Helping Others Learn to Teach: Some Principles and Techniques for Inservice Educators* (Urbana, IL: ERIC Clearinghouse on Early Childhood Education, 1979); Arthur A. Combs, *A Personal Approach to Teaching: Beliefs That Make a Difference* (Boston: Allyn and Bacon, 1982), and Arthur T. Jersild, *When Teachers Face Themselves* (New York: Teachers College Press, 1955).

16. Robert Chin and Kenneth Benne, "General Strategies for Effecting Changes in Human Systems," *The Planning of Change, Second Edition*, eds. Warren Bennis, Kenneth Benne and Robert Chin (New York: Holt, Rinehart and Winston, Inc., 1969): 32- 59.

17. Fred Erickson, "Qualitative Methods in Research on Teaching," *Handbook of Research on Teaching: Third Edition*, ed. Merlin C. Wittrock (New York: Macmillan, 1986): 119-61.

18. Margaret Gallagher, Anne Goudvis and P. David Pearson, "Principles of Organizational Change," in *Changing School Reading Programs*, eds. S. Jay Samuels and P. David Pearson (Newark, Delaware: International Reading Association, 1988): 11-39.

19. Robert M. McClure, "Individual Growth and Institutional Renewal," *Staff Development for Education in the '90s: New Demands, New Realities, New Perspectives*, ed. Ann Lieberman and Lynne Miller (New York: Teachers College Press, 1991): 221-41.

20. Charles T. Kerchner and Julia E. Koppich, *A Union of Professionals: Labor Relations and Educational Reform* (New York: Teachers College Press, 1993).

21. Nina Bascia, *Unions in Teachers' Professional Lives: Social, Intellectual and Practical Concerns* (New York: Teachers College Press, 1994).

22. Elizabeth Fennema, et al., "Learning to Use Children's Mathematics Thinking: A Case Study," *Schools, Mathematics and the World of Reality*, ed. Robert Davis and C. Maher (Needham Heights, MA: Allyn and Bacon, 1992): 93-117.

23. I first heard the term "giving reason" from Jean Bamberger and Eleanor Duckworth in the late 1970s as they explained the need to assume that student answers, while they may seem "incorrect," usually make sense within the set of assumptions being employed by the students. The purpose for the teacher is to assume that the student is being reasonable, and to determine what those assumptions are.

24. Virginia Richardson and Mary Lynn Hamilton, "The Practical Argument Staff Development Process," *Teacher Change and the Staff Development Process: A Case in Reading Instruction*, ed. Virginia Richardson (New York: Teachers College Press, 1994), 109-34. This process was based on Gary Fenstermacher's notion of practical arguments, "The Place of Practical Arguments in the Education of Teachers," *Teacher Change and the Staff Development Process*: 23-42.

25. Kay Merseth, "Cases and Case Methods in Education," Second edition, in *Handbook of Research on Teacher Education*, ed. John Sikula (New York: Macmillan, 1996): 722-44.

26. Francine Peterman, "Staff Development and the Process of Changing: A Teacher's Emerging Constructivist Beliefs About Learning and Teaching," in *The Practice of Constructivism in Science Education*, ed. Kenneth Tobin (Washington, DC: AAAS Press, 1993), 226-45; Hilda Taba and F. M. Elzey, "Teaching Strategies and Thought Processes," *Teachers College Record* 65 (1964): 524-34.

27. For example, Michael Fullan, "Staff Development, Innovation and Institutional Development," *Changing School Culture Through Staff Development*, ed. Bruce Joyce (Alexandria, VA: Association for Supervision and Curriculum Development, 1990): 3-25; Gary Griffin, "Clinical Teacher Education," *Reality and Reform in Clinical Teacher Education*, eds. James Hoffman and Sarah Edwards (New York: Random House 1986), 1-24; Susan Loucks-Horsley, et al., *Continuing to Learn: A Guidebook for Teacher Development* (Andover, MA: Regional Laboratory for Educational Improvement of the Northeast and Islands/National Staff Development Council, 1987); Milbrey W. McLaughlin, "Enabling Professional Development: What Have We Learned," *Staff Development for Education in the 90s*, eds. Ann Lieberman and Lynn Miller (New York: Teachers College Press, 1991), 61-82; Beatrice Ward, "Teacher Development: The Challenge of the Future," *Beyond the Looking Glass*, ed. Shirley Hord, Sharon O'Neal, and M. Smith (Austin: The Research and Development Center for Teacher Education, University of Texas, 1985): 283-312.

28. For example, Virginia Richardson and Peggy Placier, "Teacher Change," in *Handbook of Research on Teaching*, Fourth edition, ed. Virginia Richardson (Washington: American Educational Research Association, in press).

29. I thank the graduate students in the Teacher Development Seminar I am "facilitating" at the University of Michigan for pointing out to me that I may be projecting my own values on these content issues.

30. Allan MacKinnon and Carol Scarff-Seatter, "Constructivism: Contradictions and Confusions in Teacher Education," *Constructivist Teacher Education*, p. 53.

31. Deborah Ball, "With an Eye on the Mathematical Horizon: Dilemmas of Teaching Elementary School Mathematics," *Elementary School Journal* 93 (1993): 375.

32. MacKinnon and Scarff-Seatter, "Constructivism: Contradictions and Confusions in Teacher Education," *Constructivist Teacher Education*.

33. See Ruth M. Heaton, "Who is Minding the Mathematics Content: A Case Study of a Fifth-Grade Teacher," *Elementary School Journal* 93 (1992): 153-62; Ralph T. Putnam, "Teaching the Hows of Mathematics for Everyday Life: A Case Study," *Elementary School Journal* 93 (1992): 163-77.

34. Nancy Winitzky and Don Kauchak, "Constructivism in Teacher Education: Applying Cognitive Theory to Teacher Learning," *Constructivist Teacher Education*: 59-83.

35. For example, Kenneth Zeichner et al. asked student teachers before and after their student teaching experience to solve 18 classroom dilemmas, and analyzed the responses in terms of perspectives. Kenneth Zeichner, Robert Tabachnick and Kathleen Densmore, "Individual, Institutional, and Cultural Influences on the Development of Teachers' Craft Knowledge," *Exploring Teachers' Thinking*, ed. James Calderhead (London: Cassell, 1987): 21-59.

36. For example, Sherry Markel, *Acquiring Practical Knowledge: A Study of Development Through Observations of Student Teaching Practice and Dialogues of Community*, Unpublished dissertation (Tucson: University of Arizona, 1995).

37. Phyllis C. Blumenfeld et al., "Lessons Learned: How Collaboration Helped Middle-Grade Science Teachers Learn Project-Based Instruction," *Elementary School Journal* 94, no. 5 (1994): 539-51.

38. Two exceptions are Thomas P. Carpenter, et al., "Using Knowledge of Children's Mathematics Thinking in Classroom Teaching: An Experimental Study," *American*

Educational Research Journal 26, no. 4 (1989): 499-532; Candace Bos and Patricia Anders, "The Study of Student Change," *Teacher Change and the Staff Development Process*: 181-98.

39. Fred A. J. Korthagen, "The Influence of Learning Orientations on the Development of Reflective Teaching," *Teachers' Professional Learning*, ed. James Calderhead (Philadelphia: Falmer, 1988): 48. Korthagen, for example, suggests that students may "simulate learning behavior (*quasi adoption* to the conceptions of learning of the educators)."

CHAPTER VII

Knowing Teaching from the Inside Out: Implications of Inquiry in Practice for Teacher Education

MAGDALENE LAMPERT

For several years, I have been trying to learn about teaching and learning by teaching fifth grade mathematics in a public school classroom. The teaching and learning I have been doing occurs in an ordinary public school classroom, among one adult and many children, with constraints on time and space and other physical resources, with a responsibility to a diverse community to teach an agreed-upon curriculum, and learners who are compelled to participate. All of that is quite typical. But the teaching I have been doing is unconventional in that I am trying to make it possible for elementary school students to do different kinds of activities than those that are usually associated with learning in school, activities that will help them to understand and be able to use mathematics.

In the course of my teaching mathematics, I have been investigating pedagogical practices that are not common in American classrooms. I have also been trying to teach other teachers—new and experienced—about this kind of teaching. In my role as a teacher educator, I move from the inside of practice to the outside, attempting to communicate what I know to people who have not done the kind of teaching I have been working on. My work as a teacher informs my practice as a teacher educator in that it shapes what and how I teach teachers. It also offers a site for the common focus of others who seek to learn about teaching. By making my teaching public I can create a common text for analysis by students of pedagogy. And through the scholarly analysis I do of the practice, I create conceptual frames based in practice that may be useful to other teacher educators.

In this chapter, I explore the connections between inquiry into practice and teacher education. I investigate the problems that are encountered as one moves from knowing teaching inside the moment of a particular piece of classroom work to knowing teaching in communication with others, outside that context. This investigation continues a

Magdalene Lampert is Professor of Education at the University of Michigan.

long-term effort to understand what it means to "know teaching." Examining the contrast between how researchers thought about the problems in teaching and how practitioners thought as they confronted them, I have argued that it is often not possible simply to *use* knowledge that one brings into the classroom in the face of practical problems.[1] This does not mean that such knowledge is unnecessary, but it does mean that it is not sufficient. Teachers need to be able to manage situations in which new knowledge about what to do must be created on the spot. Teachers thus need to think in ways that enable them to create new knowledge while they work, not only as they plan what they will do beforehand or reflect on it afterward. This means that practitioners are simultaneously studying and doing teaching. What does this imply for relating inquiry in practice to teacher education? As I move out from studying what I know in and about teaching toward what I can (or what anyone can) teach someone else about this thinking in action, I recognize that knowledge of teaching has both a personal and a public character.

I have gained some insight into what it means to be in this place—somewhere between the inside and the outside—by analogy with where my fifth graders are as they study mathematics. The goal of their doing and studying mathematics in school is to learn about the relationship between creating knowledge and solving problems. They do this by creating knowledge and solving problems themselves and we reflect together on how this process goes. School learners, studying mathematics, and I, studying teaching, have two different kinds of audiences or communities of study with whom we communicate. One is local: kids talk to other kids and to their teacher as they work, asserting and giving evidence for what they know; I talk with my students' other teachers about the common problems we face, and we make statements about what we know and what we do, critically evaluating how that knowledge works in practice. In these local settings, we can all see what one another is doing and how it changes as we learn new things. These communications can be a regular part of practice, and sometimes they are even required to get the work done. The other kind of communication we engage in is public. As a teacher, for example, I want parents, employers, and taxpayers to know what school learners in my classroom are learning without having to watch them do it. I want other teachers, policymakers, and researchers to know what I am learning about teaching without requiring them to visit my classroom. My students, too, need to represent what they know to others besides their teacher and their classmates; parents and future teachers are among their "public." In communicating between the personal and the public, one moves out from the work of the practice itself and into another kind of work. The public cannot simply "see" what we do and what we learn. For school learners, educators struggle to invent performance evaluations and portfolio assessments to address this problem, but deciding what goes into portfolios and what they mean are not simple matters.[2] Teachers who write about their own teaching labor to find a voice, a language, a genre, a way of talking and writing about what they know that is not simply borrowed from more specialized academic discourses.[3] Why is it so hard?

When questions about knowing or understanding practice are juxtaposed with questions about communicating knowledge, we encounter a paradox: *if one learns to practice by creating knowledge in a practice, one knows something that non-practitioners do not know, but what is known cannot be represented to outsiders.* One way out of this paradox is to embrace "apprenticeship" models of education and to look to what "ordinary folks" do and know. In mathematics, for example, if we think of students' parents and neighbors and teachers as folks who know what students should know, then interacting with such people around doing math problems will get them an appropriate education. The learner's mathematical knowledge is created and used in practice and not represented for anyone outside the context of the problem. This approach has some merit, but avoids hard questions about equity and social mobility. How does one come to know aspects of a practice that are not part of one's everyday social intercourse? When the simple apprenticeship model for learning practice is applied to learning teaching, we have "new" teachers learning teaching from "old" teachers, leaving little room for critical analysis or innovation. Teachers who work with student teachers do not usually think of themselves as teacher educators. They assume that some kind of "teacher education" already went on back in the college classroom, although they are skeptical about its value. Rarely do the teacher and the student teacher engage in an analysis of the strategies that are used to address problems of practice or together seek new knowledge about teaching.

Another way to circumvent the paradox of learning practice, and one that has been particularly common in K-12 schools, is to argue that what students need to learn is a better understanding of the extant products of practices like mathematics. By studying representations of these products, they would learn ideas that they might not encounter in everyday problem solving.[4] The study of teaching, too, can be largely focused on the products of the inquiry of others and this is how it is often conducted in universities. Articles in research journals are amalgamated into textbooks and made into assigned reading in "foundations" and "methods" courses. Obviously, these syntheses are far from representations of knowing in practice.

Developing a Discourse of Practice

I am going to argue for another alternative as a way out of the paradox: the development of a discourse of practice, wherein insiders talk to one another about the new ideas and practices that develop as they do what they do. I do not mean to countenance the familiar "make and take" workshop in which teachers come away with a new activity to use "on Monday." Neither am I suggesting that teaching must be always new in the sense of reforming curricula or methods of instruction. Rather, I am proposing that teachers talk together to investigate the strategies they invent from moment to moment to manage the problems of practice as they come up anew in their ever-changing daily work, that they assess the appropriateness of various strategies in the context of classroom constraints, and that they generate alternative ways to make sense of what is happening in their classrooms. Such a discourse of practice could also be a medium whereby teachers communicate with those outside of teaching about teaching and bring different systems of interpretation to bear on their experience.[5] It could serve as a medium of teacher education as well as a language of practical scholarship. In developing this argument, I am deliberately avoiding the term *teacher researcher*. Instead, I am claiming that such teaching and communication of ideas are the responsibility of teachers as developing practitioners. As a form of teacher education, being a teacher involves the study of—and communication about—practice. Abdicating the responsibility for the study of teaching to academic researchers means that the focus of their study, and the resulting knowledge, will not represent what it is that teachers know.

Creating a discourse of practice in teaching has been a persistent challenge in the United States. In 1975, Dan Lortie wrote:

The preparation of teachers does not seem to result in the analytic turn of mind one finds in other occupations whose members are trained in colleges and universities. . . . One hears little mention of the disciplines of observation, comparison, rules of inference, sampling, testing hypotheses through treatment and so forth. Scientific modes of reasoning and pedagogical practice seem compartmentalized; I observed this even among science teachers. This intellectual segregation puzzles me; those in other kinds of "people work" (e.g. clinical psychology, psychiatry, social work) seem more inclined to connect clinical issues with scientific modes of thought. This separation is relevant because it militates against the development of an effective technical culture and because its absence means that conservative doctrines receive less factual challenge; each teacher is encouraged to have a personal version of teaching truth.[6]

In the past twenty years, many questions have been raised about the value of "the scientific method," including whether there ever was such a method to begin with. But the problem that Lortie calls "intellectual segregation" persists in teaching as does the rarity of observation, comparison, rules of inference, sampling, and testing hypotheses through treatment. Not only are teachers isolated from one another in their speculations about what and how to teach, but they see the "scientific" parts of the work of teaching, as well as the education of new teachers, as someone else's business. Although in some unusual settings, "action research" projects engage teachers in collaborative practical inquiry and reform, what Lortie calls "a personal version of teaching truth" exists alongside and often untouched by the "teaching truths" that are produced by university researchers.[7] Whether by encouragement or the operation of some other kind of social forces, we still live in a teaching culture where it is the norm for "each teacher . . . to have a personal version of teaching truth."

Americans have begun to recognize that this is not the norm among teachers in other societies, and to wonder what we can learn from their cultures of teaching. Looking toward Japan, for example, we find that communities of practice that educate new and experienced teachers are the norm, and have been for quite some time.[8] The structure of professional teacher education in Japan is built on the assumption that teaching is a collaborative process rather than a private enterprise, and that it is improved through teachers' collaborative inquiry, including peer planning of curriculum and instruction.[9] Similarly in China, a decades-long tradition and a well-articulated structure has new and experienced teachers collaborating in inquiry and practical problem solving.[10] The teachers who produce and communicate knowledge of teaching in these cultures are not a special brand of "teacher researchers." They do what they do as part of their everyday practice.

Commenting on these traditions of teacher learning in practice in 1997, the Research Advisory Committee of the National Council of Teachers of Mathematics observed:

Because research and development are intimately linked in the Japanese teachers' activity, theory and practice evolve together. Over the long term, a community of teachers who develop in this way can collectively build a coherent body of explanations and perspectives on students' mathematical reasoning and ways of supporting its development . . . specific instructional practices emerge as justifiable refinements and modifications of prior practices. As a consequence of this intimate relationship between research and development in their activity, Japanese teachers have collectively established a network of explanations and perspectives that is grounded in the analysis of practice.[11]

Although they are far from the national norm, communities of practice like those described here do exist in the United States, most often linked to the teaching of literacy. There are a few unusual examples of groups of teachers who meet over many years and study their own and others' practice to generate understanding and improvement.[12] These groups are sometimes associated with masters level courses in universities, but almost never institutionalized as part of the teachers' workload or organized to induct new teachers into the profession.

Problems in Teaching What One Knows of Practice

Can we make the kinds of discourse about practice that have been observed in these settings the norm in teaching in the United States? Why might it be hard to make it happen more broadly? I speculate on these matters from within the role of a teacher who is also a teacher educator. My imagination for collaborative inquiry into practice has been inspired by my participation in four unusual teacher education programs, first as a student and then as a faculty member.[13] From those experiences, I draw the following analysis of the problems associated with joining inquiry into practice and teacher education in the United States.

THE PROBLEM OF NOT-SHARED LANGUAGE

In order to study teaching and teach it to others, I have had to learn more than how to teach. I have needed to invent and learn multiple discourses. Communication about any subject usually occurs within the boundaries of a discourse community. This community shares a sense of the meaning of the terms it uses to talk about common experiences, and it also shares standards about what is accepted as evidence for assertions. To belong to such a community, one makes a tacit agreement to use its syntax and semantics. Developing a voice with which one can speak about teaching from the inside out means accepting multiple standards about what counts as justification for the statements one wishes to assert, and it raises difficult questions about how one's audience "takes" what is being asserted.[14] As I talk with other mathematics teachers who are teaching (as I do) by engaging students in mathematical activity, we assume a certain level of both mathematical and pedagogical "shared understanding." We do not always agree, but when we argue about the nature of practice, we do it within a set of common assumptions. Going out from that group to teachers with less mathematical sophistication or teachers who teach in more conventional ways. I have to figure out how to say what I want to say about my teaching in terms that respect both their knowledge and my own.

When I go out of my classroom to talk with prospective teachers, the place we are most likely to meet is the college classroom. In that setting, I need to speak about what I know in still a different language. And speaking about teaching to my fellow faculty members requires yet another kind of language, with different terms for what is going on in the classroom and different standards for supporting assertions. Parents, school board members, policymakers—all of these groups have one or another kind of interest in learning about the kind of practice I know about, and each has a different discourse that I need to learn if I am to communicate with them.

THE PROBLEM OF AUTHORITY

That some people are teachers and others are learners implies that some people know something that other people do not. We commonly refer to those who know more as "authorities" on a given matter. If we want to learn about a practice, how would we find someone who is an authority? How does one become an authority on practice? What are the differences between knowing more about *how to do* teaching and knowing how to talk about teaching? These distinctions are endlessly debatable and run through every field of endeavor. In one scenario, authority derives from quantities of experience. Someone who has been teaching longer is considered to know more than someone who is just beginning. In another scenario, authority derives from the much more ephemeral status associated with being able to say what one says in a way that others find useful. People move from being teachers to giving workshops for teachers when they demonstrate this kind of authority. And then there is the authority that derives from education, which in our field is suspect. (In my experience, it has been harder to get a classroom teaching job with an Ed.D.

in Curriculum and Instruction than it was when I had a bachelor's degree and no education courses.)

Among teachers and school administrators, there is a deep and continuing ambivalence about looking to university researchers for knowledge that might be useful in practice. Teachers do not routinely read the scholarly journals where researchers report their findings—in fact they find such journals to be almost incomprehensible, and certainly not about the same endeavor in which they are engaged. At the same time, there is a kind of mystical reverence for this work, an admission that it must be done by people who are better educated, if not "smarter."

As a teacher who has some certified, formal knowledge of teaching, I am the target of this ambivalence. I find myself in the position of trying to establish the authenticity of my ignorance and puzzlement in the face of many teaching problems while at the same time needing to justify why I am a professor and teacher educator. Part of my role as a teacher educator is to communicate to my fellow teachers and prospective teachers that teaching is a problematic and uncertain practice in which researchers' "answers" cannot simply be applied to practical questions.[15] The questions that go through my mind, and are sometimes recited aloud by someone in my vicinity, go something like this, "If you are smart enough to be a professor of education, why can't you figure out how to get everyone in your class to understand fractions? or sit still through a 45-minute lesson? or participate civilly in a discussion with their peers?" I struggle to maintain my appreciation for the creation of teaching solutions that fit the unique character of each moment of practice while living with the question, "If this is not *universally* good teaching, why teach others about it?"

THE PROBLEM OF TELLING KNOWLEDGE AS THE SUBJECT OF ONE'S OWN STUDY

Practice is doing. The study of practice begins in the setting in which a particular practitioner acts. To study practice means that one cannot succeed by limiting the focus of one's inquiry, since it is the breadth and complexity of those actions across multiple settings that are being investigated. Yet, in the course of attempting to tell about any practice, even if the telling is in the first person, one necessarily formalizes what has been learned, leaving out some aspects of the experience and highlighting others. For any inquiry into practice, there are many possible stories to tell. For every story that is told, there are many possible meanings to interpret. Stories about practice are not mirrors of experience: like all texts, they are constructed by the author with certain intentions in mind. When one is telling about oneself, no description seems adequate to the experience, and yet without description, what is learned remains private and unexamined. I have access to special knowledge as the teller of my own teaching stories, but I also am constrained by the limitations of any medium to express the multiplicity of what I know.

Although it is my aim to retain the richness and complexity of teaching when I am in the role of teacher educator, being in the middle of it makes me painfully aware of the impossibility of telling the whole story. Language, even supplemented by other media, is simply inadequate to capture my experience and knowledge of teaching practice. It is inadequate even to capture all the aspects of an event, to say nothing of representing the constellations of feelings and intentions imbedded in that event. That I can have more of a sense of the whole of what is going on than any observer is both a blessing and a curse.

Communicating between the Inside and the Outside of Practice

In an effort to address the problems I have described here, I invent stories about things that happen in my classroom. I do this to express something of the dramatic quality of what goes on, but also because narrative enables me to represent something that I think is universally important about teaching while maintaining the special qualities of knowledge created in the context of practice. The story serves as a medium for communicating about strategies invented in the moment without judging them to be ultimately correct. The stories raise universal questions about teaching, but they do not supply universal answers.

A story of teaching and learning is not a replay of what happened; it is a window on how events and relationships among the participants intertwine to produce a particular outcome. In stories of pedagogy, as in all stories, there is a narrative description of an event. But underlying this description, there is also the "state-breech-crisis-redress" cycle in which good or evil ultimately prevails.[16] As the person who both experiences the crisis and is responsible for its redress, I have the capacity to identify elements of the work of teaching that are not available to observers.[17] For example, the turning point in a piece I wrote about teaching my fifth graders the meaning of numbers written in decimal form is a moment when one of the students in the class announced (just as the lunch bell was about to ring!) that .0089 is a negative number because it is less than zero, and several of his class-mates chimed out in agreement.[18] This was a definite breech in the pedagogical conversation from my point of view as the teacher, since I know that .0089 is *not* a negative number. The students' thinking in this matter was interesting and would be recognized as such by many observers. But for me it also signaled a crisis. The kind of teaching that I am trying to do respects students as sense-makers and so I could not simply "correct" this assertion. At the same time, I want to teach in ways that honor mathematical traditions and make it possible for my students to communicate with others who honor those traditions, so I could not accept the students' assertions as a curious invention. Neither could I simply label the student "wrong" until I found out why he said what he said. At the same time, I wanted to be a good citizen of the public school in which I was teaching, and the lunch servers were waiting for my class in the cafeteria.

Studying practice in this situation is not only a matter of studying the complexity of the problems I faced. Because of the ethical responsibilities in my relationship with my students, I needed not only to recognize the potential for study in this turn of events, but to do something about it.[19] I was thrust into a domain of teaching practice that seems crucially important and valuable—trying to figure out why a ten-year-old might think that a number written as a decimal is less than zero and *at the same time* figuring out how I was going to convince him that this did not make sense while respecting him as a sense-maker, *and* doing all this without incurring the wrath of the lunch-room staff. Unlike researchers on children's thinking and learning, I did not create this problem to study it. I did what I did in order *to teach*.[20]

FROM KNOWING TO COMMUNICATING: DISSOLVING THE DUALISM?

The stories that I tell about my teaching are created after the fact with the purpose of communicating fundamental elements of my practice. There are three activities that together produce the narrative inquiry: one is doing the practice, a second is examining it, and a third is constructing a story about it.[21] Composing narratives from the perspective of practice for the purpose of teacher education cannot be one-way telling as in "announcing." Instead, it needs to be a two-way kind of storytelling: communicating one's experiences to others, checking on what is understood by the listener, and revising one's language to achieve some shared meaning. To help us understand the practice of teaching, the story needs not only to celebrate an event but also to draw out its meaning to some community of listeners who seek to learn. This requires becoming familiar with and using the language and rules of discourse of each community with whom one would communicate and creating a "language of practice" that is comprehensible to each.

To succeed in bringing a discourse of practice into teacher education, we need to create a third kind of discourse that is neither a discourse for practitioners to talk with one another about their problems, nor a discourse that mimics the focus and detachment of academia. This third kind of discourse would be built from communication in which local negotiation about meaning among speakers with differing perspectives has the potential to create a new language of practice.[22] It is not hard to imagine that creating and nurturing such a middle ground might improve both teaching and teacher learning. This somewhat romantic notion has some grounding in the social psychology of George Herbert Mead. Mead's theory of the self includes the idea that the person is both an actor and an interpreter-of-action-in-society.[23] Mead worked in the tradition of pragmatism, bent on attacking the classic dualisms—individual versus social, mind versus body, nature versus culture, fact versus value, objective versus subjective—with a harmonizing logic. This tradition of thought has given me the inspiration to imagine that it is possible to be both a practitioner and a researcher without suffering from a paralyzing personality disorder. It suggests a framework in which one can be both the protagonist, causing teaching and learning to happen, and the storyteller, interpreting that action.

In Mead's terms, the person's identity emerges from the integration of "me" and "I." "I" is the force that determines action, the will to make a unique imprint on the environment rather than simply reacting to it. "Me" is a member of various overlapping and non-overlapping social groups and understands action as it is variously interpreted by these groups. The "I" is continually involved as an agent in ongoing action, while the individual becomes aware of self through the reflective "me" which organizes the response of others to the "I." What distinguishes Mead's theory from other ways of thinking about persons-in-action that were popular when he was writing is the assertion that the person is a dynamic *integration* of the agentive "I" and the responsive "me." This assumption of integration contrasts sharply with theories of the self that understand the person as a responding organism whose behavior is a reactive product of what presses upon him or her from the outside (society) or from the inside (psyche) or both.[24] As a teacher who teaches others about teaching, I have been trying to know and tell about teaching both as the "I" who initiates action in the messy circumstances of practice and as the "me" who participates in different communities of discourse about this practice in order to understand it. The "me" part attempts to tell stories about the "I" part by describing what I do in terms that are familiar to various professional, academic and political communities.

COMMUNICATION AS AN ATTEMPT AT MUTUAL UNDERSTANDING

Perhaps it would be useful to introduce more rigorous ways of talking about what it is that is acquired from doing and studying practice. One result of studying a practice like mathematics or pedagogy is what might be called "my own understanding." This belongs to the individual practitioner and serves to justify one's actions to one's self. Representations of such understanding might be recorded in a private journal. Another kind of result of studying practice might be what is commonly called "knowledge," perhaps produced by individuals, but shored up by public argument supported by evidence. My understanding is assumed to be a product of private experience, contemplation, and reflection, while my knowledge is considered a product of intellectual work done according to a community's accepted set of rules.

Neither "understanding" nor "knowledge" in the sense that I have caricatured them here seems to be the appropriate term for what I am trying to produce about the practice of teaching. Even though it puts me in a powerful position, I am unhappy with the claim that as a practitioner I have some kind of universally applicable "knowledge" of teaching, and everyone else who teaches also ought to have this knowledge. But I also am equally unhappy with calling what I have "my own understanding," in the sense of saying that what I know is private and relevant only to the particular problems *I* face in *my* classroom.

Returning to Mead's theory of the self, what seems to be at issue in this epistemological conundrum is integrating the "I" who initiates action and the "me" who tries to understand and name action in ways that are meaningful to others. The works of Lev Vygotsky and M. M. Bakhtin and the writing of their contemporary interpreters[25] make it possible to imagine a way out of this conundrum, to understand that it is in the attempt to communicate with members of different speech communities that the "unsatisfactory stalemate between individualistic subjectivity and abstract objectivism" can be resolved.[26] What gets created in the act of trying to communicate is a new understanding, neither particular to one's private experience, nor entirely shaped by the need for universal principles, but a tool to aid all of our attempts at *mutual* understanding. In Gary Saul Morson's interpretation of Bakhtin,

Speech is *inter*locution. Understanding is active, is responsive, is a process. The process of understanding includes the listener's identification of the speaker's apparent and concealed motives and of the responses that the speaker invites and hopes to forestall.[27]

Let me try to give an example of how this helps me think about how I write or talk about my teaching. One of the things that I have been exploring in my teaching is organizing the daily agenda around multifaceted math problems instead of around a list of mathematical topics, intending the topics I want students to learn to emerge from students' work on the problems. Understanding this piece of my teaching puts me at a crossroads between the way "I" would describe what is going on and how I imagine that various speech communities might understand "me" trying to address this problem.

In an attempt to be true to both the "I" and the "me," I chose to title a paper about this aspect of my teaching "Covering the Curriculum, One Problem at a Time."[28] In my everyday work with fifth grade students, I know that just getting through the textbook is not an indication that anyone is learning anything. But as a public school teacher, I cannot only see learning mathematics in terms of constructing knowledge in the context of an attempt to make sense of a single problem; I also need to think in terms of which topics and procedures are taught and hopefully learned in which grade. If I were to speak to my fellow teachers in the same way that I speak to learning researchers about doing one problem at a time, they would be quick to point out that "it won't work in my classroom." By including the idea of "covering the curriculum" in my title, I am seeking to forestall this response, at least long enough to get my audience to listen to the "one problem at a time" part. I know, from working in a school everyday, that one cannot simply dismiss the idea of covering the curriculum, that the curriculum represents something like a treaty between the school and the community. Yet by including the phrase "one problem at a time" in my title, I seek to avoid researchers dismissing what I have to say on the basis of my being preoccupied with covering the curriculum. What I am trying to invent here is a way of talking about practice that stands back from practice but at the same time takes the point of view of practice.

Refining this kind of interlocution assumes a kind of localized exchange wherein meaning is negotiated and appropriated as such by the people who participate together in communicative events. It posits a level of study somewhere between the teacher as an individual thoughtful practitioner who keeps a private reflective journal and the teacher who views elements of practice in terms of the discourse structures of one or another public audience. In between, we might think of the teacher as collaborating with others in the thoughtful study of practice and creating a way of writing and talking about practice that satisfies *both* other practitioners and specialized non-practitioners who want to understand more of what teaching is all about.

Should Teacher Educators also Be Scholars of Practice?

This way of conceiving of teaching and the teacher's role is rare and unusual, but it is part of a tradition that was especially lively in this country at the time that John Dewey and his contemporaries were producing pedagogical scholarship and educating teachers. Fortunately for me, this tradition has survived alongside the more dominant trends to implement "teacherproof" curriculum and instructional activities and to replace teachers' engagement in intellectual practices with course requirements in the disciplines.[29]

One of Dewey's contemporaries and one of my heroes is Lucy Sprague Mitchell. Mitchell was a teacher, a teacher educator, and a researcher on teaching. She is one of a remarkable collection of educational reformers who combined scholarship with practice in America in the early part of the twentieth century. She wrote a book about teaching geography in elementary school that is considered to be a classic among teachers who regard themselves as pedagogical designers. In this little book, Mitchell ties the practical with the intellectual in her observations about what teachers need to do and learn in order for them to bring children to the point of making and understanding geographical relationships. In the section on the teacher's role in this process, she says:

It becomes the first task of a teacher who would base her program with young children on the exploration of the environment to explore the environment herself. She must know how her community keeps house—how it gets its water, its coal, its electric power, its food, who are the workers that make the community function. She must know where the pipes in her room lead to, where the coal is kept in the school, when the meters are read and by whom;

she must know the geographic features which characterize her particular environment and strive constantly to see how they have conditioned the work of
which she is a part and how they have been changed by that work.[30]

The teacher is to explore ideas first hand as a basis for knowing what
and how to teach. And there are two parts to this knowledge. One part
is the exploration itself, actually finding out the geography of the setting in which one lives and works, finding out what constitutes the
practice of geography. The other part is personalizing the findings of
that exploration by reflecting on what the study of geography enables
us to know about our own work and about how our thinking contributes to the design of our physical and intellectual environment.
There is yet a third kind of knowledge required to connect all this to
teaching. Mitchell goes on to say about the teacher's explorations of
geography:

And when she knows all this and much, much more, she must keep most of it
to herself! She does not gather information to become an encyclopedia, a
peripatetic textbook. She gathers this information in order to place the children in strategic positions for making explorations . . .[31]

If I can take a leaf from Mitchell's book, I would define my study of
teaching practice as an effort to "gather information" in order to place
myself and those others who seek to learn about *teaching* in a "strategic
position for making explorations."

Again, it is useful to make an analogy between teaching children—
this time geography—and teaching teachers. Taking Mitchell's admonitions about first-hand exploration as the basis for teaching about the
environment, we might paraphrase: "It becomes the first task of the
teacher educator who would base her program with *teachers* on the exploration of *teaching practice* to explore *teaching practice* herself." We might
agree that at least some parts of a teacher's education should entail the
exploration of teaching practice. It would be simplistic, however, to
conclude from this that teacher educators need to be school teachers.
For one, it is not enough to be a teacher. One must be a teacher who
studies practice, figuring out what one knows and how to represent
that knowledge for others. For another, doing practice and exploring
practice need not happen simultaneously. Mitchell does not suggest
that teachers of geography become professional geographers, but that
they find out what geographers *do*—what kinds of problems do they
work on and how do they work on them? It may be possible, especially

with new technologies for capturing vivid and complex information about classroom work, to study practice without doing it oneself.[32] Given some exploration of what practitioners do, teacher educators would then recast their own work to reflect an analysis of what it would take to learn that. How might we create environments in which teacher educators could learn about practice? And then how would we take the next step—using this information to place learners of teaching in strategic positions for making explorations?

NOTES

1. Lampert, Magdalene. "How Do Teachers Manage to Teach?: Perspectives on Problems in Practice." *Harvard Educational Review,* 55(2) (1995), 178-194.

2. The headline of an article on this project in *Education Week* is telling: "Even as Popularity Soars, Portfolios Encounter Roadblocks," Debra Viadero, April 5, 1995, p. 8 (Volume XIV, Number 28).

3. See Virginia Richardson, "Conducting Research on Practice," *Educational Researcher,* 23, 5 (June-July, 1994), pp. 5-10 and Marilyn Cochran-Smith and Susan Lytle, *Inside Outside: Teacher Research and Knowledge* (New York: Teachers College Press, 1993) for taxonomies of current approaches to teacher research. See Cathy Fleisher, *Composing Teacher-Research* (Albany: State University of New York Press, 1995) for an overview of scholarly arguments for the integration of teaching and research.

4. This argument has been hotly debated in mathematics education over several centuries. I have reviewed its implications in "Practices and Problems in Teaching Authentic Mathematics in School," in eds. F. Oser, A. Dick, and J. L. Patry, *Effective and Responsible Teaching: The New Synthesis.* (New York: Jossey-Bass, 1992), pp. 295-314.

5. Jennifer Gore and Ken Zeichner caution teachers against the limitations of simply reflecting on their own practice within a community of peers, suggesting that teacher's study of practice is enriched by the participation of a "critical friend." See J. Gore and K. Zeichner (1991), "Action Research and Reflective Teaching in Preservice Teacher Education: A Case Study in the US," *Teaching and Teacher Education,* 7, 2, 119-136. Joseph Schwab articulated a similar idea in his essay on "The Practical: Arts of the Eclectic," in *Science, Curriculum, and Liberal Education: Selected Essays,* Ian Westbury and Neil Wilkof, eds. (Chicago: University of Chicago Press, 1978), pp. 384-407.

6. Dan Lortie, *Schoolteacher* (Chicago: University of Chicago Press, 1975), p. 230.

7. In "Research on Teaching and Teacher Research: Issues that Divide," Marilyn Cochran-Smith and Susan Lytle examine the conceptual and practical differences in these two research traditions. *(Educational Researcher,* Vol. 19, No. 2, March 1990, pp. 2-11). The tradition of action research in education developed in the United Kingdom and has been taken up in some instances by teachers in the United States. See *International Action Research: A Casebook for Educational Reform,* ed. Sandra Hollingsworth (London: Falmer, 1997).

8. Ken Shimahara, *Learning to Teach in Two Cultures, Japan and the United States.* (New York: Garland, 1995).

9. Manabu Sato, "Japan," in H. Leavitt (Ed.), *Issues and Problems in Teacher Education: An International Handbook* (Westport, Conn.: Greenwood Press, 1992, pp. 156-168).

10. Lynne Paine and Liping Ma, "Teachers Working Together: A Dialogue on Organizational and Cultural Perspectives of Chinese Teachers," in *Teacher Collegiality and Professional Development: International Variation in Practice and Context,* ed. John Schwille, *International Journal of Educational Research,* Vol. 19, No. 8 (1993), pp. 675-698.

11. "Justification and Reform" by Research Advisory Committee of the National Council of Teachers of Mathematics in *Journal of Research in Mathematics Education*, 1996, vol. 27, no. 5, p. 518.

12. For examples, see Gail Burnaford, Joseph Fischer, and David Hobson, *Teachers Doing Research: Practical Possibilities*, NJ: Erlbaum, 1997; Joan Krater, Jane Zeni, and Nancy Devlin Cason, *Mirror Images: Teaching Writing in Black and White*, NH: Heinemann, 1996; "Teacher Professional Development as Situated Inquiry: A Case Study in Science Education," Center for the Development of Teaching Paper Series, Educational Development Center, Newton, MA, September 1997; and *Voices from Madison: Issues and Ideas from Inside Schools* (School Practitioners Speak Out on Teaching, Learning, and Knowing) Action Research Abstracts, 1990-1995.

13. I was prepared to be an elementary level teacher at The Prospect School in North Bennington, Vermont, and then taught teachers at Antioch Graduate School of Education; Buckingham, Browne, and Nichols School; and Michigan State University. The details of these experiences and how they influenced me as a teacher educator are described in Chapter 1 of Magdalene Lampert and Deborah Ball, *Investigating Teaching: New Pedagogies and New Technologies for Teacher Education*, New York: Teachers College Press (in press).

14. David R. Olson and Janet Astington, "Thinking about Thinking: Learning How to Take Statements and Hold Beliefs." *Educational Psychologist*, 28(1), 7-23 (1993).

15. There is, of course, an analogy here with what we want school learners to appreciate about problem solving in mathematics. See Magdalene Lampert, "When the Problem Is not the Question and the Solution Is not the Answer: Mathematical Knowing and Teaching." *American Educational Research Journal*, 27(1), 29-64 (1990).

16. See Jerome Bruner, *Actual Minds, Possible Worlds* (Cambridge: Harvard University Press, 1986) for a description of the nature of narrative inquiry.

17. Deborah Ball, "Special Values and Pitfalls of the First Person Perspective" (in press).

18. Magdalene Lampert, "Choosing and Using Mathematical Tools in Classroom Discourse" in Jere Brophy, ed., *Advances in Research on Teaching, Volume 1*, Greenwich, CT: JAI Press, pp. 223-264.

19. See Robert Welker, "Expertise and the Teacher as Expert: Rethinking a Questionable Metaphor," *American Educational Research Journal*, 28(1), pp. 19-35, Alan Thom, *Teaching as a Moral Craft*, and David K. Cohen, *Teaching: Practice and its Predicaments* (unpublished manuscript) for a discussion of the role of will in teacher action.

20. In contrast to others who have become teacher researchers in university settings (for example, David Wong, "Challenges Confronting the Researcher/Teacher: Conflicts of Purpose and Conduct," *Educational Researcher*, 24, 3, pp. 22-28, April, 1995), I did not decide to become a teacher in order to study problems that I was interested in as a scholar. I became a university researcher in order to better understand and communicate about a practice I had already been engaged in for more than ten years.

21. I do not wish to portray "doing" and "thinking" as separate, sequential activities. See Donald A. Schon on the role of both "reflection-in-action" and "reflection-on-action" in teaching and other practices (*The Reflective Practitioner: How Professionals Think in Action*. New York: Basic Books, 1983).

22. Joseph Schwab writes about such conversation in his series of essays about practice. See "The Practical: Arts of Eclectic," in *Science, Curriculum and Liberal Education, Selected Essays*, Ian Westbury and Neil Wilkof, eds. (Chicago: University of Chicago Press, 1978), pp. 322-364 for an analysis of the process of building such a discourse.

23. George Herbert Mead, *On Social Psychology* (Chicago, University of Chicago Press, 1956).

24. Herbert Blumer, "Sociological Implications of the thought of George Herbert Mead," in *School and Society: A Sociological Reader*, B. R. Cosin, ed. (London, Routledge and Kegan Paul, 1971). For a contemporary examination of the tensions between agency and structure in social theory, see Frederick Erickson, "Discourse Analysis as a Communication Chunnel: How feasible is a linkage between continental and Anglo-American approaches?" Proceedings of the First Annual Developments in Discourse Analysis Conference, Georgetown University, February 19, 1995 (in press).

25. See, for example, Lev Vygotsky, *Mind in Society: The Development of Higher Psychological Processes*, Cambridge: Harvard University Press, 1978; M. M. Bakhtin, *Speech Genres and Other Late Essays*, Austin: University of Texas Press, 1986; Michael Holquist, *Bakhtin and His World*, London: Routledge, 1990; Gary Saul Morson, "Who Speaks for Bakhtin?" and Caryl Emerson, "The Outer World and Inner Speech: Bakhtin, Vygotsky, and the Internalization of Language," in G. S. Morson (Ed.), *Bakhtin: Essays and Dialogues on His Work*, Chicago: University of Chicago Press, 1981, pp. 1-20, 21-40; James Wertsch (Ed.), *Culture, Communication, and Cognition: Vygotskian Perspectives*, Cambridge: Cambridge University Press, 1985.

26. See Caryl Emerson, *op cit.*

27. Morson, p. 6.

28. Research Interpretation Session, National Council of Teachers of Mathematics Annual National Conference, New Orleans, April 18, 1991.

29. See, for example, F. Michael Connelly and D. J. Clandinin, *Teachers as Curriculum Planners: Narratives of Experience*, New York: Teachers College Press, 1988; Miriam Ben Peretz, *The Teacher Curriculum Encounter: Freeing Teachers from the Tyranny of Texts*, Albany: SUNY Press, 1990.

30. Lucy Sprague Mitchell, *Young Geographers*, 75th Anniversary Edition. (New York: Bank Street College of Education, 1971), pp. 16-17, originally published, 1934).

31. *Ibid*, p.17.

32. I have written about this possibility with my colleague Deborah Ball in *Investigating Teaching: New Pedagogies and New Technologies for Teacher Education*, New York: Teachers College Press (forthcoming).

CHAPTER VIII

Professional and Subject Matter Knowledge for Teacher Education

LAUREN A. SOSNIAK

What knowledge is of most worth to prospective and practicing teachers? How should we balance and integrate the various components of a teacher education curriculum? What rules, or principles of practice, should govern work with chosen teacher education content? Each of these classic curriculum questions[1] draws us into deliberation about the nature and the place of professional and subject matter knowledge in teacher education.

In examining some of the discussion around subject matter knowledge and professional knowledge, I shall consider themes that have an enduring legacy, having been part of the conversation about teaching and teacher education from the first formal education programs or even before those programs. I shall also consider themes that have emerged as important in the last decade or so, adding new language and new ideas to a long-standing conversation.

Let me acknowledge at the start that in this chapter I will take a narrow view of professional knowledge, restricting it to knowledge, skills and dispositions associated with pedagogy. Of course, professional knowledge today is much broader than that, as one look at the chapter titles in the *Knowledge Base for the Beginning Teacher*[2] will attest. Maynard Reynolds' volume includes, for example, chapters devoted to the sociology of teaching and schooling, politics, legal rights and responsibilities, and so forth. In a broader context than I am considering, professional knowledge would include educational foundations: the development of interpretive, normative and critical perspectives on education.[3] Still, professional knowledge as defined by the theory and practice of pedagogy is an accepted boundary, explicitly and implicitly, historically and in contemporary practice. And it is a boundary that seems appropriate given the range of issues addressed in the other chapters in this yearbook.

Lauren Sosniak is an Associate Professor in the Division of Teacher Education of the College of Education at San Jose State University. She is also the coordinator of graduate programs for her division. Professor Sosniak's research focuses on curriculum enactment and students' experiences with curriculum in and out of school.

One theme running through this chapter will be the historical and ongoing acceptance of the importance of some version of both subject matter knowledge and professional knowledge for teacher education. Frequently, these commonplaces of teacher education have been supported in their most general forms without much attention to or debate about their particulars. Over time we have been willing to add on more coursework in both subject matter and professional knowledge without trying very hard to find ways of condensing, collapsing, reconceptualizing, or deleting some bodies of knowledge in favor of others.

It appears that we may be reaching the end of the line for the "more, better, newer" approach to both subject matter and professional knowledge, at least in preservice teacher education. It is hard to imagine how it could be possible to add more to already overburdened teacher preparation programs. In the final section of this chapter I will offer three possible directions for rethinking what to learn and how to learn it in the course of teacher education. I will suggest that we consider rethinking and redistributing *time* for teacher preparation; making better use of *alternative instructional technologies* for the development of subject matter and professional knowledge; and redeveloping a curriculum for teacher education more consistent with the *aims* we hold for K-12 students in the twenty-first century.

The Commonplaces of Teacher Education

In some fashion, and in some proportion, both subject matter knowledge and professional knowledge always have been part of the curriculum for teacher education. Paul Woodring points out that historically our great teachers learned both how and what to teach from their own teachers. And written advice regarding both content and method was available long before there were special schools for teacher education.[4]

Our early special schools for teacher education, the normal schools of the 1800s, included instruction in both the school subjects and the methods of teaching them. More than a century later, during the 1950s, amid controversy about the nature and quality of teacher preparation programs, both professional knowledge and subject matter knowledge again were proclaimed essential to every sound program.[5]

More recent accounts tell the same story. Judith Lanier and Judith Little reported in the 1980s that

initial teacher education conveys in its broad outlines the appearance of standardization . . . the coursework for prospective teachers is organized into three familiar strands: general education, subject matter concentrations, and pedagogical study.[6]

Also in the 1980s, "reports from professional societies . . . have been consistent in calling for teachers to have both strong (not necessarily broad) content knowledge *and* a better grasp of pedagogy."[7] It appears that both subject matter knowledge and professional knowledge not only have a long history as explicit aspects of teacher education, they also will prevail at least in the near future.

Are professional knowledge and subject matter knowledge equally important to teacher education programs? Often one or the other body of knowledge has received more attention and been given more prominence in preservice and continuing teacher education.

Lee Shulman offers us licensing tests for teacher candidates from the late 1800s that we might use as approximations for early requirements and expectations regarding teachers' knowledge. Studying those examinations, he estimates that "ninety to ninety-five percent of the test is on the content, the subject matter to be taught, or at least on the knowledge base assumed to be needed by teachers, whether or not it is taught directly."[8] The remainder of the questions, only about five to ten percent, asked about the theory and practice of teaching.

By the 1970s and 80s, the emphasis on what teachers need to know seemed to have shifted significantly from subject matter to pedagogical knowledge.[9] But today we find again an emphasis on subject matter that is similar to but not as disproportionate as that described by Shulman with respect to the teacher examinations of the 1800s. As Pamela Grossman and Susan Stodolsky write about this changing balance: "Once, teachers majored in elementary or secondary education. Today, most states require that all teachers, elementary and secondary alike, major in an academic subject."[10]

In California, for example, preservice teachers pursuing either elementary or secondary teaching certification must major in an academic subject. They also must pass a standardized subject matter examination. (Prospective elementary teachers must pass a "multiple subjects" examination.) Until very recently, no similar test for pedagogical knowledge was administered. As I write this chapter, the state is administering for the first time a standardized assessment for the teaching of reading; this assessment is required of candidates for certification in elementary education. Maryland recently has taken an alternative approach to emphasizing pedagogical knowledge; it is requiring four reading methods courses for all teachers working toward state certification.

Linda Darling-Hammond, Arthur Wise and Stephen Klein suggest the need for a different balance, one weighted toward professional knowledge. They base their argument on their interpretation of research demonstrating efficacy of instruction. They summarize a body of work this way:

> . . . subject matter knowledge is a positive influence up to some level of basic competence and familiarity with the subject but is less important thereafter . . . beyond some point, more subject matter courses do not seem to make a difference.
>
> A large number of studies have found positive relationships between education coursework and teacher performance in the classrooms. These relationships are stronger and more consistent than those between subject matter knowledge and classroom performance.[11]

There is no reason to foresee an end in the near future to the seesawing between an emphasis on subject matter knowledge and an emphasis on professional knowledge. There are instances, however, now and in the past, of a melding of professional and subject matter knowledge: academic subjects taught to teacher education candidates in a manner that calls attention to and promotes professional knowledge about teaching, and pedagogy taught in the context of, and sensitive to, the subject matter the candidates expect to teach. Reconceptualizations of subject matter and professional knowledge as two sides of a single coin do not seem to have made a significant impact on typical teacher education curricula. Instead, year after year, from the beginning of formal teacher education, preparation programs have included both components as if the two were distinct; one or the other has prominence at particular times and in particular settings.

Although the inclusion of both professional knowledge and subject matter knowledge for the preparation of teachers appears to be inevitable—historical and enduring—it is not always the focus of much attention. In the last NSSE yearbook on *Teacher Education*,[12] published in 1975, a chapter on performance-based teacher education replaces any explicit discussion of professional and subject matter knowledge, although that chapter says little about what knowledge is important in the performance-based programs.

The idea of teacher education as organized around both subject matter and professional knowledge is so taken for granted that perhaps it does not need to be talked about. Still, despite general agreement about a broad outline for teacher education, what students have an opportunity to learn appears to be "highly unstable and individualistic.

The variation among and within courses and workshops at different institutions, as well as in the same institutions over brief periods of time, achieves almost infinite variety."[13]

Alternative Conceptions of Subject Matter Knowledge

It is easy to say that subject matter knowledge is important in teacher preparation; it is more difficult to be explicit about what subject matter knowledge a teacher needs and how a teacher should acquire that knowledge. Shulman writes:

If teachers are to be certified on the basis of well-grounded judgments and standards, then those standards on which a national board relies must . . . be closely tied to the findings of scholarship in the academic disciplines that form the curriculum (such as English, physics, and history).[14]

Elsewhere Shulman and his colleagues have stated: "We believe . . . that the knowledge of subject matter that is central to teaching is also knowledge that is central to 'knowing' a discipline."[15] In this point of view Shulman represents a group of scholars and state legislators who believe that teacher preparation—and teaching—will be stronger as teachers acquire more discipline-based knowledge.

Those advocating more subject matter knowledge as part of teacher preparation argue from research that routinely finds teachers do not know enough about a discipline to teach it well. For example, the abstract for an article published in the *American Educational Research Journal* on subject matter knowledge and elementary instruction tells a common story from research in this area:

. . . the [fifth grade] teacher's knowledge of functions and graphing was missing several key mathematical ideas and . . . it was not organized in a manner to provide easily accessible, cross-representational understanding of the domain. These limitations were found to relate to a narrowing of his instruction.[16]

How much should teachers know? How much can anyone know? Although increasing teachers' subject matter knowledge is of critical importance to Shulman, he acknowledges the limits we all face as we work to develop content expertise. Reflecting on his own research question, "How does how well you know something relate to how you teach it to someone else?", he says:

. . . very few of us simply know our field deeply or don't know our field deeply. Our fields are too complex for that kind of oversimplification. In fact, we know a real lot about some parts of our fields, and damn little about others, even when we are professors thereof.[17]

We need to ask questions not only about how much a teacher should and can know, but also about who should acquire what types of subject matter knowledge. If, for example, secondary school teachers need to know their subjects well, what exactly is the content they need to learn? Should we abandon the idea of a high school science teacher, and advocate instead that we certify teachers in the more focused areas of physics or biology or chemistry? Should a secondary school history teacher be required to learn American history, European history, Eastern history and so forth, each individually or all in some combined college major? Should we be preparing separately teachers of writing and teachers of literature? What about mathematics? Should we argue for separate licenses for teachers of algebra, geometry, and statistics? And what of elementary teachers: should they be expert in one of the academic disciplines or in all of them? In other words, how much should subject matter knowledge for prospective and practicing teachers be determined by current and historical ways of organizing knowledge in post-secondary education?

There is an especially obvious problem in translating discipline-based knowledge into the elementary school curriculum. It is not at all clear how the subjects we teach in elementary classrooms are or should be related to the academic disciplines. Much to the chagrin of some academics, mathematics has become arithmetic, literature and writing are taught as language arts, history, sociology, anthropology, and psychology have been merged into the social studies. Clearly, elementary school subjects are a far cry from the academic disciplines as they are presented at the post-secondary level. If the current transformations of academic disciplines in elementary curricula are wrong, what should be the school subjects for children of 7 or 8 or 9 years of age? Can elementary teachers be well prepared to teach all school subjects? Should they be? All of these questions are important because they lead to decisions about what adults need to know in order to be well-prepared for teaching in elementary and secondary schools.

Of course, both the academic disciplines and their counterparts in K-12 curricula are social constructions. We have created ways of organizing knowledge, and ways of studying and teaching, because the order we create aids us in various ways. Is there any good reason to constrain the possibilities of K-12 education because the order created for "disciplines of knowledge" at the post-secondary level is useful at that level? Is there any good reason to believe that in-depth study of the post-secondary disciplines is the best possible preparation for persons who will teach school subjects at elementary and secondary levels? No consensus has yet been reached, only a long-standing disagreement between those who argue for discipline-based content knowledge and others who emphasize alternative constructions of knowledge.

Elementary education, in particular, does not seem to be better for an emphasis on separate subjects than it would be if it were organized around integrated work on issues of importance to youth and adults in contemporary society. However, curricula of the latter sort, like the Virginia State Curriculum program of the 1930s based on processes of life, or the 1950s program based on persistent life situations (e.g., satisfying emotional and social needs; dealing with physical phenomena; using technological resources) were short lived.[18]

In recent years the argument has been made that even at the secondary level the teaching of separate school subjects, with an emphasis on the academic disciplines, may not be what would serve our students and our society best.[19] The Coalition of Essential Schools includes among its guiding principles that schools should aim to help students learn to use their minds well and master a limited number of centrally important skills and areas of knowledge. The Coalition is explicit:

While these skills and areas will, to varying degrees, reflect the traditional academic disciplines, the program's design should be shaped by the intellectual and imaginative powers and competencies that students need, rather than necessarily by "subjects" as conventionally defined.[20]

Similarly, Susan Stodolsky argues that an orientation around academic disciplines may not be for the best:

Disciplinary lines seem to insulate those who specialize in the teaching of school subjects as much as they do practitioners of the parent disciplines. Teachers seem to be trained to teach each subject without regard to their skills in other fields of teaching. It might help to alter this usual circumstance.[21]

This is not merely an academic conversation. Teachers working with the Coalition of Essential Schools, teachers telling tales of changing practice, reportedly find themselves questioning and undoing long-standing practices such as the domination by disciplines of the curriculum in secondary schools. "They came to believe that connections between the disciplines were more potent than a single-minded focus on their own discipline."[22]

Even if there were a compelling argument for emphasizing the academic disciplines in our K-12 curriculum, it is not clear which disciplines would be most valuable to promote. Ian Westbury, writing about general education in the secondary schools, suggests that if society's values were to define the curriculum, surely the arts would have a larger place in the curriculum than mathematics or the sciences. He notes, for example:

There were more artists and commercial artists employed in Illinois in 1982 than there were civil engineers, mathematicians, or social scientists, and more musicians than chemists, psychologists, and hospital social workers. Moreover, nationwide one of every four adult Americans plays a musical instrument and secures, one can assume, pleasure in their playing that could only be enhanced by formal experience in school. In other words, like the mythical man from Mars, one can only wonder, in light of the simple-minded concern for what the tasks of general education might be, why the core curriculum is as it is.[23]

Changes in the discipline-based orientation toward K-12 teaching and toward decisions about worthwhile teacher knowledge would require change not only for teacher preparation and continuing education, but for the entire educational enterprise. After all, the subject matter knowledge of our elementary and secondary teachers is acquired almost wholly outside teacher preparation programs. It is acquired as part of undergraduate education, as part of teachers' own elementary and secondary education, and as part of their lives in homes and communities where most people think of schooling as discipline-based.

At the very least, colleges and universities would have to alter significantly their requirements for various academic majors and minors—as these signposts of work with subject matter typically satisfy subject matter requirements for admission to teacher preparation programs and for certification. There are examples of the sort of changes that might be required at the university level to be consistent with an orientation toward subject matter knowledge as suggested by the Coalition of Essential Schools, among others. Consider, for example, categories of knowledge like those of Southern Illinois University's program of general education: "Man's physical environment and biological inheritance," "Man's social inheritance and social responsibilities," "Man's insights and appreciations," "Organization and communication of ideas," and "Health and physical development." Westbury argues that such "'words' communicate intentions and purposes in ways that terms like 'science,' the 'social sciences,' and 'humanities' do not and are closer to the spirit of general education, and the needs of mass school, than our present century-old framework of 'disciplines' or subjects."[24] But education of this sort at the post-secondary level or in K-12 classrooms is the exception rather than the rule. Teacher education programs that might emphasize an approach to content knowledge like this one would be working against the grain of the entire education enterprise, including educational publishing and supplementary educational programs offered outside of the K-12 system.

Ultimately, of course, reliance on the academic disciplines for the K-12 curriculum, and then for a teacher preparation curriculum, is essentially a conservative approach, one that links us tightly with the past and makes change difficult. After all, we never create a new curriculum; all we can do is revise a curriculum that has a long history as part of our lives and part of our understanding of what counts as school. The history of academic disciplines and school subjects makes it difficult for us to appreciate alternative structures for the K-12 school curriculum and for the curriculum for teacher preparation. Many changes require that we dismantle something we know well, for the promise of something we may not even be able to fully envision.

Alternative Conceptions of Professional Knowledge

It is just as difficult to be explicit about what professional knowledge a teacher needs and how a teacher should acquire that knowledge. (As I noted at the start of the chapter, I have chosen to limit "professional knowledge" to the body of knowledge associated with pedagogy.) To begin with, professional knowledge has expanded in recent years, demanding a greater share of teacher preparation programs. There is more to know in traditional areas of professional knowledge, and there are more areas of knowledge that now are considered important for the professional education of teachers.

Where once something known as "methods of instruction" was much of the body of professional knowledge, now methods of instruction appear to be but a small part of a much larger body of knowledge, skills and dispositions associated with the profession of teaching. Darling-Hammond and her co-authors speak of knowledge acquired "in specialized education courses" as "focused on teaching, learning, and child development."[25] They are conservative in their definition compared with the chapters Reynolds includes in the *Knowledge Base for the Beginning Teacher*. Reynolds includes, for example, chapters about the school district, legal rights and responsiblities of public school teachers, and the ethical dimension of teaching.

Holding essentially to professional knowledge as bounded by pedagogical study makes no less obvious what counts as professional knowledge. One of the tensions in recent years has been between pedagogical knowledge that is broadly generalizable and pedagogical knowledge that is subject- and situation-specific. For example, is "wait time" important pedagogical knowledge or is it meaningless without details about what a teacher might be waiting for and in what situations it might make sense to wait?

Publishers of textbooks for teacher education courses appear to hedge their bets, providing texts that are oriented to either of these trends. There are, for example, general methods texts and subject-specific methods texts. I am unaware of any research that might help us understand what decisions faculty in different programs make about textbooks, or how they make these decisions.

Professional journals also seem willing to support both pedagogical knowledge that intends to be broadly generalizable as well as pedagogical knowledge that intends to be subject- or situation-specific. For the moment, though, supporters of subject-specific and situated knowledge appear to dominate the discussion in professional journals and textbooks.

Although methods classes long have been taught in relation to particular school subjects (e.g., methods of instruction in the social studies), discussions centered on subject-specific pedagogy typically derive from Shulman's 1985 presidential address to the American Educational Research Association.[26] In that address, Shulman identified pedagogical content knowledge as, "the particular form of content knowledge that embodies the aspects of content most germane to its teachability." He continued:

Within the category of pedagogical content knowledge I include, for the most regularly taught topics in one's subject area, the most useful forms of representation of those ideas, the most powerful analogies, illustrations, examples, explanations, and demonstrations—in a word, the ways of representing and formulating the subject that makes it comprehensible to others. Since there are no single most powerful forms of representation, the teacher must have at hand a veritable armamentarium of alternative forms of representation, some of which derive from research whereas others originate in the wisdom of practice.[27]

Apparently, Shulman initially conceived of pedagogical content knowledge as emphasizing subject matter and including careful attention to the representation and translation of subject matter in the course of teaching and learning. Continuing work with the idea of pedagogical content knowledge by Shulman and others seems to have moved it to more of an emphasis on pedagogy or professional knowledge and less of an emphasis on subject matter. So, for example, in 1987 Shulman identified pedagogical content knowledge as "that special amalgam of content and pedagogy that is uniquely the province of teachers, their own special form of professional understanding."[28] Shulman added: "Pedagogical content knowledge is the category most likely to distinguish the understanding of the content specialist from that of the pedagogue."[29]

Since Shulman's presentations of pedagogical content knowledge, a number of his students and other educational researchers have explored the concept in theory and practice and made it a much talked-about aspect of professional knowledge. The conversation has not yet congealed around a set of common understandings and findings. As Reynolds writes:

Of all the domains of teacher understandings, content-specific pedagogy is both the most elusive and the most discussed in the recent press. Each of the scholars who writes about content-specific pedagogy presents a definition that is slightly different from the others.[30]

Debates between general and generalizable professional knowledge versus subject- and situation-specific professional knowledge are only part of the dilemma of coming to terms with professional knowledge today. Another prominent concern has been raised by those who ask not merely what knowledge counts but also *whose* knowledge counts as professional knowledge.

Here the debate is mainly between professional knowledge derived from traditional research and that derived from the experience of teaching ("wisdom of practice," according to Shulman.) At first glance the argument seems to be about whose knowledge is of most worth: that of a researcher external to a teaching situation, or that of a teacher derived from experience.[31] But that only begins to touch the surface of the debate. There is also the question of how the knowledge is generated. Is it generated by researchers, even if it is built upon extensive work with teachers about teacher understandings? Or is it generated by teachers for teachers, without researcher involvement of any sort? It is not clear why "wisdom of practice" cannot be research-based knowledge; often, though, it seems as if "wisdom of practice" is distinguished expressly from research-based work.

Finally, there is the question of how professional knowledge is best acquired by students of teaching. Coursework in departments, schools and colleges of education is, of course, one alternative. My own experience and that of colleagues across the country suggest that the teaching of professional knowledge has grown in priority, at least in research institutions where such instruction used to take a back seat to scholarly productivity. Faculty have engaged in a variety of informal and formal efforts to make pedagogical instruction more powerful. Still there is the ever-present problem (in all professions apparently) of practitioners devaluing the pedagogical instruction they receive in professional schools.[32]

In recent years, two alternatives have become more talked about, if not necessarily more prominent, in teacher education programs. On one hand, there has been discussion about the power of arts and sciences departments for imparting simultaneously both substantive content and pedagogical technique. On the other hand, organizations like the Holmes Partnership have argued for removing pedagogical studies from college or university settings and supporting such studies in the context of Professional Development Schools.[33]

Practical efforts at developing these alternative forms of helping teachers and future teachers acquire pedagogical knowledge are still in early stages of development. Although discussion of Professional Development Schools has been prominent, to date there does not seem to be consensus about the nature of such arrangements or their effects on teachers and students.

Developing pedagogical knowledge and skill in the context of either coursework in the arts and sciences or work in Professional Development Schools requires the collaboration of individuals and institutions that have historically operated with much independence from each other. Developing incentives for collaboration and the mechanisms for working across significantly different cultures, poses as important a problem as developing innovative approaches to instruction in pedagogy through general education or Professional Development Schools.

What the Future Holds

Common sense decrees that both content knowledge and professional knowledge are essential to a teacher's education. What is not so obvious is how we should conceptualize them, how we should help beginning teachers to acquire them, or what we should expect of beginning and more experienced teachers. It seems pretty certain that some rethinking is necessary now or will be necessary in the near future.

The increasing breadth and depth of knowledge in both of these areas has been recognized but apparently has not yet led to the rethinking of courses and programs. Instead, we appear to have been willing to add prerequisites, program courses, and years of study to teacher preparation. This pattern of an increasingly complex course of action is reminiscent of two other educational programs of theory development and practical action that were once exciting but eventually became sobering.

Consider, for example, the effort, following the publication of the *Taxonomy of Educational Objectives*,[34] to become increasingly more specific in identifying and describing educational objectives. As I have written elsewhere:

Educational objectives were replaced by "instructional" objectives; these were transformed later into "behavioral" or "performance" objectives. Each shift in terminology was associated with more precise details regarding how objectives should be written and why they should be written as described. The shift in terminology also typically signaled the need for increasing numbers of carefully worded objectives to specify the goals that had been indicated earlier by a smaller number of more loosely worded intentions. In this regard, the behavioral objectives movement is said to have collapsed under its own weight.[35]

Robert Donmoyer tells a similar story about the research program on aptitude treatment interaction. What was once a promising effort to match instruction with particular learning styles eventually became a lesson in the limits of specificity for curriculum and instruction. Donmoyer cites Lee Cronbach, the leader in this large research effort, as finding himself in "a hall of mirrors that extends to infinity" as the research program became more and more detailed and specific.[36] While many educators and informed laymen alike may worry about loosely worded or general understandings about teaching and learning, over-specification (even if it seems consistent with the complexity of human beings) appears to be inconsistent with what is possible and desirable in teaching and teacher education.

Work on pedagogical content knowledge or subject-specific instruction thus seems likely to find itself at the same dead end as efforts to become increasingly more precise and specific about educational objectives or aptitude treatment interactions.[37] The research can proceed forever, of course, as scholars continue to identify slices of content knowledge to investigate. Its meaning for practice, however, likely will become less significant as the studies become overly specific and reach levels of detail that are not responsive to the daily work of teaching.

Perhaps what might help teachers and teacher educators much more than increasingly detailed work on subject-specific pedagogy would be a small number of big subject-specific ideas or concepts, well articulated and well elaborated, that have broad consequences for teaching and learning. The concept of place value, for example, might be a worthy candidate for mathematics educators to develop, as it has meaningful potential across the grades (e.g., from counting to work with exponents). So far, educators across the disciplines who have been advocating teaching toward a small number of big ideas have not yet been able to construct and promote lists of such ideas (small in number and big in importance) that are generally well accepted.

The continuing *addition* of subject matter knowledge and professional knowledge to teacher education programs would seem to be leading to a collapse of teacher education as we know it. The costs of earning teacher certification will soon outweigh the incentives for pursuing this work (if they don't already). What we face is a significant curriculum problem: how do we build teacher education programs that account for the increasing bodies of subject matter and professional knowledge without merely adding more and more pieces to a program each year and each decade?

Let me elaborate on three avenues for investigation I proposed at the outset: rethinking and redistributing *time* allotted to teacher preparation; making better use of *alternative instructional technologies* for the development of subject matter and professional knowledge; and redeveloping a curriculum for teacher education consistent with the *aims* we hold for K-12 students in the twenty-first century.

First, let us consider the distribution of the curriculum over time in the process of learning to teach. There does not appear to be any good reason to assume that teacher education needs to be "complete" prior to beginning a teaching career, or even within the first few years of teaching. Some of what we aim to teach in preservice teacher education might be best postponed until after initial preparation and practice. In fact, currently in California, for example, there is a strong movement toward systematic support and assessment programs for first year teachers. New York State is on the verge of requiring continuing education over the course of a teacher's career. At the moment, these efforts involve adding to rather than reconceptualizing teacher preparation, but as this movement takes hold, it certainly should create opportunities for rethinking the preservice and continuing education continuum.

How might we make decisions about what to move and when to introduce it? Typically, claims are made about "developmentally appropriate" learning and what beginning teachers are prepared to handle or are immediately concerned about.[38] Other possibilities for deliberation might be just as valuable. For example, we might ask about what is cost effective and/or what is generative for long-term teaching careers.

What knowledge would be most important for people who were going to teach only one or two years; what knowledge would be most important for the development of a teaching career in years three through eight; what knowledge would be most important for teachers who continue in their careers for fifteen or more years?

Or we might deliberate about what knowledge must be taught explicitly versus what knowledge is likely to be learned on the job. Deborah Ball and G. Williamson McDiarmid write: "The experience of coming to understand, for example, the division of fractions, or the causes of the American Civil War, or the meaning of 'In a Station at the Metro' while actually teaching is probably fairly common."[39] How much of the subject matter knowledge that teachers need to teach can be acquired in its richest sense in the context of preparing for instruction and then teaching?

Rethinking the distribution of curriculum over time in the process of learning to teach would allow for *more* growth in both content and pedagogy. Perhaps more important, it would allow for a *redistribution* of professional and subject matter education. A redistribution could take into account what may be developmentally important in helping more beginning teachers stay longer with careers in education. A redistribution also could provide support for increasing the understanding and skill that comes from teachers' learning on the job. Perhaps most interesting, a redistribution of teacher education across the span of a teacher's career could help to develop a cadre of teachers who share current subject matter and professional knowledge irrespective of when they did their initial teacher preparation and what policies and practices were prominent at that time.

The second avenue for investigation that I am proposing is that we make better use of alternative instructional technologies for the development of subject matter and professional knowledge. In this category we can consider the Internet and other tools of distance learning. These technologies would support spreading teacher preparation over time, with teachers working and living in school districts far from colleges of education. At the least, the Internet or other distance learning technologies could allow for initial exposure to important concepts and practices, exposure that could be developed later, and over time, in the company of peers and instructors from universities or school districts. And, of course, the Internet is useful now to students who are on campus on a regular basis.

Less technical alternatives may be even more valuable. Consider, for example, the power of the National Council of Teachers of Mathematics

Standards[40] for generating teacher study groups and shared conversation within and across school districts and states. National (not federal) texts like these—small in number, big in content, moderate in size, promoted and supported by leading educators and informed laymen— could serve as powerful vehicles for the continuing development of both subject matter and professional knowledge.

These texts would allow teachers to learn individually as well as in study groups (self-created or created by school districts or colleges of education). These texts (and related professional journals) could provide a community of practice for teachers who do not find or are not comfortable with study groups in their immediate vicinity. If teachers were required by their districts or their states to belong to one or more such communities of professional practice and growth, and required regularly to describe the impact of their membership in one or more of these communities on their work in the classroom, continuous development of professional and subject matter knowledge throughout a teacher's career could become a reality. Further, this form of teacher education would support the work of teachers as "honest brokers between the ideas, skills, and dispositions contained in national and state curriculum frameworks, and the specific conditions, understandings, and interests of students, schools, and communities."[41]

The third avenue for investigation that I propose is that we consider redeveloping a curriculum for teacher education more consistent with what we value and less beholden to an historical competition between subject matter knowledge and professional knowledge for time in the curriculum. To what extent is the acquisition of discipline-based knowledge one of the most important or prominent aims of K-12 education? If we hold other aims equally, or even more strongly, as I believe that many of us do, then teacher preparation needs to be consistent with our best hopes for K-12 education.

When we develop teacher education curricula largely around subject matter knowledge and its representations, we assume the aims of K-12 schools to be efficient and effective communication of content knowledge, understandings, and skill. If the acquisition of subject matter knowledge and skill in the most efficient and effective manner is *not* the only or the most important aim for public education, then teacher preparation programs are at best partial and at worst headed in the wrong direction. Ralph Tyler has suggested: "The most generally accepted goal of American education is to help all young people learn the attitudes, knowledge, skills, and habits necessary for citizens who are to participate intelligently in the responsibilities of a democratic society."[42] If this is an acceptable statement of the purposes of K-12 education, one can imagine very different ideas and practices regarding professional and subject matter knowledge for teacher preparation than we typically hold today. Examples I provided earlier—from Westbury, regarding Southern Illinois University's program of general education, and of curricula based on persistent life situations—begin to suggest possibilities for K-12 curricula and for relevant teacher education programs that respond more strongly to the aims Tyler voices than to the more traditional aim of acquiring discipline-based knowledge.

A potentially helpful mechanism for rethinking teacher education curriculum is the use of principles like those the Coalition of Essential Schools demonstrates in its reform efforts.[43] Principles serve as a "platform"[44] of sorts, or a "value-position . . . something more basic and stable than a list of objectives."[45] Statements of principles provide an intermediary vantage point from which curriculum developers are helped to think about the goals they truly want to aim toward, the activities that might serve well in support of those objectives, and the relationships between goals and activities. Principles point to both the theory that guides us and the practice that follows logically. Principles make explicit what too often is hidden in the titles of courses, in the particulars of assigned (and unassigned) readings, in the focus of class sessions, in the manner in which content is communicated.

Faculty could use a small number of important principles to define their teacher education programs for themselves and for their students. Across the country or a state or even a county, we may find teacher education programs aligned with different sets of principles: this could reflect a natural variation in values, and it could provide an opportunity for examining thoughtfully the means and the ends of alternative programs for teacher education.

Attention to principles serves as a powerful reminder of the values underlying, or embedded in, all curriculum decisions. In other words, decisions about the amount and nature of subject matter and professional preparation in teacher education are not merely technical decisions and are not amenable simply to empirical research and demonstration. Decisions about what knowledge is of most worth for teacher education, about how we should balance and integrate the various components of a preservice teacher education curriculum, and about what rules or principles of practice should determine the content of teacher education are decisions about what we value and how we believe we can best serve those values. When we become more explicit about our values for teachers and teaching, and about the role of values in making decisions about curriculum, perhaps we will also be able to become more inventive in working with the enduring issue of defining professional and subject matter knowledge for teacher education.

NOTES

1. Herbert M. Kliebard, "Systematic curriculum development, 1890-1959," in *Values Conflicts and Curriculum Issues*, eds. Jon Schaffarzick and Gary Sykes (Berkeley: McCutchan, 1979).

2. Maynard C. Reynolds (Editor), *Knowledge Base for the Beginning Teacher* (Oxford: Pergamon Press, 1989).

3. Kathryn M. Borman, "Foundations of Education in Teacher Education," in *Handbook of Research on Teacher Education*, ed. W. Robert Houston (New York, Macmillan, 1990). Nowadays, Borman notes, the majority of teacher education students are required to take only one course devoted to foundations, and recent efforts to change teacher education, including the work of both the Holmes Partnership and the Carnegie Forum on Education and the Economy, largely ignore foundations in their discussions of proposed changes.

4. Paul Woodring, "The Development of Teacher Education," in *Teacher Education*, Seventy-fourth Yearbook of the National Society for the Study of Education, Part II, ed. Kevin Ryan (Chicago: University of Chicago Press, 1975).

5. Ibid., p. 19.

6. Judith E. Lanier and Judith W. Little, "Research on Teacher Education," in *Handbook of Research on Teaching*, 3rd ed., ed. Merlin C. Wittrock (New York: Macmillan Publishing Company, 1986), p. 546.

7. David Jenness, "National Concerns and Goals as Viewed On-Site," in *Teacher Preparation Archives: Case studies of NSF-Funded Middle School Science and Mathematics Teacher Preparation Projects*, eds. Robert Stake et. al. (Urbana: Center for Instructional Research and College of Education, 1993), p. 239.

8. Lee S. Shulman, "Those Who Understand: Knowledge Growth in Teaching," *Educational Researcher*, 15, no. 2 (1986): p. 5.

9. Ibid.

10. Pamela L. Grossman and Susan S. Stodolsky, "Considerations of Content and the Circumstances of Secondary School Teaching," in *Review of Research in Education*, 20, ed. Linda Darling-Hammond (Washington: American Educational Research Association, 1994), p. 179.

11. Linda Darling-Hammond, Arthur E. Wise, and Stephen P. Klein, *A License to Teach: Building a Profession for 21st-century Schools* (Boulder: Westview Press, 1995), p. 24.

12. Kevin Ryan (Editor), *Teacher Education*, Seventy-fourth Yearbook of the National Society for the Study of Education, Part II (Chicago: University of Chicago Press, 1975).

13. Lanier and Little, "Research on Teacher Education," p. 546.

14. Lee S. Shulman, "Knowledge and Teaching: Foundations of the New Reform," *Harvard Educational Review*, 57, no. 1 (1987): p. 5.

15. Pamela L. Grossman, Suzanne M. Wilson, and Lee S. Shulman, "Teachers of Substance: Subject Matter Knowledge for Teaching," in *Knowledge Base for the Beginning Teacher*, ed. Maynard C. Reynolds (Oxford: Pergamon Press, 1989), p. 24.

16. Mary Kay Stein, Juliet A. Baxter, and Gaea Leinhardt, "Subject-matter Knowledge and Elementary Instruction: A Case from Functions and Graphing," *American Educational Research Journal*, 27, no. 4 (1990): p. 639.

17. Lee S. Shulman, "Aristotle Had it Right: On Knowledge and Pedagogy," Occasional Paper #4. (East Lansing, MI: The Holmes Group, 1990), p. 3.

18. Hilda Taba, *Curriculum Development: Theory and Practice* (New York: Harcourt, Brace and World, 1962).

19. See, for example, Theodore R. Sizer, *Horace's School: Redesigning the American High School* (Boston: Houghton Mifflin, 1992), or Theodore R. Sizer, *Horace's Compromise: The Dilemma of the American High School* (Boston: Houghton Mifflin, 1984).

20. Patricia A. Wasley, *Stirring the Chalkdust: Tales of Teachers Changing Classroom Practice* (New York: Teachers College Press, 1994), p. 5.

21. Susan S. Stodolsky, *The Subject Matters: Classroom Activity in Math and Social Studies* (Chicago: University of Chicago Press, 1988), p. 132.

22. Wasley, *Stirring the Chalkdust*, p. 189.

23. Ian Westbury, "Who Can Be Taught What? General Education in the Secondary School," in *Cultural Literacy and the Idea of General Education:* Eighty-seventh Yearbook of the National Society for the Study of Education, Part II, eds. Ian Westbury and Alan C. Purves (Chicago: University of Chicago Press, 1988), p. 180.

24. Ibid., pp. 194-195.

25. Darling-Hammond, Wise and Klein, *A License to Teach*, p. 22.

26. Shulman, "Those Who Understand: Knowledge Growth in Teaching," p. 5.

27. Ibid., p. 9.

28. Shulman, "Knowledge and Teaching: Foundations of the New Reform," p. 8.

29. Ibid.

30. Reynolds, *Knowledge Base for the Beginning Teacher*, p. 5.

31. See, for example, F. L. Elbaz, *Teacher Thinking: A Study of Practical Knowledge* (London: Croom Helm, 1983).

32. Lee S. Shulman, "Theory, Practice, and the Education of Professionals," *Elementary School Journal*, 98, no. 5 (1998).

33. See, for example, The Holmes Group, *Tomorrow's Schools: Principles for the Design of Professional Development Schools* (East Lansing, MI: The Holmes Group, 1990).

34. Benjamin S. Bloom et al., *Taxonomy of Educational Objectives, The Classification of Educational Goals, Handbook I: Cognitive Domain* (New York: David McKay, 1956).

35. Lauren A. Sosniak, "The Taxonomy, Curriculum, and Their Relations," in *Bloom's Taxonomy: A Forty-year Retrospective*, Ninety-third Yearbook of the National Society for the Study of Education, Part II, eds. Lorin Anderson and Lauren Sosniak (Chicago: University of Chicago Press, 1994), pp. 117-118.

36. Robert Donmoyer, "Theory, Practice, and the Double-edged Problem of Idiosyncrasy," *Journal of Curriculum and Supervision* 4, no. 3 (1989): pp. 257-270.

37. Interestingly, Shulman has compared work in the area of aptitude treatment interaction studies with his developing agenda of work on the school subjects. See Shulman, Lee S. "The psychology of school subjects: A premature obituary?" *Journal of Research in Science Teaching* 11, no. 4 (1974): pp. 319-339.

38. For a summary of this work, see Paul R. Burden, "Teacher Development," in *Handbook of Research on Teacher Education*, ed. W. Robert Houston (New York: Macmillan, 1990).

39. Deborah Loewenberg Ball and G. Williamson McDiarmid, "The Subject-Matter Preparation of Teachers," in *Handbook of Research on Teacher Education*, ed. W. Robert Houston (New York: Macmillan, 1990).

40. See, for example, National Council of Teachers of Mathematics, *Curriculum and Evaluation Standards for School Mathematics* (Reston, VA: National Council of Teachers of Mathematics, 1989).

41. Lee S. Shulman, "Conclusion," in *Detachment and Concern: Conversations in the Philosophy of Teaching and Teacher Education*, eds. Margaret Buchmann and Robert E. Floden (New York: Teachers College Press, 1993), p. 260.

42. Ralph W. Tyler, "Progress in Dealing with Curriculum Problems," in *Critical Issues in Curriculum*, Eighty-seventh Yearbook of the National Society for the Study of Education, Part I, ed. Laurel N. Tanner (Chicago: University of Chicago Press, 1988), p. 267.

43. See, for example, Appendix A in Sizer, *Horace's School*.

44. Decker Walker, "A Naturalistic Model for Curriculum Development," *School Review*, 80 (1971): p. 51-65.

45. William A. L. Blyth, "One Development Project's Awkward Thinking about Objectives," *Journal of Curriculum Studies* 6, no. 2 (1975): pp. 99-111.

CHAPTER IX

Caring and Competence

NEL NODDINGS

It is sometimes suggested that caring and competence are somehow in opposition or, even if they are not, that teacher education can address only academic competence. Caring, from this perspective, is a virtue naturally possessed by some teacher candidates, not a type of relationship that can be promoted by sound practices in teacher education and supervision. After brief analyses of caring and competence in teaching, this chapter addresses two large domains of competence in which teacher education may be failing to prepare its candidates adequately. The first is the domain of subject matter considered from the perspective of students' needs; the second is the domain of moral life and civility in classrooms. Teacher effectiveness in both of these domains requires the establishment of caring relations and a high level of competence.

Caring

There are two main ways in which "caring" is used today. In everyday language, it usually refers to a broad virtue or constellation of admirable qualities belonging to an individual or group. For example, we say, "He is a caring person," "They are a caring family," or "Nurses are more caring than doctors." In all of these expressions, we credit an individual or group with *caring* in much the same way we might credit them with honesty, decency, or loyalty. *Caring* is a virtue or set of virtues.

Not only does common language encourage us to construe caring as a virtue; traditional philosophy does also. The major moral orientations have long been described as deontological (duty-based), teleological (consequence-based), or virtue-based. Thus, when feminist philosophers began to write seriously about caring as a moral orientation, it is not surprising that other philosophers (and even some writing on caring) decided that, since caring was neither deontological nor

Nel Noddings is the Lee L. Jacks Professor of Child Education at Stanford University and is affiliated also with Teachers College, Columbia University.

teleological (although it exhibits qualities of both), it must—by elimination—fall into virtue theory. But this is a mistake.

A more theoretically powerful use of caring is relational. We need not discard the virtue use. Indeed, we have to recognize that the word "caring" is regularly used to refer to a virtue, and we will find many occasions on which to use it that way even in a relational framework. When we have established what it means for a relation to be properly called caring, we will be able to say that a "caring teacher" is one who quite regularly establishes caring relations over a broad range of individuals, groups, and situations. Thus there is clearly a form of competence involved here, and such teachers must possess a set of qualities that we rightly call virtues or excellences. But we cannot begin by describing these. We must first analyze the caring relation to see what it requires.

There are, minimally, two elements in a caring relation (A,B)—a carer (A) and a recipient of care or one who is cared-for (B). Each contributes to the relation in a distinctive way. Of course, relations may be represented as brief encounters or as long sequences of encounters over time. To make the basic definitions clear, let's concentrate on the encounter.

In an encounter that may rightly be described as a caring relation, what may be said of the first element or carer? First, by reflecting on our consciousness in such situations, we know that the carer is attentive or receptive to the cared-for.[1] When we care, we listen openly without laying on structures activated by our own needs and desires. Simone Weil comments on this way of meeting the other:

This way of looking is first of all attentive. The soul empties itself of all its own contents in order to receive the being it is looking at, just as he is, in all his truth. Only he who is capable of attention can do this.[2]

Weil's remarks capture a familiar experience. In a caring encounter, we put aside (temporarily) our own interests and immediate concerns.

Next, if the relation is to be one of caring *now* for *this* one who addresses us, our motive energy must begin to flow toward the other and his or her needs. We feel our own needs and purposes receding (however briefly), and we want to help or share in the experience described. I have called this "motivational displacement." Receptivity and motivational displacement always mark the consciousness of carers in caring relations, but their presence does not tell us what carers will actually do. What is done depends on the situation, on what is requested, and what the carer is capable of doing.

Whatever is done, however, must be recognized (explicitly or implicitly) by the cared-for as an act of caring. Sometimes, the acknowledgment of the cared-for is seen directly in a verbal thank-you, a smile, a nod, a handshake, or a hug. Other times, it is conveyed by the clear improvement in the cared-for's condition: the patient is no longer in pain, the infant relaxes and sleeps, the student finishes a problem successfully, the traveler moves off in the right direction. If carer and cared-for are in a long-term relationship, the cared-for's contribution becomes more obvious. Milton Mayeroff writes of such relations: "To care for another person, in the most significant sense, is to help him grow and actualize himself."[3] The cared-for's contribution is made, in part, by his or her own growth.

In formal terms, then, we may say that a relation (A,B) is a *caring relation* if and only if:

1. A, the carer
    a.) is nonselectively attentive, receptive, to B
    b.) experiences and exhibits motivational displacement
2. B, the cared-for, acknowledges that A cares.

Why is this relational analysis of caring more powerful than the description of caring as a virtue? One great strength is that it forces us to look at both parties. We can't evaluate a relation or encounter as caring simply on the basis of acts performed by the carer or of intentions proclaimed by the carer. Clear-eyed observation of the world reminds us that cruel, thoughtless, and clumsy acts are often performed by people who claim to care. The sort of theory to be avoided is one that directs our attention to the carer as an isolated agent, the sort that prompts a list of caring behaviors or tries to describe a caring attitude that can be discerned without looking at the cared-for. Second, even when the relation fails to be one of caring, we can still credit a carer with trying to care, and we might draw heavily on virtue theory in deciding whether this credit is due. But, more important, when the relation fails to be one of caring because the cared-for denies that he or she has been cared for, we must probe more deeply. Is the carer at fault? Is the cared-for selfish and obtuse? Or is the situation itself so uncongenial that it is virtually impossible for the carer's efforts to be completed successfully? A relational analysis is thus more accurately attuned than is the virtue approach to the complexity of real human relationships.

At least one more advantage of a relational analysis should be mentioned. When we ourselves, as people who want to care, fail to establish a caring relationship or find such a relation weakening, we are pressed to find out why. We cannot sit back and rest on our good intentions and rule-abiding behavior. Rather, we must use the feedback—positive or negative—that comes from the cared-for to monitor our competence as carers. We may occasionally be too hard on ourselves, and that is a definite risk. To lessen it, we should remember to scrutinize the situation as carefully as our own behavior. This analytic competence becomes part of what it means to care in the virtue sense.

The relational perspective has already generated interesting empirical studies. In education, such studies ask students to describe caring teachers.[4] They ask students to tell researchers when they have felt cared for by teachers and when they have felt caring to be absent. In an alternative method, researchers act as "caring jurors" and make judgments on the basis of observing what teachers do and how students respond. Both approaches acknowledge the relational nature of caring by looking at the cared-for as well as the carer.

We can make some useful generalizations about caring teachers—teachers who regularly establish caring relations. They are respectful toward students, have fair rules that they do not apply rigidly, create safe emotional environments, and give personal attention to students who need it.[5] Sometimes professional (subject matter) competence is named as a form of caring, but students often do not recognize their own need for such competence in their teachers.

Where we can make dependable generalizations, we should follow up by demonstrating these behaviors and attitudes in teacher education. We should treat our own students with respect, make it safe to question and to err, modify our rules to meet individual circumstances, and give personal attention when it is requested explicitly or implicitly by the student's behavior. But we must also respond to inferred needs—those needs that we as adults conclude students have although they show no signs of recognizing them and may even deny having them. This complicates matters further. What is an inferred need? When do students have needs that they fail to articulate or even recognize?

Identifying such needs is a risky business, but caring teachers have to try. Students may not realize that they need to make connections between the discipline under study and other disciplines. Some may, in fact, not need such connections, but pedagogical experience suggests that many will profit from them. It seems clear that all students can profit from connecting academic subject matter to existential questions: What is the meaning of life? How should I live? What does it mean to love? How should I look at death? It also seems to many of us that students need to have their political consciousness raised.

There is no way they can express this need directly because, by definition, they are not aware of this set of needs. An especially important
inferred need is the one for competence in a given subject matter.
Young students often see no reason why they should learn certain
material. The caring teacher should worry about this. Is the material
really so important that students should become aware of their need
for it? Or is this a time to politicize the classroom and help students to
understand the gate-keeping function of certain studies? Responding
to inferred needs requires great sensitivity and a willingness to back
off when pressing forward is clearly impeding the satisfaction of mutually recognized needs. The identification and analysis of needs and
modes of response to them all require considerable competence.

Competence

Three decades ago, many scholars were interested in a distinction
between *competence* and *performance*, and competence theories directed
much of the work in psycholinguistics and developmental psychology.[6]
Competence was used to describe the capabilities of an idealized speaker/
hearer in linguistics and of a thinker in stage theories of mental development. Errors made by native speakers of a language or by thinkers
in everyday logic were said to be *performance* errors. The idea was that
there was nothing wrong with the underlying mental machinery that
generates language or logic in such cases but simply that people make
errors. Misunderstanding the theoretical distinction, some educators
attempted to strengthen competence directly by teaching the various
transformations described in transformational grammar. Others,
somewhat more realistically, tried to hasten mental development by
introducing students to tasks a bit ahead of their measured stage.
Some of these attempts strike us now as ludicrous; others retain a
degree of respectability—as in the use of Kohlbergian dilemmas in
moral education.

While competence theorists generated hypotheses to be tested empirically, some educational theorists warned against mixing the language of competence with that of performance. Advocates of behavioral objectives advised teachers not to state objectives in terms of what
students "will be able" to do but, instead, to say exactly what students
"will do" under specified conditions.[7] This advice, too, strikes many of
us as humorous in its naive neglect of what students *want* to do.

As the distinction faded in importance, goals once stated as behavioral objectives became "competencies," and these were often gathered

into long sets describing what students (and teachers) should be required to know, do, or somehow display. This approach, applied to teachers, was part of a much longer and broader movement to define the competent teacher.[8] Under the guidance of behaviorists, competencies were to become observable and measurable performances. However, in practice, statements of competencies often included somewhat abstract global capacities as well as hosts of trivial performances.

This very brief history of *competence* reminds us that misguided policies can often be traced to lack of care in defining our terms and impatience with the sort of analysis that might lead to reasonable recommendations for practice. Suppose we start with an ordinary use of the word "competence." In everyday language, we usually think of competence contextually. A person is competent in everyday life if he or she can function adequately in his or her usual setting. In making a determination of competence, we allow for a range of disabilities and required help, but at bottom, the competent individual must at least be aware of his or her need for various forms of assistance and able to profit from such help. We think in categorical terms of physical, mental, and financial competence, but our judgments are closely connected to the demands of a person's everyday life.

Competencies, within this broad context, are acquired, maintained through practice, lost through impairments of health and age, and sometimes rendered obsolete because of drastic changes in the environment. For example, young children gain competence in walking and climbing stairs and, as this competence grows, their physical domain enlarges. Elderly people may lose the capacity to climb stairs, and then their physical domain becomes more restricted. Psychiatric patients may function normally in some settings and under certain conditions, and display dramatic incompetence in other settings. Thus the demands of the setting are as important as the capacities of the person in determining competence. We recognize this today when we try to place students with disabilities in the "least restrictive" environment compatible with their continued growth and that of others.

When we move from everyday life to more specialized settings, the general criterion of competence remains useful: Does the person in question function adequately in this setting? In making our judgments, we still must ask what the setting demands, whether a person can meet these demands, and whether the demands can be safely and reasonably changed so that someone struggling with present demands can be assessed as fully competent in a closely related domain. For example, a brilliant young M.D. may be incompetent in general medicine (alienating patients with his gruff manner and handling them roughly) but with sufficient training he may become highly competent in, say, pathology. In teacher education, we regularly suggest lateral shifts in program. A candidate who is incompetent in the classroom may be entirely capable in a program focused on education but not for teaching. He or she may go into educational publishing or work in an education-related agency of some kind. At our most sensitive, we also recognize that some teacher candidates who cannot function in the public school classroom to which they have been assigned may perform more than adequately in the smaller, well-ordered classrooms characteristic of many independent schools. Similarly a student teacher who seems incompetent with high school students may perform adequately with elementary school students.

Thus, before making long lists of competencies (and we may want to refuse this task entirely), we need to ask what the enterprise of teaching requires. What does it *always* require? Clearly, teaching always involves subject matter (even if the curriculum is co-constructed by teachers and students), and it always involves interactions between teacher and student and, usually, among students. It also necessarily involves some connection with an institution or social milieu. Even in tutoring, a teacher must interact with a parent, guardian, school, or other agency. Every act of teaching takes place in a setting that involves subject matter, students, and a social/institutional context. Caring teachers want to do their best for each student. This means, at least, that the handling of subject matter will address the needs of students and that interpersonal exchanges will be monitored and guided so that harm and hurt are minimized. In what follows, I will integrate discussion of the social context with my analysis of subject matter and social interaction. In a lengthier treatment, the institutional context would properly receive much greater attention.

Competence in Subject Matter

Subject matter belongs to the setting of teaching and makes its own demands. In the days when I was a high school mathematics teacher, I would have been dismayed to learn at the start of a school year that I had been assigned to teach biology or Latin instead of mathematics. I was prepared for the demands mathematics placed on me as a teacher but not for those of biology or Latin. Yet today many teachers are forced to teach outside their field of preparation and, although the custom is deplored, it seems to be tacitly held that a person prepared to teach can teach anything with just day-to-day preparation. Possibly no other false idea has done so much damage to the professional status of teaching.

But what do we mean by "demands of the subject matter"? Educational theorists and practitioners have given far too little attention to this question. Usually we think in terms of majoring or minoring in a given subject. But how does such concentration fit one to answer the demands made by subject matter in, say, secondary schools? The insistence that teachers present a major in mathematics to qualify for a mathematics teaching position has more to do with professional status than with genuine professional preparation. As a semi-profession (a step up from carpentry, Thorndike suggested), teaching has always had a status problem. One way to address that problem, some have thought, is to insist that students preparing to teach study exactly the same curriculum as anyone else majoring in a given subject.[9] Such a move says to the public, "See, teachers are as smart as any college graduates." This practice hasn't done much to improve the status of teaching, and it has done little to address the demands of the subject matter in teaching situations.

Since the demise of teachers' colleges (around 1950), departments in the liberal arts have been largely responsible for the subject-matter preparation of teachers, and in many cases they have not differentiated between the needs of prospective teachers and other students. Indeed, with some admirable exceptions, it has been common for departments in the liberal arts to regard courses specially designed for teachers as watered down, easier, designed for mediocrity. Professional schools, usually lacking the personnel to teach basic subject matter (what university would endorse such redundancy?), have contented themselves with teaching process and method. Sometimes this is done so well that subject matter is addressed rigorously, but often professional schools have to assume that the candidates prepared in the liberal arts are already competent in subject matter. This may be a false assumption.

The demands of the subject matter for high school teaching appear in textbooks and courses of study. (There are, of course, demands that arise as students interact with subject matter, and I will address these a bit later.) A simple criterion for subject matter competence at the high school level is this: Teachers should be able to do anything that students are asked to do (anywhere in the curriculum) in the subject they teach. By that I mean that high school mathematics teachers should be able to perform adequately in every mathematics course offered at their school. Their "expertise" should not be restricted to first-year algebra and/or plane geometry. With a little brushing up and immediate preparation, competent high school mathematics teachers should be able to step into any mathematics course without experiencing great difficulty with the subject matter.

Why is this important when we consider caring and competence? If we look seriously at the development of care theory in education, we see that continuity is an important condition for the establishment and maintenance of caring relations.[10] It is recommended that teachers and students stay together (by mutual consent) for several years so that teachers will be able to respond better to the individual needs of students and students will be more likely to trust the advice and guidance their teachers give. Clearly, such continuity is impossible if a teacher cannot move upward with his or her students. Further, if teachers who cannot meet the demands of subject matter attempt to do this, they risk losing credibility. If a special mark of caring is the caring response, then it would not be unreasonable for students to suspect that teachers do not care when they cannot respond to their needs with respect to subject matter.

The "taking" of lots of mathematics, characteristic of a strong mathematics major, does not guarantee that a teacher can meet the subject matter demands of high school teaching. He or she may have had advanced calculus but no geometry whatever, abstract algebra but no carefully designed course on the structure of the number system, differential equations but no history or philosophy of mathematics. For elementary school teachers, the case may be even worse. A course or two in college mathematics may add little to their mathematical knowledge, and what is learned in such courses—typically cut off from pedagogical purposes and disconnected at both ends—decays rapidly. Indeed, what remains may be lack of confidence, even fear of mathematics.

It is small wonder, then, that potentially powerful reforms in mathematical pedagogy so often fail. It is not only that the structure of teaching as a profession tends to block reform (the isolation of teachers, tenure, superficial methods of evaluation that encourage mere compliance, mountains of paper work, the historically supported conviction that "this, too, shall pass"); in addition to all this, teachers are often simply not prepared to answer the demands of subject matter. How can a teacher encourage and guide open-ended problem exploration if she is herself unsure of what constitutes an adequate mathematical response?

What can teacher education do about this situation? As I pointed out earlier, the chasm between subject matter preparation and professional (pedagogical) preparation has widened and deepened since the disappearance of teachers' colleges. A return to that structure is probably impossible and perhaps undesirable because along with their one great strength—the integration of subject matter and pedagogy—teachers' colleges had many weaknesses. But the problem clearly needs to be addressed. Recognition of the problem has prompted John Goodlad and his associates to promote three-way partnerships as essential to educational renewal.[11] Schools of education must, of course, work with school people, but they must also work effectively with colleagues in the liberal arts if teachers are to meet the demands of subject matter.

It is worth noting, before leaving this part of the discussion, that teacher education in other parts of the world operates in much the way I am suggesting here.[12] Teachers are prepared in depth on the material they will actually teach. It is not supposed that the mathematical preparation of teachers should be identical to that of engineers, nurses, business managers, economists, and mathematicians. The mathematics in a program designed for teachers can be wonderful and sophisticated. It can provide a deep understanding of elementary mathematics from a higher standpoint; that is, it can treat elementary content in such a way that teachers gain in both pedagogical strength and knowledge of higher mathematics. Clearly, it must provide a thorough knowledge of the subject matter that is taught in schools.

I have claimed that the subject matter itself makes demands on teachers' competence. But students also create demands related to subject matter. It is not just that they learn differently and need appropriately different methods, although these differences are important. At a more universal level, students need to make connections among the various subjects they are forced to study and, even more vital, to life itself. What has mathematics to do with the meaning of life? With how one should or might live? How does it fit into the whole scheme of education, and what is the purpose of education anyway? Does the learning of mathematics contribute to a better life? How? Is it possible that the requirements of schooling serve political purposes? Who benefits and who is harmed?

Teachers are poorly prepared to engage in such questions with their students and, tellingly, they often protest that they are not employed to do this. "I teach math," some will say and insist that they are not (and, presumably, should not be) prepared to engage in moral education, general studies, political consciousness raising, aesthetic appreciation, or any of a list of topical areas long regarded as part of a fully human education. The supposition seems to be that schools should offer all the bits and pieces, and when these are accumulated in a given student, he or she is well educated. But students would be hard pressed to find models of such "well-educated" people among their teachers. The bits and pieces are almost never assembled into a coherent picture, and teachers, who urge their students to study all the subjects forced on them for the sake of a good education, can rarely draw upon any subject but their own in their teaching, and even in that their knowledge is often limited.

Competent teachers who, as carers, want to respond to the voiced and unvoiced needs of their students need what might be called latitudinal knowledge. They should be able to draw on literature, history, politics, religion, philosophy, and the arts in ways that enrich their daily teaching and offer multiple possibilities for students to make connections with the great existential questions as well as questions of current social life. Further, engaging such material should be legitimized. It should not be considered a distraction from the particular subject matter scheduled for a test on Friday. No one topic so introduced or pursued by a teacher will attract all of her students, but the vast multitude of direct references, allusions, stories, poems, anecdotes, jokes and names will make it likely that most students will find the connections they so badly need to come fully awake.

At least two important changes will have to occur if teachers are to acquire competence in subject matter as discussed here. First, faculty from arts and sciences will have to work closely with education faculty to design rigorous and exciting courses for teachers. They will have to overcome the arrogant and outdated notion that there is only one form of respectable preparation in each discipline. Glenn Irvin has noted that a person is not usually recognized as "a chemist, or a physicist, or a historian" unless that person has earned a Ph.D. in the subject. This concern for longitudinal subject mastery "is often reflected in the arts and sciences' insistence that prospective teachers pursue the same curriculum as students majoring in the arts and sciences; otherwise they have not mastered the subject matter and methodology appropriate to the degree . . . as the arts and sciences conceive it."[13] In opposition, I have suggested that there are multiple approaches to every subject matter and that powerful alternative models of curriculum in a given subject should not be ordered hierarchically. A well-designed curriculum for teachers is not inferior to one designed for mathematicians. Curricula should be matched to the purposes and interests of the students.

Second, subject matter offered for prospective teachers should be stretched from within. By this, I mean that mathematics courses for teachers should incorporate material similar to that which we hope teachers will use in their own classrooms. Such courses should be rich in history, literature, philosophy, and the other fields that teachers might draw upon. The competence aimed at by doing this is hard to acquire from a "bits and pieces" curriculum. It can be done, and some polymathic teachers exhibit wonderfully rich repertoires. But if such competence is to become a regular expectation, teacher education programs will have to be redesigned.

Civility in Classrooms

From the perspective of care, the purpose of subject matter competence is to establish teachers' "response-ability." The subject matter makes its own demands, and the needs of students increase the demands on teachers to broaden and deepen their competence. However, students have needs that go beyond the demands of subject matter, and some of these needs must be met by teachers.

As persons, students should be treated with care and respect, and as young, inexperienced people they need to learn how to treat others with care and respect. This double need has always created tension for caring adults. The temptation—and sometimes even the expectation—is for adults to use authoritarian methods to coerce proper behavior from the young. It is sometimes reasonable to use coercion in the best interests of children and teenagers, but from the care perspective every act of coercion raises a question. What justifies us in treating children in ways we would not treat adults? Sometimes the answer is clear, but often it is not; we simply use our power neglecting even to ask the question.

Let's consider first the issue of treating students with care and respect. Teacher education programs today properly spend time on problems of multicultural education, gender, special education, and community-school relations. The message is clear in all of these areas: respect and care for *all* of our children, not just the favored few. Although we have a long way to go on these problems, it seems accurate to say that teacher education programs are attending to them vigorously. As a result, teacher-student interactions today are almost certainly more evenhanded than they were two decades ago.

But a paradox arises. Current demands for improved student test scores drive teachers to ignore many of the social and individual needs of students. This emphasis on academic mastery is paradoxical because, as I noted earlier, teachers are not as well prepared in subject matter as they should be. When teachers are not broadly prepared to relate subject matter to the individual and social needs of students, they may resort to authoritarian methods and dull, repetitious work in the conscientious desire to raise test scores. When I suggest to teachers that they should make greater use of stories, the arts, and dialogue on the great existential questions, they respond with initial enthusiasm but then lapse into doubt. How, they ask, can they do these wonderful things when the school demands that they "cover" the curriculum and produce high test scores? Thus the *school* demands on subject matter are seemingly at odds with the two demands I identified earlier. Resolution of the paradox requires the sort of preparation that will enable teachers to incorporate stories, conversation, experiences with the arts, and intellectual dialogue in their regular instruction, but it may also require a careful analysis to see whether some schooling demands can be reduced or eliminated. The current emphasis on academic achievement is doubly paradoxical because it may not be possible to attain high levels of achievement without attending to the needs of students as persons; that is, the establishment of caring relations may be essential to the development of student competence.

Teacher educators are to be commended for their great emphasis on equality, but it may be time to ask whether we have become satisfied with treating everyone equally badly. From the care perspective, we should be asking serious questions about many of the schooling demands that may in fact impede learning. Do our classroom testing practices enhance learning? Teachers should be encouraged to put aside complaints about standardized and district-wide testing and examine their own practices carefully. Are teacher-student interactions respectful? Should teachers "keep students on their toes" by using "cold calling" and other methods that many students find frightening? I do not intend to dictate answers to these questions. Reasonable people can differ in their responses. But teachers who do not consider such issues deeply are not fully competent. Every classroom practice should be subjected to the basic question of care: Does this practice help me to respond to the needs of these students? of *this* student?

Treating students with care and respect is but one side of the problem of civility in classrooms. Surely students should not be afraid of their teachers or fearful of any activities their teachers plan for them. But they should not be afraid of one another either. Many reports today suggest that students, especially at the middle and high school levels, treat others badly. I cannot undertake a review of the empirical literature on this problem here, but there is no reason to doubt that the problem exists. The question is whether teachers are addressing it competently.

Consider the following hypothetical scenarios. In each, we may assume that the teacher has overheard enough of the conversation between two students to understand its content. Each conversation is illicit in the sense that it takes place without the teacher's permission.

1. Sue says to Amy, "Don't worry about your book. I'll help you look for it at lunch time." As Sue says this, she pats Amy's arm, and a worried look on Amy's face gives way to a smile.

2. Bill asks Joe whether he saw "that great game" last night and both boys emit exclamations of admiration for a player's performance. They laugh and gesture enthusiastically but not disruptively.

3. Tom makes an obscene comment to Jill and suggests that she should welcome it since no other boy would bother with "such a cow."

Suppose in all these cases, the teacher responds by saying, "Okay, let's settle down and pay attention. Quiet please." Is the teacher being respectful and evenhanded? Or is she neglecting a clear obligation to teach her students what it means to care for one another? Incidents of this sort are often held up as examples of teacher management in which the teacher properly keeps the class focused on the lesson's learning objective. In contrast, from the care perspective, such lack of discrimination is a sign of incompetence. In all these cases, the teacher has an opportunity to help her students understand the demands of civility.

In the first case, the teacher might compliment Sue for her compassion and solicit the help of her classmates. What book is missing? Has anyone seen it? What will happen if it isn't found? Can we depend on our community when such problems arise? Should we be able to? Can we set aside a time later in the day to discuss this in greater depth?

In the second case, the teacher's generic comment seems appropriate. However, even in that case, she might recognize the boys' interests and suggest some connection to their school work. For youngsters who are pinning all their hopes on athletic careers, she might refer to the film *Hoop Dreams* or some other account of the tragedy of preparing too narrowly for an uncertain future. Responding appropriately to these particular boys is important not only for the boys but for the whole class. Such a response demonstrates civility. It shows that people who treasure civility respond to one another as persons. The teacher can quickly return to the lesson, and the students will probably follow her more willingly than they might otherwise.

I would not have included the third case if I had not actually heard of such cases recently. What excuse can a teacher offer for ignoring Tom's harassment of Jill? One legitimate response might be that the teacher decided to handle it later rather than risk further embarrassment to Jill. This response could be persuasive, but teacher educators should be sure to explore thoroughly with their students what should be done "later." Did other students hear Tom's comments? If so, is a later, individual treatment still appropriate?

The excuse offered more often is that the principal (or other disciplinary authority) "would not do anything" if the teacher sent Tom to the office. But why should teachers suppose that the only solution to disciplinary problems must be formal and hierarchical? Most classroom social problems—certainly this one is a prime example—are matters of civility. It might be effective for the teacher to say to Tom (so that everyone can hear), "Decent people do not talk that way to others. In this classroom, we *never* do that. Your classmates and I will not stand for it." Other students may never know exactly what was said or to whom, but the message is clear: In this classroom at least, we will be civil in our interactions. Later, the teacher may well want to have another conversation with Tom, and she will certainly want to assure Jill that she deserves respect and has a right to object to such treatment. Too many young people suffer these offenses silently, resigned to what seems a fact—"this is how it is in middle school."

The question arises once again: How can we take time to handle situations with sensitivity and care when we are pressed to cover so much material? The answer has to be that it is never wasteful to use time to establish relations of care and trust. Everything else goes better when such relations are in place. If teachers, with great artistry, can relate social incidents to the subject matter at hand, the rewards are clearly enormous. But even if the subject matter must be set aside temporarily, the results in terms of emotional safety and social growth are worth the brief sacrifice.

Conclusion

I have argued that caring requires competence. A caring teacher must be prepared to respond to the needs of students as both learners of subject matter and young persons learning to live meaningful lives. In analyzing the competence required for this "response-ability," I have suggested that teacher educators should work toward strengthening the preparation of teachers in two great domains central to teaching—subject matter and moral/social life.

This is only the beginning of what should be a much more extensive analysis. Besides the demands made by subject matter and moral life, the conditions of current schooling make tremendous demands on teachers. Perhaps teacher educators put too much effort into preparing new teachers to meet these special schooling demands. Perhaps we should do more to reduce those demands and help teachers to reconcile the paradoxes that arise as the demands inherent in teaching clash with the daily demands of schooling.

NOTES

1. In much longer analyses, I have referred to this attention as "engrossment." See Nel Noddings, *Caring: A Feminine Approach to Ethics and Moral Education* (Berkeley: University of California Press, 1984), *Women and Evil* (Berkeley: University of California Press, 1989), and *The Challenge to Care in Schools* (New York: Teachers College Press, 1992).

2. Simone Weil, *Simone Weil Reader*, ed. George A. Panichas (Mt. Kisco, NY: Moyer Bell Limited, 1977), p. 51.

3. Milton Mayeroff, *On Caring* (New York: Harper & Row, 1971), p. 1.

4. See, for example, Deborah Eaker-Rich and Jane Van Galen, eds., *Caring in an Unjust World* (Albany, NY: State University of New York Press, 1996).

5. See the special issue on "Youth and Caring," *Phi Delta Kappan*, May 1995; see also Mary Poplin and Joseph Weeres, *Voices from the Inside: A report on Schooling from Inside the Classroom* (Los Angeles: Institute for Education in Transformation at the Claremont Graduate School, 1992).

6. See ed. Edmund Short, *Competence* (Lanham, MD: University Press of America, 1984).

7. See, for example, Robert Mager, *Preparing Instructional Objectives* (San Francisco: Fearon Press, 1962).

8. For an historical analysis of teacher competency movements, see Henry C. Johnson, "Teacher Competence: An Historical Analysis," in *Competence*, pp. 41-69.

9. See Holmes Group, *Tomorrow's Teachers* (East Lansing, MI: Author, 1986).

10. See Noddings, *The Challenge to Care in Schools*.

11. See John I. Goodlad, *Educational Renewal: Better Teachers, Better Schools* (San Francisco: Jossey-Bass, 1994).

12. This is especially clear in China. See Liping Ma, "Profound Understanding of Fundamental Mathematics," Unpublished doctoral dissertation, Stanford University, 1996.

13. Glenn Irvin, "The Role of Arts and Sciences in Teacher Education," *Record in Educational Leadership* 15, no. 2 (1995): 21.

Section Three
THE FUTURE OF
TEACHER EVALUATION

CHAPTER X

Educating Teachers for the Next Century: Rethinking Practice and Policy

As the twenty-first century approaches, it is increasingly clear that schools must become dramatically more successful with a wide range of learners if many more citizens are to acquire the sophisticated skills they need to participate in a knowledge-based society. Most reformers now agree that increasing teachers' expertise and effectiveness is critical to the success of ongoing efforts to reform American education. The kind of pedagogy needed to help students to think critically, create, and solve complex problems as well as to master ambitious subject matter content is much more demanding than that needed to impart routine skills. And teachers are being asked to achieve these goals for *all* children, not just the ten or twenty percent who have traditionally been selected into "gifted and talented" or "honors" programs. Only very knowledgeable and skillful teachers who are able to respond differentially and appropriately to students' needs can enable diverse learners to succeed at these much more challenging learning goals.

It is also becoming increasingly clear that the capacities teachers need in order to succeed at teaching more challenging content to more diverse students can only be widely acquired throughout the teaching force by greater investments in teacher preparation and development. Such reforms, many policymakers and practitioners believe,

Linda Darling-Hammond is Charles E. Ducommun Professor of Education at Stanford University, where she teaches education policy and teacher education. She is also executive director of the National Commission on Teaching and America's Future, the blue-ribbon panel that issued the influential report, *What Matters Most: Teaching for America's Future*.

will in turn require comprehensive restructuring of the systems by which states and school districts license, hire, induct, support, and provide for the continual learning of teachers.[1]

Central to any discussion of teacher preparation is a judgment about what it is that teachers must be prepared to do. If teaching is viewed primarily as the transmittal of information to students—and if not all students are expected to learn well—one could argue that teachers need little more than the basic subject matter knowledge needed to string together comprehensible lectures. For this kind of teaching, it is easy to believe that a liberal arts education alone could be sufficient preparation. But if teachers need to be able to ensure successful learning for students who bring different levels of prior knowledge and learn in different ways, then teachers need to be diagnosticians and planners who know a great deal about the learning process and have a large repertoire of teaching methods at their disposal. This kind of teaching is not learned intuitively. And it is this kind of teaching that current social demands increasingly require.

Although American schools have tended to treat teachers as semi-skilled workers, success in the American classroom requires high levels of knowledge and a broad range of skills. Students are more diverse in their needs and backgrounds and many are less supported in their communities than ever before. In 1996, for example, about 11 percent of students were identified as handicapped or learning disabled[2] and the vast majority of them (73 percent) were served in regular classrooms,[3] although most teachers have had no training to address their needs. At the same time, about 5 percent of American students were identified as limited English proficient,[4] yet just one-fourth of the teachers serving these children had received any training in strategies for teaching new English language learners.[5] In addition to these specific needs, students bring with them a wide range of approaches to learning, prior experiences, and types of knowledge that teachers must understand in order to be effective. In today's schools, more than one-third of students are members of racial/ethnic minority groups or recent immigrants from a wide variety of cultures; more than one-fourth live in households below the poverty line; and more than half live in families that have experienced divorce, absence, or death of at least one parent.

Thus, in a typical classroom of 25 students, today's teacher will serve at least four or five students with specific educational needs that require professional expertise previously reserved to a few specialists. In addition, he or she will need considerable knowledge to develop curriculum and teaching strategies that address the wide range of learning approaches, experiences, and prior levels of knowledge the other students bring with them, and an understanding of how to work within a wide range of family and community contexts. And he or she will need to know how to help these students acquire much more complex skills and types of knowledge than ever before.

Current education reforms also create a broader range of roles for teachers in developing curriculum and assessments of student performance, coaching and mentoring other teachers, and working more closely with families and community agencies. Finally, school-based management and shared decision-making initiatives rely for their success on the capacity of education practitioners to make knowledgeable judgments about teaching, program design, and school organization.

How can we prepare teachers for this daunting mission? What kinds of programs can help teachers learn to practice in ways that are both *learner-centered*—that is, ways that are responsive to individual students' academic needs, intelligences, talents, cultural and linguistic backgrounds—and *learning-centered*—that is, ways that support in-depth learning that results in keen thinking and proficient performances? And what kinds of policies would be needed to provoke and enable universities and schools to create these programs of powerful teacher education?

In this chapter, I outline the case for investments in teacher education, review some recent findings about the features of particularly powerful programs of preservice teacher preparation, and discuss the policy changes that would be needed to create such programs on a wide scale. The goal of universal, high-quality teacher education is one that has never been adopted in the United States, with its long tradition of pursuing small-scale innovations while operating large numbers of other programs that provide decidedly mediocre preparation and admitting still other teachers with no training whatsoever. Adopting such a goal reflects the aspirations of the National Commission on Teaching and America's Future:[6] that every child should have the right to be taught by a caring, competent, and qualified teacher, and that every teacher should enjoy the right to high-quality preparation and ongoing professional development. New policy, as well as reformed practice, is critical to this objective.

What Teaching Knowledge Matters?

What do teachers need to know to teach all students in the way new standards suggest? First of all, teachers need to understand *subject matter* in ways that allow them to organize it so that students can create useful cognitive maps of the terrain under study. They need more than formulaic or procedural understanding of the core ideas in a discipline and how these help to structure knowledge, how they relate to one another, and how they can be tested, evaluated, and extended. Teachers also need to be able to use their knowledge of subject matter flexibly to address ideas as they come up in the course of learning. They need to understand how inquiry in a field is conducted and what reasoning entails—such as what counts as "proving" something in mathematics as compared with proving something in history.[7] And they need to see how ideas connect across fields and to everyday life, so that they can select and use examples, problems, and applications well.

Understanding subject matter in this way provides a foundation for *pedagogical content knowledge*,[8] which enables teachers to represent ideas so that they are accessible to others. Knowledge of the domain of study is critical: the teacher needs to understand what ideas can provide important foundations for other ideas and how they can be usefully linked and assembled. The audience is also key: people understand ideas differently depending on their prior experiences and context. A skillful pedagogue figures out what a particular audience is likely to know and believe about the topic under study and how learners are likely to "hook into" new ideas, so as to create productive learning experiences. Knowledge of cognition, information processing, and communication are also important so that teachers can shape lectures, materials, learning centers, projects, and discussions in useful ways.

Interpreting learners' statements and actions and framing productive experiences for them requires knowledge of *development*—how children and adolescents think and behave, what they are trying to accomplish, what they find interesting, what they already know and what they are likely to have trouble with in particular domains at particular ages in particular contexts. This knowledge includes an understanding of how to support further growth in a number of domains— social, physical, and emotional, as well as cognitive.

Teaching in ways that connect with students also requires an understanding of *differences* that may arise from culture, language, family, community, gender, prior schooling, or other factors that shape people's experiences, as well as differences that may arise from developed intelligences, preferred approaches to learning, or specific learning difficulties. Teachers need to be able to inquire sensitively and productively into children's experiences and their understandings of subject matter so that they can interpret curriculum through their students' eyes and shape lessons to connect with what students know and how they learn well. To get non-stereotypic information that can help them come to understand their learners, teachers need to know how to listen carefully to students and look at their work as well as to structure situations in which students write and talk about their experiences and what they understand. This builds a foundation of *pedagogical learner knowledge*[9] which grows as teachers examine how particular learners think and reason, where they have problems, how they learn best, and what motivates them.

An understanding of *motivation* is critical in teaching for understanding because achieving understanding is difficult. Teachers must know how to structure tasks and feedback so as to encourage extensive effort without either relinquishing the press for understanding when the going gets tough or discouraging students so that they give up altogether. Motivating students not only requires understanding general principles about how to engage young people and sustain their interest at different ages, but also understanding what individual students believe about themselves and their abilities, what they care about, and what tasks are likely to give them enough success to encourage them to continue to work hard to learn.

Teachers need several kinds of knowledge about *learning*. Since there are many kinds of learning—for example, learning for recognition or appreciation versus learning for various kinds of applications or performances—teachers need to think about what it means to learn different kinds of material for different purposes, how to support different kinds of learning with distinctive teaching strategies, and how to make judgments about which kinds of learning are most necessary in different contexts. Not everything can be learned deeply—that is, with opportunities for extensive application—but some things must be deeply understood as foundations for work that is to follow and as a means for developing specific skills and performances. Other ideas may be understood more superficially to create a map of the domain, but learned so that they connect to concepts that are meaningful.

Teachers need to understand what helps children (or anyone) learn in these different ways. They need to be able to construct and use a variety of means for *assessing* students' knowledge as well as for evaluating students' approaches to learning. To be effective, they must be able to identify the strengths of different learners while addressing their weaknesses—those who rely more on visual or oral cues; those who tend to reason from the specific to the general or vice versa; those who use spatial or graphic organizers and those who are more text-oriented; those who bring a highly developed logical/mathematical intelligence and those who bring a strong aesthetic sense.

Using this information well requires a command of *teaching strategies* that address a variety of ways to learn and a variety of purposefully selected goals for learning. Strategies that regularly use multiple pathways to content are one major part of a teacher's repertoire. In addition, more than ever before in the past, all teachers need tools to work with the students in their classrooms who have specific learning disabilities—the estimated fifteen to twenty percent of students who are dyslexic or dysgraphic, who have particular visual or perceptual difficulties or difficulties with information processing. There are useful teaching strategies for these relatively commonplace problems, but they have been rarely taught to "regular" (rather than special education) teachers. And because language is the gateway to learning, teachers need an understanding of how students acquire language, both native English speakers and students who start from other languages, so that they can build language skills and create learning experiences that are accessible. This may mean strategies ranging from explicit teaching of key vocabulary or use of an array of visual and oral cues and materials to the creation of collaborative learning settings in which students use language extensively.

Teachers need to know about *curriculum resources and technologies*. They need to be able to connect their students with sources of information and knowledge that extend beyond textbooks, that allow for the exploration of ideas, the acquisition and synthesis of information, and the development of models, writings, designs, and other work products. The teacher's role will be to help students learn to find and use a wide array of resources for framing and solving problems, rather than to remember only the information contained in one source.

And they need to know about *collaboration*. They need to understand how interactions among students can be structured to allow more powerful shared learning to occur. They need to be able to shape classrooms that sponsor productive discourse that presses for disciplined reasoning on the part of students. They need to understand how to collaborate with other teachers to plan, assess, and improve learning within and across the school, as well as how to work with parents to learn more about their students and to shape supportive experiences at school and home.

Finally, teachers need to be able to *analyze and reflect* on their practice, to assess the effects of their teaching, and to refine and improve their instruction. When teaching for understanding, teachers must maintain two intertwining strands of thought at all times: How am I doing at moving the students toward high levels of understanding and proficient performance? How am I taking into account what students know and care about in the process of moving them toward these curriculum goals and developing their talents and social abilities? Teachers must continuously evaluate what students are thinking and understanding and reshape their plans to take account of what they have discovered as they build curriculum to meet their goals.

These demands that derive from the desire to teach a much wider range of students for much higher standards of performance are new ones for most teachers. With few having experienced this kind of learning themselves, how can it be possible to create a different kind of teaching on a wide scale? The only plausible answer is to develop much more powerful forms of teacher education—both before entry and throughout the teaching career—that systematically provide experience with the kinds of knowledge and forms of practice described above, and then to make that kind of education available to all teachers, not just a few. As Gary Fenstermacher observes:

> In a time when so many advocate for restructured schools, for greater decision autonomy for teachers, and for connecting the schools more intimately with homes and communities, it is more important than ever that teachers have the capacity to appraise their actions, evaluate their work, anticipate and control consequences, incorporate new theory and research into practice, and possess the skills and understanding needed to explain their work to other teachers, and to students and their parents. . . .
>
> These reflective capacities are not innate to human beings, nor are they acquired quickly. They are not acquired during a planning period sandwiched somewhere in between classes, or during evening "mini-courses" after a full day's work. They are, rather, the outcome of sustained and rigorous study, and of dialogue and exchange with master teacher educators.[10]

Developing the kinds of knowledge I have described requires that most teachers move far beyond what they themselves experienced as students, and thus that they learn in ways that are more powerful than simply reading and talking about new pedagogical ideas.[11] Learning to practice in substantially different ways from what one has oneself experienced can occur neither through theoretical imaginings alone nor unguided experience alone. It requires a much tighter coupling of the two. This tighter coupling of theory and practice in the context of a broader and deeper base of knowledge about learning, development, and teaching is perhaps the key feature of teacher education for the twenty-first century.

How Teachers' Knowledge Matters

Even when agreeing that there are desirable knowledge and skills for teaching, many people sincerely believe that anyone can teach or, at least, that knowing a subject is enough to allow one to teach it well. Others believe that teaching is best learned, to the extent it can be learned at all, by trial-and-error on the job. The evidence strongly suggests otherwise. Teacher expertise—what teachers know and can do—affects all the core tasks of teaching. What teachers understand about content and students shapes how judiciously they select from texts and other materials and how effectively they present material in class. Their skill in assessing their students' progress also depends on how deeply they understand learning, and how well they can interpret students' discussions and written work. No other intervention can make the difference that a knowledgeable, skillful teacher can make in the learning process. At the same time, nothing can fully compensate for weak teaching that, despite good intentions, can result from a teacher's lack of opportunity to acquire the knowledge and skill needed to help students master the curriculum.

A growing body of research finds that teacher expertise is one of the more important school factors influencing student achievement, followed by the smaller but generally positive influences of small schools and small class sizes.[12] That is, teachers who know much about teaching and learning and who work in environments that allow them to know students well are critical elements of successful learning. Studies of student achievement in Texas,[13] Alabama,[14] and New York,[15] for example, have concluded that teachers' qualifications (based on measures of knowledge, education, and experience) account for a larger share of the variance in students' achievement than any other single factor. Two of these studies found that, in combination, differences in teacher expertise and class sizes accounted for more of the measured variance in achievement between high- and low-scoring districts than did poverty, race, and parent education.[16]

National studies and local research in Georgia, North Carolina, Michigan, and Virginia have found that students achieve at higher levels and are less likely to drop out when they are taught by teachers with certification in their teaching field, by those with master's degrees, and by teachers who are enrolled in graduate studies.[17]

These findings are reinforced by those of a recent review of sixty production/function studies which found that teacher education, ability, and experience, along with small schools and lower teacher-pupil ratios, are associated with increases in student achievement.[18] This study's estimates of the achievement gains associated with different kinds of expenditures found that spending on teacher education swamped other variables as the most productive investment for schools.

What matters for teacher effectiveness? Other research confirms that teacher knowledge of subject matter, student learning and development, and teaching methods, along with skills developed through expert guidance in clinical settings are all important elements of teaching effectiveness. Reviews of research incorporating more than two hundred studies contradict the long-standing myths that "anyone can teach" and that "teachers are born and not made." This research also makes it clear that teachers need to know much more than the subject matter they teach. Teacher education, as it turns out, matters a great deal. Teachers who have more background in their content areas and have greater knowledge of learning and teaching methods are more highly rated and more successful with students in fields ranging from early childhood and elementary education to mathematics, science, and vocational education.[19]

If it is increasingly clear that teacher learning is a linchpin of school reform, it is equally apparent that if teachers are to negotiate the demands of new standards and new students, they must have access to a deeper base of knowledge and expertise than most teacher preparation programs and staff development programs now provide. While individual projects already demonstrate that new models of teacher development can be successfully launched and that they make a difference for what teachers can do in schools, these occasional exemplars have not yet provoked more far-reaching efforts to create systemic change.

Teacher Education in the United States: The Luck of the Draw

In contrast to many other countries that the United States thinks of as peers or competitors, prospective teachers here must fund their own preparation and frequently are allowed to decide how much training they will undertake. In addition, by virtue of weak accreditation policies, universities in many states are allowed, in turn, to decide on the content and quality of the training they offer. Because requirements for teacher education are dramatically uneven across the country, and because most states lower or ignore their standards whenever districts have trouble filling vacancies, teachers get radically different kinds and qualities of preparation depending on where and how they choose to enter the profession.

Schools, colleges, and departments of education have been severely criticized during much of the past century.[20] One major aspect of the critique of teacher education is that, particularly after normal schools were incorporated into university departments in the 1940s and '50s, many teacher education programs seemed to separate theory and application to a large extent. In some places, teachers were taught to teach in lecture halls from texts and by teachers who frequently had not themselves ever practiced what they were teaching. Students' courses in subject matter were disconnected from their courses on teaching methods, which were in turn disconnected from their courses on foundations and psychology. Students completed this coursework before they began student teaching, which was a brief taste of practice typically appended to the end of their program with few connections to what had come before. In the classrooms where they were student teaching many encountered entirely different ideas from those they had studied, because university- and school-based faculty did little planning or teaching together. Sometimes their cooperating teachers were selected with no regard for the quality or kind of practice they engaged in. When new teachers entered their own classrooms, they could remember and apply little of what they had learned by reading in isolation from practice. Thus they reverted largely to what they knew best: the way they themselves had been taught.

The often-repeated critiques of traditional teacher education programs include:

- **Inadequate Time.** The confines of a four-year undergraduate degree make it hard to learn subject matter, child development, learning theory, and effective teaching strategies. Elementary preparation is considered weak in subject matter; secondary preparation, in knowledge of learning and learners.

- **Fragmentation.** Elements of teacher learning are disconnected from each other. Coursework is separate from practice teaching; professional skills are segmented into separate courses; faculties in the arts and sciences are insulated from education professors. Would-be teachers are left to their own devices to put it all together.

- **Uninspired Teaching Methods.** For prospective teachers to learn active, hands-on and minds-on teaching, they must have experienced it for themselves. But traditional lecture and recitation still dominate in much of higher education, where faculty do not practice what they preach.

- **Superficial Curriculum.** "Once over lightly" describes the curriculum. Traditional programs focus on methods and a smattering of educational psychology. Candidates do not learn deeply about how to understand and handle real problems of practice.

- **Traditional Views of Schooling.** Because of pressures to prepare candidates for schools as they are, most prospective teachers learn to work in isolation rather than in teams and to master chalkboards and textbooks instead of computers and CD-ROMS.[21]

Over the past decade, many schools of education and school districts have begun to change these conditions. Stimulated by the efforts of the Holmes Group and the National Network for Educational Renewal, more than three hundred schools of education have created programs that extend beyond the confines of the traditional four-year bachelor's degree program, thus allowing more extensive study of the disciplines to be taught along with education coursework that is integrated with more extensive clinical training in schools. Some are one- or two-year graduate programs that serve recent graduates or mid-career recruits. Others are five-year models that allow an extended program of preparation for prospective teachers who enter teacher education during their undergraduate years. In either case, because the fifth year allows students to devote their energies exclusively to the task of preparing to teach, such programs allow for year-long school-based internships that are integrated with coursework on learning and teaching.

Programs that provide a bachelor's degree in a disciplinary field plus intensive study of teaching at the graduate level are often better able to resolve several traditional dilemmas of teacher education: They create time for study of both subject matter and pedagogy, rather than trading off one against the other. They create room for much more extensive clinical experience—typically 30 weeks or more rather than the traditional 8 to 10 weeks of student teaching. And they reduce fragmentation of the curriculum by interweaving coursework with practical experiences, rather than frontloading theory disconnected from practice.

A number of recent studies have found that graduates of extended (typically five-year) programs are not only more satisfied with their preparation, they are viewed by their colleagues, principals, and cooperating teachers as better prepared, are as effective with students as much more experienced teachers, and are much more likely to enter and stay in teaching than their peers prepared in traditional four-year programs.[22]

Many of these programs have joined with local school districts to create professional development schools where novices' clinical preparation can be more purposefully structured. Like teaching hospitals, these schools aim to provide sites for state-of-the-art practice which are also organized to support the training of new professionals, extend the professional development of veteran teachers, and sponsor collaborative research and inquiry. In the most highly developed sites, programs are jointly planned and taught by university-based and school-based faculty. Cohorts of beginning teachers get a richer, more coherent learning experience when they are organized in teams to study and practice with these faculty and with one another. Senior teachers report that they deepen their knowledge by serving as mentors, adjunct faculty, co-researchers, and teacher leaders. Thus these schools can help create the rub between theory and practice that teachers need in order to learn, while creating more professional roles for teachers and building knowledge in ways that are more useful for both practice and ongoing theory-building.[23]

These institutions join those in a growing number of countries whose teachers are now prepared in programs that extend to the graduate level with clinical experiences that closely link schools with universities. Among those that have moved much of the teacher education enterprise into two-to-three-year graduate school programs are France, Finland, Germany, Ireland, Italy (secondary), Luxembourg, the Netherlands, New Zealand, and Portugal.[24] In most of these countries, teacher education is heavily subsidized by the government and candidates pay little or nothing for this extensive training. Although many institutions in the United States are taking this step because they believe it will enable them to prepare more effective teachers, they lack the systemic policy supports for candidate subsidies and programmatic funding that their counterparts in other countries enjoy.

What may be a critically important feature of these new programs in the United States and elsewhere is that they allow teachers to learn *about* practice *in* practice,[25] in settings that deliberately construct integrated studies of content, learning, and teaching and create strong connections between theory and practice. Learning to teach diverse learners for deep understanding requires approaches to professional development that help teachers negotiate the web of interactions that lie between general propositions about learning, development, and teaching and the situated realities of subject matter, students, and classrooms. Without an opportunity for genuine praxis, abstract theoretical ideas seem inadequate to the complexities and idiosyncrasies of students; meanwhile, the outcomes of classroom efforts seem random and unpredictable.

Situated learning about teaching in curriculum contexts also appears to be an important attribute of inservice education. Studies have found that changes in teaching practice and student achievement appear to occur when teachers participate in sustained collaborative professional development grounded in the curriculum they teach and emphasizing the examination of teaching methods and student work.[26] For example, in a study of teachers' implementation of the California mathematics curriculum framework, teachers who exhibited the most "reform-oriented" practice and whose students scored highest on the state assessment (student characteristics and school conditions held constant) had had the most access to professional development in which they worked directly with one another and with experts on new student curriculum materials related to specific concepts in the framework. Over time, teachers collaboratively studied these materials, developed and tried lessons, and discussed the results with their colleagues, treating issues of mathematics content, instruction, and learning simultaneously.[27]

Other evidence about the characteristics of more successful teacher education programs emerged in a study by the National Commission on Teaching and America's Future, which researched extraordinary teacher education programs that prepare teachers who are successful at teaching diverse learners effectively. The programs, at public and private universities across the country, operate at Alverno College in Milwaukee; Bank Street College of Education in New York City; Trinity University in San Antonio; University of California at Berkeley; University of Southern Maine; University of Virginia; and Wheelock College in Boston. The outcomes collected included reputational evidence about quality from scholars and from practitioners who hire program graduates; surveys and interviews of graduates about their perceptions of their preparation compared with a group drawn randomly from beginning teachers across the country; surveys and interviews of principals about their perceptions of the graduates' preparation and performance; and observations of graduates' practice in their classrooms. Based on evaluations and observations of their practice, the graduates of these programs have developed pedagogical skills that enable them to teach the challenging material envisioned by new subject matter standards aimed at higher levels of performance and greater understanding.

These teacher education programs share several features that directly distinguish them from many others:

- a common, clear vision of good teaching that is apparent in all coursework and clinical experiences;
- a core curriculum grounded in substantial knowledge of child and adolescent development, learning theory, cognition, motivation, and subject matter pedagogy taught in the context of practice;

- extended clinical experiences (at least 30 weeks) which are carefully chosen to support the ideas and practices presented in simultaneous, closely interwoven coursework;
- well-defined standards of practice and performance that are used to guide and evaluate coursework and clinical work;
- strong relationships, common knowledge, and shared beliefs among school- and university-based faculty;
- extensive use of case study methods, teacher research, performance assessments, and portfolio evaluation to ensure that learning is applied to real problems of practice.[28]

While progress in some institutions is evident, there are still many programs that operate with inadequate resources, knowledge, and motivation to improve. The National Commission's report noted the long-standing problem that many universities have treated teacher education as a "cash cow" which is conducted on a shoestring and used to fund programs in other fields. This problem continues to exist. A 1997 study confirms earlier research which found that education programs are funded well below the average, generally near the bottom ranks of departments and well below the level of most other professional preparation programs.[29] In addition, the National Center for Education Statistics reports that teacher educators receive lower salaries than other education faculty, who, in turn, earn significantly lower salaries than noneducation faculty.[30]

These conditions make it hard to improve the quality of teacher education, while the lack of enforcement of quality standards in many states removes much leverage for change. Only three states require professional accreditation of education schools, and few state agencies have the resources or capacity to evaluate programs and enforce high standards through their program-approval process. Candidates are licensed if they graduate from a state-approved program, and virtually all programs, regardless of their quality, are state-approved. In addition, 42 states continue to hire candidates on emergency licenses whenever districts claim recruitment difficulties.

As a consequence, teachers' qualifications in the United States are tremendously uneven. Whereas many new teachers who attend redesigned programs are better prepared for teaching than ever, many others—particularly those who teach low-income children in high-minority schools—have little or no training for their work. In 1994, about 20 percent of all new entrants to teaching were hired with a master's degree, an indication that they probably attended the kinds of

extended programs described above. Most of these more intensively prepared teachers taught in relatively wealthy schools. At the same time,
about 10 percent of new hires in public schools had no license at all, and
another 17 percent had not completed the requirements for a license in
their main assignment field. These teachers were disproportionately
assigned to the most disadvantaged students in low-income schools.[31]

On virtually every measure, teachers' qualifications vary by the status of the children they serve. Students in high-poverty schools are
still much less likely to have teachers who are fully qualified, and much
more likely to have teachers who lack a license and a degree in the
field they teach. They are also least likely to have teachers with higher
levels of education—a master's, specialist, or doctoral degree.[32] Whereas only 8 percent of public school teachers in low-poverty schools
taught without a minor in their main academic assignment field, fully
one-third of teachers in high-poverty schools did so and nearly 70 percent taught without a minor in their secondary teaching field.[33]

Out-of-field teaching remains a serious concern nationwide. In 1994,
among public high school teachers in academic fields, 21 percent lacked
a minor in their main assignment field, including 28 percent of mathematics and 22 percent of English teachers and 18 percent of both science
and social studies teachers. Roughly 20 percent of secondary teachers in
each academic area also lacked state certification in that field, ranging
from 17 percent of science teachers to 24 percent of mathematics teachers. State-by-state differences in teacher preparation are huge. For
example, whereas 84 percent of Wisconsin's high school mathematics
teachers have a major and full certification in their field, only 39 percent
of Alaska's do.[34] The differences among teachers in their content area
preparation as well as their training in education are a function of differences in state licensing standards and university program requirements,
as well as of the willingness of states to bypass their standards—whatever
they are—and allow candidates to teach who are not fully prepared.

Policy Issues in the Improvement of Teacher Education

Policy is the tool by which a society seeks to spread practices that
are deemed beneficial and sufficiently important to justify social investments. It is also a means to guarantee access to opportunities
deemed critical to citizens' ability to function. As adequate education is
increasingly viewed as a student right rather than an option, and as the
importance of teaching to student achievement is increasingly clear,
students' guaranteed access to well-prepared teachers is an issue of

growing concern. In this context, critical policy issues include how to ensure that teachers get access to adequate opportunities to learn, how to encourage the spread of more productive approaches to preparing teachers, and how to support the continued advancement and use of knowledge in the field.

In pursuing these goals, federal and state governments can play a direct role by establishing and enforcing elementary and secondary students' rights to school resources, including qualified teachers, and by making investments in the education of teachers, for example, by subsidizing candidates' studies and by paying for program improvements. In other respects, the most appropriate role for government is indirect. The development of teaching knowledge that is made widely available to teachers to support high-quality teaching is not something that can be easily mandated or bureaucratically enforced. Because knowledge is always growing and its appropriate application is contingent on many different factors, the process of developing and transmitting a complex knowledge base and ensuring its appropriate use is better managed by members of the profession itself.

The genre of policymaking that delegates substantial authority to a profession while holding the profession more accountable for the outcomes of its actions might be called "professional policy." This kind of policy relies more on professional standard setting than direct regulation by the state.[35] It emphasizes the development of expertise to be used for problem solving rather than the imposition of standardized prescriptions for practice that impede teachers' ability to handle the diversity. As Richard Elmore and Susan Fuhrman note:

As equality of opportunity comes to rest more squarely on the need for quality instruction, issues of how to enhance the professional competence of educators become more important. To ensure equal opportunity in today's context means enhancing, not limiting, the professional nature of teaching, and for that task state policy as it has been conceived in the past is hardly the best instrument, . . . We need new ways of conceiving the state's role and the strategies at the state's disposal.[36]

In organized professions, the major lever for professionwide transfer of knowledge and continual improvement is the use of standards to guide preparation and practice. Professions generally set and enforce standards in three ways: (1) through professional accreditation of preparation programs; (2) through state licensing, which grants permission to practice; and (3) through certification, which is a professional recognition of high levels of competence.*[37] In virtually all professions other than teaching, candidates must graduate from an accredited professional school in order to sit for state licensing examinations that test their knowledge and skill. The accreditation process is meant to ensure that all preparation programs provide a reasonably common body of knowledge and structured training experiences that are comprehensive and up to date. It is because of this process that consumers can rest assured that their doctor has studied anatomy, physiology, pathology, and a host of other topics; their lawyer understands civil and criminal law, torts, contracts, and so on; and their architect knows about the physical requirements for constructing safe structures as well as the aesthetic features of design.

Licensing examinations are meant to ensure that candidates have mastered the knowledge they need to practice responsibly. Developed by members of the profession through state standards boards, the tests generally include both surveys of specialized information and performance components that examine aspects of applied practice in the field: Lawyers must analyze cases and, in some states, develop briefs or memoranda of law to address specific issues; doctors must diagnose patients via case histories and describe the treatments they would prescribe; engineers must demonstrate that they can apply certain principles to particular design situations.

In addition, many professions offer additional examinations that provide recognition for advanced levels of skill, such as certification for public accountants, board certification for doctors, and registration for architects. This recognition generally takes extra years of study and practice, often in a supervised internship and/or residency, and is based on performance tests that measure greater levels of specialized knowledge and skill. Those who have met these standards are then allowed to do certain kinds of work that other practitioners cannot. The certification standards inform the other sets of standards governing accreditation, licensing, and relicensing: They are used to ensure that professional

---

* In education, the term "certification" has often been used to describe states' decisions regarding admission to practice, commonly termed licensing in other professions. Until recently, teaching has had no vehicle for advanced professional certification. Now, advanced certification for accomplished veteran teachers is granted by a National Board for Professional Teaching Standards (NBPTS; hereafter the National Board). To avoid confusion between the actions of this professional board and those of states, I use the terms licensing and certification as they are commonly used by professions: "licensing" is the term used to describe state decisions about admission to practice and "certification" is the term used to describe the actions of the National Board in certifying accomplished practice.

schools incorporate new knowledge into their courses and to guide professional development and evaluation throughout the career. Thus, these advanced standards may be viewed as an engine that pulls along the knowledge base of the profession. Together, standards for accreditation, licensing, and certification comprise a "three-legged stool" that supports quality-assurance in the mature professions.[38]

This three-legged stool is quite wobbly in teaching, where each of the quality assurance functions is still underdeveloped. Until recently, there was no national body to establish a system of professional certification. Meanwhile, states have managed licensing and the approval of teacher education programs with little involvement of the profession itself using widely varying standards and generally weak enforcement tools. Since the 1920s, most states have licensed teachers based primarily on their graduation from a state-approved teacher education program. Thus, a critical check on quality that exists in other professions—a system for individual candidate assessment against common standards of knowledge and skill—has been missing for many decades in teaching. The program approval process, generally coordinated by the state's department of education, typically assesses the kinds of learning situations in which prospective teachers have been engaged and the time spent therein rather than what they have actually learned.

Admitting individuals into practice based on their graduation from a state-approved program was a wholesale approach to licensing. It assumed that program quality could be well defined and monitored by states; that programs would be equally effective with all of their students; and that completion of the courses or experiences mandated by the state would be sufficient to produce competent practitioners. The state approval system also assumed that markets for teachers were local: that virtually all teachers for the schools in a given state would be produced by colleges within that state, a presumption that has become increasingly untrue over time. Much of the hiring of unprepared teachers in communities that claim shortages is really a function of the poor distribution of teachers between and among states and districts with large surpluses and those with greater demand but lower levels of supply. Lack of reciprocity in state licensing requirements, along with lack of pension portability and salary credit, limit the mobility of teachers in a labor market that is now decidedly national.[39]

One problem with state approval of teacher education, according to some critics, is that the standards in many states have been out-of-touch with advances in knowledge about teaching and learning.[40] Another is that many state education agencies have inadequate budgetary resources and personnel to conduct the intensive program reviews that would support enforcement of high standards.[41] In state departments with few resources, reviews of programs are infrequent and perfunctory, revealing little about the quality of experience provided by the institutions. For example, teacher education programs in some states have been approved for more than fifteen years without any active external review.

A third problem is that, even when state agencies find weak programs, political forces within states make it difficult to close them down. Teacher education programs bring substantial revenue to universities and local communities, and the availability of large numbers of teaching candidates keeps salaries relatively low. As George Dennison notes, "The generally minimal state-prescribed criteria remain subject to local and state political influences, economic conditions within the state, and historical conditions which make change difficult."[42]

Meanwhile, many policymakers' suspicions about the quality and utility of teacher education have led them to create special routes into teaching that avoid teacher education and bypass standard licensing requirements altogether, either because they believe these are unnecessary or ineffective[43] or because they want to fill vacancies at below market wages.[44] For various reasons, then, the traditional system of teacher licensing based upon completion of specified courses in state-approved programs of study has left most practitioners, members of the public, and policymakers unconvinced that licensing standards separate out those who can teach responsibly from those who cannot. Furthermore, this system has not provided a means for the growth and transmittal of knowledge in the field or for the widespread improvement of programs.

New Standards for Teaching

In recent years, new standards for teacher education accreditation and for teacher licensing, certification, and ongoing evaluation have been promoted as a lever for promoting systemwide change in teaching.[45] The National Commission on Teaching and America's Future argued that:

Standards for teaching are the linchpin for transforming current systems of preparation, licensing, certification, and ongoing development so that they better support student learning. (Such standards) can bring clarity and focus to a set of activities that are currently poorly connected and often badly organized. . . . Clearly, if students are to achieve high standards, we can expect no less from their teachers and from other educators. Of greatest priority is reaching agreement on what teachers should know and be able to do to teach to high standards.[46]

Efforts currently underway to develop and implement more meaningful standards for teaching include the move toward performance-based standards for teacher licensing,[47] companion efforts to develop more sophisticated and authentic assessments for teachers, and the development and integration of national standards for teacher education, licensing, and certification.[48] These national efforts are being led by the new National Board for Professional Teaching Standards, an independent organization established in 1987 as the first professional body—comprised of a majority of classroom teachers—to set standards for the advanced certification of highly accomplished veteran teachers; by INTASC, a consortium of states working together on "National Board-compatible" licensing standards and assessments; and by the National Council for Accreditation of Teacher Education (NCATE), which has been strengthening standards for teacher education programs, recently incorporating the performance standards developed by INTASC.

An analogue to the bodies that offer board certification in medicine, architecture, and accounting, the mission of the National Board is to "establish high and rigorous standards for what accomplished teachers should know and be able to do, and to develop and operate a national, voluntary system to assess and certify teachers who meet these standards."[49] The Board's standards and performance-based assessments—much more thoughtful and rigorous than any that preceded them—have been the engine behind the standard-setting movement. The standards developed by the National Board, INTASC, and NCATE are linked to one another and to the new student standards developed by professional associations such as the National Council of Teachers of Mathematics. These initiatives incorporate knowledge about teaching and learning that supports a view of teaching as complex, contingent on students' needs and instructional goals, and reciprocal—that is, continually shaped and reshaped by students' responses to learning events.

The new standards and assessments take into explicit account the teaching challenges posed by a student body that is multicultural and multilingual, that possesses multiple intelligences, and that represents diverse approaches to learning. By reflecting new subject matter standards for students and the demands of learner diversity, as well as the expectation that teachers must collaborate with colleagues and parents in order to succeed, the standards define teaching as a collegial, professional activity that responds to considerations of subjects and students. By examining teaching in the light of learning, they put considerations of effectiveness at the center of practice. This view contrasts with that of the recent "technicist" era of teacher training and evaluation, in which teaching was seen as the implementation of set routines and formulas for behavior, unresponsive to either clients or curriculum goals.

Another important attribute of the new standards is that they are *performance-based*: that is, they describe what teachers should know, be like, and be able to do rather than listing courses that teachers should take in order to be awarded a license. This shift toward performance-based standard setting is in line with the approach to licensing taken in other professions and with the changes already occurring in a number of states. This approach aims to clarify what the criteria are for a determination of competence, placing more emphasis on the abilities teachers develop than the hours they spend taking classes. Ultimately, performance-based licensing standards could enable states to permit greater innovation and diversity in how teacher education programs operate by assessing their outcomes rather than merely regulating their inputs or procedures. Well-developed assessments of candidates, if they actually measured the important attributes of teaching knowledge and skill, could open up a variety of pathways and types of preparation for entering teaching without lowering standards as current emergency licensure provisions and many alternative certification programs do.

The INTASC standards call for a staged set of examinations that evaluate subject matter knowledge and knowledge about teaching and learning in paper-and-pencil tests at the end of preservice education, and then assess applied teaching skills when the candidate is practicing under supervision during an internship or induction year through a portfolio assessment much like that of the National Board. The portfolio assessments are scored by trained experienced teachers and used as the basis for awarding a professional license at the end of the probationary teaching period. The portfolio tasks examine how teachers plan and guide instruction in the light of new standards for student learning, evaluate student work and learning and adapt teaching accordingly, use a variety of curriculum materials, and handle problems of practice. Candidates who have been licensed through this process will be well positioned to sit for National Board certification later in their careers.

The possibilities for pursuing these new assessments are strengthened by the creation of a program for state partnerships for performance-based licensing and accreditation through NCATE, which has developed several strategies by which states can work with the Council to review and approve programs. NCATE's standards revision in 1987 aimed to ensure that teacher education programs were grounded in knowledge about teaching and learning; another revision in 1994 incorporated the model INTASC standards for what beginning teachers should know and be able to do; an initiative launched in 1997, "NCATE 2000," aims to create a performance-based system that takes into account graduates' performance in the accreditation decision. While continuing to examine what programs do in the course of preparing teachers, the system will also use performance measures ranging from education schools' internal assessments of students, including portfolios, videotapes, and performance events of various kinds, to scores on performance-based state licensing examinations that are compatible with NCATE's standards. In addition to incorporating the INTASC standards for preservice teacher education programs, the standards for advanced programs are expected to reflect those for accomplished teaching established by the National Board.

As a result of these combined initiatives, systems of licensing and certification that directly assess what teachers know and can do could ultimately replace the traditional methods of requiring graduation from an approved program or tallying specific courses as the basis for granting program approval, a license, or credit for professional growth. Furthermore, because the three sets of standards described above are substantively connected and form a continuum of development along the career path of the teacher, they conceptualize the main dimensions along which teachers can work to improve their practice. By providing vivid descriptions of high-quality teaching in specific teaching areas, "they clarify what the profession expects its members to get better at. . . . Profession-defined standards provide the basis on which the profession can lay down its agenda and expectations for professional development and accountability."[50]

Uses and Effects of the New Standards

In a short time, the new teaching standards have achieved a noteworthy consensus among policymakers and members of the profession: By 1997, 35 states belonged to INTASC and at least 24 had formally adopted or adapted the INTASC standards for beginning teacher licensing. Nearly twenty states were involved in developing or piloting INTASC assessments for either the preservice Test of Teaching Knowledge or the portfolio for beginning teachers. Twenty-six states and more than 70 school districts had established incentives for teachers to pursue National Board certification, including fee supports, professional development offerings, and stipends or advancement opportunities for those achieving certification. Seventeen states had agreed to accept National Board certification as the basis for granting a license to out-of-state entrants or as the basis for granting "recertification" to experienced teachers. Eight had agreed to offer higher salaries, sometimes significantly so, to teachers successful in achieving certification. School districts like Cincinnati, Ohio and Rochester, New York had incorporated the National Board standards into teacher evaluation criteria, using them as one basis for recognition as a "lead teacher" who mentors others and as a basis for salary increments in a performance-based compensation schedule.

In addition, by 1997, 41 states had established partnerships with NCATE—more than double the number engaged in such partnerships three years earlier. These partnerships include various approaches to the use of national professional standards, ranging from the possibility of joint institutional reviews by state and NCATE teams to permission for teacher education programs to become state-approved by meeting NCATE accreditation standards. Fifteen states were using NCATE standards to approve all of their teacher education institutions, a five-fold increase over the previous three years. And several were making plans to participate in NCATE's new performance-based accreditation plan that will approve institutions using data about the performance of their graduates on assessments like those developed by INTASC.

More states are creating induction programs to provide mentoring and support for beginning teachers. Among teachers with less than five years of experience, 55 percent report that they experienced some kind of formal induction program during their first year of teaching. By contrast, only 16 to 17 percent of teachers with more than ten years of experience had had such help when they entered the profession.[51] Like all other education policies, however, access to induction programs varies widely across the country. More than three-fourths of beginners report having experienced induction supports in states that put such programs in place several years ago—Connecticut, Florida, Indiana, Kentucky, Missouri, North Carolina, Oklahoma, and Pennsylvania. However, in states like Rhode Island and Massachusetts that have relied only on local initiatives, fewer than 15 percent of beginning teachers have received any kind of systematic mentoring.

Finally, by 1997, 14 states had established fully independent or quasi-independent professional standards boards for teaching like those that exist in other professions. Most of these boards were created after

1990. In these states, teachers, other educators, and public members who sit on the standards board have assumed responsibility for setting standards for program approval and licensing. New boards like those in Indiana, Georgia, Kentucky, and North Carolina have adopted the continuum of teaching standards represented by NCATE, INTASC, and the National Board as a foundation for redesigning the preparation, licensing, induction, and ongoing professional development of teachers.

These actions, collectively, lay the groundwork for what Ingvarson calls a standards-guided model of professional development, which would include:

1. Profession-defined *teaching standards* that provide direction and milestones for professional development over the long term of a career in teaching;

2. An *infrastructure for professional learning* whose primary purpose is to enable teachers to gain the knowledge and skill embodied in the teaching standards;

3. Staged career structures and pay systems that provide *incentives and recognition* for attaining these teaching standards; and

4. A credible system of *professional certification* based on valid assessments of whether teachers have attained the levels of performance defined by the standards.[52]

Although some of these components have begun to be put in place, the real impact of standards—widespread use for professional development, as well as for making decisions about which institutions are allowed to prepare teachers, which individuals are allowed to enter teaching, and how advancement in the field will be acknowledged—has yet to occur.

Thus far, only Connecticut has a nearly fully functioning system of INTASC-based performance assessments, although several other states are moving ahead rapidly with pilots. As of mid-1998, just under 2,000 teachers had been certified by the National Board, although 6 percent of public school teachers (about 160,000) had participated in professional development to prepare for certification.[53] Federal funds were appropriated late in 1997 to support candidate fees, with an intention to underwrite the costs of 100,000 candidacies for Board certification by the year 2005. And just over 40 percent of institutions offering teacher education programs are professionally accredited, although a growing number of institutions have entered the accreditation system.

If policies are enacted to encourage their use, there are reasons to believe that the new standards could exert greater leverage on practice than program approval and licensing systems have in the past. For one thing, the standards offer a conception of teaching that is linked to student learning, and they use performance-based modes of assessment. These two features together engage teachers in activities that help them evaluate their effects on students and actively refine their practice, a much different outcome from that associated with the completion of multiple choice tests. The standards envision licensing, certification, and accreditation systems that are structured to *develop* more thoughtful teaching rather than merely to *select* candidates into or out of teaching. They do this by engaging teachers in the individual and collective analysis of teaching and its effects, and in professional decision making. They offer new roles for teachers that involve them more deeply in the processes of assessment. For example, in addition to being assessed themselves, teachers:

- sit on boards and committees in charge of developing and reviewing the standards and assessments;

- participate in the writing, piloting, and refinement of assessment tasks;

- analyze the practice of exemplary teachers to develop standards, tasks, benchmarks, and professional development materials aimed at helping other teachers meet the standards;

- serve as assessors for the assessments;

- act as mentors for teachers who are developing their portfolios.[54]

Because these activities center around authentic tasks of teaching which are examined from the perspective of standards within the contexts of subject matter and students, they create a setting in which serious discourse about teaching can occur. Because evidence of the effects of teaching on student learning is at the core of the exercises, candidates and assessors are continually examining the nexus between teachers' actions and students' responses. Focusing on the outcomes of practice while making teaching public in this way creates the basis for developing shared norms of practice.

Connecticut's process of implementing INTASC-based portfolios for licensing beginning teachers illuminates how this can occur. Connecticut's licensing system is designed as much as a professional development system as a measurement activity, and educators are involved in every aspect of its development and implementation, so that these opportunities are widespread. Each assessment is developed with the assistance of a teacher in residence in the department of education;

advisory committees of teachers, teacher educators, and administrators guide the development of standards and assessments; hundreds of educators have been convened to provide feedback on drafts of the standards. Still more educators have been involved in the assessments themselves as cooperating teachers and school-based mentors who work with beginning teachers on developing their practice, as assessors who are trained to score the portfolios, and as expert teachers who convene regional support seminars to help candidates learn about the standards and the process of developing portfolios. Individuals involved in each of these roles are engaged in preparation that is organized around the examination of cases and the development of evidence connected to the standards.

Raymond Pecheone and Kendyll Stansbury, who are system developers in Connecticut, explain how the standards are used in professional development settings for beginning and veteran teachers:

The state support and assessment system must be centered around standards that apply across contexts and that embrace a variety of teaching practices. Teaching is highly contextual, however, varying with the strengths and needs of students, strengths of the teacher, and the availability of resources. The support program needs to help beginning teachers see how to apply general principles in their particular teaching contexts. The design currently being implemented in the Connecticut secondary projects begins support sessions by modeling selected principles, then having teachers discuss work they have brought (e.g., a student assignment, a videotape illustrating discourse, student work samples) in light of the principles presented.

For experienced teachers who will become the assessors and support providers the reverse is true. They typically understand contextual teaching practices well. Although they are acquainted with the general principles at some level because they keep abreast of developments in their teaching specialty, they do not generally have extensive experience in either articulating the principles to others or in seeing their application across multiple contexts. An intensive training program for both assessors and mentors ensures similar understandings among individuals and gives them opportunities to articulate how these principles are applied in classrooms.[55]

Teachers report that the process of analyzing practice in this way has transformational influences on their ongoing work. Embedded in state teacher assessment policy, these processes can have far-reaching effects. By one estimate, more than 40 percent of Connecticut's teachers have served as assessees, assessors, mentors, or cooperating teachers under either the earlier beginning teacher performance assessment or the new portfolios. By the year 2010, 80 percent of elementary teachers, and nearly as many secondary teachers, will have participated in the new assessment system as candidates, support providers, or assessors.[56]

In states like Indiana, North Carolina, or Maryland that have recently adopted a comprehensive approach to professional standards-based reform, a continuum for teacher development is formed by the requirement of NCATE accreditation for teacher education programs, the development and state funding of professional development school partnerships for the preparation of all prospective teachers, the adoption of INTASC standards and assessments for beginning teacher licensing, the establishment of financial and educational incentives for veteran teachers to pursue National Board certification, and encouragement for school districts and colleges to use National Board standards as a basis for ongoing professional development opportunities. These steps hold promise for creating a professionwide conversation and set of learning experiences that could dramatically transform the ways that teachers look at and develop their craft.

Teaching Standards, Supply, and Inequality

While new teaching standards may pose possibilities for raising the quality of teacher preparation, these advances will have little import for the education of the nation's most vulnerable students if they continue to be taught by teachers who are unprepared, assigned out of field, or quick to leave in the face of difficult conditions and few supports. While disparities in salaries and working conditions make teacher recruitment more difficult in central cities and poor rural areas, many states and districts continue to lower or eliminate standards for entry rather than to create incentives that will attract an adequate supply of teachers. The bi-modal teaching force that has developed in rich and poor communities poses the risk that the nation may experience heightened inequality in opportunities to learn—with all of the social dangers that implies—at the very time it is crucial to prepare all students more effectively for the greater challenges they face.

A legitimate question can be raised as to whether improving standards will create or exacerbate teacher shortages and whether standards will limit access to historically underrepresented groups, as the professionalization of medicine did many years ago. Interestingly, the reverse has historically been true in teaching. As Michael Sedlak and Steven Schlossman found in their historical overview:

It has proved possible, time and again, to raise standards during periods of protracted shortage. Not only has the raising of standards not exacerbated teacher shortages, it may even—at least where accompanied by significant increases in teachers' salaries—have helped to alleviate them and, at the same time, enhanced popular respect for teaching as a profession.[57]

During these periods of raised standards and salaries, representation of women and minorities remained stable or increased. Declines in the entrance of minority candidates to teaching occurred during the 1970s and '80s primarily because, as other professions previously closed to such students opened up and teaching salaries declined, able students of all backgrounds defected from teaching in large numbers, and those who continued to choose teaching were less academically prepared. As teaching salaries increased once again, along with standards, in the late 1980s and early 1990s, the number of minority entrants to teaching has increased once again, although not to levels that mirror the growing share of children of color in the nation's schools.[58]

Today there is no absolute shortage of teachers, but there are distributional problems that create apparent shortages in specific fields and locations. In fact, the United States prepares many more teachers each year than actually enter teaching, and many states have large surpluses of teachers whom they cannot hire. Spot shortages occur in part because some states prepare relatively few teachers but have rapidly growing student enrollments and/or high teacher turnover, and because there is little reciprocity in licensing across states. Hence, it is difficult to get teachers from where they are prepared to where they are needed. In addition, spot shortages occur because of inequalities in salaries and working conditions across states and districts; inattention to planning and recruitment; inadequate national and regional information about vacancies; and inadequate incentives for recruiting teachers to the fields and locations where they are most needed.[59] Moreover, nearly 30 percent of new teachers leave within five years of entry. With even higher rates in the most disadvantaged districts that offer fewest supports, this revolving door of recruits leads to continual pressure for hiring.

It is also true that standards that count can be uncomfortable because they highlight shortcomings in current practice and meeting them requires change. Thus it is often the case that as standards are raised loopholes are created. This has occurred in a number of states as they have raised licensing standards: the higher standards simultaneously gave rise to temporary or alternative routes that allowed many candidates to avoid meeting the new standards. In virtually every case, the less-prepared candidates are hired to teach to the least-advantaged students, thus denying them the benefits of the intended reforms. On the other hand, some states have simultaneously enacted incentives and created development opportunities while raising standards, thus enhancing the quality of practice and equality of opportunity across the board.[60] Similar efforts to avoid the discomforts of change associated with higher standards have occurred with regard to teacher education accreditation. As NCATE has raised its standards, alternative accreditation proposals have been put forward to allow schools to continue to practice with the imprimatur of accreditation without having to meet external scrutiny against rigorous professionwide standards.

States and communities that have reversed these trends have equalized resources for teachers' salaries and have created proactive recruitment and induction systems with appropriate incentives and supports for teaching in high-need areas.[61] A key question is whether other states and communities are willing to invest in these kinds of strategies in lieu of lowering standards for the teachers of the most vulnerable and least powerful students. Among the strategies with the greatest potential for addressing supply imbalances and achieving greater equity in students' access to high-quality teachers are the following:

1. **Raising and equalizing teachers' salaries while raising standards:** Connecticut's 1986 Education Enhancement Act created a minimum beginning teacher salary level and offered state funds to districts on an equalizing basis to reach that target. Meanwhile standards for licensing were strengthened with more rigorous requirements for teacher education, carefully designed teacher licensing examinations, and a beginning teacher internship and assessment program. Within three years, Connecticut's cities went from having shortages to having surpluses of teachers, and the quality of teacher preparation and practice rose steadily, along with levels of student achievement.

2. **Establishing reciprocity across states,** using common standards and assessments like those developed by INTASC, as a number of states are now beginning to do. This would enable new and veteran teachers in states with surpluses, like Maine, Minnesota, Wisconsin, and Iowa, to move more easily to states that experience shortfalls, like California, Texas, and Florida.

3. **Creating national recruitment initiatives and developing on-line information technologies** for reaching teachers who are interested in moving and for managing their applications in a timely, efficient way, as districts like New Haven, California[62] and Fairfax, Virginia[63] have done.

4. Granting a license to out-of-state entrants who have achieved National Board Certification. About twenty states have enacted rules granting a license to any teacher who has met the rigorous standards of the National Board. With about 160,000 public school teachers across the nation who have engaged in professional development to prepare them for Board certification, and the prospect of 100,000 Board-certified teachers by the year 2005,[64] this would help create a national labor market of excellent teachers and provide incentives for others to develop their skills by pursuing Board certification.

5. Creating service scholarship programs to prepare high-ability candidates in shortage fields. Research has found that scholarship programs that function like forgivable loans have been very successful in getting fully prepared candidates into high-need fields and high-need locations in professions like medicine as well as teaching. One of the most successful state programs is the North Carolina Teaching Fellows, which fully underwrites the college education of thousands of high-ability students who prepare to teach and who teach for at least four years in North Carolina schools. This program has increased the supply of male and minority teachers as well as individuals in shortage fields like mathematics and science.[65]

6. Expanding teacher education programs in high-need fields. In many states there are inadequate numbers of teacher training slots in particular high-need areas, such as mathematics, physical science, special education, and English as a Second Language. Targeted incentives to expand the number of slots programs offer in shortage fields would ensure that there are programs available for candidates to attend. There is substantial precedent for this in medicine where the federal government subsidizes the creation and expansion of training programs to increase the supply of physicians in high-need areas.

7. Providing incentives for the establishment of more extended teacher education programs. Studies have found that teachers prepared in extended teacher education programs enter and remain in teaching at higher rates than teachers in traditional four-year programs and remain at much higher rates than those prepared in short-term alternative certification programs. The National Commission on Teaching estimated that the costs of preparing teachers in extended programs is actually $1000 less per candidate remaining in the profession after three to five years than the costs for preparing candidates in shorter programs who leave much sooner. States that want to develop a stable, high-quality teaching force can invest their training resources more wisely by emphasizing program models that prepare effective career teachers.

8. Providing incentives for community college/college pathways that prepare paraprofessionals for certification. Another high-yield source of teacher supply, especially of minority teachers, is the pool of current paraprofessionals who are not yet in college. A number of successful programs now exist to help these individuals who are already committed to education complete their undergraduate education and certification requirements in a streamlined, supported fashion through pathways that take advantage of both community colleges and universities working in partnership.[66]

9. Creating high-quality induction programs for beginning teachers. Beginning teachers who have access to intensive mentoring by expert colleagues are much less likely to leave teaching in the early years. A number of districts, like Cincinnati, Columbus, and Toledo and Rochester (New York) have reduced attrition of beginning teachers from more than 30 percent to only 5 percent by providing expert mentors with released time to coach beginners in their first year on the job.[67] These young teachers not only stay in the profession at higher rates but quickly become more competent than those who must learn by trial and error.

10. Creating incentives for districts to hire fully qualified teachers. School districts often have disincentives to hire qualified teachers or have inadequate systems for doing so. On the financial side, some districts refuse to hire more experienced qualified teachers who cost more when they can hire less expensive unqualified teachers. Some let go of large numbers of qualified teachers in early retirement buyouts to reduce salary costs, and then hire unqualified new teachers. Many have cumbersome, non-automated hiring procedures with built-in delays that make early, efficient hiring almost impossible, thus losing qualified candidates. Some prefer to hire patronage candidates rather than qualified teachers. States that do not allow the hiring of unqualified teachers have careful management systems and legislated incentives to ensure a highly qualified teaching force. Among these are policies that allow salary reimbursements only for qualified teachers; require districts to hire qualified teachers who have applied or reassign other fully certified teachers not currently in classrooms before hiring less-qualified teachers; and require specific procedures for recruiting and advertising before an uncertified teacher can be hired. In addition, states can provide assistance for districts to automate and streamline their personnel functions to facilitate early, efficient identification and hiring of qualified personnel.

States and communities that have chosen to invest in the recruitment, support, and retention of well-prepared teachers in all schools have been able to pursue excellence and equity in tandem. These efforts appear to have substantial payoff. For example, one recent study found that, after controlling for student characteristics like poverty and language status, the strongest predictor of state-level student achievement in reading and mathematics on the National Assessment of Educational Progress was each state's proportion of well-qualified teachers.[68] With carefully crafted policies that rest upon professional standards, invest in serious preparation, and make access to knowledge a priority for all teachers, it is possible to imagine a day when each student will, in fact, have a right to a caring, competent, and qualified teacher working in a school organized to support his or her success.

NOTES

1. Carnegie Forum on Education and the Economy, *A Nation Prepared: Teachers for the 21st Century* (Washington: Author, 1986); Holmes Group, *Tomorrow's Teachers: A Report of the Holmes Group* (East Lansing, MI: Author, 1986); National Commission on Teaching and America's Future (NCTAF), *What Matters Most: Teaching for America's Future* (New York: Author, 1996).

2. National Center for Education Statistics (NCES), *National Assessment of Educational Progress 1996 Mathematics Report Card for the Nation and the States* (Washington: U.S. Department of Education, 1997): Table D.1.

3. National Center for Education Statistics (NCES), *Condition of Education, 1997* (Washington: U.S. Department of Education, 1997): pp. 294-296.

4. National Center for Education Statistics (NCES), *Schools and Staffing in the United States: A Statistical Profile, 1993-94* (Washington: U.S. Department of Education, 1996): p. 154.

5. National Center for Education Statistics (NCES), *America's Teachers: Profile of a Profession* (Washington: U.S. Department of Education, 1997): p. 141.

6. National Commission on Teaching and America's Future (NCTAF), *What Matters Most: Teaching for America's Future.*

7. Deborah Ball and David K. Cohen, "Developing Practice, Developing Practitioners: Toward a Practice-based Theory of Professional Education" in *Teaching as the Learning Profession: A Handbook of Policy and Practice*, eds. Linda Darling-Hammond and Gary Sykes (San Francisco: Jossey Bass, in press).

8. Lee Shulman, "Knowledge and Teaching: Foundations of the New Reform," *Harvard Educational Review* 57, no. 1 (1987): pp. 1-22.

9. Peter Grimmett and Allen M. MacKinnon, "Craft Knowledge and the Education of Teachers," in *Review of Research in Education*, ed. Gerald Grant, Vol. 18 (Washington: American Educational Research Association, 1992): pp. 385-456.

10. Gary Fenstermacher, "The Place of Alternative Certification in the Education of Teachers," *Peabody Journal of Education* 67, no. 3 (1992).

11. Ball and Cohen, "Developing Practice, Developing Practitioners: Toward a Practice-based Theory of Professional Education."

12. For reviews, see: Linda Darling-Hammond, *Doing What Matters Most: Investing in Quality Teaching* (New York: National Commission on Teaching and America's Future [NCTAF], 1977); Linda Darling-Hammond, *The Right to Learn: A Blueprint for Creating Schools that Work* (San Francisco: Jossey Bass, 1996); and National Commission on Teaching and America's Future (NCTAF), *What Matters Most: Teaching for America's Future.*

13. R. F. Ferguson, "Paying for Public Education: New Evidence on How and Why Money Matters," *Harvard Journal on Legislation* 28, no. 2 (Summer 1991): pp.465-498.

14. R. F. Ferguson and H. F. Ladd, "How and Why Money Matters: An Analysis of Alabama Schools," in *Holding Schools Accountable*, ed. Helen Ladd (Washington: Brookings Institution, 1996), pp. 265-298.

15. Eleanor Armour-Thomas, et al., *An Outlier Study of Elementary and Middle Schools in New York City: Final Report* (New York City Board of Education, 1989).

16. Ferguson, "Paying for Public Education: New Evidence on How and Why Money Matters"; Ferguson and Ladd, "How and Why Money Matters: An Analysis of Alabama Schools."

17. Parmalee Hawk, Charles R. Coble, and Melvin Swanson, "Certification: It Does Matter," *Journal of Teacher Education* 36, no. 3 (1985): p. 13-15; National Assessment of Educational Progress, *1992 NAEP Trial State Assessment* (Washington: U.S. Department of Education, 1994); G. A. Knoblock, "Continuing Professional Education for Teachers and its Relationship to Teacher Effectiveness," Unpublished dissertation, Michigan State University, 1986, *Dissertation Abstracts International* 46 (02), 3325A, University microfilms no. AAC8529729; Sandra L. Sanders, S. D. Skonie-Hardin, and W. H. Phelps, "The Effects of Teacher Educational Attainment on Student Educational Attainment in Four Regions of Virginia: Implications for Administrators," Paper presented at the Annual Meeting of the Mid-South Educational Research Association, November 1994.

18. Rob Greenwald, Larry V. Hedges, and R. D. Laine, "The Effect of School Resources on Student Achievement," *Review of Educational Research* 66 (1996): pp. 361-396.

19. Patricia Ashton and Linda Crocker, "Does Teacher Certification Make a Difference?" *Florida Journal of Teacher Education* 38, no. 3 (1986): pp. 73-83; E. G. Begle, *Critical Variables in Mathematics Education* (Washington: Mathematical Association of America and National Council of Teachers of Mathematics, 1979); Linda Darling-Hammond, A. E. Wise, and Stephen P. Klein, *A License to Teach: Building a Profession for 21st Century Schools* (Boulder: Westview Press, 1995); C. A. Druva and R. D. Anderson, "Science Teacher Characteristics by Teacher Behavior and by Student Outcome: a Meta-Analysis of Research," *Journal of Research in Science Teaching* 20, no. 5 (1983): pp. 467-479; Carolyn Evertson, Willis Hawley, and Marilyn Zlotnick, "Making a Difference in Educational Quality through Teacher Education," *Journal of Teacher Education* 36, no. 3 (1985): pp. 2-12; National Commission on Teaching and America's Future (NCTAF), *What Matters Most: Teaching for America's Future.*

20. For recent analyses see John Goodlad, *Teachers for Our Nation's Schools* (San Francisco: Jossey Bass, 1990); Kenneth R. Howey and Nancy L. Zimpher, *Profiles of Preservice Teacher Education* (Albany: State University of New York, 1989); Kenneth M. Zeichner, "Traditions of Practice in U.S. Preservice Teacher Education Programs," *Teaching and Teacher Education* 9 (February, 1993): pp. 1-13.

21. National Commission on Teaching and America's Future, *What Matters Most*, p. 32.

22. Michael D. Andrew, "The Differences Between Graduates of Four-Year and Five-Year Teacher Preparation Programs," *Journal of Teacher Education* 41 (1990): pp.

45-51; Michael D. Andrew and Richard L. Schwab, "Has Reform in Teacher Education Influenced Teacher Performance?: An Outcome Assessment of Graduates of Eleven Teacher Education Programs," *Action in Teacher Education* 17, no. 3 (1995): pp. 43-53; Jon J. Denton and William H. Peters, "Program Assessment Report Curriculum Evaluation of a Non-Traditional Program for Certifying Teachers" (Unpublished report, College Station, TX: Texas A and M University, 1988); A. B. Dyal, "An Exploratory Study to Determine Principals' Perceptions Concerning the Effectiveness of a Fifth-Year Preparation Program," Paper presented at the annual meeting of the Mid-South Educational Research Association, New Orleans: 1993; H. Shin, "Estimating Future Teacher Supply: An Application of Survival Analysis," Paper presented at the Annual Meeting of the American Educational Research Association, New Orleans, 1994.

23. Linda Darling-Hammond, *Professional Development Schools: Schools for Developing a Profession* (New York: Teachers College Press, 1994).

24. Organization for Economic Cooperation and Development (OECD), *Education at a Glance* (Paris: 1995); National Commission on Teaching and America's Future (NCTAF), *What Matters Most*.

25. Ball and Cohen, "Developing Practice, Developing Practitioners: Toward A Practice-Based Theory of Professional Education."

26. C. A. Brown, M. S. Smith, and M. K. Stein, "Linking Teacher Support to Enhanced Classroom Instruction," Paper presented at annual meeting of the American Educational Research Association (New York 1995); David Wiley and Bokhee Yoon, "Teacher Reports of Opportunity to Learn: Analyses of the 1993 California Learning Assessment System," *Educational Evaluation and Policy Analysis* 17(3): 355-370.

27. David Cohen and Heather Hill, "Instructional Policy and Classroom Performance: The Mathematics Reform in California," in Darling-Hammond and Sykes, eds., *Teaching as the Learning Profession*.

28. Linda Darling-Hammond, *Doing What Matters Most: Investing in Quality Teaching*.

29. Richard Howard, Randy Hitz, and Larry Baker, *Comparative Study of Expenditures per Student Credit Hour of Education Programs to Programs of other Disciplines and Professions* (Montana State University-Bozeman, 1997). See also: Howard Ebmeier, Susan Twombly, and D. J. Teeter. "The Comparability and Adequacy of Financial Support for Schools of Education," *Journal of Teacher Education* 42 (1991): pp. 226-235.

30. National Center for Education Statistics (NCES), *America's Teachers: Profile of a Profession*, p. 31.

31. Linda Darling-Hammond, *Doing What Matters Most: Investing in Quality Teaching* (New York: National Commission on Teaching and America's Future (NCTAF), 1997).

32. National Center for Education Statistics (NCES), *America's Teachers: Profile of a Profession*, p. 30.

33. Ibid. Tables 3.5 and A3.2.

34. Darling-Hammond, *Doing What Matters Most: Investing in Quality Teaching*.

35. Darling-Hammond, Wise, and Klein, *A License To Teach*; Richard Elmore, and Sarah Fuhrman, "Opportunity to Learn and the State Role in Education," in *The Debate on Opportunity-to-Learn Standards: Commissioned Papers* (Washington: National Governors Association, 1993).

36. Elmore and Fuhrman, "Opportunity to Learn," p. 86.

37. Darling-Hammond, Wise, and Klein, *A License To Teach*.

38. National Commission on Teaching and America's Future (NCTAF), *What Matters Most*.

39. National Commission on Teaching and America's Future (NCTAF), *What Matters Most*.

40. Darling-Hammond, Wise, and Klein, *A License To Teach*.

41. R. F. Campbell, G. E. Sroufe, and D. H. Layton, *Strengthening State Departments of Education* (Midwestern Administration Center, University of Chicago, 1967); J. L. David, *Transforming State Agencies to Support Education Reform* (Washington: National Governors' Association, 1994).

42. George M. Dennison, "National Standards in Teacher Preparation: a Commitment to Quality," *The Chronicle of Higher Education*, A40, 1992.

43. Linda Darling-Hammond, "Teaching and Knowledge: Policy Issues Posed by Alternative Certification for Teachers," *Peabody Journal of Education* 67, no. 3 (1992), pp. 123-154.

44. Goodlad, *Teachers for Our Nation's Schools*.

45. Darling-Hammond, Wise, and Klein, *A License to Teach*.

46. National Commission on Teaching and America's Future (NCTAF), *What Matters Most*, p. 67.

47. Interstate New Teacher Support and Assessment Consortium (INTASC), *Model Standards for Beginning Teacher Licensing and Development: A Resource for State Dialogue* (Washington: Council for Chief State School Officers, 1992).

48. Darling-Hammond, Wise, and Klein, *A License To Teach*.

49. National Board for Professional Teaching Standards (NBPTS), *Toward High and Rigorous Standards for the Teaching Profession* (Detroit: NBPTS, 1989).

50. Lawrence Ingvarson, *Teaching Standards: Foundations for Professional Development Reform* (Monash University 1997): p. 1.

51. Darling-Hammond, *Doing What Matters Most: Investing in Quality Teaching*.

52. Ingvarson, *Teaching Standards*.

53. Darling-Hammond, *Doing What Matters Most: Investing in Quality Teaching*.

54. Darling-Hammond, Wise, and Klein, *A License to Teach*.

55. Raymond Pecheone and Kendyll Stansbury, "Connecting Teacher Assessment and School Reform," *Elementary School Journal* 97, pp.172-173.

56. Ibid., p. 174.

57. Michael Sedlak and Steven Schlossman, *Who Will Teach? Historical Perspectives on the Changing Appeal of Teaching as a Profession* (R-3472). (Santa Monica, CA: The Rand Corporation, November, 1986), p. 39.

58. Linda Darling-Hammond, Mary Dilworth, and G. K. Bullmaster, "Recruiting and Retaining Educators of Color," prepared for United States Department of Education Conference on Teacher Recruitment, Washington, 1996.

59. National Commission on Teaching and America's Future (NCTAF), *What Matters Most*.

60. Ibid.

61. Ibid.

62. *Investing in Quality Teaching: The Case of New Haven, California* (New York: National Commission on Teaching and America's Future [NCTAF], in press).

63. National Commission on Teaching and America's Future (NCTAF), *What Matters Most*.

64. Darling-Hammond, *Doing What Matters Most*.

65. National Commission on Teaching and America's Future (NCTAF), *What Matters Most*.

66. Recruiting New Teachers, *Breaking the Class Ceiling* (Belmont, MA: Author, 1996).

67. National Commission on Teaching and America's Future (NCTAF), *What Matters Most.*

68. Linda Darling-Hammond, *Teacher Quality and Student Achievement: A Review of State Policy Evidence*, Center for the Study of Teaching and Policy (forthcoming).

CHAPTER XI

Of Promises and Unresolved Puzzles: Reforming Teacher Education with Professional Development Schools

BETTY LOU WHITFORD AND PHYLLIS METCALF-TURNER

A Professional Development School in Action

It's the first day of the new school year for teachers (not students) at Garden Grove Elementary School, a Chapter One school for students in an urban neighborhood in Louisville, Kentucky. About 45 adults are slowly entering the library where a meeting is about to begin. Several pairs of teachers are talking excitedly about workshops they attended during the summer, while others are gathered around the coffee-and-pastries table.

Already seated together at one of the tables in the far left corner of the room are six University of Louisville graduate students who have been assigned to Garden Grove for their "professional year field experience" as a result of the Professional Development School partnership between the school and the university. The students' graduate status and the "professional year field experience" are a radical departure from what Garden Grove teachers had been accustomed to in years past. These Master of Arts in Teaching students are not doing eight weeks of student teaching at the end of their program; nor are they there for shorter practicum or observation assignments. Rather, the MATs, as they are often referred to, will be at Garden Grove for most of the year on a regular basis.

These six students are part of a larger cohort of about thirty students divided into small groups for assignment to one of five elementary schools working with the University of Louisville in Professional Development School partnerships. Like the other members of the larger cohort, the six students at Garden Grove—three females and three males—already hold degrees in disciplines other than education. Many in the program are making a career change in seeking initial certification in elementary education. The teacher preparation program they have entered was collaboratively designed by classroom teachers and education faculty.

Betty Lou Whitford is Professor of Education at the University of Louisville. She currently co-directs the Leading Edge Professional Development School Network affiliated with NCREST. Phyllis Metcalf-Turner is Assistant Professor of Early and Middle Childhood Education at the University of Louisville, where she serves also as a University Liaison for a Professional Development School.

After introducing the MAT students, the university liaison updates the faculty on the features of the teacher education program for the benefit of teachers who are new to the building and unfamiliar with the Professional Development School partnership, which is now in its third year.

The liaison shares highlights of the upcoming "professional year," pointing out that the students are required to "live the life of a teacher" during the year. This means they are expected to attend all meetings the faculty attend, including professional development sessions, committee meetings, and parent-teacher conferences. MAT students will have experiences at both primary and intermediate grade levels, they will attend teacher education courses at the university on a "block" schedule, and they will rotate to a rural elementary school for five weeks during the spring semester while the MAT students in the rural school spend those five weeks at Garden Grove.

During the next two hours, the MATs and the university liaison along with the school's faculty listen to announcements about school and district issues, committee work, and classroom reassignments. After the meeting, the MATs and their mentor teachers come together with the university liaison to talk about programmatic as well as school-based expectations and requirements. It is during this meeting that the students ask the teachers for ideas they may have for a collaborative leadership project.

Required in the MAT program, this project addresses one of the nine "Standards for Experienced Teachers" issued by the state of Kentucky. Teacher education students in Kentucky must provide evidence of meeting all nine standards during their programs. Right away, several of the teachers mention the lack of parent involvement and the school's low rating by Chapter One evaluators on this issue. During their discussion, the MATs learn that there is a low literacy rate in the community and at least some of the teachers feel that this is a reason for the lack of parent involvement. Another reason offered is the "cross-cultural communication problem"; that is, many teachers at Garden Grove frequently experience difficulty discussing students' problems with their parents.

Together, the MATs and the mentor teachers sketch out several potential strategies for a project aimed at improving parent involvement. These include introducing literacy learning activities to both students and parents, such as applying for a library card, visiting the local branch library for storytelling activities, visiting a book store to purchase a book of the child's own choosing, inviting parents to school for a "read-in" where students read and dramatize a story; designing activities which invite parents into their child's classroom; and improving teachers' awareness about cross-cultural communication differences.

After roughing out these strategies, the MATs and mentor teachers turn their attention to what it will take to implement the project. One of the teachers mentions grant development; another observes that nothing will improve if they do not address the cultural problems. One of the teachers turns to the university liaison and asks, "What do you think will help in this area?" The liaison tells them that several faculty members at the university have expertise in issues of diversity and classroom management. Another teacher suggests that their professional development workshops already scheduled for the year might be the venue for addressing these needs.

One of the mentor teachers volunteers to work with the liaison in preparing a grant proposal to fund the project. They also decide that three professional development workshops should focus on literacy instruction for students from diverse cultural, economic, and ethnic backgrounds; classroom management; and cross-cultural communication.

Later in the year, the grant proposal is funded jointly by the school system and university. Three professors from the university including the liaison are invited to facilitate the workshops, which are presented over a three-day period and attended by both certified and non-certified staff. Evaluation data reported by Garden Grove's teachers and staff indicate a high level of satisfaction.

Beginning in late fall, the MAT students along with their mentor teachers begin to implement plans for the literacy project. The two activities designed to increase parent involvement prove to be a great success. Parents have the opportunity to accompany students on a field trip to the local book store and to participate in the schoolwide "read-in." At the end of their experiences at Garden Grove, the MAT students have achieved the dual goals of the program: providing leadership in the PDS and addressing one of the school's pressing concerns.

This vignette illustrates several of the complex reforms that are occurring in many Professional Development School partnerships across the United States. In partnerships like this one, teacher preparation has become a collaborative responsibility of university professors and classroom teachers who are coordinating and pooling their talents as teacher educators. At the University of Louisville and many other institutions, teacher preparation is now a graduate degree program with a year-long intensive internship. School personnel, school systems, higher education faculties, and universities share resources to support teacher preparation as well as the continuing professional development of experienced educators.

In the last ten years, hundreds of sites, partnerships, and programs have begun calling themselves "Professional Development Schools." What do we know about these new arrangements and what do we need to know? To address these larger concerns, this chapter examines four questions about Professional Development Schools: (1) What is a Professional Development School? (2) What conditions affect the relationships among PDS partners? (3) What characterizes PDS-related research? (4) What are some persistent and emerging PDS puzzles?

Before we begin the discussion, a word about the terms we use is in order. When innovation aimed at significant reform is underway, the language used to describe and examine what is going on often varies widely across sites. This condition complicates communication in two ways: there are many different arrangements using the PDS label, and at the same time, there is much similar work going on that is rarely or never referred to as "PDS." New terms with clear meanings have not yet been established, and old language fails to capture all of the nuances of the emerging roles and ways of working.

In this chapter, we often rely on traditional terms even though we realize that these are sometimes inadequate. For example, we use "university" to refer to any unit of higher education engaged in PDS work, though we know that some liberal arts colleges are also involved in this work and some education units have little support from their larger university communities. We use "professor" for those in tenure-track positions in higher education, and we use "teacher" for those in K-12 settings. When we want to include teachers and professors in the role of "teacher educator" we try to make that clear in the writing. To some, this usage emphasizes status differences that many involved in Professional Development Schools strive to ameliorate. We use the terms, not to negate those efforts, but to be as clear and efficient as we can be within the limits of one chapter addressed to a wide audience interested in teacher education.

What Is a Professional Development School?

Since the publication of *A Nation At Risk* in the early 1980s, multiple approaches to education reform have been promoted.[1] Early reform agendas focused on doing more of what was already occurring in schools—longer school days and years, more homework, more classes, and the like. In what became known as the "second wave" of reform, characterized by calls for changes in kind rather than degree, some reformers began tackling the complex and multifaceted issues related to linking school reform with reform of teacher education. Most reformers argued that new forms of collaboration were essential.

Some of the organizations at the center of this continuing work include the Holmes Partnership, the National Network for Education Renewal (NNER), and the National Center for Restructuring Education, Schools, and Teaching (NCREST).[2] Each of these groups, and others as well, presented ideas on how collaborations between schools and universities should be designed to promote reform, labeling these new collaborations variously: Professional Development Schools, Professional Practice Schools, Site-Based Professional Schools, school-university partnerships, or simply partnership schools.

While the different ideas discussed under these various labels have historical roots,[3] the definition of a Professional Development School formulated by the Holmes Group in 1986 seems to be used more frequently than others. In *Tomorrow's Schools*, a PDS is defined as a "regular elementary, middle, or high school that works in partnership with a university to develop and demonstrate" improved quality in teacher preparation, faculty development (at both the K-12 and university level), and student achievement. Toward those ends, Holmes also presented six underlying principles to guide the work of PDS's. These are:

1. Teach for understanding so that students learn for a lifetime.

2. Organize the school and its classrooms as a community of learning.

3. Hold these ambitious learning goals for *everybody's* children.

4. Teach adults as well as children.

5. Make reflection and inquiry a central feature of the school.

6. Invent a new organizational structure for the school.[4]

The reforms that would be required to enact these principles were ambitious and culturally transformational. School and university educators working collaboratively in Professional Development Schools would create and implement constructivist curriculum and instructional strategies to support academic success for all students, decrease or eliminate the effects of an unequal society, engage in thoughtful long-term inquiry into teaching and learning to promote reflection on practice, and produce useful knowledge. The collaboration, based on open communication, would redefine the roles of teacher educators and teachers as well as alter schedules and organizational structures to provide more time for reflection.

Along these same lines, in 1993, the NCREST PDS Network drafted a vision statement that pulled together connecting themes from an array of reform agendas. These were then organized into a set of goals, commitments, and enabling conditions in support of PDS's. The commitments include centering schools on learners and learning, communication and collaboration, connection and community, developing knowledge and promoting inquiry, sharing responsibility for the learning of all members of the PDS community, parity in partnerships, and continual renewal and improvement.[5] To realize these commitments, the network representatives emphasized that "changes in

current organizations, attitudes, and practice will require commitment, time, and resources," including rethinking the regularities of
schooling and the allocation of resources, and creating new patterns of
governance and leadership.[6]

A further specification defining a PDS comes from the PDS Standards Project of the National Council for Accreditation of Teacher
Education (NCATE). The project's draft standards document states
that a PDS is a:

Collaboration between schools, colleges or departments of education, P-12
schools, school districts, and union/professional associations. The partnering
institutions share responsibility for (1) the clinical preparation of new teachers; (2) the continuing development of school and university faculty; (3) the
support of children's learning; and (4) the support of research directed at the
improvement of teaching and learning.[7]

To address this mission, the project argues that PDS relationships are
developed over time and suggests at least three stages to describe this
development: pre-threshold, threshold, and quality attainment. Prior to
assessing a PDS with the proposed standards that cover the latter two
stages, the project suggests that partnerships should work toward certain "pre-threshold" conditions. This early stage, where relationships
develop among key stakeholders—primarily administrators, teachers,
researchers, and teacher educators—as they attempt to build a partnership, precedes an institutional commitment by any party. Accordingly,
in this conception, a PDS begins with participants identifying mutual
values and understandings about the types of activities that best integrate the four main functions of a PDS; that is, preservice teacher
preparation, staff development, research, and support of children's
learning.[8]

In the second stage of development, the project suggests that the
partners focus on "threshold" conditions. These are primarily the institutional commitments that develop the support needed for the partnership to be successful. The project suggests that the following threshold
conditions are critical:

1. An agreement which commits school, school district, union/
professional organization, and the university to the basic mission of a
PDS;

2. A commitment to the critical attributes of a PDS (learning community; collaboration; accountability and quality assurance; organization, roles, and structure; and equity);

3. A positive working relationship and a basis for trust between partners;

4. The achievement of quality standards by partner institutions as evidenced by regional, state, national, or other review;

5. An institutional commitment of resources to the PDS from the school and university.[9]

To best address the mission of the PDS, the standards project argues that the four functions must be integrated; thus, the draft standards are tied to "critical attributes" relevant to the four functions rather than to each function independently. The critical attributes are: learning community; collaboration; accountability and quality assurance; organization, roles, and structure; and equity. Standards and indicators of the standards are provided for both the threshold conditions (those focused on institutionalizing the partners' commitments to the PDS mission) and for the critical attributes.

Two examples of standards and indicators that the Project has drafted are provided here. The first refers to one of the threshold conditions: "an institutional commitment of resources to the PDS from school and university." One of three suggested indicators of this standard is: "Resources are clustered to create new roles, structures, and opportunities to learn." Examples of the indicators for this standard are:

- University faculty spend no less than one day per week at PDS.
- PDS has a critical mass of school and university faculty and educators committed to mission.
- School faculty have time to work outside their classrooms.
- Commitments to PDS work are long term. Partners spend regular time together.
- Interns are clustered in school sites.[10]

The first of the critical attributes which apply to PDS's in the "quality attainment" stage is "learning community." The standard for this attribute is:

The PDS is a learning-centered community characterized by norms and practices which support adult and children's learning. Indications of a learning-centered community include: public teaching practice; integration of intern and teacher learning with school instructional program; collegiality; inquiry; and dissemination of new knowledge. Opportunities to learn are equitably supported.[11]

One of the indicators for learning community is: "The PDS provides the opportunity for interns, residents, school and university faculty, and educators to develop their knowledge, skills, and understandings related to working with diverse students." Examples of this indicator include:

- PDS supports development of diverse learners.
- Interns work in multiple classrooms.
- PDS participants share responsibility and accountability for all children.
- PDS participants know and know about children's families.[12]

There are ten standards in all, one for each of the five threshold conditions and the five critical attributes. The document also provides three to ten indicators of each standard and examples of each indicator that characterize a PDS if the threshold conditions are met and the critical attributes are present. The Standards Project has received additional funding to begin testing these standards in twenty PDS partnerships over a three-year period beginning in the fall of 1998.

Other reform groups, while not using the PDS label, have articulated goals and priorities similar to those promoted by Holmes, NCREST, and the NCATE Standards Project. For example, the four major goals of the National Network for Education Reform are:

1. *Educator preparation*: collaboration between partners to ensure that those entering the education profession are prepared to serve all students effectively.

2. *Professional development*: collaboration between partners to provide opportunities for teachers to strengthen their ability to contribute to the students they serve.

3. *Curriculum development*: collaboration between partners to improve the education and school experiences of all students.

4. *Research and inquiry*: collaboration between partners to raise questions and conduct research that will promote educational renewal at both the school and the university.[13]

A precise definition of a PDS is elusive in part because the manifestations are distinctly local. That is, many of those doing this work place high value on the importance of shaping the relationships and substance of the work in ways that best fit the particular school site and partner university. This means that a single university in partnership with multiple schools can be working under several distinctive, customized relationships simultaneously.[14] Even with an overriding model or theme, as is encouraged by the NCATE accreditation process (e.g., "teachers as learners and leaders"), the work will still "look different" in each school site and those participating will have somewhat different experiences.

With hundreds of partnerships claiming to be "doing PDS," variety is inescapable. Despite the differences, Lee Teitel, in his review of about two hundred papers on PDS, finds "strong convergence around four goals: improvement of student learning, the preparation of educators, the professional development of educators, and research and inquiry into improving practice."[15] It is also clear that these goals are to be achieved within the context of *regular schools* (as opposed to university laboratory schools) and *partnerships* primarily between schools and universities, sometimes including teachers' unions.

What Conditions Affect Relationships among PDS Partners?

If a PDS is both a place—generally a public school—and a partnership, the nature of the institutional alliances and the relationships among the individuals in these diverse settings are crucial to understanding how the partnerships are developing and how they may be assessed and sustained.

PDS partnerships are forms of institutional collaboration that can vary widely depending on the individuals involved as well as the cultures of their home institutions. They can also ebb and flow, expand and recede because of variance in the content of specific projects, the duration of the mutual work, the degree of support provided, and how central the work is not only to the agenda of the partnership but also to the missions of the member institutions and the interests of individual participants.

To capture the significance of some of the different possibilities, Phillip Schlechty and Betty Lou Whitford describe three types of collaboration: (1) *cooperative*—short-term relationships occurring between or among individuals; (2) *symbiotic*—institutional relationships emphasizing mutual self interest; (3) *organic*—where the member institutions develop and support a common agenda, a common good.[16]

Cooperative relationships generally focus on short-term projects with clear beginnings and endings. They grow out of friendship or professional networks and receive little or no institutional support. A physics professor visits the middle school classroom of a neighbor to demonstrate scientific experiments. A high school English teacher meets with her former professors to explain how she scores writing

portfolio entries. Symbiotic relationships may be identical to cooperative ones, but they are reciprocal and supported institutionally with
released time, merit pay, small in-house grants, and the like.[17] Organic
relationships span boundaries. They form around a common agenda,
mutually owned problems "that no party to the collaboration can solve
alone or over which no party has an exclusive monopoly."[18]

While PDS partnerships must have some form of institutional
commitment to survive, the specific examples of collaborative work
occurring within the partnerships can vary on the degree to which they
are primarily cooperative, symbiotic, or organic, particularly when
PDS goals other than teacher preparation are addressed. For example,
many action research projects where a professor and a teacher work
together in the teacher's classroom are symbiotic collaborations. The
professor's primary interest may be a publication while the teacher's
primary interest is improving the learning of children. Without the
institutional partnership, the relationship would be cooperative. If the
teacher and the professor were equally committed and institutionally
supported and rewarded for both publication *and* improving the learning of the children, the work would be organic.

Because of institutional support and the long-term association of
individuals, a PDS provides a context for the development of relationships and commitments that can help sustain such joint activities.
When the collaboration is organic, the partnership is less fragile and
less dependent on the particular needs and interests of the individuals
and individual agencies involved. But if the collaboration primarily
serves only one partner's interests, the partnership will not likely be
sustained over time.

In reality, of course, since PDS partnerships are relatively recent
innovations, these relationships are "a work in progress." Moreover,
the development of the relationships is rarely continuously progressive; rather, there are gains and setbacks, plateaus and slippage, leaps
forward and crashes. When there is low turnover of key individuals—
teacher leaders, administrators, teacher educators—and the school
sites are relatively stable, the likelihood of creating and sustaining
agreed-upon common work and ways of doing it over time are greater.
Where the individuals and the sites change, understandings must be
negotiated and renegotiated, sometimes many times with key leadership and staff changes. In these cases, the partnership may alternately
expand and shrink or fail completely depending on which individuals,
and how many, embrace the work. Because of higher turnover among
students and staff, there is less stability in urban sites than is typical in

other schools, complicating the progress toward sustained collaboration even more.

Few examples of fully organic partnerships exist at present. However, there are examples of partnerships making progress on establishing common expectations and mutually agreeable ways of addressing key elements of Professional Development Schools such as developing common understandings about teaching and learning, creating a reform agenda that includes both K-12 and higher education, demonstrating mutual respect for each other's expertise, sharing decision making, and assessing the focus of the collaboration against explicit values and standards. For example, from a survey of 28 "highly developed" PDS sites, Roberta Trachtman reports for at least 25 sites collaborative planning of teacher education and professional development experiences, shared supervision of student teachers, and joint participation in school renewal.[19] Just under 20 of these sites also report joint participation in university renewal. In fewer cases, 16 and 11 respectively, teachers hold university appointments and professors teach K-12 students.

There are other examples of establishing boundary-spanning roles and common work across schools and universities. At the University of Southern Maine, for example, preservice teachers (interns) work simultaneously with pairs of teacher educators (site coordinators), one university-based and the other school-based, in addition to their classroom teacher mentors. Over time, roles of the site coordinators have come to span both organizations. For example, school site coordinators have voting rights in the university's teacher education department, and in at least one district a USM professor serving as a university site coordinator is an active member of the district's leadership team. In addition, USM methods courses are often taught by practicing classroom teachers as well as university professors.[20]

At the University of Louisville, both tenure-track and tenured full-time faculty spend an average of one day a week in schools serving as PDS sites. These faculty work directly with students, teachers, and teacher candidates, conduct school-based research, and help design and lead schoolwide planning and reform projects. Other tenured faculty, not directly involved with teacher preparation, also work with professional development and research projects related to the PDS sites. School district representatives, including many teachers, are full participants on the design teams developing new graduate programs for experienced educators. These programs, culminating in a graduate degree as well as salary enhancement, will integrate substantial school- and district-based professional development experiences with university coursework as students and faculty in the programs work on authentic education problems.

Making progress in these directions requires, among other factors, persistence and a long-term view of change. Leaders, formal and informal, in each partner institution must behave in ways that contradict long-held, often negative views of their partners' work. And, at least as important, they must find ways to support others for doing likewise.

Making progress also means PDS leaders must work to overcome a history in which those in higher education and those in K-12 schools have not routinely seen either symbiotic or self-interested reasons for collaborating.[21] Rather, the professor in higher education has traditionally been seen as the teacher or provider of services while the K-12 teacher has been seen as the student or receiver of services. In this situation, those in higher education are cast as possessing superior or "privileged" knowledge, which is publicly disciplined by theory and research, while the mostly tacit and privately held expertise of those in schools is unrecognized but powerful in guiding teaching and decisions about schooling.

These and other difficulties are encountered along the way toward creating mutual reform agendas. For example, higher education partners, especially those in arts and sciences, are often criticized by their colleagues as "cavorting with the enemy" or wasting time that should be spent on "real" scholarship. Institutional support for such work—beyond a pat on the back for being responsive to community needs—may be hard to secure. Rarely is such work rewarded in university promotion, tenure, and merit policies in the same way as are refereed journal articles.

Likewise, teachers' and principals' participation in PDS work is generally treated by their districts as an "add-on" to existing roles rather than being supported with additional school-based positions or salary supplements. Moreover, many schools serving as PDS sites are also involved in multiple reform projects and may view PDS as just one of several. All of these conditions affect the priority given PDS work and affect how scarce resources are distributed by the partnering institutions. Under such circumstances, there is little likelihood that the partnership can grow beyond a few committed individuals.

In the more successful partnerships, it is likely that two conditions are at play. First, some of the cultural differences between schools and universities are less evident among those directly engaged in PDS work.

Those active in the partnerships are *exceptions to* rather than *examples of* the oft-mentioned differences. Anecdotally, in informal conversations and in working sessions at conferences, those with extended experience with Professional Development Schools cite evidence of a developing PDS culture that blends the values of the academy with those of practice. For example, at a session sponsored by the PDS Standards Project in 1996 and attended by representatives of PDS's identified by the project as "highly developed," several participants commented that while cultural differences remain, they seem to be increasingly evident between those school and university educators doing PDS work and those not involved rather than simply between school and university educators generally.

A second condition found in successful PDS partnerships is that the partnering *institutions*, not just the individuals involved, find value in their collaboration. The functions most likely to be seen as valuable to both institutions are those concerning the preparation and continuing professional development of teachers. Less central and of lower priority as *shared institutional goals* are educating children, a high priority for schools, and research and inquiry, a high priority for universities. Thus, even with institutional support, PDS partnerships are fragile because each institution has compelling goals that have not become demonstrably central in the PDS relationship. It remains to be seen whether school-university collaboration can build commitments to PDS goals which are related to educating all students well, including producing enough high-quality novice teachers to supply the growing needs of school systems, and creating, capturing, and disseminating professional knowledge that is both highly valued by universities and useful to schools.

What Characterizes the Research and Inquiry Related to PDS?

Research reported in the literature generally appears to be one of three types: (a) descriptions of changes that have occurred in preservice teacher education programs as a result of collaboration among school and university educators, (b) analyses of the process of collaboration and partnership development, especially regarding conditions that support or inhibit it, and (c) studies conducted by university and/or school faculty focused on improving practice in elementary and secondary school classrooms.

What is absent from the literature is also significant. Teitel[22] reports very few studies focused on evaluation of the PDS model however defined. Also missing from the literature are the many action research studies reportedly conducted by school and university educators and/or teacher education students in many PDS programs. Such studies may have been shared locally but have not been disseminated widely.

Those best positioned to be interested in producing and disseminating reports of innovative inquiry are precisely those who are doing the *other* work of PDS's—creating and developing new teacher preparation programs, engaging in professional development, working on school reform strategies, dealing with new sets of interpersonal relationships, including putting out (or sometimes setting) fires that arise from these new ways of working. Another factor contributing to the lack of systematic examinations of effects and effectiveness is the recency of PDS as an innovation. That we need more data on the effectiveness of the model and its effects on universities, schools, participants, children, districts, and so on is obvious. Such evidence is vital to evaluating and improving the approach and to decisions regarding whether PDS's can or should be sustained, an issue addressed more fully in the last section of the chapter.

Another consideration is that schools and universities create enormous amounts of data in a variety of forms such as institutional reports, surveys of graduates, job placement surveys, test scores, samples of student work, parent surveys, course evaluations, reflective journals, and school district hiring information that could constitute useful data about PDS's, but for various reasons, these data, for the most part, remain unexamined and so have not often found their way into conference presentations or published papers. Sometimes, researchers inclined to write such reports do not trust the adequacy of institutional data collected by busy administrators; in other cases, no one has been able to carve out the time it would take to make sense of extant data.

At the same time, there is another, more basic issue about examining what characterizes research and inquiry related to Professional Development Schools. How are research and inquiry defined? Most conceptions of the PDS model show a marked preference for the term "inquiry" over the term "research." Two types of differentiation are suggested in the literature. Frank Murray, for example, argues that research of a particular type is to be conducted in these schools:

PDS inquiry is about understanding the particular case, while traditional university-based inquiry seeks more universal explanations and contributes to general theory. . . . PDS research is directed at local action and the particular child. . . .[23]

This focus for PDS-related inquiry reflects, to some extent, the disdain with which many educators in schools and universities view traditional hypothesis-testing research. Among the many criticisms that have been leveled at such research are these: that it is inaccessible to all but experts on quasi-experimental design or multi-variate statistical models, it is too theoretical and narrowly focused, it attempts to control for rather than take context into account, and as a result, it is not helpful in determining what should be done in classrooms and schools.

A second observation about the preference for "inquiry" is that the term indicates a broader view of the forms and purposes of "the systematic examination of evidence" than has been traditionally conveyed with the term "research." This broader conception enhances attention to the PDS research-and-inquiry function, both by increasing the vehicles for capturing contextual knowledge and effects of practice and by broadening the base of who participates in research and inquiry to include more K-12 educators.

For example, Barnett Berry and Katherine Boles distinguish three types of PDS inquiry, suggesting that each has a different purpose: *inquiry in* PDS, *inquiry on* PDS, and *inquiry as* teaching and learning.[24] *Inquiry as* teaching and learning refers to a mindset about teaching and learning. Good teaching practice requires constant reflection and is embedded in the daily work of teachers. This mindset, Berry and Boles argue, facilitates a transition to *inquiry in* teaching and learning where, in some manifestations, classroom teachers become teacher researchers focusing on the systematic collection and public analysis of evidence about teaching and learning. Thus, for them inquiry *in* teaching and learning is an extension of inquiry *as* teaching and learning. The former is likely to be collaborative and thus more public (and perhaps more systematic) since the latter can occur privately in an individual teacher's classroom.

Inquiry on teaching and learning is concerned with effects of the PDS itself and its various components and functions. In their review of the evidence about inquiry presented in Trachtman's survey of 28 "highly developed" sites, Berry and Boles found that *inquiry on* PDS "was the least described dimension, with less than a handful of the 28 site respondents describing specific research that informs both practice and policy in a significant and sustained manner."[25]

Thus, there remains much to find out about Professional Development Schools. What is their impact on school goals for reform? On student learning? Are teachers prepared in PDS sites better equipped, more knowledgeable, and more effective than those prepared in more traditional programs? Do PDS graduates stay in teaching at higher rates than graduates of other programs? What are the effects of PDS on educators' learning? Has practice in these schools improved? How are university faculty and programs affected? What effects has PDS inquiry had on practice?

Comparative analyses across various sites and institutions in terms of degrees of change and examination of the effects and effectiveness constitute a logical direction in which to proceed to address such questions. The findings from this type of inquiry would help determine the strengths or limitations of the various models and lead to a dialogue for addressing strategies for improvement. Moreover, until we put the PDS model on the research agenda, the likelihood of institutionalization is not very great.

Some Pieces that Remain Puzzling

In *Tomorrow's Schools*, the Holmes Group presented a model for the design of new organizational arrangements—Professional Development Schools—in which a number of education reforms could be implemented in a coordinated fashion. The PDS was to be a place in which inquiry would be an integral component, used to examine instructional practice, teacher preparation, professional development, and their interrelationship.

Since the PDS concept was introduced, a growing body of literature has addressed the different activities within PDS's and the processes employed to form these new partnerships. However, this literature contains very little evidence bearing on the effectiveness of PDS activities. Consequently, some question whether the vision for the PDS put forth by the Holmes Group was sufficient to guide its development so that it could live up to ambitious expectations.

While the innovation is fairly recent and the research is still quite limited, enough experience has accumulated to indicate some trends. What is evident in the literature is that school and university educators who have initiated and sustained a dialogue have, in fact, created new arrangements for themselves and new programs for their students. These conversations are characterized less by the university's need for research and more by the school's need to improve student achievement. The interaction has led to new roles and relationships that have promoted the perception among participants that each group has valuable knowledge and expertise to bring to the effort. University professors and administrators are beginning to see school teachers and administrators as colleagues; and this view is reciprocated. The Professional Development School has also cultivated the view that the task of teacher preparation is a joint venture no longer to be considered as the domain of the university alone.

Yet many issues remain. We address three here: equity, sustainability, and comprehensiveness. We cast them as puzzles to encourage the mindset that they can be solved even though some are quite daunting.

EQUITY

One of the more troubling puzzles is how to insure equity. In *Tomorrow's Schools*, the Holmes Group stated, "A major commitment of the Professional Development School will be overcoming the educational and social barriers raised by an unequal society."[26] Yet in their recent review of PDS research, Linda Valli, David Cooper, and Lisa Frankes concluded that "most PDS partners have either not attempted or are floundering in this undertaking."[27] Are the inadequacies identified by Valli and colleagues enough to indicate that PDS partnerships have failed on the equity agenda? Was the expectation unrealistic and inadequately supported? Is there progress on equity issues that has not been reported in the literature? Has enough time passed for evidence to accumulate?

While there are many such concerns related to equity, we will describe only one here—an apparent contradiction in PDS goals which may account, in part, for the observed inadequacies related to equity. On the one hand, there is an expectation that those learning to teach should be placed with superb teachers in schools meeting quality standards. However, given social class differences and the neglect to which urban schools are often subjected, it is likely that larger numbers of high-quality settings will be found outside urban areas than inside. Those inside urban districts are likely to be "magnet" schools or other privileged schools.

This is not to say that there are no good urban schools, and certainly, it is not to say that there are no good urban teachers. Yet when PDS sites are selected, they are less likely to be located in urban schools than in other settings. For one thing, the turnover of staff and students in urban schools makes them less attractive as places to build long-term commitments. Students in urban schools are also likely to have diverse learning problems, thus presenting teachers with greater challenges, especially in secondary schools. Teaching practices that succeed with middle class students may not work as well with students exhibiting greater diversity in learning styles and ethnic, racial, and socioeconomic backgrounds. Moreover, many teacher education students are white, middle class women and men who received their own schooling in non-urban settings. Their limited exposure to the issues of diversity in urban schools complicates the challenges of internships in urban schools.[28]

The effect is that the need to place teacher candidates in schools demonstrating "best practices" conflicts with the goal of improving teaching and learning for all students, especially in those schools that traditionally report low achievement and high dropout rates. If urban schools present more challenges, then it is a given that urban PDS's will as well. Yet if few partnerships are based in schools with high degrees of diversity, or if they are not sustained as long as are those in less diverse schools, the development of better learning strategies for all children is short-circuited. Can a PDS serve the diverse needs of urban schools effectively? Can PDS staffs invent ways of providing high-quality education to all students?

SUSTAINABILITY

Sustainability is another challenge for institutions using the PDS model. There are several issues involved in this puzzle, including staffing, financing, and the ebb and flow of collaboration.

Regarding staffing, in most cases a minority of a school's faculty is directly involved in preparing teachers. Likewise, probably less than a third of a university's education faculty is involved.[29] Inventing new programs, creating new roles and relationships, and learning to work in two worlds simultaneously—the school and the university—is time-consuming, labor-intensive, exhilarating, energizing, and stressful, often all at the same time.

Moreover, much of the work of PDS staff centrally involved in teacher preparation depends on the idiosyncratic characteristics of individuals rather than on well-established roles. The departure of an individual in a leadership role may call for a make-over of the program. In any case, relationships and common understandings must be developed anew.

The idiosyncratic approach to PDS work makes its continuity especially vulnerable to staff turnover. The lack of institutionalization of roles is also exacerbated by a limited pool from which to recruit replacements, especially among teacher leaders and university faculty. Similar problems arise with turnover of mentor teachers but since there are potentially many more of them, that aspect of the problem is not quite as critical.

Many of those involved are deeply committed to supporting the activities and achieving the goals of PDS. These key participants also have many opportunities to become involved in other exciting projects related to school reform, some of which are not central to their PDS efforts. If other parts of their jobs are not flexible, (such as teaching required courses), when grants are secured, faculty are tempted to switch from PDS responsibilities to the project supported by the grant.

Moreover, burnout is a constant concern for overextended PDS faculty from both schools and universities. Because leaving a PDS position has programmatic effects, faculty are confronted with difficult choices. Staffing problems are not likely to be resolved by routinization of the work, given the idiosyncratic nature of collaboration.

Financial needs also beget puzzles. Universities place a high value on securing outside funding. And indeed some PDS partnerships have relied on such soft money throughout their existence, in some cases short-lived. Outside funding can be both a blessing and a curse. Developmental projects typically require additional start-up funding to build new relationships and ways of working, create new materials, and secure equipment and other resources (such as e-mail links). Some of this cost is reduced once a program is invented and is operating. In these cases, outside funding is a blessing.

An obvious pitfall of using soft money to create new programs is, of course, the curse of "when the money is gone, so is the program." To avoid this pitfall, careful thought must be given from the earliest stages as to how to move the program into the mainstream of the partners' staffing and funding structures. Planning for institutionalization is at least as important as planning for development and innovation. But with scarce resources, new programs often mean educators simply add work rather than substituting new work for old, creating the threat of role-overload.

A third component of the sustainability puzzle concerns the ebb and flow of collaborative relationships. Gaining commitments from *institutions* to support collaboration is usually a hard-won accomplishment, essential to sustaining PDS partnerships. Yet carrying out institutional commitments depends on developing trust and openness among individuals. Authentic collaboration cannot be mandated; it must be built around work all of the partners believe in.

Thus a hallmark of effective collaboration is that it is voluntary. Yet volunteerism is a fragile base on which to build teacher education programs. Enough volunteers must stick with the work for extended periods of time in order to form a cadre of teachers and professors who can begin to transform the culture of teaching and learning. What are the consequences of operating a PDS without whole-school involvement? How is authentic collaboration to be encouraged and maintained without mandates?

COMPREHENSIVENESS

A third set of puzzles concerns how time, energy, and commitments are divided among the four functions of the PDS: teacher preparation, continuing professional development, quality education for all students, and inquiry. Assuming the literature on PDS activities is representative, clearly much more attention is being paid to the first two than to the last two.

The current imbalance in attention to the four functions may simply reflect the developmental stage of the PDS innovation; it may arise from how particular partnerships came about in the first place. Generally, but not exclusively, higher education institutions have initiated these partnerships, and PDS activity has begun with the redesigning of teacher preparation programs, which naturally connects with issues of teaching and learning for more experienced teachers.

Another possibility is that teacher preparation and continuing professional development are the places where collaboration can happen most vigorously. These areas are clearly boundary-spanning and connect well with work that has traditionally gone on in both institutions separately. Both school districts and universities have long provided opportunities for continuing professional development. While universities have been the official sites for teacher preparation, many would argue that novices really learn to teach when they get their first teaching jobs. Moreover, those interested in the reform of teacher education have acknowledged that in the long run the teaching practices supported in schools overwhelm those practices taught in preparation programs. So both institutions can rightfully lay claim to educating novices.

But when it comes to the other two functions expected of the PDS —inquiry and educating all children well—it is clear that the university's mission favors research, while the school's mission is the education of students. Thus it is not surprising that sustained collaboration focused on these two functions has yet to develop. While almost everyone working in PDS's believes that partnerships between universities and schools are indeed a good thing, we must come to a better understanding about both the limits and the possibilities, particularly when resources are tight. Is it realistic to expect PDS's to effect change in all four areas? Given that a number of PDS's have been operating for about ten years without developing all functions well, is it possible that such an expectation is unrealistic without substantially increased resources—time, money, and personnel?

What is the promise of Professional Development Schools? Over the last ten years or so, university and school educators have demonstrated that they can indeed collaborate in ways that provide those entering teaching with experiences that blend theory, research, and practice in novel ways. Many doing this work characterize it as "letting the genie out of the bottle." Just as the genie cannot be coaxed back into the bottle, those engaged in reforming teacher education through the creation of Professional Development Schools have expressed little desire to return to former practices, despite increased work loads and scarce resources. PDS work has been compelling enough to sustain conversations among school and university educators so that respect for ideas originating in each organization has had a chance to grow. Out of these sustained conversations may come additional reform that comes closer to the promise—educating all children well.

NOTES

1. National Commission on Excellence in Education. *A Nation at Risk* (Washington, DC: US Department of Education, 1983).

2. Key publications related to the work of these groups include *Tomorrow's Schools: Principles for the Design of Professional Development Schools*, The Holmes Group (East Lansing: Michigan State University, 1990); John I. Goodlad, *Teachers for Our Nation's Schools* (San Francisco: Jossey-Bass, 1990); John I. Goodlad, *Educational Renewal: Better Teachers, Better Schools* (San Francisco: Jossey-Bass, 1994); "Vision Statement of the Professional Development Schools Network" (New York: National Center for Restructuring Education, Schools, and Teaching, April 8, 1993); Marsha Levine, ed., *Professional Practice Schools* (Washington, DC: American Federation of Teachers, November, 1988).

3. The roots of PDS work can be found in John Dewey's laboratory school, the work of Lucy Sprague Mitchell, and others. In the mid-1970s, Phillip Schlechty began arguing for "Site-Based Professional Schools" which would be governed by an organization affiliated with but independent of the those currently in control of teacher education (see, for example, Phillip C. Schlechty, Julius R. George, and Betty Lou Whitford, "Reform in Teacher Education and the Professionalization of Teaching," *The High School Journal*, Vol. 61, No. 7, April, 1978, pp. 313-320.

4. The Holmes Group, *"Tomorrow's Schools: Principles for the Design of Professional Development Schools,"* p. 1.

5. National Center for Restructuring Education, Schools, and Teaching, "Vision Statement: Professional Development Schools Network: Purposes, Commitments, and Enabling Conditions for Professional Development Schools," New York: Author, April 8, 1993.

6. Ibid., p. 5.

7. National Council for Accreditation of Teacher Education, *Draft Standards for Identifying and Supporting Quality Professional Development Schools* (Washington, DC: NCATE, September, 1997), p. 4.

8. Ibid., p. 2

9. Ibid.

10. Ibid., p. 9

11. Ibid., p. 11

12. Ibid.

13. R. T. Osguthorpe, R. C. Harris, M. F. Harris, and S. Black (eds.), *Partner Schools: Centers for Educational Renewal*. (San Francisco: Jossey-Bass), 1995, p. 5.

14. Lee Teitel, "Changing Teacher Education through Professional Development School Partnerships: A Five-year Follow-up Study," *Teachers College Record*, Vol. 99, No. 2, Winter, 1997, pp. 311-334.

15. Lee Teitel, "Professional Development Schools: A Literature Review" (Washington, DC: NCATE PDS Standards Project, unpublished manuscript), p. 6.

16. Phillip C. Schlechty and Betty Lou Whitford, "Shared Problems and Shared Vision: Organic Collaboration," in Kenneth A. Sirotnik and John I. Goodlad (eds.), *School-University Partnerships in Action: Concepts, Cases, and Concerns* (New York: Teachers College Press, 1988), pp. 191-204.

17. Betty Lou Whitford, "Collaborations Are Relationships," in *Learning to Collaborate: Lessons from School-College Partnerships in the Excellence in Education Program*. (Report prepared by Policy Studies Associates, Inc. for the John S. and James L. Knight Foundation, November 1996), pp. 2-3.

18. Schlechty and Whitford, 1988, p. 192.

19. Roberta Trachtman, *The NCATE Professional Development School Study: A Survey of 28 PDS Sites* (Washington, DC: National Council for Accreditation of Teacher Education, May, 1996).

20. Betty Lou Whitford, Gordon Ruscoe, and Letitia Fickel, *Knitting It All Together: Collaborative Teacher Education in Southern Maine*. (Washington, DC: American Association of Colleges for Teacher Education, and New York: National Commission on Teaching and America's Future, forthcoming).

21. Sirotnik and Goodlad, 1988.

22. Teitel, 1997.

23. Frank Murray, "All or None—Criteria for Professional Development Schools," *Educational Policy*, Vol. 7, No. 1, 1993, pp. 61-73.

24. Barnett Berry and Katherine Boles with Kellah Edens, Annalee Nissenholtz, and Roberta Trachtman. *Inquiry and Professional Development Schools* (New York: National Center for Restructuring Education, Schools, and Teaching, forthcoming).

25. Barnett Berry and Katherine Boles with Kellah Edens, Annalee Nissenholtz, and Roberta Trachtman (forthcoming), pp. 4-5.

26. The Holmes Group, *Tomorrow's Schools*, p. 7.

27. Linda Valli, David Cooper, and Lisa Frankes, "Professional Development Schools and Equity: A Critical Analysis of Rhetoric and Research," in Michael W. Apple (ed.) *Review of Research in Education 22* (Washington, DC: American Educational Research Association), p. 299.

28. Nancy Zimpher, "The RATE Project: A Profile of Teacher Education Students," in *Journal of Teacher Education*, Vol. 40, No. 6, pp. 27-30, 1989.

29. Phyllis Metcalf-Turner, "Toward Establishing Professional Development Schools: Faculty Perceptions in Colleges and School of Education in the Holmes Group." Unpublished dissertation, University of Minnesota, 1993.

CHAPTER XII

Pervasive Problems and Issues in Teacher Education

KENNETH R. HOWEY AND NANCY L. ZIMPHER

As earlier chapters have illustrated, teacher education today confronts numerous problems. In this concluding chapter we address those problems that appear not only most troublesome but are also pervasive and persistent. We concentrate on the critical *initial* phases of teacher education, the cornerstone for what hopefully will become a *continuum* of professional growth. We focus on initial teacher preparation because we have studied this phenomenon for almost a decade as investigators in the Research About Teacher Education (RATE) study sponsored by the American Association of Colleges for Teacher Education (AACTE). From the mid-80s to the mid-90s we annually surveyed faculty and students in programs of teacher education across the United States.

The challenge for us in writing this chapter was not so much framing the problems although in some instances we have identified problems that have not been widely acknowledged. Rather, our challenge was to respond to these problems with suggestions that are bold and interrelated. Such strategies are warranted for problems that are of considerable magnitude and intertwined. In the past narrowly focused and less potent strategies have not effected needed changes in teacher education.

From our perspective, it is paradoxical that far too many persons, both within and outside the education professions, believe that teaching and learning and hence teacher education are really neither very complex nor expensive endeavors. Yet among many who know better, a common response is not a more complex portrayal and manifestation of teaching and teacher education; instead, they offer a rather romantic and facile notion of inquiry and reflection as the means to move these endeavors forward. In contrast, these problems suggest to us a reform agenda and a redesign process that are multifaceted and coordinated nationally. Our position is that a strong, new legal-political infrastructure must be put in place over the next several years to undergird a more potent and seamless form of teacher education.

Kenneth R. Howey is Professor of Education at the University of Wisconsin, Milwaukee, and Nancy L. Zimpher is Chancellor of the University of Wisconsin, Milwaukee. At the time this chapter was written, they were members of the faculty of the College of Education, The Ohio State University.

We hardly profess to have all the answers for advancing teacher preparation, but we can assert what we believe should be some of the major planks in a reform agenda. We have identified seven problems, each of which is discussed in what follows. We begin with what we view as the root problem—the perceptions and the reality surrounding the nature of teaching.

Discrepancies between Perceptions and the Reality of Teaching

Many view teaching as the relatively effective transmission of important information. However, there is considerable evidence that a reception-accrual model of learning, the reciprocal role for such teaching, is unlikely to result in significant understandings.[1] What constitutes high-performance learning and, correspondingly, teaching? Scholarly inquiry is informative here. There is a confluence of research findings on how and why individuals learn in a deep and conceptual manner, alone and in groups. Much of the former is embedded in cognitive psychology and the latter in constructivist principles. In reviewing research for the American Psychological Association Patricia Alexander and P. Karen Murphy identified five learner-centered principles:

- One's existing knowledge serves as a foundation of all future learning by guiding organization and representations, by serving as a basis of association with new information, and by coloring and filtering all new experiences. (*the knowledge base principle*)
- The ability to reflect upon and regulate one's thoughts and behaviors is essential to learning and development. (*the strategic processing principle*)
- Motivational or affective factors, such as intrinsic motivation, attributions for learning, and personal goals, along with the motivational characteristics of the learning tasks, play a significant role in the learning process. (*the motivation/affect principle*)
- Learning, while ultimately a unique adventure for all, proceeds through common stages of development influenced by both inherited and experiential/environmental factors. (*the development principle*)
- Learning is as much a socially shared undertaking, as it is an individually constructed enterprise. (*the context principle*)[2]

What attributes of learning do these principles suggest? Since learning is first and foremost a process of inquiry and active problem solving, the disposition and ability to examine in a continuing manner how one goes about learning is essential. Inquiry by good learners examines the effort they put forth and the specific procedures they employ in their learning. Documentation and evaluation are ongoing activities integrated into learning, just as they are integral aspects of teaching. Teaching and learning are reciprocal: roles and responsibilities are at times formally exchanged and at other times naturally blended. Conceptual learning calls for thinking out loud and sharing with others. Members of a learning community understand what responsibility they have for their own learning and also their responsibility for assisting others in their learning as well. Thus, both effort and strategies for learning and abilities and attitudes toward socially responsible behavior are monitored by the class or learning community as well as by the individual. High-performance learning is highly transportable and often applied in contexts outside of the classroom on authentic tasks calling for individual and often collective problem solving.

While there are many pockets of excellence that reflect the types of teaching that engender such learning, they are nonetheless uncommon. For example, in a recent visit to classrooms in his urban school district, a new superintendent characterized most teaching he observed as "stand and deliver," with students engaged in passive, individual seat work. He found a great deal of what occurred in these classrooms to be "boring, repetitive, unengaging and vapid, seemingly intended to kill time."[3]

Uneven, often mediocre teaching occurs as well in colleges and universities and surely in teacher education classes. Neither of us, for example, can recall anyone—ever—coming to observe us in our classrooms as teacher educators. Much of the teaching we observed during the field studies of programs of teacher education in connection with the RATE studies could be characterized as pedestrian in nature with lecture and discussion invariably the staple.[4] Teachers do teach as they are taught.

Admittedly, this portrayal of teaching generally might be too harsh. Frankly, there are not enough *large-scale* observational studies framed in fine-grained analyses of teaching and learning to accurately gauge the depth and breadth of the problem. Nevertheless, we assert that it is a problem, and one of major proportions. Far too many view teaching as the maintenance of order and the transmission of information efficiently and effectively. Given the latter goal, the former concern understandably often takes priority.

Obviously, a great many teachers—including teacher educators— don't construe teaching in this manner, but they often exhibit in their

own teaching a fundamental discontinuity between beliefs and practice. This is because most of us have limited abilities to engage learners in multiple potent pathways to learning that is conceptually
framed, problem-oriented, and experientially relevant. Thus, what too
often exists is a vicious cycle of mediocre teachers teaching teachers
who are in turn mediocre. For us this is the bedrock problem, and in
order to break this cycle we believe that the following types of activities must be at the center of a reform strategy for teacher education.

We need to address first the teaching of teacher educators. The
"reculturing" of teacher education faculties especially with regard to
improving their teaching over time will demand that we start at the
beginning. Guidelines and standards are being developed for carefully
structured, core experiences in doctoral programs to extend and refine
pedagogical abilities.[5] We strongly support this idea. The time devoted to these core activities in doctoral programs should be similar to
the amount of time devoted at present to acquiring competence in research design and methodology.

Beyond this, we suggest that beginning teacher educators (that is,
any beginning professor who has major responsibilities teaching
prospective or veteran teachers) should be the beneficiaries of structured entry-year or transitional educative, supportive, and evaluative
activities, just as is commonly advocated for the beginning teacher. In
these arrangements a "mentor" or consulting professor would be
assigned to work with the new professor at the beginning of his or her
work in a teacher education program. The centerpiece of this structured induction or enculturation activity, as with the reconceptualized
doctoral program, would be the mutual investigation of the effects of
teaching on learning. These on-going investigations would employ
multiple theoretical perspectives and a range of analytic observational
tools. While we harbor some reservations, the distance of such practice from present reality suggests to us that it will be necessary to
develop relatively explicit standards along these lines for approval of
teacher education programs. Workshops for deans, department heads,
and directors of education would be needed also to move toward graduate preparation focused strongly on developing teaching abilities.

In a related vein, our second recommendation is that a national dialogue be initiated involving provosts, deans of education, and teacher
education faculty addressing the effete and often invalid criteria and
procedures which purport to assess the quality of teaching for performance reviews and decisions regarding promotion. Toward strengthening the assessment of teaching there are a number of obvious directions

to consider including peer review of course syllabi as a product of scholarly activity, periodic peer engagement in and examination of teaching, random third-party sampling of students' learning and, perhaps most fundamentally, a collegial review of the learnings expected in courses and course-related activities and an examination of how these, in fact, are assessed. Organizations such as the Holmes Partnership or the American Association of Colleges for Teacher Education could promote this dialogue, which must result in specific recommendations regarding evidence on quality of teaching and how it can best be obtained. The nature and quality of teaching is not a priority in many research-oriented institutions, and in many institutions where it is a priority it is more often defined in terms of teaching load than in the kinds of teaching expected.

Finally, our third recommendation has to do with the development of teaching standards for teacher educators and a voluntary process for applying for advanced certification similar to the procedures that veteran teachers engage in when standing for advanced certification from the National Board for Professional Teaching Standards.[6] This parallel process would document teacher educators' ability to teach adults as well as youngsters. Teacher educators, at regular intervals and for reasonable periods of time such as a quarter or semester, need to teach in K-12 classrooms like those for which they are preparing their students to teach. This is essential. A variety of personnel exchanges can be negotiated in the formal partnerships between schools and colleges which over time will be responsible for teacher preparation extending into the early years of teaching. Highly select classroom teachers will assist in teaching prospective teachers on campus as well as in schools, and professors will teach periodically in schools as a precondition to their eventually seeking certification as accomplished teacher educators.

In summary, we assert that the prevalent perception of teaching is the ultimate core problem of teacher education and one with far-reaching consequences. The perception of teaching held by many outside of education as a relatively facile and straightforward exercise unfortunately squares with much of the reality. We don't believe that we will change this prevailing public perception and gain more support for teaching, and hence *teacher education*, unless and until a professional culture develops that makes the challenges and complexities of teaching and teacher education much more transparent than at present. Teaching that is primarily a form of transmission of personal knowledge must be replaced by teaching that engages learners with powerful understandings that have to be negotiated and applied in diverse social and cultural contexts. Such a process is especially suited to our diverse public schools. To move forward the types of learning and concomitant teaching we have attempted to portray here calls for strong measures and, we believe, a coordinated, *national* reform agenda.

Inadequate Resources

In this section we examine a host of conditions that have contributed to funding inadequacies. We also pose a set of strategies for revenue enhancement. The sixth annual RATE study (1992) revealed that the conditions in most schools, colleges and departments of education are essentially inadequate. Ironically, "both teacher education faculty and deans report that the recent reform era in education and teacher education has commonly resulted in a more favorable view of their school, college, or department of education . . . than that previously held by their central administration." Nonetheless, in most instances ". . . financial support and resources for desired changes are simply not forthcoming from these sources."[7] Over 1200 colleges and universities nationally house a school or department of education; several states have as many as 50 to 60 state-approved programs.[8] It is no wonder then that they compete ineffectively for scarce resources, both from state and federal funding sources, as well as within the institutional contexts in which they reside.

Further, RATE studies repeatedly documented the rise in enrollment in these programs, with baccalaureate institutions increasing enrollments in their teacher education programs by as much as 44 percent, and institutions formerly offering only the baccalaureate degree rapidly adding offerings at the master's level as well. Competition for prospective students continues to create more programs within institutions preparing teachers.[9] In the United States, the teaching profession exceeds by five times the number of training institutions for law, medicine, engineering, and business. Such scale constrains the dispersal of adequate resources, especially for state-supported institutions, to intolerably low levels. In Ohio, for instance, the state's formula for allocating resources to various professional and academic programs places education in the lowest strata of the funding model; "Baccalaureate I" at $3,430 per full-time-equivalent student, in contrast to "Baccalaureate III" for nursing, engineering and pharmacy at $8,123 per enrolled full-time student.[10]

The resource problem can be seen in terms of not only the quality but the type of facilities typically found attached to schools and colleges of education. The perception of what teaching is and what it means to learn to teach also contributes to the resource problem. What facilities are needed to learn to teach effectively? While the classroom is the ultimate laboratory, we suggest that laboratories and clinics designed specifically for *learning to teach* are needed. The nursing profession has often been identified as a reasonable comparison group to the teaching profession. However, the contrast between facilities, resources, and equipment employed in the preparation of nurses and the archaic facilities and dearth of modern equipment in colleges of education is stark. Further, the RATE studies clearly revealed attrition over time in the use of laboratory facilities and modern communications technology in the preparation of teachers.[11] Facilities in our colleges of education reinforce teaching practices that often result in narrow and sterile instruction. We need more teaching clinics such as those employed in the widely acclaimed Reading Recovery® program where teacher trainees observe tutoring sessions and then engage in detailed, conceptually grounded analysis of learner performance and teacher decision making. Laboratory facilities are needed which can draw on a rich library of videos and case material which could be developed over time in a coordinated manner through national consortia. The type of laboratory facility for beginning teachers described below has obvious implications for the continuing development of the professoriate as well:

For example, our prospective teachers should view dozens of hours of video representing both principles which guide the teaching profession and the pervasive problems teachers encounter. As we indicated earlier, they should examine teaching and learning episodes from the vantage point of and with the concomitant conceptual lenses provided by the psycholinguist, political scientist, social psychologist, cognitive scientist and cultural anthropologist, as well as, of course, the classroom teacher, student, and parent. These multiple perspectives brought to bear on video representation of teaching and learning in a laboratory setting lead to informed professional judgment. Taking on critical, multiple perspectives of teaching and learning demonstrates applied research and theories in use and vividly illustrates the scholarly bases for separating professional judgment from conventional wisdom. . . . Again, preservice teachers [read teacher educators as well] should be able to engage in these early preparatory activities in a context in which complex phenomena can be represented from multiple perspectives, through several media, and at a time and in a manner conducive to learning. They should be able to critically inquire in a setting and at a pace that fosters such activity.[12]

We recommend a federally supported national competition for the development of case material and teaching protocols around both exemplars of best practice and persistent classroom problems. These could be developed within a limited number of domains framed initially by core propositional knowledge and abilities such as those posited in the INTASC standards.[13]

Economic conditions in teacher education are further exacerbated by the general inability to manage enrollments and adequately calibrate the supply of teachers with the needs of specific regions and disciplines. And there is no sign that the quality control problem, compounded by the issuance of emergency licenses in areas lacking a pool of well-prepared teachers, will ease any time soon. This is especially the situation in large urban areas. Lack of responsiveness to pressing needs also militates against adequate funding.

Still other common practices and conditions within the academy seriously constrain resources. "By the standards of other professions and of teacher education in other countries, teacher preparation in the United States has historically been thin, uneven, and poorly financed. Although many schools of education provide high-quality preparation, others are treated as 'cash cows' by their universities, bringing in revenues that are spent on the education of doctors, lawyers, and accountants rather than on their own students."[14] The Holmes Partnership foreshadowed this concern in 1995 as it asked:

Why do so many institutions want to prepare teachers and other educators? . . . Many people besides the quality-conscious mount teacher education programs because they are profitable. The education of teachers and other educators is big business in a nation that employs over three million educators. Dollar signs flash in the eyes of those looking for good market opportunities. Where else can you produce something, or offer services, and not have to be accountable for the quality of the product or services?[15]

The resource problem is inextricably linked with the lack of performance standards and accountability.

How can schools and colleges of education begin to redress these problems? Geraldine Clifford and James Guthrie call attention to the need for "professionalization" of schools of education, stating unequivocally:

Schools of education, particularly those located on the campuses of prestigious research universities, have become ensnared improvidently in the academic and political cultures of their institutions and have neglected their professional allegiances. They are like marginal men, aliens in their own world. They have seldom succeeded in satisfying the scholarly norms of their campus letter and science colleagues and they are simultaneously estranged from their practicing professional peers.[16]

Since an increasing number of colleges of education aspire to "research-oriented" status, this is not the problem exclusively of Category I research institutions.[17] We agree that schools of education should exist on university campuses primarily in the service of the teaching profession broadly defined. We believe that greater clarity of mission will lead to better understanding of needed resources and other capacity issues. This type of professional school image is echoed, for example, in John Goodlad's notion of a "center of pedagogy."[18] More recently, the Holmes Partnership articulated a concept of tomorrow's school of education.[19] Each of these fosters a vision of a school of education designed much like a school of medicine, law or business.

Essentially, a professional school of education is characterized by a vision of service to the profession with a set of core values that manifest that vision. Framing such a vision can take many paths. Recently the College of Education at the Ohio State University undertook a three-year process of restructuring wherein it derived a set of core values. This process resulted in more coherent programming in professional preparation and the simultaneous and coordinated review of the college and the K-12 schools with which it is partnered. Personnel from those schools were fully involved in these endeavors.[20] Also emphasized was a commitment to continuing faculty development to resolve the incongruities between beliefs and practices previously discussed in this chapter. Finally, a commitment to inquiry in all aspects of these programs and services was underscored. Achieving a more focused mission in partnership with elementary and secondary schools is the signal objective of the newly formed Holmes Partnership.[21]

An affirmation or reaffirmation of professional teacher preparation as the *primary* focus of a school of education—which is also driven by scholarly inquiry—should lead to a revisiting of the resources needed. First aspects of teacher preparation to be addressed are the academic and didactic, and these require such resources as lecture halls, space for discussion groups, study areas, and, increasingly, facilities to accommodate new technologies.

Two other critical components of professional preparation include on-campus laboratories and clinics. Just as prospective doctors must have biology and anatomy laboratories and law and business majors need access to a case library that draws on both text and technology, future teachers need special facilities. While the resources necessary to hire a chemistry or physics professor include significant laboratory start-up costs, such allowances are not made for education professors.

On the Ohio State University campus a laboratory for a bench scientist is factored from one hundred thousand to one million dollars. Recently an entire floor was added to a medical facility in order to recruit a top-drawer team of two professors in heart and lung diseases. Today most teacher educators are hired with a start-up package of an office and sometimes, but hardly always, a computer. Rarely do administrators factor in access to on-campus teaching laboratories or other technologies, including two-way video to interact with students and colleagues in K-12 settings. Present facilities in colleges of education are a disgrace, and we recommend federal funding for the development of lighthouse models of pedagogical laboratories and clinics.

Off campus as well as on campus, teacher preparation programs are squeezed by financial shortages. For example, most field experiences, student teaching assignments, and internships are provided through the good graces of local school systems, sometimes with a small stipend to reimburse the cooperating teacher, or with a tuition voucher to be used for a course at the school of education.[22] In short, field preparation is assumed to be basically a no-cost factor in the preparation of teachers. In many universities, clinical faculty designations are also limited to the health professions, preventing education departments from developing formal, dignified, and reimbursable appointments for key faculty in the K-12 sector who play key roles in the preparation of teachers. Until and unless we begin to assert forthrightly the necessary ingredients of professional preparation which go unquestioned in the more established professions, we will not be able to deliver the kind of quality experience for teachers that our nation's schools demand.

Moreover, many technologies commonplace in the private sector are, at least for the moment, beyond the financial reach of colleges of education. For instance, colleges preparing teachers in workforce education and educational technology need access to laser-driven machinery, cutting-edge computer technologies, video telephoning and teleconferencing, and kinesiology and physiology laboratories that exist in business and industry and in the health and communications fields. To meet this need, schools of education may develop partnerships with business and industry and across campus with medical, allied medical, and communications programs, but such arrangements may be less than satisfactory. In many institutions, developing capacity in distance education is severely limited by inadequate resources. A case in point: on one of the largest single campus sites in the United States, there exist only five distance-learning facilities or "smart" classrooms. To offset inadequate resources, teacher education programs have to be aggressive in identifying facilities (and opportunities for learning) that can be shared.

Fund raising is a third strategy. Whereas fund development was once conducted chiefly at the central university level, more recently many schools of education have established their own development offices. Strategies include making use of the college's mission statement to build a case for funding needs. Faculty participate by clarifying their values and articulating the school's mission, by helping to identify constituents capable of giving back to the college at differentiated levels, and by cultivating potential donors. However, few schools of education have had outstanding success in fund raising without investing in a development staff to plan events, prepare brochures, and remain in close contact with donors.

Differentiated Roles for Teachers in Schools and in Teacher Education

If becoming a teacher spans an entire career, it is appropriate to examine closely the forces that influence each stage, from recruitment and selection through preservice and entry-level preparation, and on to continuing professional development. Many voices have advocated such an examination. In 1986, the Holmes Group (now Partnership) underscored the view that conditions in teaching will not be improved until there is universal acknowledgment that those who excel in teaching can achieve leadership roles among their colleagues. To achieve this goal, the Group recommended specialization in the teaching force. A relatively small, select cadre would be career professionals—individuals at the top of their profession who had proved their excellence in teaching, in knowledge of subject matter, and in examinations and assessments. Professional teachers, comprising the majority of the teaching force, would have proven competence in their work and would have met rigorous standards for entry and continuance. Beginning teachers, designated *instructors*, would be exploring careers in teaching under the tutelage of professional teachers.

A decade later, the National Commission on Teaching and America's Future revisited this issue of role definition and proposed a new career continuum, recommending that teachers and administrators be given options over time for multiple professional roles. The Commission advised that "school districts should create more fluid and varied roles for educators throughout their careers so that knowledge and talent can be more widely shared."[23] Concomitantly, the Commission called for school districts to structure time and responsibility so that teachers could be involved in peer coaching and mentoring, curriculum and assessment development, teacher education, and various forms of school leadership.

Reconceptualizing the work of teacher education within the context of a career continuum requires that we also examine what professors do on campus and in schools, as well as what teachers do in schools and on campus. From analysis of education professors' self-reported activities, the RATE studies drew a common profile showing varying degrees of involvement in research and in participation in K-12 schools. While there are considerable variations within institutions and surely by institutional type, repeated iterations of these studies revealed that teacher education faculty increasingly report engagement with elementary and secondary schools, mostly in the supervision of student teachers and not in their scholarly activities or the renewal of K-12 schools.[24]

The most traditional and enduring manifestation of classroom teachers' involvement in initial teacher preparation is, of course, their role as cooperating teachers. Typically, the cooperating teacher participates in a triadic relationship with the student and the university supervisor. The limitations of this arrangement are well documented and range from clashes in expectations between university and school supervisors, differences in conceptions of teaching and appropriate supervisory roles, and inadequate preparation, recognition, and reimbursement for the cooperating teacher.

New views of the relationship between schools of education and K-12 schools, and the introduction of the Professional Development School (PDS) and professional practice or partner schools, have brought into focus the need for a reexamination of traditional roles. Many schools of education are creating new roles and role-relationships that more fully acknowledge the important contribution of K-12 teachers in the conduct of initial teacher education. At the same time, standards for tenure and promotion are being examined to bring about a more appropriate reward system for education faculty who spend significant amounts of time at PDS or partner school sites.

We recommend that a panel of distinguished leaders from relevant teacher education organizations—including the NEA and the AFT—meet on a continuing basis and revisit the issues attendant to the selection, further preparation, and reimbursement of various K-12 personnel playing key roles in the preparation of preservice and novice teachers.

Additionally, we suggest that a process of certification for teacher educators, analogous to that for board-certified teachers, should be put in place. This panel would consider the type and duration of K-12 teaching experiences teacher educators should have, and would recommend how school-based responsibilities should be credited in performance reviews and promotion criteria.

Finally, state-supported, boundary-spanning prototype roles should be piloted to establish stronger links between standards and innovations in the education of teachers and evolving standards in elementary and secondary education. These roles would be filled by individuals from schools of education and K-12 schools who for specified periods of time would experiment with blending responsibilities in the two sectors and would critically examine how blended roles can advance partnership arrangements.

Emerging designations for teachers who participate in on-campus and school-based teacher education are Resident Teacher, Clinical Educator, Faculty Associate, Hub Teacher, Field Professor, and Clinician. Increasingly, the roles of teachers in PDS's, teaching academies, and peer assistance and review programs are being clarified and chronicled, paving the way for the reconceptualization of teacher *leader* roles in school renewal and in the redesign of teacher education. Thus, a basic strategy for improving initial teacher education, promoting school renewal, and enabling continuing professional development is to provide accomplished teachers with opportunities to develop further their potential for leadership roles.

We believe that several new school-based leadership roles will evolve over time. Teachers will assume these new roles while maintaining reduced teaching responsibilities. At the same time, a new vision of the principal's role will emerge as the following six types of key *leadership* roles are strengthened to ensure continuing school renewal: (1) examining and evaluating professional practice; (2) integrating information and communications technologies; (3) engaging parents and community; (4) improving professional practice; (5) developing goals-based instructional materials; (6) helping students learn with and from one another. Venture funds at both the federal and state level should be allocated on a competitive basis to partnerships designed specifically to develop new lead teacher roles and reinvent administrative teams. These pilot programs would also designate specific and significant school-based roles in K-12 schools for university faculty, thus advancing the idea that they are legitimately engaged in schools beyond initial teacher preparation.

While the revision of criteria for tenure and promotion has been widely discussed since the publication in 1989 of Ernest Boyer's *Scholarship Reconsidered*, changes in academic guidelines that embrace multiple views of scholarship, including collaborative forms of inquiry in schools, are slow to evolve.[25] These conditions must be faced directly if lasting educational partnerships are to be built.

Inadequate Socialization of Teachers

It has been the tendency of a number of school reform initiatives to treat initial teacher education as an intervention too weak and too little related to the daily vicissitudes of teaching to be factored into their reform strategies in any major way. What, rather, are these reform initiatives about? Some would argue they are about "reculturing" existing school faculties. While there are many variations on the theme of school reform, good schools have at their core cultures and conditions that enable continuous learning not only for students but for all school personnel, especially teachers. Such schools are characterized by learning communities among students and high degrees of collaboration among teachers. In 1982 Judith Little identified four critical practices in defining teacher collaboration:

1. Teachers engage in frequent, continuous, and increasingly concrete and precise talk about teaching practice.
2. Teachers are frequently observed and provided with useful (if potentially frightening) critiques of their teaching.
3. Teachers plan, design, research, evaluate, and prepare teaching materials together.
4. Teachers teach each other the practices of teaching.[26]

Such critical practices are not the norm in most schools. How might "reculturing" occur to bring about these four patterns of behavior? We argue that initial teacher preparation is central here and does indeed have an impact on the organization and staffing of schools. The teaching practices that prevail in schools result from the way teachers are prepared initially. If collaborative cultures and collective self-renewal are at the heart of school reform, or better, of a self-renewing school, then teachers should be socialized initially so that there is a direct and powerful link to this type of school culture and concomitant instructional practice.

The primary emphasis in preservice education should be on generating the abilities and the disposition for *learning* to teach, not only as an individual but also as a member of a professional community. In short, more attention needs to be focused on how preservice teachers are socialized as professionals. To be sure, they need to acquire a repertoire of technical abilities—at an entry level—to be refined and extended over time through a related repertoire of learning-to-teach strategies. But these important technical aspects of teaching will be developed further—most likely during the first five years of teaching when a rapid learning curve can occur—but only if teachers are socialized to continue to learn with and from one another.

Bold new staffing patterns are needed in elementary and secondary schools with more diverse teaching roles than exist at present, designed to provide more challenging learning opportunities for students. A reduction in the scope of teachers' responsibilities and a better division of labor at the school site should result. This idea needs to be addressed first in programs of teacher education. As it stands now, teachers are prepared to work independently and without thought as to *why* and *how* they might best function in teams for the planning, implementation, and assessment of teaching. Elementary teachers especially have too great a scope of responsibility, which limits their capacity to teach multiple subjects well. Neither elementary or secondary teachers benefit in any sustained manner from working with colleagues who have high degrees of expertise in such critical activities as the development of timely, high-quality instructional materials or the valid evaluation of conceptual or applied learnings. For reasons such as these, teacher education programs need to be grounded in different conceptions of teacher roles and role relationships than at present.

As it stands now, most "regular" teachers and special education teachers are prepared independently of one another, although modest progress is being made in a number of preparation programs with blending these two roles. We know of no cross-role program prototypes, however, wherein teachers, administrators, counselors, and media specialists are engaged together during their preparation in activities that would socialize and prepare them to work together effectively in schools. Equally rare are preparation activities of an *interprofessional* nature which would be especially relevant for city schools which serve as hubs for integrated or inter-agency services to students and their families. Break-the-mold programs are needed for the preparation of all school-based professionals, not just teachers. Even though cross-role and interprofessional experiences are only one aspect of teacher preparation, they should be an integral part of the program. However, time restrictions in most preservice programs suggest that much of this learning will have to come as integrated transitional or induction experiences extending into the first years of teaching.

Most fundamental to the improvement of teacher education is addressing how all teachers are prepared to work with one another. Many promising practices in this regard can be observed in preservice programs currently, and the nucleus exists from which to build a nationally coordinated program of development and research. Teacher educators in partnership with professionals in elementary and secondary schools can design more powerful strategies than exist at present for the socialization of beginning teachers. For example, short-term cohort arrangements lasting days, weeks, or months can contribute to (1) interpersonal development; (2) cooperative planning for instruction; (3) cooperative learning; (4) collaborative action research; (5), and most fundamental, peer reviews of videotaped teaching, examining the actions and thinking of both teachers and learners. While such arrangements are indeed possible, at present it is rare that program architects plan cohort arrangements in sustained, coherent ways to achieve the purposes of socialization.[27]

A national program of development and research could be framed by an overarching research question such as: What is the impact of different programs designed to prepare teachers specifically to learn with and from one another both in terms of their performance and subsequently their pupils' performance? Specific domains in this coordinated research agenda would be defined by variations in how these programs socialize prospective teachers. Individuals and teams pursuing similar program development and research interests from across different teacher preparation programs would convene on a periodic basis to share progress on their mutual or related inquiries and over time would contribute to data-based prototypes for how to prepare teachers in quite different ways than they are at present. These program innovations would necessarily have to be *partnership* endeavors between schools of education and K-12 schools since new patterns of preparing education personnel, and especially teachers, demand new staffing patterns in schools. New staffing patterns in schools, in turn, demand new forms of preparation.

The Knowledge Base for Teacher Education

Our position is that initial teacher preparation has a twofold mission: (1) an intensive socialization process that disposes teachers to learn with and from others as *school-based* professionals and (2) assistance to preservice teachers in the acquisition of core strategies not just for teaching but for learning to teach *over time*. These abilities are derived from an understanding of how students learn on their own and how they learn from one another.

This orientation to teacher education speaks directly to what we believe constitutes an important aspect of the knowledge base of the teaching profession. It is long past time that some initial consensus be reached on a set of basic approaches to teaching, both content specific and applicable to all domains. These, in turn, should be augmented by a similarly basic set of strategies for learning to teach over time. These obviously should be derived from and coupled with some consensus about what constitutes high-performance learning for youngsters, a general construct which we addressed earlier. The teacher education profession's inability to reach even a tentative agreement about a knowledge base for teaching and learning has resulted in perceptions of an infantile, often highly confused "wanna-be" profession.

We understand that teaching is much more than a set of skills. We stated at the outset and throughout have argued that reform of teacher education is severely constrained by a simplistic view of teaching. Teaching is a very complex activity that often reaches beyond the confines of the classroom. Characterized by myriad face-to-face interactions, it is laced with unique interpersonal dimensions and continuing moral considerations. In its best manifestations it is highly clinical in nature and rooted in an intellectual exercise that has distinctive properties of *teacher* reasoning. But it also has a critically important skill base.

We feel compelled to underscore this point because from our perspective discourse surrounding teacher education has drifted towards viewing teaching solely as a clinical activity. It is as if surgeons were prepared to rigorously reflect on practice but without the technical means or abilities to operate in any sophisticated manner. Increasingly, we have ignored the technical teaching abilities which should be the focus of much of our inquiry and analysis. Beyond that, we have not been thoughtful enough about what the technical properties of reasoning and reflection may be, notwithstanding the very helpful formative typologies put forward by scholars such as Lee Shulman.[28]

Our contention is that we need to focus on a combination of core teaching abilities—what *all* teachers know and can do—with concomitant attention to when, where, and exactly how these should be employed. We agree with Richard Arends, who identified five initial approaches to teaching: (1) presentation, (2) concept teaching, (3) direct instruction, (4) cooperative learning, (5) discovery and discussion.[29] A limited repertoire of teaching models applicable to any subject matter such as Arends advocates, perhaps three to five in number, are a reasonable expectation for an entry-level teacher. The ability of teachers to appropriately utilize a number of teaching approaches during the course of an instructional episode of any length appears to impact both the extent and quality of student engagement in instruction.[30]

While much pedagogical artistry is obviously related to a teacher's depth of understanding of the subject matter of a lesson, domain-general teaching models serve as a powerful supporting infrastructure. An analog would be the limited number of offensive patterns that a basketball team practices over again and again. These eventually take on myriad variations and are mediated powerfully by the team with which the player is engaged. Just as it is on the basketball court, a repertoire of teaching models is very much the framework for the action which unfolds in the classroom.

In addition to developing these core abilities at an *entry level*, teacher preparation needs to provide the novice teacher with a limited number of strategies for refining and extending these teaching abilities. We have long advocated models of teaching that can be naturally embedded in the on-going activities of the school day. The teacher educator's ability to socialize students to work together in preservice courses is essential to their acquiring a second, related repertoire of strategies for refining teaching over time that would include:

- Peer observation and self-observation and analysis of various dimensions of teaching and learning
- Case development around persistent problems
- Engagement in several variations of action research
- Systematic study of students
- Utilization of coaching strategies and guided practice with specific models of instruction
- Participation in study groups
- Examinations of student work and the relationships of this to teacher actions.

Engagement with these two intertwined patterns of instructional behavior should continue into the early years of teaching. They are critical components of the knowledge base undergirding teaching and teacher education, and they are a visible link between the first two stages of a teacher's professional development.

We recommend that a major aspect of pre-tenure assessment of beginning teachers focus on their ability to demonstrate a reasonable repertoire of instructional approaches appropriate to particular lessons and that they have guided practice in inquiring into the effects of alternative means of instruction. The INTASC standards being adopted for beginning teachers in several states should be refined and expanded to ensure that continuing attention is given to the instructional abilities enumerated above. NCATE's continuing developmental work on standards should also address how these core abilities are addressed in programs of teacher preparation.

Connecting Two Different Worlds

There is no shortage of documentation about the problems of forming partnerships, including the profound cultural differences between faculties in schools of education and those in K-12 schools that must be negotiated in order to create the ultimate professional continuum.[31] The cultures differ in use of time, role identification, collegial affiliation, incentives and rewards, and in the very structure of work within the two institutions. Further, the various design stages of the teacher education continuum still hold properties that are essentially the purview of either one institution or the other. That is, preservice education remains mostly an on-campus responsibility. While school-based clinical educators are increasingly involved, and literally hundreds of institutions are experimenting with Professional Development School sites, the design of the initial teacher preparation program emanates largely from the school, college, or department of education. Further, school personnel generally refer to the PDS as a college-initiated platform for preparing beginning teachers, and rarely cite its potential for continuing professional development, inquiry, or school reform. This attitude challenges educators who would serve the needs of beginning teachers and the professional development of other school staff.

Nowhere is the absence of a seamless continuum in teacher education more evident than in the early years of teaching. At the same time, no point in the continuum has more potential to bring the worlds of the schools and the academy into a true symbiotic partnership than this induction stage. While the problems and frustrations of beginning teachers are well documented, little systemic reform in approaching these problems has materialized. Beginning teachers are often placed in the most difficult teaching situations, long ago abandoned by career teachers seeking more stable conditions; they are given little advice or collegial assistance and, in some instances, are not so subtly encouraged to keep their problems to themselves. They are often frustrated by a lack of self-efficacy and have but limited means for assessing the actual impact of their practice. And they are typically held to the same standards as veterans. With respect to improving the condition of beginning teachers, the National Commission on Teaching and America's Future states:

Like doctors in their medical residency, teachers who have the support of more senior colleagues and opportunities for continuing their learning become more skilled more quickly. Research shows that beginning teachers who have had the continuous support of a skilled mentor are much more likely to stay in the profession and much more likely to get beyond classroom management concerns to focus on student learning.[32]

The design of entry-year programs necessarily hinges on three essential services: (1) continuing personal support; (2) regular and responsive educative experiences which both extend and enrich their initial preparation and address the particular demands of their teaching situation; and (3) ongoing feedback and assessment of their performance over the first year, culminating in a summative decision as to whether they should be relieved of their teaching responsibilities, continue on an initial licensure track, or be placed on a regular licensure track.

Such a design assumes the assignment of a veteran teacher, prepared to provide clinical training and personal support, who is partially released from instructional responsibilities to work in a continuing manner with the beginner. Ideally, the novice teacher will be assigned to an experienced teacher in the same building and in the same subject specialty or at the same grade level. Also ideally, beginners should have some say in the selection of this consulting veteran teacher. Finally, beginning teachers should experience a reduced load, perhaps sharing a classroom or teaching assignment, so that specific times during the school day can be dedicated to working with their mentor in the assessment of their teaching.

This is a big order and such reforms will not be achieved without positive responses to the following types of recommendations:

1. Universities and schools have to realize that true partnership is a high-stakes investment. Each entity must put into the equation improvement strategies that are meaningful to their respective organizations; that is, they need to identify areas where they truly need help from one another. Then, *institutionally* and *programmatically*,

they have to find ways to work together to make those intended improvements a reality. All other recommendations stem from this principle.

2. The design of preservice programs must acknowledge that the time required to prepare fully competent teachers extends beyond the initial teacher education program. Thus, teacher education programs must be mutually designed by persons who understand what knowledge, abilities and attitudes are best cultivated (a) in preservice; (b) during the initial phase of teaching; and (c) later in the teacher's career development.

3. Personnel from schools of education must work in tandem with school practitioners to create conditions of mentoring and monitoring that will truly extend initial preparation into the beginning years of teaching. Assumptions about university roles versus school roles must be examined by staff from both institutions.

4. School districts and teacher unions have to accept responsibility for adjusting the conditions, roles, and responsibilities of beginning teachers to create the time needed to extend professional preparation, support, and evaluation in the first years of teaching. Continuing support may well require adjustments in salary for both beginners and lead teachers, thus illustrating a key aspect of the career ladder.

5. Colleges of education, school administrations, and unions have to be willing to carve out a strategy for releasing expert veteran teachers to work with both preservice and novice teachers. Peer Assistance and Review (PAR) programs, as implemented in Toledo, Columbus, Cincinnati, and Rochester are models to build on.[33] More work is needed on the criteria for selection and on robust preparation for peer consultants, however. Schools should work in tandem with local universities to create preparation programs for PAR consultants and to design continuing developmental experiences for beginning teachers. Funding for prototype programs is needed.

6. Development of mentoring and assessment models would also be the joint responsibility of school-university partnerships, including decisions about using PRAXIS, INTASC, or other current assessment procedures and protocols.[34]

7. Finally, the partnership should work toward the achievement by PAR consultant teachers of National Board Certification, just as we recommended for university-based teacher educators.

These recommendations, and the profound implications they carry, highlight how far apart are the worlds of university and school personnel. School districts are, in fact, ill equipped to vary the instructional roles of beginning teachers. Few have embraced a peer assistance model or mentoring program. Universities tend not to think of their preparation programs as only a beginning; they rarely find authentic ways to bridge these programs with the early years of teaching. Contract language that speaks to these issues is rare. Teacher leadership remains an informal process. Many other problems and responsibilities in both sectors are placed ahead of developing a seamless continuum for teacher development. And this situation will not change markedly until the above recommendations are addressed. We are optimistic that the newly funded National Partnership for Excellence and Accountability in Teaching (NPEAT) will assist in bridging the policies and practices of the two worlds of school and university.[35]

Assessment and Accountability

This is a problem of considerable proportions and far-reaching ramifications. One reason that teacher education is such a massive, uneven, and often suspect enterprise is that we ultimately have little solid evidence as to the quality of teachers graduating from the more than 1200 institutions professing to prepare teachers. As a field, teacher education has spider-danced all around the issue of what constitutes quality. This problem will not be redressed either through institutional or state initiative, but rather calls for nationally coordinated research and development. Our recommendations are threefold and relate to earlier recommendations.

First, we must establish clear and clearly differentiated benchmarks for teacher understandings and abilities along a continuum from preservice preparation into the early years of teaching. These benchmarks should be framed in a professional consensus as to what constitutes high-performance teaching. For now the INTASC standards could serve as a framework.[36] But the corpus of knowledge guiding both our understanding of teaching and teacher education will undergo continuing modifications and should be regularly reviewed (perhaps every three years) by prestigious panels of researchers, teacher educators, and teachers. These panels might be sponsored by Division K of the American Educational Research Association in collaboration with NPEAT. Their task would be analogous to that of consensus panels employed by agencies such as the National Institutes of Health, which evaluate on a regular basis available scientific information and biomedical technology.

Second, the emphasis in assessment must be squarely on coupling teacher performance and teacher learning with *pupil learning*. This demands that prospective and novice teachers acquire the ability to assess student performance against *criterion-referenced, teacher-developed standards* along with clear understanding of the norm-referenced standardized measures. We recommend national competition among teachers and teacher educators to do two things: first, develop item banks for assessment that reflect high-performance learning; second, produce innovative materials and procedures to promote student achievement on specific measures. With respect to advancing teachers' abilities to develop criterion-referenced measures, we refer the reader to the pioneer work of Del and Mark Schalock undertaken over the last two decades in Oregon.[37] Their theoretical and empirical work is anchored in the premise that teacher effectiveness is determined primarily by the learning *gains* of their students. This conception of teacher effectiveness is based on outcomes and dependent on context. These scholars insist that one cannot look at student learning either rationally or ethically as a measure of teachers' effectiveness without factoring in the classrooms, schools, homes, and communities in which teaching and learning occur. Consequently, they have developed a work sample methodology (WSM) as a sustaining guide to teacher education and as an essential measurement strategy. With WSM prospective teachers develop plans for instruction and assessment that are aligned or coupled, and then collect, interpret, and reflect upon evidence of student progress. In twenty years of developing WSM the Schalocks and their colleagues have addressed major psychometric issues in terms of the multiple factors which impact student learning.

Third and finally, emphasis needs to be directed to multiple measures of teacher development over time. Obviously, it makes sense to measure relevant teacher knowledge and understandings prior to student teaching and again just before the first year of teaching or internship. However, we cannot condone the use of the PRAXIS III criteria developed by the Educational Testing Service to do a limited number of "dipstick" observations of the performance of beginning teachers.[38] In some states as few as two teacher observations are being proposed to determine licensure.

Our position is that institutions preparing teachers demonstrate with rigorous cut-off scores that their prospective graduates: (1) possess requisite knowledge of subject matter; (2) can effectively assess student gains over time on criterion-referenced measures; (3) understand norm-referenced proficiency tests and can teach to key items on these tests through a variety of approaches; and (4) can develop a portfolio measuring their own *development* over time. This portfolio would be framed in something like the INTASC core propositions. Evaluations would be continued into the first years of teaching with an emphasis on examining *multiple measures* of teacher performance against the forms of evidence in (2), (3), and (4) above. Assessment of teachers' *development* would proceed over time from an examination of their performance as teachers *per se* to an analysis of their students' behavioral patterns and achievement in relation to their patterns of behavior as teachers. A second indicator of teachers' development would be their reasoning about teaching and learning. Evaluations would examine a teacher's progression from largely unexamined assumptions and unsupported teaching decisions and actions to decisions that are repeatedly subjected to public examination and are supported by various types of information and data. A third major pattern would consider the congruity of beliefs and practices, looking for the application of beliefs to such practices as grouping and grading.

Improving the assessment of teachers and teacher educators calls for both further growth of professionalism and major influence on state policies. It calls for some coordination nationally between educators and policymakers and could test NPEAT as to whether, in fact, any viable type of national partnering can be brought to bear on the measurement of teaching effectiveness. NPEAT could bring together key representatives from NEA and AFT, AACTE, the Holmes Partnership, and NBPTS in an education summit designed to move rigorous assessment of teachers forward. This is a task which embraces not only major conceptual and methodological challenges, but legal-political and economic ones.

Summary

In this chapter we have attempted to examine a number of pervasive and interrelated problems associated with teacher education. We advocate as do others in this volume a seamless extension of teacher education into the first years of teaching. We have attempted to provide recommendations (or at least directions to be considered) in response to the several issues and problems identified. While the resolution of many of the inadequacies of teacher education lies ultimately with individuals and institutions, there is little evidence that the needed initiative and collective action will *emanate* from them. Similarly, while the legal framework and political forces exist at the state level to influence teacher education, history reveals a lack of positive initiative at this level, too. Hence we advocate professional and political alliances that are national in character for achieving a bold, coordinated, long-term reform agenda and strategies for change.

The problems of teacher education should not be underestimated. We have a long, long way to go if the goal is a more potent and protracted form of teacher preparation intersecting in central ways with school renewal. Multiple major changes are in order. These include fundamental changes in the way professors are recruited and prepared. When professional schools of education become partnership enterprises, they will incorporate different types of training facilities from those that exist at present and hence will need an expanded resource base. Another change calls for differentiated assignments for graduates in their first years of teaching with correspondingly differentiated roles for lead teachers assigned to work with them. Each of these changes has conceptual, methodological, legal, and political dimensions.

Realistic preparation of teachers demands *first* a fundamental rethinking of teachers' roles and responsibilities, leading to a clearer vision of high-performance teaching, which will be manifest in the practice of classroom teachers and teacher educators. Teacher education programs need to emphasize forms of professional socialization and teaching strategies that at present are little in evidence. Beyond this, the teaching profession must address more squarely and forcefully than heretofore the nature and extent of the knowledge base which gives direction to their work.

Finally, the enterprise is beset with the pervasive problem of accountability. Trustworthy assessment of teaching practice should start with an examination of those who view themselves as teacher educators. Evaluation of teaching must move from a concentration on the ability of a teacher to perform on limited occasions to gauging development over time through multiple measures focused especially on related patterns of student learning. Additionally, resolving the problem of accountability demands that teachers themselves demonstrate versatile assessment abilities and also address the reality of norm-referenced measures through innovative instruction that is aligned, if not blended, with these standardized measures.

NOTES

1. Linda M. Anderson, "Learners and Learning," in *Knowledge Base For the Beginning Teacher*, ed. M. C. Reynolds (New York: Pergamon Press, 1989).

2. Patricia Alexander and P. Karen Murphy, "The Research Base for APA's Learner-Centered Psychological Principles," in *Issues in School Reform: A Sampler of Psychological*

Perspectives on Learner-Centered Schools, eds. N. L. Lambert and B. L. Combs (Washington, DC: The American Psychological Association, 1998).

3. James H. Lytle, "The Inquiring Manager," *Phi Delta Kappan* 77 (June 1996): p. 666.

4. K. R. Howey and N. L. Zimpher, *Profiles of Preservice Teacher Education* (Albany: State University of New York Press, 1990).

5. K. R. Howey, "Three Domains in a Common or Core Doctoral Experience for Prospective Education Professors: Learning, Teaching and Learning to Teach" (paper presented at the annual meeting of the Committee on the Preparation of the Education Professoriate, Land Grant Deans of Education, Albuquerque, NM, October, 1997).

6. National Board for Professional Teaching Standards, *What Teachers Should Know and Be Able to Do* (Detroit: National Board for Professional Teaching Standards, 1994).

7. American Association of Colleges for Teacher Education, *The Context for the Reform of Teacher Education*, RATE VI (American Association of Colleges for Teacher Education, Washington, DC, 1992): pp. 26-27.

8. Nancy L. Zimpher, "Right-sizing Teacher Education: The Policy Initiative," in *Teachers for the New Millennium*, eds. L. Kaplan and R. A. Edelfelt (Thousand Oaks, CA: Corwin Press, 1996).

9. American Association of Colleges for Teacher Education, *Teaching Teachers: Facts & Figures*, RATE II (American Association of Colleges for Teacher Education, Washington, DC, 1988).

10. Matthew V. Filipic, *State Funding for Higher Education in Ohio: A Brief Introduction* (Columbus: Higher Education Funding Commission, 1996).

11. American Association of Colleges for Teacher Education, *Teaching Teachers: Facts & Figures*, RATE IV (American Association of Colleges for Teacher Education, Washington, DC, 1990).

12. Kenneth R. Howey and Vivienne Collinson, "Cornerstones of a Collaborative Culture: Professional Development and Preservice Teacher Preparation," *Journal of Personnel Evaluation in Education* 9 (1995): p. 29.

13. Interstate New Teacher Assessment Consortium, *Model Standards for Beginning Teacher Licensing and Development: A Resource for State Dialogue* (Washington, DC: Interstate New Teacher Assessment Consortium, 1992).

14. National Commission on Teaching and America's Future, *What Matters Most: Teaching for America's Future* (New York: National Commission on Teaching and America's Future, 1996): p. 15.

15. The Holmes Group, *Tomorrow's Schools of Education* (East Lansing: The Holmes Group Inc., 1995): p. 1.

16. Geraldine Jonçich Clifford and James W. Guthrie, *Ed School: A Brief for Professional Education* (Chicago: University of Chicago Press, 1988): pp. 3-4.

17. The March-April, 1997 edition of *Academe* offers a comprehensive look at various institutions' research status.

18. John I. Goodlad, Roger Soder, and Kenneth A. Sirotnik, eds., *Places Where Teachers are Taught* (San Francisco: Jossey-Bass, 1990).

19. The Holmes Group, *Tomorrow's Schools of Education*.

20. College of Education, The Ohio State University, *College of Education Restructuring Plan* (Columbus: Unpublished Report, 1994).

21. The Holmes Partnership Board of Directors, "The Holmes Partnership Strategic Action Plan: 1998-2003," working paper, Columbus, OH: 1997.

22. RATE IV (American Association of Colleges for Teacher Education, Washington, DC, 1990).

23. *What Matters Most*, pp. 96, 98.

24. RATE IV.

25. Ernest L. Boyer, *Scholarship Reconsidered: Priorities of the Professoriate* (Princeton: Carnegie Foundation for the Advancement of Teaching, 1990).

26. J. W. Little, "Norms of Collegiality and Experimentation: Workplace Conditions of School Success," *American Educational Research Journal* 19 (1982): pp. 325-340.

27. American Association of Colleges for Teacher Education, *The Context for the Reform of Teacher Education, RATE VI*.

28. Lee S. Shulman, "Knowledge and Teaching: Foundations of the New Reform," *Harvard Educational Review* 57 (1987): pp. 1-22.

29. Richard I. Arends, *Learning to Teach*, 2nd ed. (New York: McGraw Hill, 1991), p. 228.

30. Patricia A. Wasley, Robert L. Hampel, and Richard W. Clark, *Kids and School Reform* (San Francisco: Jossey-Bass, 1997).

31. Marilyn Johnston et al., eds., *Collaborative Reform and Other Improbable Dreams*, in press, 1998.

32. *What Matters Most*, pp. 80-81.

33. "The Columbus Education Association's Peer Assistance and Review, PAR: An Award Winning Teacher Evaluation Model for Ohio . . . and the Nation." Unpublished Report: 1997.

34. Carol Anne Dwyer, *Development of the Knowledge Base for the PRAXIS III: Classroom Performance Assessments Performance Criteria* (Princeton: Educational Testing Service, 1994).

35. The National Partnership for Excellence and Accountability in Teaching, NPEAT (Washington, DC: NPEAT, nd).

36. Interstate New Teacher Assessment Consortium, *Model Standards for Beginning Teacher Licensing and Development: A Resource for State Dialogue* (Washington, DC: INTASC, 1992).

37. Del Schalock and Mark Schalock, *Advances in Theory and Research on Teacher Effectiveness: An Invitational Conference and Seminar: Conference Proceedings* (Monmouth, OR: Western Oregon State College, 1995).

38. *Development of the Knowledge Base for the PRAXIS III.*

Name Index

Subject Index

Academic knowledge, 88-89, 106. *See also*, Subject matter knowledge.

American Association of Colleges of Teacher Education (AACTE), 105, 279, 283, 302

American Educational Research Association (AERA), 105, 194, 300

American Federation of Teachers (AFT), 68, 104, 290, 302; changes in direction of, 78

American Psychological Association (APA), 280

Assessment: of teacher education graduates, 300-302; of teachers, 234-235, 283; of teachers, related to student learning, 300, 301, 302. *See also*, Praxis III.

Association of Teacher Educators (ATE), 105

Caring: as commonly defined, 205; as defined in traditional philosophy, 205-206; as mark of teacher effectiveness, 208, 209; relational analysis of, 206-208. *See also*, Competence of teachers.

Certification, 187, 237; advanced teacher, 98-99. *See also*, Licensure.

Charter Schools Initiative (CSI), of National Education Association, 74-76

Chicago Public Schools: dilemmas experienced by teachers in, 37, 41-44; reform movements in, 40-41; statistics on, 37-38, 39

Civility in classrooms, 216-219

Coalition of Essential Schools, 191, 192, 201

Competence of teachers: compared with performance, 209, 210; in caring, 207, 216, 217, 219; in subject matter, 211-216

Constructivist learning theory, 146-149; as related to Dewey's view of language, 148; as related to teacher education, 145, 146; compared with non-constructivist learning theory, 146; Piaget's view of, 147; Vygotsky's view of, 147-148

Constructivist teacher education, 151-155; as reform movement, 149-151; exemplified in Cognitively Guided Instruction Program, 156; issues in, 158-162; process of, compared with non-constructivist

teacher education, 152, figure, 153, 154-155; research on, 161-162

Continuum in teacher education, 21, 51, 54-56, 199, 200, 232-233. *See also*, Staff development.

Council of Chief State School Officers, 98

Dilemmas: definition of, 30, 34; in the classroom, 34-35; management of, in Chicago Public Schools, 37-39, 41-44; related to purposes of schooling, 35; related to school change, 35-36; teaching the management of, 44, 52

Direct instruction in teacher education, 152

Discourse communities, 172-173, 177

Frankfort School of Critical Theory, 116

Handbook of Research on Teaching, 105
Handbook of Research on Teacher Education, 105

Holmes Group/Partnership, 49, 98, 104, 105, 110, 196, 231, 260, 261, 264, 272, 273, 283, 286, 287, 289, 302

Inquiry: as part of teaching for social justice, 133-138; as teaching and learning, 271; collaboration in, about practices, 171, 172; into teaching practices, 170, 171

Interstate New Teacher Assessment and Support Consortium (INTASC), 96, 98, 99, 100, 102, 104, 105, 240, 241, 242, 244, 247, 249, 286, 297, 299, 300

Knowledge Base for the Beginning Teacher, 105, 185, 193

Learning, constructivist principles of, 280; in communities of learners, 281; relation of, to teaching, 281

Learning communities of teachers, 263, 264, 292, 293, 294

Licensure, 96, 97, 101, 234, 235, 237, 238, 239; Connecticut's process of, 245, 246, 247; for beginning teachers, 99-101

RECENT PUBLICATIONS OF THE SOCIETY

1. The Yearbooks

97:1 (1998) *The Adolescent Years: Social Influences and Educational Challenges.* Kathryn Borman and Barbara Schneider, editors. Cloth.

97:2 (1998) *The Reading-Writing Connection.* Nancy Nelson and Robert C. Calfee, editors. Cloth.

96:1 (1997) *Service Learning.* Joan Schine, editor. Cloth.

96:2 (1997) *The Construction of Children's Character.* Alex Molnar, editor. Cloth.

95:1 (1996) *Performance-Based Student Assessment: Challenges and Possibilities.* Joan B. Baron and Dennie P. Wolf, editors. Cloth.

95:2 (1996) *Technology and the Future of Schooling.* Stephen T. Kerr, editor. Cloth.

94:1 (1995) *Creating New Educational Communities.* Jeannie Oakes and Karen Hunter Quartz, editors. Cloth.

94:2 (1995) *Changing Populations/Changing Schools.* Erwin Flaxman and A. Harry Passow, editors. Cloth.

93:1 (1994) *Teacher Research and Educational Reform.* Sandra Hollingsworth and Hugh Sockett, editors. Cloth.

93:2 (1994) *Bloom's Taxonomy: A Forty-year Retrospective.* Lorin W. Anderson and Lauren A. Sosniak, editors. Cloth.

92:1 (1993) *Gender and Education.* Sari Knopp Biklen and Diane Pollard, editors. Cloth.

92:2 (1993) *Bilingual Education: Politics, Practice, and Research.* M. Beatriz Arias and Ursula Casanova, editors. Cloth.

91:1 (1992) *The Changing Contexts of Teaching.* Ann Lieberman, editor. Cloth.

91:2 (1992) *The Arts, Education, and Aesthetic Knowing.* Bennett Reimer and Ralph A. Smith, editors. Cloth.

90:1 (1991) *The Care and Education of America's Young Children: Obstacles and Opportunities.* Sharon L. Kagan, editor. Cloth.

89:2 (1990) *Educational Leadership and Changing Contexts of Families, Communities, and Schools.* Brad Mitchell and Luvern L. Cunningham, editors. Paper.

88:1 (1989) *From Socrates to Software: The Teacher as Text and the Text as Teacher.* Philip W. Jackson and Sophie Haroutunian-Gordon, editors. Cloth.

88:2 (1989) *Schooling and Disability.* Douglas Biklen, Dianne Ferguson, and Alison Ford, editors. Cloth.

87:1 (1988) *Critical Issues in Curriculum.* Laurel N. Tanner, editor. Cloth.

87:2 (1988) *Cultural Literacy and the Idea of General Education.* Ian Westbury and Alan C. Purves, editors. Cloth.

Order the above titles from the University of Chicago Press, 11030 S. Langley Ave., Chicago, IL 60628. For a list of earlier Yearbooks still available, write to the Secretary, NSSE, 5835 Kimbark Ave., Chicago, IL 60637.

2. The Series on Contemporary Educational Issues

This series has been discontinued.

The following volumes in the series may be ordered from the McCutchan Publishing Corporation, P.O. Box 774, Berkeley, CA 94702-0774. Phone: 510-841-8616; Fax: 510-841-7787.

Academic Work and Educational Excellence: Raising Student Productivity (1986). Edited by Tommy M. Tomlinson and Herbert J. Walberg.

Adapting Instruction to Student Differences (1985). Edited by Margaret C. Wang and Herbert J. Walberg.

Choice in Education (1990). Edited by William Lowe Boyd and Herbert J. Walberg.

Colleges of Education: Perspectives on Their Future (1985). Edited by Charles W. Case and William A. Matthes.

Contributing to Educational Change: Perspectives on Research and Practice (1988). Edited by Philip W. Jackson.

Educational Leadership and School Culture (1993). Edited by Marshall Sashkin and Herbert J. Walberg.

Effective Teaching: Current Research (1991). Edited by Hersholt C. Waxman and Herbert J. Walberg.

Improving Educational Standards and Productivity: The Research Basis for Policy (1982). Edited by Herbert J. Walberg.

Moral Development and Character Education (1989). Edited by Larry P. Nucci.

Motivating Students to Learn: Overcoming Barriers to High Achievement (1993). Edited by Tommy M. Tomlinson.

Radical Proposals for Educational Change (1994). Edited by Chester E. Finn, Jr. and Herbert J. Walberg.

Reaching Marginal Students: A Prime Concern for School Renewal (1987). Edited by Robert L. Sinclair and Ward Ghory.

Restructuring the Schools: Problems and Prospects (1992). Edited by John J. Lane and Edgar G. Epps.

Rethinking Policy for At-risk Students (1994). Edited by Kenneth K. Wong and Margaret C. Wang.

School Boards: Changing Local Control (1992). Edited by Patricia F. First and Herbert J. Walberg.

The two final volumes in this series were:

Improving Science Education (1995). Edited by Barry J. Fraser and Herbert J. Walberg.

Ferment in Education: A Look Abroad (1995). Edited by John J. Lane.

These two volumes may be ordered from the Book Order Department, University of Chicago Press, 11030 S. Langley Ave., Chicago, IL 60628. Phone: 312-669-2215; Fax: 312-660-2235.